STUDIES

IN

HISTORICAL

CHANGE

STUDIES
IN
HISTORICAL
CHANGE

ॐ

EDITED AND
WITH AN INTRODUCTION BY
RALPH COHEN

University Press of Virginia
Charlottesville and London

THE UNIVERSITY PRESS OF VIRGINIA
Copyright © 1992 by the Rector and Visitors
of the University of Virginia
First published 1992

Library of Congress Cataloging-in-Publication Data

Studies in historical change / edited and with an introduction
by Ralph Cohen.
p. cm.
ISBN 0-8139-1374-8 (cloth).—ISBN 0-8139-1375-6 (pbk.)
1. Literature—History and criticism. 2. Literature and
history.
3. Civilization, Modern. I. Cohen, Ralph, 1917–   .
PN50.S78   1992
809—dc20   91–36668
CIP
Printed in the United States of America

CONTENTS

ह्य

STUDIES

IN

HISTORICAL

CHANGE

INTRODUCTION: ON STUDIES OF HISTORICAL CONTINUITY AND CHANGE

Ralph Cohen

MERELY TO BE ALIVE is to undergo change and merely to be alive is to live with continuity. Whether change and continuity are cognized, narrativized, theorized, or recognized, indeed, even if they are not recognized and cognized, human beings and the environment have change and continuity inscribed in them. In this sense, human beings reflect and act upon nature that acts upon them. So obvious has the relation between continuity and change become that descriptions, explanations, or interpretations of nature and nurture, genres and culture, scientific change and continuity are taken as clichés.

Discussions of continuity and change limited to the human sciences are commonplace so that a collection of studies that illustrate the interrelationships would appear redundant. If this were the case, it would be unnecessary to publish additional essays on the subject. But this collection has somewhat different aims from those anthologies that provide diverse views of a single text or a single trope or subject, or even studies of a period or movement. It provides a series of essays that deal with particular explanations of change in art history, political science, European and

American history, philosophy, anthropology, architecture and criticism, and theory in feminist, generic, and African-American studies.

These essays are not intended to be representative of all disciplinary approaches to change; nor do they offer a range of possible methods or subjects. Rather, they focus upon processes of change in explanatory or interpretive essays. Eight of these appeared unrevised earlier in a prize-winning issue of *New Literary History:* those of David Boucher, Murray Krieger, Berel Lang, Richard Lehan, R. K. Meiners, Linda Orr, Ann Rigney, and Cushing Strout. Five and the introduction are here published for the first time.

My use of "continuity and change" can be considered as a mode of critical discourse, that is, a use of terms that are not confined by genre. Although this is not a history of these terms, it is an attempt to clarify how they function in contemporary criticism and theory, how they relate to each other and the various texts in which they have a place.

I begin with Norman Bryson's essay entitled "Art in Context," because it offers a reformulation of "change" in the study of a single term and concept, namely, *context.* This essay serves several purposes in establishing the contribution the collection makes. It takes a term that has persistence and stability in art criticism; the term itself introduced as a change in relating a text to its interpretation by bridging the gap between the visual object and its pertinent external productive connections. As context became a part of traditional art history in the twentieth century, its validity as a concept ceased to be questioned.

Bryson's inquiry into context results from his commitment to semiotic theory and to the analytical procedures that a semiotic theory entails. He sets out not to replace context but to reformulate it for a more compre-hensive practice. He questions assumptions taken for granted by histori-ans themselves, about the framing of art, its inclusions and exclusions. He insists, however, that context is not an empty concept, but has been one that asked the wrong questions and gave the wrong answers in relat-ing an artwork to forces outside the discipline. He writes: "For what is not at stake is that 'context' be abandoned as a working concept, in the supposed free play of 'anything goes'; rather, what visual semiotics pro-poses is that the concept be problematized and reformulated, and not just incidentally but as a central and continual activity within the discipline."

Bryson lists thirteen examples of the inadequacy of the misconceived practice of context. He draws attention to the need to reformulate context criticism of past works. Art historians need to examine and interrogate their own contextual determinants and to speak "from what they might eventually decide to be their *actual* context."

> It is only by seeing from within our own context that institutional forces within art history have worked to silence the whole question of the roles played by gender and sexuality in the field of vision, that we are able *now* to begin to see the ellipses and silences within the archive. *Our* context has latterly enabled us to realize different contexts, and that it is we who set them up. Which should, rationally, lead us to inspect our own contextualizations within the discipline of art history at least as much as to create historical contexts for the visual texts the discipline deals with. The same historiographic scruple that requires us to draw a distinguishing line between "us" and the historical "them"—to see how they are different from us—should by the same token urge us to see how we are different from them, and to use context not as a legislative idea but as one that will help us to locate ourselves.

The significance of Bryson's study about context is its demonstration of the antithetical character of words and contexts pertinent to change. Context introduced a change in interpretation and then became itself a stable and continuing term. For Bryson's reformulation of the term leaves context in place but offers a different kind of stability for the future.

Bryson indicates some of the consequences of his reformulation in relation to interpreting works of the past. One is that any context is a human construction and thus requires an examination of the constructs historians of art impose. Another is that a reformulated context draws attention to the differences between past texts and present, a result that helps art historians to locate themselves on the map of art history.

As context undergoes reversal, so do continuity and change. But reversibility is not a necessary procedure. There exist many practices that define different relationships between continuity and change. Continuity does not imply an essential characteristic and change does not imply an improvement. If Norman Bryson writes of a methodological issue in the varied genre of art history, Franco Moretti's essay deals with one specific European genre, the bildungsroman, 1898–1914. His argument is that a change occurs in this genre during these years, a change marked by the loss of continuity. The European bildungsroman was before this time a well-formed genre and he analyzes the change that takes place when novels of this kind begin to present "erratic and unsteady structures," when they cease to be well formed. They are, he declares, "literary failures." He writes:

> To the inevitable question, "Would you mind explaining what exactly *is* a literary failure?" I would reply, although sketchily, that it is the sort of thing that occurs when a form deals with problems it is unable to solve. This definition presupposes in its turn the idea that symbolic forms are fundamentally problem-solving devices: that they are the means through which the cultural tensions and paradoxes produced by social conflict and historical change are disentangled (or at least reduced). Here lies the so-called social function of literature, with its so-called aesthetic pleasure: solving problems is useful and sweet. So much for my personal convictions, which I have tried to justify more at length elsewhere, and which are of course thoroughly questionable. But if they strike you as plausible, then a form that addresses problems it cannot solve is indeed a failure, socially, and aesthetically.

In placing the study of a genre as the framing device for his analysis of change and continuity, Moretti makes aesthetic quality a criterion for adequate instances of the genre. This is not the concern of Bryson who aims to correct an inadequate formulation of a critical concept; Moretti deals with a group of fictive texts. Literary texts denominated "failures" require some explanation of this negative change. A stable bindungsroman provides an equilibrium between features that permit changes of subject or rhetoric within the functions that fit. Failure is marked by a loss of this equilibrium. Moretti puts his discussion of a stable text in terms of problem solving. European novels of education are at a stage of equilibrium when "they are the means through which the cultural tensions and paradoxes produced by social conflict and historical change are disentangled (or at least reduced). Here lies the so-called social function of literature, with its so-called aesthetic pleasure: solving problems is useful and sweet."

A bildungsroman that addresses problems it cannot solve is a failure socially and aesthetically. This failure is the undoing of continuity. So long as the genre dealt with the conversion and resolution of appropriate social and aesthetic problems, it was successful. But failure to handle social and aesthetic problems adequately was less an authorial than a social problem. Failure to deal with such problems derives from a sickness in the body politic. Moretti suggests that certain features of the well-made bildungsroman persist but they now introduce "discontinuity within novelistic temporality, generating centrifugal tendencies toward the short story and the lyric."

Moretti does not pursue the relation of a failed genre to other genres that assume some of its features and themselves propose proper construction of questions for their own genre. But it is significant that Moretti's version of change is directly related to the adequate or inadequate narrativizing of cultural tensions and social conflicts. Moretti also points out that literary change in a general study "does not occur as a straight growth (*Stephen Hero,* then *Portrait,* then *Ulysses*), but as a branching process (*Stephen Hero,* and then either *Portrait* or *Ulysses*). Joyce chose the *Portrait* way, as we know, but it led nowhere. Far from preparing *Ulysses, Portrait* delayed it, and in order to invent Bloom, Joyce had to forget his *Künstlerroman* and retrace his steps all the way back to that initial bifurcation near Eccles St. It is an arabesque that may be taken as a miniature for the late bildungsroman as a whole: every tree has its dead branches, and this, alas, was one of them."

Moretti's assumption that a text is generic indicates that it has filiations with other genres that complicate the relation of continuity to change. If a critical or theoretical text contains within it discourses, quotations, illustrations, even philosophical propositions, then the relation between it and texts outside the discipline is no longer simple. Moretti's assumption that novels of education are structured by social and cultural questions and answers leaves open the possibility that other genres are equally involved in such procedures. But it is questionable, as Moretti knows, whether problem solving can adequately characterize the many different kinds of changes that govern bildungsromane.

The problem is clearly raised by Ann Rigney in her discussion of historical actions and their representation in historical narratives. For her, historical discourse has a *referent,* an event or character or separation. She explores "the nature of historical reference and how it influences the actual composition of historical narratives." Her point is that events become a part of the discourses that describe them; they thus involve decisions about the making of a context, about the greater or lesser details appropriate for the discourse. That a particular subject should be selected for discussion by numerous critics of the same time indicates, she says, that certain subjects are mediated by ideological factors of a given place, time, and society. In this respect they share a continuity. She is also aware that certain statements made by participants in particular situations are often quoted in different texts. They remain quotations, discrete units in different ideological texts. These, claims Rigney, are used to guarantee authenticity, provide local color and the illusion of dramatic immediacy. So, too, for topoi. They ensure common ground, assumptions of continuity. These continuities create readers' expectations and thus make possible the introduction of new knowledge or change. "In any case, it is apparent that historical narratives are perhaps more complex and heterogeneous in structure than has hitherto been realized; that their role in configuring-representing events may be inseparable from other functions such as interesting their readers, explaining events to them, and persuading them of the truth of the representation given."

Linda Orr pursues the study of the relation between history and literature in the writings of nineteenth-century historians who argue that the two genres are not interrelated. The pertinence of this study for continuity and change is that history and literature have a long history in which interrelatedness was assumed. What had at times been seen as continuous had in the nineteenth century become—for many historians—discontinuous.

Orr declares that as a result of this break, the "historical object has multiplied spatially and temporally. It has proliferated culturally and socially, entering into previously invisible realms like death, childhood, and the imaginary. The territory of history has in fact grown enormous and vertiginous, that is 'universal.'" But she notes that at the same time "it appears that the more history presses toward science, the more literature, or a has-been history, is produced." Orr presents us with the paradoxical phenomenon of a history that emphasizes its scientific bias, while it produces more "literature" than before. Orr points out that archival research and the writing of history "are not only in tension at certain periods of history but are perhaps by nature antagonistic." When historians find that rhetorical writing debauches research, they not only make claims about demystifying and purifying the language in which they write but they substitute figures and graphs that are aspects of the rhetorical. Orr puts the issue of change between the genres of literature and history as follows: "Is the difference—no less important—between the two genres that historians and their readers believe in their prefaces whereas in fiction we suspend disbelief? (Do we need, then, both a history of our belief in our own historical and linguistic representations—for example, Foucault's *Les Mots et les choses,* Genette's *Mimologiques*—and more *Rezeptionsgeschichte* or sociology of literature?)"

Orr outlines the paradoxical, complicated intertwining of history and historical change in terms of the historian's choice in relating the past to the present: "One is left with the double bind imperative: you cannot ignore the past (or it will return to haunt you . . .), and you must ignore the past if you want to live." Since historical change as narrative involves the writing of a history that the historian desires, what, asks Orr, is the status of nonverbal material in an account that includes *groups* and *figures?* Her conclusion that history is a narrative of events might be based on the assumption that the last new history missed again. The newest new history, however, need not lead to a return to the last, but to a series of questions that constantly require examinations and reexaminations of the relation between writing history and rereading the documents. "Would such stories," she asks, "be remarketed as novels?" It is, she believes, the very dynamic of history's failure that leads to another kind of history.

One wonders whether Orr is developing a theory of historical change in which historical change is always located in a narrative that has its gaps and discontinuities just as fiction does. But if this is the case, then Orr is offering an approach to history and fiction in which history and fiction become one genre at some times while at others they remain separate, related only by some features of narrativization. Such a genre theory would then take account of such nonnarrative features in history as graphs and statistics, illustrations, typographical and visual devices. The question of external reference thus becomes internal because the references are inserted into the narrative. I analyze an example of this procedure in Dell Hymes's essay that relates change to continuity in oral and written narrative.

Orr's discussion and that of the other essayists thus far presented deal with problems normally identified as the relation between past objects and their narrativization and past narratives and present critics and theorists. By placing these problems in terms of continuity and change I want to argue that the various pasts we construct are no less temporally situated than our own present. Historicists sometimes point to the obvious phenomenon that every past was once a present. The process by which a narrative once present becomes past is what some of these essays trace.

The terms in which Bryson or Moretti or Rigney or Orr seeks to rewrite the past involve debates about the construction of past narratives, considering the diversity of constructions of present narratives and the disagreements these elicit. Thus Bryson's reformulation of "context," Moretti's redescription of the text of a bildungsroman, Rigney's view of continuity in quotations and historians' shared use of rhetorical devices, Orr's analysis of the shifting paradoxes in the relations between history and literature among nineteenth-century historians all attempt to examine the interrelationship of present to past narratives, of continuity to change.

The contributors deliberately avoid generalizations about all texts and confine themselves to their own disciplines in order to control the reliability of their conclusions. But this procedure leaves the reader without any agreement upon whether a text is a series of signs or a member of one or more genres, or a collection of discourses, or all of these. The readers will be challenged to locate the relation of change to continuity in the essays they select to read. The essays deal with numerous themes so that they can be read as analyses of historical writing or the use of theory by black women writers or the functions of philosophy in postmodernism.

Such an anthology permits the readers to enter the collection at any point with any text they wish. There is no deliberate order other than what the reader makes. The practice is itself an example of the constructed order that the authors and editor have made. Thus David Boucher's essay "Conversation and Political Thought" here connected with historical texts can be connected with orality as it is presented in Dell Hymes's essay or in Deborah E. McDowell's references to Sojourner Truth. Boucher directs his remarks against the revisionist historians of political thought—Quentin Skinner, J. G. A. Pocock, and John Dunn, who assume a dialogic transaction between past and present texts:

> The historian makes an imaginative leap back to a past where he becomes privy to the conversations of others. However, the historian is not an interlocutor in the dialogue, nor a participant in the sense that he contributes to the substantive details. The historian in this respect appears to have a different role, and that is as a custodian of the then current meaning of what was said. Nevertheless, although the historian does not contribute to the conversation, he imagines himself to be a spectator who is familiar with the prevailing linguistic conventions and can detect nuances of meaning because of this familiarity.

Boucher resists this assumption because he believes it mistakenly identifies "understanding spoken discourse with the activity of understanding written texts." He denies that understanding written texts of the past "can fruitfully be conceived in terms of a conversational or dialogical relationship." But his own view of the changes imposed by historians upon past texts resembles that of the historians he criticizes. For he, like them, is guided by the evidence of the times in which past thinkers lived and in which they developed their methods of scholarship and inquiry.

> Thus, as far as I can see, there are two constraints upon the meanings achieved in the history of political thought. First, there is textual evidence, and by this I mean both the inscriptions of political thinkers and the evidence we have of the times in which they lived. And, secondly, we have the manner or mode of inquiry in terms of which the interpretation is formulated. Texts, indeed, are the bedrock to which interpretations must be anchored, but they point to nothing more beyond themselves than a possible world of meanings achievable through subscription to the current standards of scholarship and procedures of inquiry governing the mode of inference employed.

Boucher's conflict with the revisionists rests on his claim that historians do not recover the past, but provide acceptable substitutes for it. If all that is meant by recovering the past is that it is covered once again, this time by an applicable conception of the present, then Boucher and the revisionists have no debate. If, however, Boucher means that Skinner and his corevisionists believe that they reveal the past as it "truly" was, then he does his opponents an injustice. His notion of "substitution" would itself be a body of modern texts and would thus involve the very problem he seeks to eliminate.

If texts are "the bedrock to which interpretations must be anchored," Boucher assumes that a text is continuous in time because the words remain the same. But texts are differently anchored even in their own time. Moretti suggests that texts of bildungsromane are forms of problem solving; can critics agree upon continuity despite different conceptions of a text?

The problem of the text as continuous is addressed by Dell Hymes in "Notes toward (an Understanding of) Supreme Fictions." Hymes urges the reader to accept the continuity of particular oral Indian texts as a genre that not only is folklore, but also has the characteristic of a written literary text. The tales become members of two genres, not one. Hymes attributes the characteristic of literariness to oral narratives told by Indians from the North Pacific Coast of the New World. And he applies his claims for continuity and change to the constituents of the genre, to its narrative units, to its performance and reception. The plot, characters, and constituents of the original narrative are recognizable, but their functions now place them as instances of written literary genres. Hymes demonstrates the interconnection between continuity and change so that the added genre changes the interpretation of the text by reformulating it while retaining as well the received Indian text. This intertwining of negation with affirmation accounts for the possibility of ideological mixtures that are contradictory.

"Much of the current study of oral narratives," writes Hymes, "focuses on the event of narration itself, on narrators as performers. Focus on occasion brings attention to change as between one performance to another, one performer and another, and within a performance itself." Changes can refer to narrative order, to narrative units (lines, verses, stanzas, scenes), of the relation between narrator and audience. Stories can vary by incorporation into larger narratives. Such changes may move from mere variations of a narrative to a new version. Thus change is analyzed in terms of variations within a narrative to changes that remake the narrative into a new production or genre: "Change for which the narrator is not so much witness, or performer, as 'remaker,' interpreting fundamentals, deconstructing and reconstructing both." Some of the changes in the narratives told by Victoria Howard, the last speaker of the Clackamas Chinook language of the Willamette Valley of Oregon, seem to rethink the role of women in them and Hymes finds that again and again "these tellings seem to show the effect of growing up in a shattered culture, one in which caretakers are uncertain, unreliable, and in which women must muster what strength they can." Hymes points to the use of widespread myths about the ending of a world and relates these historically to the distribution of communities in particular places (such as western Oregon). Myths thus become more than mere versions of the past. Communal listeners who have heard more than one performance or performer will understand "that myths have only partly to do with the past, that myths are a dialogue between past, present, and future."

Oral narratives, Hymes argues, share with written poems and other literary structures principles of composition. His essay, therefore, opposes the received stability that assumes a strict opposition between oral and written narratives. In the first section of the paper Hymes selects the arguments of three literary critics—Robert Alter, Michael Riffaterre, and A. J. Greimas—to demonstrate the correlation of oral texts with written literary ones. And in the last section dealing with the tale-teller's artistic construction and performance and the audience's reception of oral texts, Hymes takes as his basis for comparison Wallace Stevens's titles to his three sections of *Notes toward a Supreme Fiction:* It Must Be Abstract, It Must Change, It Must Give Pleasure.

Hymes joins Moretti in recognizing the value of generic theory for the analysis of criticism and change. His major contribution in his essay is to demonstrate how an oral folklore genre can also be understood as an exemplar of a written literary narrative. It is not unusual that written works belong to more than one genre: the process of continuity that keeps them in two genres is as important as the changes that make it possible to differentiate among them. But oral and written discourses have not previously been aligned. Indeed, Hymes's argument is (so far as I know) the first attempt to connect the oral Indian narratives of the Northwest with written English literary genres. That texts perceived as opposite can in time, and occasionally even at the same time, be perceived as similar, supports the need to analyze change and continuity in generic terms of exchange and interchange.

There are obvious examples of power claims and power announcements involved in the concept of change. Rachel Blau DuPlessis draws attention to Mina Loy's "Feminist Manifesto" ("conjecturally dated 1914") and she states that "Loy's forthright critique of a 'mental attitude' deemed 'superstition,' not to speak of her forthright willingness to discuss sex (sexuality, gender, sexual intercourse are all mingled in the term), are clear ruptures with dominant ideology." Manifestos, whether feminist or communist or Dadaist, announce ruptures with the past, but the very announcements indicate a sameness, a repetition that defies the change. Yet the change may be present in the writer's own writing without providing a basis for an innovative continuity of poetry or prose. This is often the case of prefaces that announce the change which the text will introduce, but the reader discovers only too often that the authority of the preface is unreliable, even contradictory, when compared with the text itself. This, I take it, is Linda Orr's point about prefaces to history.

Finally, the concepts of continuity and change belong to the production of texts. Critics, no less than poets or novelists, reject or repress certain texts. Whatever the reasons for continuing a practice or abandoning it, they cannot be sought merely in the published texts. Whether oral as described by Dell Hymes or written in the drafts discussed by DuPlessis, selective generic or metaphoric choice ought not be overlooked. Governments can put a sudden and immediate stop to the production of particular texts; by law or censorship they may permit changes to take place gradually.

It is not, however, my desire as editor in this introduction to go into detail on the critical methods implied by the practice of contributors. It is apparent, however, that Bryson, for example, proceeds from semiotic assumptions since he makes this claim himself. The historians apply methods from intellectual history. Moretti proceeds from a Marxist approach to genre and Hymes from a literary-theoretical version of genre mixed with ethnographical hypotheses. Other critics prefer to make disciplines the basis for the study of change and thus refer to inside and outside the discipline.

In an illuminating example, Murray Krieger offers a study of the change within literary theory from the New Criticism to the present critical and cultural theory in literary study. Krieger examines the theoretical changes that Cleanth Brooks underwent from his early *Modern Poetry and the Tradition* (1939) to his *The Well Wrought Urn* (1947). He declares that change is not the consequence of any history of progress but "a sequence of wayward accidents, each subject only to local forces and not a rationalized, timeless pattern."

> Indeed, we can look at the history of recent criticism—especially as it is related to the privileging of one or another kind of literary work—as a succession of would-be empires, movements that have gone through similar stages in their rise and—too soon thereafter—their fall. If we take the word *movement* literally, in thinking of literary and critical movements, we find in it this group commitment to change, to forgo rest for activity itself. This need of a movement to keep moving finds itself in continuing conflict with its desire to establish itself as a dominant, unchanging institution.

Krieger divides a movement into three parts: the first movement—the most radical—puts a new conception or critical "empire" in place by including texts and excluding poems previously included. The second movement recasts a number of the new inclusions and moves to the argument that a universal sameness exists in all literature. The third movement marks the disintegration of the universalist assumption.

Krieger and Moretti both describe continuity and change in terms of cycles that apply to texts that become part of a movement. Thus the New Criticism applies to poetry primarily rather than to tragedy or comedy and Moretti takes as his subject the bildungsroman, not the romance. Moretti relates his cycle to cultural forces in the state whereas Krieger draws attention to a universalizing impulse to theorize one's differentness while casting it in a repetitive model and imposing it upon others who thus become theoretical clones: "For the human mind cannot allow history to unroll without projecting a form upon it: our formal, universalizing impulse would make theorists of us all. The need to proclaim the differentness brought by each agent of revolutionary change is always in conflict with the sameness of the enterprise that proclaims it. This need is also in conflict with the imperialistic desire—and hence the program— to impose this special version of differentness upon others, thus making it their sameness."

Krieger emphasizes the rapidity with which theoretical positions can gather supporters. He points to the changes that were introduced by the deconstructionists, the neo-Marxists, and feminist versions of these and sees these as conforming to his triadic model. But the issue of fashion becomes for him a force for unexamined change, and an analysis of a current operation of fashion can be found in Deborah E. McDowell's essay.

But there are critics who are less interested in the historical rise and fall of movements than in the continuity of contributions that are passed on. R. K. Meiners, who also discusses the New Criticism, writes about the critical rhetoric it produced: "This includes the way the writer of the New Critical essay takes his relationship to his ostensible subject (including the texts he questions), the way the critic marks himself out from his opposition and then absorbs it, and the way in which Rhetoric itself may be seen both in concert with and opposed to Dialectic." Meiners agrees with Krieger that the critics and theorists have been rejected. But he warns of the dangers of dismissing the writers of the past too readily. Individual writers compose the New Criticism; if we are to point to continuities in the movement, we should distinguish those who provide the continuities from those who don't. Meiners presents a close reading of some of Allen Tate's early criticism and some of R. P. Blackmur's late essays. Tate and Blackmur did indeed have some of the cultural awareness that most New Critics lacked. Meiners lays out in detail what he takes to be the reasons for the failure of the New Criticism and he explains what they needed in their criticism to prevent its rejection:

> What was needed was a more direct political understanding of the way criti-
> cism appropriated the languages of poetry and other literary discourse; but
> beyond that an understanding of the way that poetry, and "literature" gener-
> ally, appropriated and triumphed over, in its own imperialism, the rejected
> languages and marginal voices of the culture (including critical discourse),
> and used those to subvert the dominant languages. And above all, it needed
> a more constantly critical and political knowledge of how critics, once they
> allow their marginal intelligences to become co-opted by central concerns of
> institutions, run the continual risk of becoming what Gramsci called "experts
> in legitimation."

The claim that these critics needed a more adequately critical and cultural knowledge in order to have a greater continuity raises the question: Are assertions about continuity and change merely contingent upon "adequate" information or also on some "adequate" perceptual framework into which the information fits? In my discussion of the contributions to this collection I have cited contemporary disagreements about such key concepts as contexts, oral and written discourse, history and fiction. A particular critical theory may explore a particular continuity, but what specific kinds of continuity are decisive for future directions? Other theories contemporary with it may use terms like *appropriation, triumphed, imperialism, co-opted* for quite different continuities. There are examples of theory that account for changes in terms of combinatory rather than combative choices. And in urging continuity, can we deny that different criticisms in using the same or similar terms have different continuities because they connect the terms with different aims?

This is apparent in McDowell's essay, "Recycling." She points to the example of Sojourner Truth, the nineteenth-century black woman, whose short oral text, "Ain't I a Woman?" has often in our time become for some black and white women critics no more than a token. And so, too, her name. "But the repetition of Sojourner's name makes no *real* difference. In dominant discourses it is a symbolic gesture masking the face of power and its operations in the present academic context. As a figure summoned from the seemingly safe and comfortable distance of a historical past, Sojourner Truth is removed from the present social context and can thus act symbolically to absorb, defuse, and deflect its conflicts. However, 'Sojourner Truth' stirs up far more controversy than it settles, preventing any easy resolution of feminism's conflicts."

Sojourner Truth is for McDowell an example of the failure of many black feminist critics to historicize their past, to fill the gap in criticism between the mid-nineteenth century and the late twentieth. Uttering the name Sojourner Truth is not followed by study of her actions and her role in the lives of black women. It performs "for some an absolution of critical guilt, but the utterance is all."

What McDowell offers as a valuable and necessary project for connecting contemporary black feminist discourse to its past is to proceed "from the commonplace assumption that no consideration of *any* intellectual project is complete without an understanding of the process of that project's formation. And thus any responsible accounting of the work of black women in literary studies would have to provide a history of its emergence and to consider that emergence on its own terms." This is an important step, but it is not without its dilemmas. There is no reason to assume that the history of emergence is any less liable to be co-opted or subordinated to strategies of dominance than the hollowing of the name. In the effort to relate past acts or statements to present theory, McDowell is aware, we need to try to know what has slipped away from the past as well as what we have recuperated from it. And are we not already reformulating what we have recuperated?

The recovery of a past text that disappeared or failed to establish continuity has its analogue in Cushing Strout's inquiry about Tocqueville's prophecy in 1840 "that modern democratic writers would, by focusing on 'passions and ideas' in 'the hidden depths of man's spiritual nature,' illuminate by exaggeration, as he put it, 'certain dark corners of the human heart.'" Discontinuity finally leads to continuity after a long gap. But Cushing Strout points out that a body of critics in the nineteen thirties and forties provided numerous explanations that continued and supported the paradigm. McDowell's effort to recover the values of Sojourner Truth would seem to require some unified effort at constructing a history of black women critics. And it requires, too, societal and institutional (university) support as well. The underlying theme is the construction of a community by black women writers.

Richard Lehan's essay, "Urban Signs and Urban Literature: Literary Form and Historical Process," explores some of the issues involved in constructing a narrative of the city. His approach to historical change involves the relation of fact to narrative, of urban architecture and governmental institutions and laws as they affect the people that are controlled or contained by them. The issue of change between events and their narration was treated by Rigney and Orr. When statements, aphorisms, propositions, and quotations are involved, these can form continued elements of narratives. But converting vision into verbal statements involves highly complicated practices of perceptual transformations.

In pursuing the relation of fact to fiction, Lehan observes the continuity of narrative patterns in Gothic novels and contrasts this continuity of structure with that of earlier novels in which there was a symbiosis between city and countryside that is now breaking down: "When the historical signs of this breakdown were translated into literary codes, what we got was the Gothic novel." Not only was the relationship between city and countryside unsettled, "what was going on beneath the surface of the city was equally unsettled and unsettling." These remarks resemble Moretti's in that they assume a relation between internal structure and external social and political behavior. But Moretti refers to the bildungsroman whereas Lehan refers to the Gothic novel. What about the fiction of Charlotte Lennox and Fanny Burney? Are there only specific genres that respond to social and economic changes? Lehan provides a remarkable series of examples describing the unsettled characters and situations in the subsurfaces of the city in the nineteenth- and twentieth-century versions of novels. As he moves from examples drawn from British novels to those of the Russian and French, the relation of continuity to change becomes more and more challenging.

The implication might very well be that the texts which deal with urban life provide the continuing factor for fiction whereas changes in fictional strategies result not from changes in urban life but from new combinatory features of narratives. The essay recognizes that the city provides data for narratives, but there seems no feedback indicating that our view of the city is changed by them, as argued by Orr and to a more limited extent by Rigney. Lehan gives a dense description of the surface and subsurface of the city beginning with Defoe. For him, narratives interpret the city, but they continue the structures that are already in the signs of the city. "As Jacques Ellul has shown, as these societies became more technologically sufficient, they also found the means of controlling the masses, the information that reached the masses, and the liberties that were allowed them."

What about change and continuity in the history of philosophy? Berel Lang in his essay, "Nostalgia for the Future, Waiting for the Past: Postmodernism in Philosophy," plays upon the reversibility of time, of the future in the past and the past in the future. What can now constitute a history of philosophy when, in Lang's view, such a philosophy is "either hopelessly amorphous or, still worse, that bears an uncanny resemblance to the past—that is, a 'new' present in which nothing has changed." Neither of these is adequate as a historical conception, for no useful generalization can come from them. What Lang offers as a possibility is that the history of philosophy began "by setting out from particular moments of experience."

What this amounts to, then, is the appropriation into the present of "a past that can be advanced, subverted—or, with the tactics of postmodernism, turned on its side: certainly not for the first time, probably not for the last, but nonetheless. Thus, everything *is* possible—including philosophy when it flatly asserts that not everything is possible."

Thus the procedures of the history of philosophy indicate that continuity and change are intricately involved in a series of nongeneralizable relations. But with regard to a specific argument or a particular experience, continuity and change are possible.

What implications can be drawn from my discussion of continuity and change? The first is that the theme I have selected is treated at different levels and given different emphases and importance by contributors. Moreover, each contributor locates the discussion of change among a variety of discourses. For critics like Rachel Blau DuPlessis, Deborah McDowell, Dell Hymes, the analysis of continuity and change is less important than the issues of orality and writing or the discourses of black feminist writers or the analysis of a poem by Mina Loy as a sexually powerful feminist document. For other critics, the discussions of change have primary or ancillary functions.

The combinations give each contribution a specific identity. I have pointed out in my discussion that the essays employ various strategies to deal with continuity and change. But many other strategies remain to be examined. These essays indicate that the combinatory features of critical writing lead to more than one kind of change. As I have indicated, both "change" and "continuity" embrace multiple discourses. Moreover, lyrics and history and bildungsromane, when considered as instances of a generic system are examples of changes.

This collection suggests some of the varied directions that change can take in criticism and theory. By helping us to understand how continuity and change have functioned, these essays lead us to consider the possibilities of change before us. Which of these directions are returns, which are dead ends, which redirect writing, and which of these cause us to rethink the relation of writing to our nonverbal world?

1

ART IN CONTEXT

ॐ

Norman Bryson

IT IS A BATTLE CRY, a command, a whole program. Yet some of its assumptions might well give grounds for disquiet. What it liberates with one hand it legislates with the other. At the same time that it guides art history forward, it drives it back. "Context" is just that, a double operation of advance and containment.[1] At the center of art-historical endeavor, it is nevertheless a concept that one is not supposed to question. How could one possibly be against it?

In what follows I attempt to sketch some of the difficulties that "context," as an idea, entails; my general perspective is that of visual semiotics, which discusses art and viewing as activities of the sign. I would not want to claim that other points of view would not lead to the same or to similar conclusions, or that to start from the proposition that visual art is a matter of signs supplies any particular advantage for an inquiry into the context-idea. It is simply where I happen, given my own formation, to start from. On the way I encounter a number of operations in the rhetoric of contextualization that I call, for want of a better term (and to avoid worse terms) "slides." They are not systematically presented; they do not, for example, always correspond to the figures named in rhetoric. I leave them as incidental punctuation, merely numbered, with the hope they may be more suggestive than irritating.

Perhaps the strongest resistance on the part of traditional art history to the perspectives opened up by semiotics occurs at the initial moment of encounter, when the emphasis on visual *signs* is misheard and misread as a call to retire one of the key terms of the art-historical apparatus, namely, "context." One of the most reliable predictions that can be made about the transactions between a classical art history department and the visiting speaker from a "neighboring" discipline where semiotics has a history, or the graduate student in the department whose dissertation proposes to engage with semiotic issues, or the unfortunate spokesperson for semiotic theory at, say, a National Endowment for the Humanities Institute on Interpretation and the Visual Arts, is that within minutes it will be alleged that the perspective of semiotics is deficient in that it cannot address the context in which works of visual art are historically produced. What typically ensues is that the semiotician, at last cornered by traditional art history, is denied the time even to sketch the reasons why "context," so far from being irrelevant to visual semiotics, is vital to its mode of inquiry. For what is not at stake is that "context" be abandoned as a working concept, in the supposed free play of "anything goes"; rather, what visual semiotics proposes is that the concept be problematized and reformulated, and not just incidentally but as a central and continual activity within the discipline.

A number of assumptions operate within the word *"context"* itself, which the term is rarely required to unpack or declare. First, there is the implied opposition between context and work of art, context and visual text; these are taken as predestined antonyms, in that the text is something to be explained by the context: here lies the visual text, waiting for the context to come to order its uncertainties, and over there is the context, as that which shall act upon the text and transfer to the latter its own certainties and determinations. Context and text are thus established in the guise of a separation that is at the same time an evident hierarchy, for the expectation is that context will *control* the text; once their opposition is staked out the terms taken together are made to form an economy in which context is active and the text or work of art passive. Insofar as the text is assumed to be exactly a *work* of *art* (wrought, elaborated, heightened) the context that will operate upon it will do so from a place that is not constructed and made, but acts as a natural ground on which the text may be laid out; here the opposition becomes that of nature versus artifice. Since context is credited with the status of a given, or a series of givens, once the text is placed within its orbit the text's vagaries and waywardness can be brought to an end, by replacing these features with the context's univocality and rectitude. One knows what the context is: it is a question of transferring to the text the context's own properties, of determinate form, givenness, and ground. Perhaps one can locate here one of the primary figures in the rhetoric of contextuality. (Slide 1: context is that which will *pass* its qualities to the text, in a transfer that is also a substitution: text is only that which still awaits its conversion into context.)

The limitations of the text-context pairing begin to emerge quite quickly if one attends to a home truth of historiography—though it is one that intellectual historians in particular are often taken to task for ignoring: that it cannot be taken for granted that the evidence which makes up "context" is going to be any *simpler* than the visual or the verbal text on which such evidence is to operate. Dominick LaCapra is especially sharp in pinpointing the "simplicity" postulate, which he describes as "the tendency of professional historians to see texts as documents in the narrow sense of the word and, by the same token, to ignore the textual dimensions of documents themselves, that is, the manner in which documents 'process' or re-work material in ways intimately bound up with larger sociocultural and political processes."[2] In practice the danger here, built into the text-context distinction from the beginning, is that the contextual document is identified directly with what it seems to represent or say—"with its propositions, themes, or characterisations."[3] The evidence classed as "context" is placed, by the text-context hierarchy, as not requiring to be *read* in the same fashion as the verbal or visual text in question: if text is posited as "textual" in the senses of elusive, complex, veiled, then context is somehow exempted or protected from such involuted textuality. One is not dealing here with negligence but with the structural necessities of the text-context model, one of which is that text be systematically opposed to context (even when no difference in complexity between them may be expected in advance), resulting eventually in the turning of "context" into *non*-text.

In art history the practical dangers here may be especially acute, since the contextual texts that it draws upon are so often both highly complex in their organization, and rhetorically calculated to project particular effects into their sociocultural milieux. In a "high" category art history confronts such classes as ekphrastic commentary, theological summae, the philosophical or linguistic treatise, sermons, parliamentary acts, histories, novels, poems, dramas. And, again, it cannot be assumed in advance that texts in the "low" category, in popular culture, will by virtue of that be any less semantically complex: diaries, letters, memoirs, maxims, chronicles, travelogues, etiquette books, graffiti. An opposition may at the outset be posited between a context, held to be determinative in its effects upon a work of art, and the artwork, held to be lacking in determination. But context here is not different in kind from text; in Jonathan Culler's famous phrase it is "just more text": "context is not given but produced; what belongs to a context is determined by interpretive strategies; contexts are just as much in need of elucidation as events; and the meaning of a context is determined by events."[4] In place of context, Culler proposes a much more useful term: *frame,* which has the virtue of reminding one that framing is something we do, not something we find, that it is a process of making—and thereby avoids the positivistic connotations of "givenness" that are inseparable from the context-idea. Of itself, the appeal to context does not yet solve the problem it points to, but only displaces it: "context" purports to be the controlling term for text, but in fact it only shifts the problem sideways. (Slide 2: denial of complexity on one side, in "context," *appears* as containment of complexity on the other side, in "text.")

This points to a further vicissitude in the context-idea, and one that does not, I think, require a specifically semiotic critique for it to emerge, in that it does so even if the whole question of textuality, visual and verbal, is bracketed. The difficulty here is that the very certainty of ground that the word *context* appeals to is undone by its own operation, which is nothing but a movement of regression. The context-idea invites us to *step back* from the uncertainties of text to "context" posited as platform or foundation. But once this step is taken it is by no means clear why it may not be taken again; that is, "context" entails from its first moment a regression "without brakes." Lawyers, one suspects, may have a special professional familiarity with the problem, in that the context in a legal dispute is not a given of the case but something that lawyers themselves precisely make: the nature of evidence is such that there is always more of it, subject only to the external limits of their own stamina, the court's patience, and the client's means.[5] But art historians, too, have to confront and negotiate the problem on a daily basis. In his wonderfully elegant chapter on art-historical forensics, which takes as its historical object the engineer Benjamin Baker's Forth Bridge (1889), Michael Baxandall draws up an initial compilation of twenty-four factors acting as the determinant context upon the bridge's construction. Here I present just the opening and the conclusion of the list:

1. East-coast estuaries of Scotland
2. Location of towns
3. Railway's need of continuity of line
4. Railway's independent companies
21. Steel's sensitivity to shear stress
22. William Arrol's executive virtuosity
23. A gamut of public taste
24. Baker's functional expressionism[6]

Out of these twenty-four determinants Baxandall is able to fashion a convincing and rational case—a model of what goes on when causal narratives are assembled. Yet just as he is winding up, he cannot resist adding to the list: on the final page of his analysis the reader hears, for the first time, of long-span metal bridges as a feature of Benjamin Baker's late style; of Baker's interest in symmetry (encasing weights in the stone piers to avoid revealing an imbalance between the side cantilevers); of the Fourth Bridge as a national publicity exercise, promoting an image of the technical expertise of British engineers over their French and German rivals; of the Bridge as taking as its audience not the public or the directors of the railway company but Baker's professional colleagues.

What can be the status of these afterthoughts, which extend the list to perhaps twenty-eight factors, if not that of supplements that are added to the list in order to bolster it up, to make it even more rounded and complete; but which reveal thereby an uncurtailability in the list, exactly the impossibility of its closure. Once begun, the enumeration of contextual determinants knows no point of finality within its own domain. What is more, it cannot know at what point the contextual determinants for one event (for the building of the Forth Bridge) in fact become determinants in another distinct event (though "distinctness" is exactly in question here), such as the history of railway companies, of Victorian taste, of publicity, of professions, of steel; no procedure within the list can ascertain when the context that is being constructed is in fact being constructed not for the Forth Bridge but for some quite other entity. The sheer ostensibility of the bridge (an object apparently disclosed in full just by pointing at it) cannot overcome the way that context, in its infinite expansiveness, blurs the edges of the bridge, dissolves its boundaries, and enters the orbit of another term or entity, itself no less subject than the bridge to the same eventual dissolution of outline.

But surely *adding* to a list of determining factors only strengthens the case? Why else would lawyers, who must presumably know what they are doing, devote such efforts to expanding the context they must present in court? It would seem that one is starting to argue that the very principle that adds weight to the analysis, enumeration, in some way lightens it. But addition cannot be a guarantee here of explanation's gravitas. Suppose that one tries to engineer an ideal causal narrative, a utopian explanation in which all the key domains of context are combined; let us say that the object for causal explanation is a painting. Perhaps one would want to combine the areas of determination that are currently thought to be the principal ones, starting with the painter's intention; the internal logic of the unforeseen problems that the actual work of painting brings into being, together with their solutions; the factors of patronage or of the market; the ideological components at work in the image; its references to tradition; its dealings with the generic expectations of its audience; the role of prestige or cultural capital in shaping the work's decisions; its relation to institutions of pedagogy, and professional or other social structures within the community of painters. While the accumulation of determining factors may seem at first sight to tend toward the ideal of complete causal accounting, what troubles the account here is difference between the various orders of explanation. To move from intention to the problematics of execution, to patronage, to intertextuality, and the rest, is to invoke areas whose mutual articulation is far from clear. In order to tend *toward* the goal of complete explanation, the account must know what counts as strong and what as weak determination; it must also be able to establish lines of causality within the various domains involved, and the direction in which those lines run. But the attempt to combine a plurality of domains and kinds of explanation in fact announces its limits in its opening move, of aggregation, the adding together of different registers or domains;[7] for what this points to is precisely conflict of interpretation and diffraction among the factors of determination.[8]

In practice, and to cope with this situation, causal explanations tend to adopt a convention that excuses them from the need to establish the mode of articulation between domains: it will be enough to make a list. Within the list there now appear factors that are extraordinarily unrelated, factors at times having in common *only* that they can be made to point roughly toward their supposed outcome: the painting, the Forth Bridge. (Slide 3: the unity of the "determined" object stands in for the missing unity of the causal account.) As one passes from the Scottish estuaries, to the railways' need for continuity of line, to the shear stress of steel, to Baker's professional standing, and so on, one's journey through the list is a bit like the Chinese encyclopedia in Borges's story.[9] Unless the account also specifies factors of weighting and of mutual dynamics among the domains of the explanation, the result is not a statement about determination (to determine: to make up one's mind, decide; fix as known; be the deciding factor in) but about *difference* at work in the account's causal order—differences which, without the arbitrations and specifications that are needed, are not even clearly on the map.

Ascertaining the direction in which the lines of causality run may sometimes be difficult, for art history as for philosophy. Cause is supposed to be logically and temporally prior to effect. Yet there are obvious instances where the sequence is actually inferred from its end point, from the effect, leading to the kind of metalepsis Nietzsche called "chronological reversal."[10] "Suppose one feels a pain. This causes one to look for a cause and spying, perhaps, a pin, one links and reverses the perceptual or phenomenal order, *pain . . . pin,* to produce a causal sequence, *pin . . . pain.*"[11] In this case the pin as cause is located after the effect it has on us has been produced. The terrain in which art history faces the phenomenon most acutely is that of influence, since causal accounts of art are likely to include as determinants not only "events in the world" but earlier representations whose traces may be found in the particular work subjected to causal analysis. (Slide 4: it is assumed by causal narration that every determinant will leave a trace; catalytic transformations, conversions of the determinant into new forms, the historical disappearance of the determinant, all these are excluded from the picturing of what must remain causal *lines* and contiguities. A cult of metonymies appears here as the hallmark of modernity and scientific explanation, though science itself knows others models of determination.)[12] The problem is that of knowing how to evaluate the links between earlier and later works which the analysis finds, or constructs.

Suppose that such a link is made, between two paintings that have in common a similar handling of a particular feature or range of features. What is the most appropriate move here for the art historian to make? The model of causality, as art history proposes it, provides an immediate answer, modulated through a key art-historical technology, namely, source analysis: the earlier image stands as "origin" to the later image. Students of classical art history are apt to develop a sharp eye for possible sources, and source analysis may be one of the discipline's most effective instruments in training the eye to make extremely fine distinctions and observations. But one may well be worried about the compatibility between the skills thus generated and the causal model that those skills are made to serve. (Slide 5: source analysis transposes to a causal plane observations originating at a comparative plane of analysis.) It can come as a surprise to the outsider from another discipline, even from places of such soft forensics as literature departments, to realize that the control upon what may constitute a source in art history has the latitude it does, and that it employs only a negative or subtractive check: that it would *not have been impossible* for the painter of image Y to have seen the earlier image X. Of course the case can be made more persuasive if more positive proof of the painter of Y having actually seen X is put forward, but it is by no means essential within art historical discourse. And to the extent that the negative or subtractive convention applies, one is dealing with "chronological reversal" in a form that only appears to respect the logical and temporal priority of cause to effect. The "context" in which the work is placed is in fact *being generated out of the work itself,* by means of a rhetorical operation that nonetheless purports to regard the work as having been produced by its "causes" and not as producing them. (Slide 6: metalepsis, substitution of cause for effect.)

When cause and effect oscillate in this way there is grave danger of discursive disruption, since reversal of the lines of causality threatens the coherence both of the causal model (from cause *to* effect) and of the context-idea (context is that which acts *upon* the visual text). And typically what happens when such disruptions occur is that the analysis quickly shifts to another interpretive level where the threat may be evaded or contained. (Slide 7: with the causal model not under siege, the *narration* intervenes through diversionary tactics, by rerouting the commentary away from cause-to-effect sequences; as when, in conversation, one changes the subject.) Frequently met with is the following: at the exact point where causal lines threaten to go into reverse, there is invocation to a higher unity, whether to the creative artist-subject, or to the organic unity of traditions, or, often, both at once.

Appeal to the unity supplied by the creativity of the artist-subject typically takes the form of saying that, despite the (apparent) causal dependency on an earlier work X, artist Y in fact "goes beyond" the source, assimilating it and successfully transforming it into something new.[13] The success of the transformation will now justify it as self-originating and thereby *account* for its status as cause rather than effect; the appeal to creativity actively reorders and explains the disruption at the lower plane of analysis, where what was supposed to be "effect" threatened to become "cause." (Slide 8: an operation at a second level of discourse can rework and *pacify* what had been turbulent at the first causal level.) Related to this move is its opposite, the verdict that the work may have *tried* to transform its source X, but failed to do so (mediocrity). Here the judgment issues from the same diversionary plane of analysis as before, that of the full artist-subject, only now the work is said to fail at this level; the mediocre work is that which is unable to transcend the *mechanical* nexus of cause and effect. The outcome is, again, containment of the disturbance present within the causal account, since the mediocre work is discovered after all never to have actually made the causal lines to reverse; it was not strong enough to become self-originating, and so it was after all only an effect, an echo.

Appeal to the unity supplied by "tradition" works in a rather different way. Here the work that could not be placed as effect to cause, but made the causal operation to go into reverse gear, is recuperated by the idea of organic accommodation within a field of (always unitary) tradition. The work of Picasso is not simply an addition to the European tradition, it transforms our perception of everything that had gone before; looking at Francis Bacon will make us see the portraits of Velázquez with different eyes; Ingres makes us go back to Raphael and see in Raphael's works qualities to which only Ingres can sensitize us, and so forth. Here the figure of causality, of chains that are supposed to run unidirectionally but are constantly threatening to reverse, is abandoned in favor of a quite different figure, the network. "The existing order is complete before the new work arrives; for order to persist after the supervention of novelty, the whole existing order must be, if ever so slightly, altered; and so the relations, proportions, values of each work of art toward the whole are readjusted; and this is conformity between the old and the new."[14] Where linear chains and concatenations lose their coherence as their operations go into reverse, and are weakened and defeated by metalepsis or chronological reversal, "network" as a concept thrives when such reversals happen; it is defined exactly by its capacity to allow its components to switch from active to passive roles. To pass from Velázquez as influence and Bacon as receiver of that influence, to the opposite situation, Bacon as refashioner of Velázquez's work, is the very movement which brings "network," as a rhetorical figure, into being. More elastic and comprehensive than the causal model, the network-idea, Eliot's organic tradition and all its variants, steps in to absorb the tensions created when the derivation from cause to effect cannot be analytically produced. In a sense it is parasitic upon cause-to-effect as a model, since "network" can only begin its rhetorical work when the linearity of cause-to-effect breaks down; in another sense it subsumes the causal model, the latter emerging as a special case within the network itself.

Although the phenomenon of the verbal or visual text that generates its own context, of the work that shapes its own "sources," emerges with unusual clarity in the terrain of influence, it is by no means confined there. The paradoxes of source analysis may be only a particular instance of a more general chronological reversal that haunts art-historical discourse. To locate this larger field, I would like to turn to Michael Holly's recent inquiry into Burckhardt's reconstructions of Renaissance history.[15] What Holly finds is a striking congruence between the Renaissance as represented by its painters and the Renaissance as reevoked in Burckhardt's historiographic enterprise. On the one hand Burckhardt writes, as Hayden White has also observed, in such a way as to frustrate his readers' expectation of a linear historical narrative.[16] His study of the Renaissance is a *satura,* or miscellany; it breaks with the nineteenth-century historian's imperative, to tell a story. It is through an abundance of details and through unmotivated juxtapositions—bloodthirsty tyrannicides against Petrarchan love sonnets—that his account is built. Yet at the same time Burckhardt's abundance, Holly argues, is held within a fixed optical framework. Nothing is excluded from its scope of vision—in principle there is no object which the writing could not embrace. But what reorders the miscellany is exactly a look, a viewpoint whose function and result is to supply through its own masterful overview the unity that is absent at the level of the historical object. The Renaissance passes before and within a single, monocular, seigneurial gaze. It is impossible to miss the resemblance between this unifying, mastering prospect and the jewel of Renaissance painting, Albertian perspective, with its capacity to see and to represent any object, with its folding of vision around the single, centralized spectator, and its aesthetic balance between the abundance and detail of *copia* and the unity and coherence of *compositio.* "Venice . . . the jewel-casket of the world . . . where the business of the world is transacted, not amid shouting confusion, but with the subdued hum of many voices; where in the porticos round the square and in those of the adjoining streets sit hundreds of money-changers and goldsmiths, with endless rows of shops and warehouses above their heads. . . . Before . . . the great Fondaco of the Germans . . . ships are drawn up side by side in the canal; higher up is a whole fleet laden with wine and oil, and parallel with it, on the shore swarming with porters, are the vaults of the merchants."[17] Burckhardt's representation elides with Renaissance representation, in an account characterized not by distance from the historical object but heightened implication and involvement. Burckhardt's history is "anticipated by the structure of the objects it labors to illuminate"[18]—in this case, Carpaccio; there is a sense in which Renaissance paintings have *predicted* the form of the historian's later portrayal. The outcome is a collaborative production created both by those who, during the Renaissance, attempted to fix a picture of their own historical milieu, and by the historian coming afterwards who looks back to them to see how, for them, their world was organized.

When the historian's account appears to be the continuation of a performance that was begun in the period that is to be accounted for, the situation could perhaps be treated as an aberration, a regrettable surrender of the detachment that should shape the historian's enterprise. Yet the metalepsis present in Burckhardt, which works to make text and context change places, may be able to point toward a much more general phenomenon within art-historical discourse. Imagine a contemporary account of, say mid-Victorian painting; one which aims to reconstruct the context for the paintings in terms of social and cultural history. The works themselves depict such social sites as racetracks, pubs, railway stations and train compartments, street scenes where well-to-do ladies pass by workmen digging the road, interiors in which domestic melodramas are played out, the stock exchange, the veterans' hospital, the church, the asylum. It would not be thought unusual for the art historian to work from the paintings out toward the history of these sites and milieux, in order to discover their historical specificity and determination, their detailed archival texture. Just this sort of inquiry is what the word *"context"* asks for; such reconstruction would be fitting, and, one might say, indicated by the nature of the visual materials to hand.

But there are senses in which the procedure is still strange, despite its familiarity and its aura of professionalism. A primary difficulty is that those features of mid-Victorian Britain that do *not* find themselves pictured by mid-Victorian painters do not necessarily feature here as part of the context that is to account for the works of art. A social history that set out, unassisted by pictures, to discover the social and historical conditions of mid-Victorian Britain might well attend to quite other milieux, different social sites, and indeed many other kinds of historical objects that do not readily lend themselves to pictorial representation. A harder social analysis might treat the pictures incidentally, in passing, as one sort of evidence among many—if one is going to do social history, why privilege works of art in such a way that the findings of historiography must be bound to the mise-en-scène of painting? What is perplexing about the kind of context that is asked to be produced here is, first of all, its regulation by an unspoken trope, the part for the whole: those sites that are represented in pictures will stand for that larger entity, the context behind them, Victorian Britain (or Renaissance Italy, or seventeenth-century Holland, or Edo Japan). Moreover, what counts as the sites that, in the form of context, are to act as determinants upon the paintings, have in fact been determined by the visual texts they are to explain, in a substitution of cause for effect that is, nevertheless, rhetorically presented as a causal account. (Slide 9: synecdoche: context is necessarily conceived as a totality; it is everything in the world that could possibly count as context—everything, that is, except the visual text.)

By a further trope or rhetorical production, the paintings from which the context had been derived are then able to act as confirmation of the truth of the analysis. The crucial action performed here by the rhetoric is the postulation of an *interval* between the text and the context, such that the two, having been separated, may come together in a moment of proof. Yet how could the context *not* fit the text, under these conditions, since it is from the visual text, from the paintings themselves, that the terms of the context were in the first place established? (Slide 10: a spiral is at work here—elements of visual text migrate from text to context and back; but recognition of such circulation is prevented by the primary cut of text-stroke-context.) The work, the labor of the rhetoric, consists in the creation of a phantasmic cleavage between text and context, which is followed by an equally uncanny drawing together of the two sides that had been separated. This break or cut is exactly what the text-context model wants from the beginning, from the moment is breathes its name. The stroke dividing "text" from "context" is the fundamental operation on which all else is built. It is what Derrida calls "the *sans* of the pure cut,"[19] a cutting of the field that will be so sharp as to leave no traces of its own incision; a conceptual blade so acute that when the two sides of the cleavage are brought together the edges will perfectly rejoin. From one point of view (that of the "parergon") this cut is precisely the operation that establishes the aesthetic as a specific order of discourse. From another point of view, the cut is that which creates a discourse of art historical explanation; it is because the blade can so cleanly separate the two edges, of text and context, that one seems to be dealing with an order of explanation at all, explanation on one side and *explanandum* on the other.

Three rhetorical stages have been sketched here: the metaleptic substitution, cause for effect; the presentation of the part for the whole; the double action of separating text from context, followed by the two coming together in a veridical fit (the account must be true; the paintings prove it). Perhaps they have been familiar steps in other kinds of academic reasoning, in other disciplines. But the discourse of art history goes on to supply a last and culminating stage that may be peculiar to itself. For the situation of art history entails that the order of explanation be related to a *visual* object. Where literary critics or historians join text and text the art historian joins text and image, and the conjunctions and disjunctions between these enable a distinct set of procedures to arise. The final operation, and the most uncanny, is that the commentary is eventually made to assume iconic form, *as* the pictures. In the move from context to visual text, the commentary comes to *picture itself,* to merge with and become the paintings it analyzes: picture and commentary stand in a mimetic rather than an analytic relation, the context copying the visual text, and the visual text iconizing or imaging the context. Taken together, the semiotic maneuvers at work in such a discourse add up to a set of procedures, naturalized as a common professional language, that is perhaps specific to the generic form of the *illustrated* text. An image, thought to be the product of a series of causal chains, in fact shapes those chains. The detailed contextual account that is worked out as relations of contiguity is then reexpressed in terms of the totality that is inscribed in the word *context,* as part-for-the-whole. (Slide 11: from metonymy to synecdoche, from the drudgery of clue-finding and of causal chains down below to the great simultaneous vista from on high, the total prospect: the Renaissance, mid-Victorian Britain, Edo Japan, and so forth.) In its concluding stages the analysis then looks to the image for confirmation or proof of its own truth (the splicing and rejoining of the primary cut of text and context); and finally the detailed historical account is iconized as the picture. (Slide 12: from analysis to ekphrasis.)

One of the key issues in the construction of context that so far has not been touched on is that of reception: the way that visual texts were apprehended by actual viewers in a given historical period. Introduction of reception does a great deal to call into question the notion of a "timeless" response to paintings; by the very act of describing the responses of viewers in another period, accounts that are in actuality constructed and guaranteed by particular cultural and institutional forces in the present find it that much the harder to represent themselves as transcendent, as outside and above contingency, in the purity of aesthetic contemplation. Moreover, to focus on the difficulties raised by the question of reception can have a salutary effect in another way. Imagine the following: an artist (for example, LeBrun) produces a painting *(The Queens of Persia at the Feet of Alexander)*; at the same time an official commentary is produced, describing ways in which the image is to be viewed (Félibien). If the question of how actual viewers responded to this double pressure upon viewing—from the work and from its authorized commentator—is bypassed, it becomes possible to treat the commentary as though the visual responses it describes could be identified, via synecdoche, as the "period" response that contextual art history needs. The need may be particularly strong when the emphasis on such a period response is made in order to combat the sort of transcendental viewing that reckons itself to be ahistorical (the line that passes, perhaps, from the *Critique of Aesthetic Judgment* to Kenneth Clark's *Civilisation*); it administers a sharp rebuke to universalist musings. The risk here is that without looking to what actual historical viewers made of this doubly reinforced pressure upon their viewing (from the *Premier peintre* and from the authorized ekphrasis) the official commentary may then be placed in such a way as to regulate viewing now, in the discourse of art history. (Slide 13: "stolen authority.")

Perhaps the question of reception can be rephrased in such a way as to break this circle. When reconstructing the actual responses of historical viewers, as opposed to responses that were officially prescribed, becomes a central aim in art history, a certain narcissism comes to an end. One sees more clearly what has happened so often in art history's past: that, in the absence of conceptual space for actual historical viewers—who may have reacted to the official, prescribed way of viewing with varying degrees of assent, dissent, and indifference—the art historian presented the official view of the painting as an ideal toward which viewing in the later period should also aspire, if it wished to escape from "transcendental" viewing. I have in mind the kinds of account which, in order to reconstruct the responses of medieval viewers, turned to the highest authority, the promulgations of the Church; in order to reconstruct Renaissance viewing, turned to the most learned and lettered communities of theologians and humanists; to reconstruct the viewing of still life in the Netherlands in the seventeenth century, turned to the biblical allegories they allegedly encoded in order to discover their key. This was reconstruction based on just two terms: the authorized rationales, mandates, and programs that highly privileged or specialized groups supplied to painters; and the art historian who, by an act of elision, presented the official picture then as the properly historicized view now.

The foregrounding of reception may signal a profound restructuring of art-historical discourse. But it is not without its problems, some of which are touched on here as part of the present engagement with the difficulties presented by the context-idea. Many of these can be seen to stem from a core problematic, that of the "representative sample."

The first I want to mention derives from historiographic scruple. In order to avoid gross historical error, it is essential that a line be drawn between "them" and "us," between the members of a past culture and ourselves; only then can the sense of historical difference begin to emerge. The members of the past culture had skills that are not our skills, and these have a role to play in our reconstruction. Yet the distinction between the knowledge of the participants in a culture, and our own reconstruction of their expertise, while impeccable as a rationale, can easily lead to rhetorical moves that are exactly productive of power relations within art-historical discourse—relations that at the same time they also serve to conceal. The distinction between participation and observation, though

perhaps necessary, already inscribes ideas of the naturalness and spontaneity of "culture." Where we who come later have to reconstruct a skill that
is alien to us, which we could never perform with ease, the very awk-
wardness and scruple that characterizes the labor of archival reconstruction can then be inverted and projected, across a slide, as the instinctive
grace of the members of past cultures. We move in broken stages, intellectually, never inside the skills we are trying laboriously to piece together: they move naturally, with flexibility and confidence, at home in
their native cultural language.

This grace, that of people thought to be completely grounded in their
world, so contrasts with the observer's gaucherie that the antithesis is
stark, though its implications are seldom pursued. The clumsiness of
scholars and the naturalness inherent in membership of past cultures *need*
one another: it is not an accidental but a constitutive contrast. Grace and
gaucherie support each other in a continuous rhetorical operation: the
maladroitness of the historian is needed to establish the past culture in its
unity and coherence, which confer ease of movement on all its members;
that naturalness, the ability to inhale the culture as freely as air, to inter-
nalize its conventions as instinctual spontaneity, underwrites that scruple
of the historical endeavor, its brokenness and externality to what it describes. At the same time this double movement conceals the operation
of an unspoken synecdoche. For the sample out of which the skills are
reconstructed will be that of specific groups: for example, particular professions with expertise that cannot be generalized; women whose skills are
related to social positions that are different from those created for men;
castes and ethnic groupings whose skills are asymmetrical with regard to
the surrounding groups. To move from the difference of groups (however
these are named) to the unity of culture, or the period eye, is to produce,
embellished with the themes of naturalness and spontaneity, a unity that
comes from within the discourse and out of its own resources. Partly the
discourse employs synecdoche to solve its own difficulties, those of the
representative sample: how to move from specific types of visual response,
whose traces are found in the archive, to the more general propositions—
how, in fact, to unify the analysis. But the rhetorical slide, from difference
to unity through the operation of synecdoche, is obviously open to appropriation by numerous ideological determinants, from conservative nostalgia (their past grace, our modern brokenness) to the play of the scholarly

imaginary (both positive and negative idealizations: their athletic grace, our bookworm maladroitness; their instinctive and unreflecting spontaneity, our higher rationality).

The idea of a diffracted response, of visual reception as a term that must be broken down according to group affiliation, is an evident improvement here, both rhetorically and politically, on the idea of a grace of cultural membership conferred at once by historical birthright. But there are further difficulties, again stemming from the core problematic of the representative sample. Let us suppose that analysis of reception discloses different social groups whose visual responses to particular works of art vary; that different groups (again, however these are defined) possess different codes for viewing even the same work. But the idea of *possession* of codes of viewing cannot be taken for granted: if one is really going to address reception, it must be recognized that possession of codes of viewing is a process, not a given, and that members of groups acquire their familiarity with codes of viewing, and their ability to operate those codes, to varying degrees. Access to the codes is a matter of unevenness: codes have to be learned and their distribution varies (and changes) within a group, even in those cases in which a group defines itself through its ability to manipulate visual codes in distinct ways. That is, even when attention to the conditions of reception discloses a particular group that operates codes of viewing in a distinctive way, analysis of reception must still distinguish between degrees of *access* to those codes. If it does not do so, it is substituting an ideal case (full possession of cultural skills, expertise, naturalness) for what is in fact an uneven process. A familiar rhetorical operation may still be at work here, in which "group" as a concept acts as a synecdoche: in fact members of the group have different levels of access to the group's codes, varying degrees of competence and expertise; but the condition of expertise is generalized to all of them, precisely so that the term *group* can operate in the discourse.

So far as the historical record goes, the viewing of pictures is a largely silent activity. Of course it was far from being literally silent. I am looking at an engraving from the eighteenth century, depicting an Academy exhibition. It is a representation with its own conventions: the panoptic point of view, showing three walls of the great saloon and part of its ceiling; the pictures stacked in ranks from the smaller works crammed together at eye level to the great machines five stories above; when it comes to the pictures themselves there is an overall indistinctness, but enough detail to identify, here and there, a familiar or half-familiar image. My attention shifts to the multitude that throngs through this space, men, women, and—surprisingly—children. One does not see the hush of the church. The figures are gesticulating and craning to see, are busy talking in couples or in groups, are admiring or criticizing what is around them, are looking detached from the crowd or are quizzing the paintings as connoisseurs.

How much of this commotion has entered the historical record? Not much. What *has* entered it are highly specialized responses to the exhibition, literary productions that promoted or defended particular artists and schools, and entered into various running debates about questions of taste. Such traces do not speak of their viewing in a straightforward manner. Constrained by often deeply restrictive literary conventions, leaving little room to register the viewing response of their authors in any detail, they become expressive only when "enhanced" by reading between the lines, and between those lines, and by carefully sounding their turns of phrase, their ellipses, to determine what by implication they may be giving voice to. If we meet with such obstacles within the public and recorded responses, and if we wish to develop further our concept of reception, what of all the other microscopic acts of viewing, each local and infinitesimal, which in their unseen trajectories failed to give rise to a discursive configuration that could survive? If such difficulties arise even with the molar groups that reception analysis is able to identify, what of all those other practices of looking, those swarms of viewers who left no trace of their ways and moments of seeing? There are many other viewers besides the ones who compose a treatise, publish pamphlets, or pen their memoirs. Those are only a fraction, the smallest percentage, of actual reception. And how should we view this immense *reserve?*

Above all, by remembering it is there, even when it cannot be retrieved; and by noticing the absences in the record as much as what survives. For example . . . the absence of women. In my engraving of the Academy exhibition women are a visible and active presence. Yet as a group without access to the machinery of the aesthetic treatise and of official taste, the archival traces of women's spectatorship are minimal. The movement of synecdoche in art-historical discourse, which looks only to the small fraction of male viewers who left their treatises, pamphlets, and memoirs, is deeply political; synecdoche may be the master trope of patriarchy, always installing at its center Man—a trope without which patriarchal discourse could not function. When one sees it produce those great apparatuses, the culture, the style, the period, one knows who in the first place the trope will set to one side and efface. The identification of empirical reception with archival traces is a tropical movement that can only reenact the exclusions the archive has already performed; it can even naturalize them further.

Does this point to an extension of the archival project, to a more comprehensive history of reception that would ideally and eventually uncover the hidden traces of other codes of viewing than those we are currently attuned to? From one point of view, certainly: as a canon has its exclusions, and can be countered by making it now admit those it had set aside, so has an archive; though we may need to look away from the obvious, the official records of reception in order to do so. Surrounding those forms of looking that have given rise to discursive configurations that actually figure in the archive are other, submerged series of procedures that addressed other needs. Such series will include codes of viewing that represent residual practices edged out by the rise of those later codes that eclipse and replace them; and, conversely, codes that are hardly yet formed, emergent ways of seeing whose coherence has not yet been established and whose energies have not yet taken root, still tentative and faltering configurations that still have to find each other and lock together to form a configuration that may, perhaps, emerge into the historical record.[20] Staying just with those fully configured codes of seeing, the ones that have made it into the arena of public taste and debate, there will be those that also exist in "debased" versions of the official protocols of viewing. On one side, there is the practice of seeing works of art that seeks, but has not yet attained, confidence within a dominant visual discourse, that stammers and is not yet there, does not fully grasp which responses do and which do not fall within the orbit of the sanctioned, yet seeks instruction and admission. On the other side are decaying versions of dominant practices of viewing, those that drift from the official model, through lapses of memory, disaffiliation, random variation, memory lapses, and so forth. As to the practices of resistance to dominant regimes of viewing, we know these are legion, and perhaps—comparatively—they are better understood: they range from polite parody to outright defacement, from the clandestine inversion of existing rules of viewing to the invention of wholly new sets of rules, from subtle violations of propriety to blank refusal to play the game.[21] In a separate category are complete idiolects of viewing, private languages of memory and habit that reorder the dominant codes into secret configurations of desire and identity, which may or may not be revealed to another human being, whose nature may or may not be consciously recognized. The reserve of visual practices will perhaps be as Foucault describes power, as a swarm of points that, separating and coming together in ways that public discourse may be entirely unaware of, sometimes move in a common direction uniformly enough to become organized as a dominant regime.

Alongside the pamphlets and the memoirs we must posit another world of looking, even before we can specify it; against the "monotheism" of synecdoche, and its molar constructions (style, period, culture), we have to assume the persistence of a "polytheism" of hidden and dispersed practices of looking at works of art, which while never giving rise to the consolidated forms of the review, the essay, the treatise, nevertheless constituted reception and context as historical realities.[22] One cannot know in advance what might enter into reconstructions of silent practice. What counts as much as what might eventually fill the space of the reserve is that such a space be created. It is not enough to escape the enclosure of synecdoche if the archive is simply extended toward as yet silent groups, for as each of these is identified and brought in, the logic of the representative sample is not yet challenged, only confirmed. In the same way that extension of canons to include, for example, the work of women artists or artists of color, nevertheless stays within the bounds of canonicity, so the discovery of previously unrecognized modes of visual practice stays within the logic of synecdoche unless the trope is deliberately confronted. The advantage of "reserve" as a concept here is precisely its negativity and emptiness. "Reserve" is dark. Once "reception" goes beyond being a discourse based on other prior discourses, and ventures out into domains where there are only viewing practices without accompanying discourse, a sudden vista appears that is that of night. A space is opened up that cannot be scanned, compounded, and generalized, for it is a space that nothing visible fills. An image of Michel de Certeau comes to mind: "a car at the edge of cliff. Beyond, nothing but the sea."[23] "Reception," when profoundly thought, will always take us to this point; all of its paths will lead to it. But at the same time "reception" is typically intercepted within art-historical discourse long before this happens.

Among other things, this "edge" is where "reception" confronts the dimension of semiotic play. Until it does, in fact, reach that point, "reception" remains a primarily repressive and *legislative* idea, like so much of the context-idea in which it plays a conspicuous role. Take the case of the "classic" literary text. Literary historians, as well as critics, are far more at ease than art historians with the possibility of a text that changes through time, becoming different as it passes from one milieu and period to another, changing as different generations of readers bring to bear upon the text the discourses that constitute them as readers. Admittedly, the openness of such a text can be and has been appropriated and used in the name of a number of ideological operations: the rehabilitation of the concept of the canon in literary criticism is one (the open text turning out to coincide with the shelf of masterworks, the rest remaining ephemeral and merely *lisible*); the cult of the reader as hedonistic consumer is another (a consumer who never reflects on the preconditions of his consumption). Obviously the plurality attributed so selectively to the "classic" text is not an excess it has because it is a masterpiece, as hagiography would have it. Rather the opposite: its openness is that constitutive lack that it shares with all texts, masterworks or not; the text cannot exist outside the circumstances in which the reader reads the text, performs it, and nothing the text is able to do can fix in advance the outcome of its future encounters with other contexts and later times. Literary criticism tends to be sanguine about this situation; perhaps it exploits it. Art history tends to react with super-Hirschean indignation: these *later* readings are inessential, they belong to a separate subdomain of art history, the history of taste. What counts is "context," defined as the place and year of the work's first appearance or exhibition. That is the *one and only* true context; and it has to be, because art-historical discourse, having committed itself to causal narration as its dominant form of writing, and once it has enumerated all those causal chains needs a place where the chains will terminate. The quest for causes can range so freely in that discourse precisely because it always has that one fixed enclosure, where all the causal chains converge and come to an end.

But even this rigid delimitation of reception as the place at which the metonymic chains all reach their termination cannot succeed in concealing the fundamental *motility* of viewing. Let us take a case of extreme delimitation of reception, its confinement to the *season* in which a particular work of art appeared. In discussion of French painting the word *Salon* has an important rhetorical function here, for it localizes reception to a single, contained space; to a narrow band of time—those few months

when the Salon opened its doors; it then identifies reception and context
as this splendidly ostensible locus; and it iconizes context and reception
through the image of the Salon that everyone carries in their head, of a
lofty room with four walls and a ceiling. Now the fly is in the fly-bottle!
But if we look down from those walls what we *might* also see in the crowds
who swarm through the space is the reserve, the sea; the unarrestable
energy of the glance, of the myriad moments of looking that open out not
on to quadrilateral space but beyond it, into the polytheism of hidden
and dispersed practices that make up semiotic play. Even in the chamber
and season of its first appearance, the visual text enters networks of semiotic transformation as volatile and as tangled as the glances of a crowd in
any given minute. Nothing can stop the movement of signifier to signifier
in a visual text as it is actually being viewed. To do so one would have to
be able to overcome something that cannot be eradicated from texts—
whether visual, verbal, written, or the "general text": that at the moment
when a text is made, enunciation and enunciated cleave at the most fundamental level, and the visual text sets out on its numberless trajectories
of seeing, none of which will exhaust the mobility of signification.

Does this semiotic play mean that, for an art historian, anything goes?
By no means. At least two principles are at work: the contextual determination of meaning, and the infinite extendability of context. Derrida:
"This is my starting point: no meaning can be determined out of context,
but no context permits saturation."[24] It is true that the two principles do
not sit easily together; they do not interact in a classical or topologically
familiar fashion. What their conjunction does *not* point to is that infinite
extendability of context overrides or cancels out the principle of contextual determination (though that is a common misreading of Derrida).
Rather, the principles coexist in such a way that the extendability of context, as an idea, provides a conceptual space from which to problematize
context as having any kind of legislative force. It highlights that "context"
is never naturally given; it is something we make, whether we are viewers
at a Salon or art historians working in our own institutional contexts.

I have left until last what may be the most unproductive usage of the
context-idea, which occurs when "context" is pronounced as an imperative that is to locate contextuality in a cleanly demarcated moment in the
past. This necessarily conceals context as the contextuality of the present,
the *current* functioning of instituted art-historical discourse. It is from this
context that, among other things, the *context!* imperative itself comes.

Perhaps this is the most disturbing of the many slides that occur in the rhetoric of contextualization, because it is the one that takes away from those who work in art-historical discourse the grounds both for examining and interrogating their own contextual determinants, and for speaking from what they might eventually decide to be their actual context. A plain example will make this clear. How is it that female spectatorship has not been, from the beginning, a primary object of art-historical inquiry? I have already given one, rather generous set of answers: that it was because the archive was lacking in evident traces of women viewers, and then because the archive was conceptually mishandled by those whose procedures were governed by synecdochal thinking, and that, because *incidentally* the representative sample typically concerned only male viewing, the latter was extrapolated from the archive and presented as the self-evident context. But obviously this is an insufficient explanation. It suggests more innocence than we know was there: it is as if "the fault lay in the archive, not in ourselves; had the traces been those of some other privileged group, we would have privileged them instead!" It is only by seeing from within our own context that institutional forces within art history have worked to silence the whole question of the roles played by gender and sexuality in the field of vision, that we are able *now* to begin to see the ellipses and silences within the archive. *Our* context has latterly enabled us to realize different contexts, and that it is we who set them up. Which should, rationally, lead us to inspect our own contextualizations within the discipline of art history at least as much as to create historical contexts for the visual texts the discipline deals with. The same historiographic scruple that requires us to draw a distinguishing line between "us" and the historical "them"—to see how they are different from us—should by the same token urge us to see how we are different from them, and to use context not as a legislative idea but as one that will help us to locate ourselves.

NOTES

1. The quotation marks around "context" ("reserve," "network," etc.) are meant to designate that at this place the word appears as an object of methodological reflection.

2. Dominick La Capra, *History and Criticism* (Ithaca, N.Y., 1985), p. 38.

3. Ibid.

4. Jonathan Culler, *Framing the Sign: Criticism and Its Institutions* (Norman,

Okla., 1988), p. xiv. See also Mieke Bal's discussion of context in relation to Rembrandt criticism, in her introduction to *Reading Rembrandt: Beyond the Word-Image Opposition* (Cambridge, 1991).

5. Culler, *Framing the Sign*, p. 148.

6. Michael Baxandall, *Patterns of Intention: On the Historical Explanation of Pictures* (New Haven, 1985), p. 26.

7. It must be said that Baxandall's own account rejects "aggregation" as a description of the proposed relationship among determining factors; *alloy* is the term preferred (Baker "alloyed them all into a form" [*Patterns of Intention*, p. 32]). All I would point out here is the rhetorical complexity of Baxandall's text, and its "inner" games with key terms. One can perhaps be guided by Baxandall's own directions: in his opening pages he directs his reader's attention to the title of his study: "a title in which the multiple puns (I count three or four) are important to me"; but it is not only in the title that complex conceptual transfers occur in this extremely rich and fascinating text. Is it too much to see in "alloy" a metaleptic slide, whereby the key property of the object under investigation, the strength of the alloy steel, is transferred to the field of explanation?

8. Culler, *Framing the Sign*, p. 148.

9. As glossed by Foucault, *Les mots et les choses* (Paris, 1966), p. 7.

10. "The fragment of the outside world of which we become conscious comes after the effect that has been produced on us and is projected *a posteriori* as its 'cause.' In the phenomenalism of the 'inner world' we invert the chronology of cause and effect. The basic fact of 'inner experience' is that the cause gets imagined after the effect has occurred" (Friedrich Nietzsche, *Werke*, ed. Karl Schlechter [Munich, 1986], 3:804; cited in Culler, *On Deconstruction: Theory and Criticism after Structuralism* (London, 1983), p. 86.

11. Culler, *On Deconstruction*, p. 86.

12. ". . . full causes without effects, immense effects with futile reasons, strong consequences from insignificant causes, rigorous effects from chance occurrences" (Michel Serres, *The Parasite* [Baltimore, 1982], p. 20).

13. At its best, the move away from influence as a model that assumes the *passivity* of the object being influenced, toward a different conception in which influence is thought of as the selective transformation of prior material, can act as a powerful critique of the "mechanical" idea of cause-to-effect. Baxandall's account of influence is a case in point; see *Patterns of Intention*, pp. 58–62.

14. T. S. Eliot, "Tradition and the Individual Talent," in *Selected Essays* (New York, 1950), p. 5.

15. Michael Ann Holly, "Past Looking," *Critical Inquiry* 16 (1990): 371–96.

16. Hayden White, *Tropics of Discourse: Essays in Cultural Criticism* (Baltimore, 1978), pp. 44, 62.

17. J. Burckhardt, *The Civilization of the Renaissance in Italy,* 2 vols., ed. B.

Nelson and C. Trinkaus (New York, 1958), pp. 83–84; cited in Michael Ann Holly, "Burckhardt and the Ideology of the Past," *History of the Human Sciences* 1, no. 1 (1988): 50.

18. Holly, "Past Looking," p. 373.

19. Jacques Derrida, *The Truth in Painting* (Chicago, 1987), pp. 83–118.

20. See, for example, Raymond Williams, "Base and Superstructure in Marxist Cultural Theory," *New Left Review* 82 (1973): 3–16.

21. For two very different theorizations of "local resistance" to dominant regimes, see Michel de Certeau, *The Practice of Everyday Life* (Berkeley, 1984); and Pierre Bourdieu, *Esquisse d'une théorie de la pratique: Précédée de trois études d'ethnologie kabyle* (Geneva, 1972), tr. Richard Nice as *Outline of a Theory of Practice* (Cambridge, 1977).

22. On "monotheism" and "polytheism" see de Certeau, *Heterologies: Discourse on the Other* (Minneapolis, 1986), p. 189; and idem, *The Practice of Everyday Life*, p. 48.

23. De Certeau, *Heterologies*, p. 188, and *The Practice of Everyday Life*, p. 61.

24. Jacques Derrida, "Living On: Border Lines," in *Deconstruction and Criticism*, ed. Harold Bloom et al. (New York, 1979), p. 81.

2

"A USELESS LONGING FOR MYSELF": THE CRISIS OF THE EUROPEAN BILDUNGSROMAN, 1898–1914

&

Franco Moretti

Youth, BY JOSEPH CONRAD, IN 1898. *Tonio Kröger,* by Thomas Mann, in 1903. *The Perplexities of Young Törless,* by Robert Musil, in 1906. *Jakob von Gunten,* by Robert Walser, in 1909. *The Notebooks of Malte Laurids Brigge,* by Rainer Maria Rilke, in 1910. *A Portrait of the Artist as a Young Man,* by James Joyce, written between 1904 and 1914. *Amerika* (or *The Lost One*), by Franz Kafka, written between 1912 and 1914.

That such an unusual concentration of wonders should not open a new phase in the history of the European bildungsroman, but bring it to a sudden close, is at first glance an enigma. Then one notices the year Joyce completed, and Kafka abandoned, their novels: 1914. "No one shall come out of this war"—wrote a German volunteer—"if not as a different person." And indeed, as Fussell and Leed have shown, the initial feeling of European youth was that of being on the verge of a collective, immense initiation ritual. Rather than fulfilling the archetype, though, the war was to shatter it, because, unlike rites of passage, the war killed—and its only mystery didn't decree the renewal of individual existence, but its insignificance. If one wonders about the disappearance of the novel of youth, then, the youth of 1919—maimed, shocked, speechless, decimated—provide quite a clear answer. We tend to see social and political history as a creative influence on literary evolution, yet its destructive role may be just as relevant. If history can make cultural forms necessary, it can make them impossible as well, and this is what the war did to the bildungsroman. More precisely, perhaps, the war was the final act in a longer process—the cosmic coup de grace to a genre that, at the turn of the century, was already doomed. Before discussing the interrelated tendencies that had undermined the form of the bildungsroman, however, I will briefly recapitulate the reasons for its previous significance.

In the course of the nineteenth century, the bildungsroman had performed three great symbolic tasks. It had contained the unpredictability of social change, representing it through the fiction of youth: a turbulent segment of life, no doubt, but with a clear beginning, and an unmistakable end. At a micronarrative level, furthermore, the structure of the novelistic episode had established the flexible, antitragic modality of modern experience. Finally, the novel's many-sided, unheroic hero had embodied a new kind of subjectivity: everyday, worldly, pliant—"normal." A smaller, more peaceful history; within it, a fuller experience; and a weaker, but more versatile Ego: a perfect compound for the Great Socialization of the European middle classes. But problems change, and old solutions stop working. Let us then turn to our group of novels—which, for lack of anything better, I shall call the late bildungsroman—and see what the new problems were.

Whereas previous novels tended to personalize social relations, presenting them as relations among individuals, in the late bildungsroman social institutions began to appear as such: the business bureaucracy of *Amerika,* the Church of *Portrait,* and above all the School of Mann and Musil, of Walser and Joyce. The growth of institutions was a massive historical fact, of course, which a realistic narrative could hardly ignore: acknowledging it, though, proved just as difficult. "One is not supposed to say so"—complains Törless—"but of all we are doing all day long here at school, what does have a meaning? What do we get out of it? For ourselves, I mean. . . . We know we have learned this and that . . . but inside, we are as empty as before." But inside . . . this is the trouble with the school: it teaches this and that, stressing the objective side of socialization—functional integration of individuals *in* the social system. But in so doing it neglects the subjective side of the process: the legitimation *of* the social system inside the mind of individuals, which had been a great achievement of the bildungsroman. What the school deals with are means, not ends; techniques, not values. A pupil must know his lesson, but he doesn't have to believe in its truth. Convincing the subject that what he must do is also symbolically right is, however, exactly what modern socialization is all about. If this does not happen, and shared values are replaced by sheer coercion (how many arbitrary and unfair punishments in these novels!), the individual will hardly feel at home in his world, and socialization will not be fully accomplished. When Tonio Kröger returns to the home of his childhood, he finds in its place a public library; and think of Karl Rossmann, the lost one, banished by his parents across the ocean; of Törless's enforced exile ("A small station on the line to Russia. Four parallel rails run straight, out of sight, in opposite directions"), and of Stephen's deliberate one. "The time has come," writes Malte Laurids Brigge, "when all things are leaving the houses. . . ." No wonder that in 1916, writing *The Theory of the Novel,* Lukács should define the novel as the genre of "transcendental homelessness," a questionable statement for the nineteenth century—but quite true for the late bildungsroman, with its rootless heroes and inhospitable environments. Malte's anxious loneliness, Jakob's abject submission, Karl's blank passivity, Stephen's contemptuous isolation: here are some versions of Lukács's homelessness. But the most uncanny result of a merely functional socialization, and of its disregard for a shared symbolic universe, is Törless's nonchalant violence, which flatly rejects all notion of a common humanity: "One last question. What do you feel now? Pain? Mere pain, which you would wish to stop? Just this, with no complications?" And that the best pupil of a "renowned boarding school" should announce the brown shirts—what a setback for the civilizing machinery of liberal Europe!

Lothar and Jarno in *Meister,* De la Mole and Mosca in Stendhal, Jacques Collin in the *Comédie Humaine,* Austen's and Eliot's narrator: in the nineteenth century, the wisdom of adults had been a constant, critical counterpoint to the hero's adventures. But from Mann onwards countless stolid professors will suggest that, as soon as they become professional teachers, adults have nothing left to teach. Youth begins to despise maturity, and to define itself in revulsion from it. Encouraged by the internal logic of the school—where the outside world disappears, while grades overdevelop the sense of the slightest age difference—youth looks now for its meaning within itself: gravitating further and further away from adult age, and more and more toward adolescence, or preadolescence, or be-

yond.[1] If twentieth-century heroes are as a rule younger than their predecessors, this is so because, historically, the relevant symbolic process is no
longer growth but regression. The adult world refuses to be a hospitable
home for the subject? Then let childhood be it—the Lost Kingdom, the
"Domaine mystérieux" of Alain-Fournier's *Meaulnes*. Hence Malte's longing for his mother, or Jakob's anguished final cry ("Ah, to be a small
child—to be that only, and forever!"); or, in a more militant vein, Törless's devastating sense of omnipotence: that most regressive of features,
out of which will arise—through *Le grand Meaulnes* (1913), *Le Diable au
corps* (1923), and *Lord of the Flies* (1954)—a veritable tradition of counter-
bildungsroman. "What is the matter," asks the hero of *Meaulnes*, "are
children in charge here?" They are, and readers of Golding know the end
of this story, where childhood may well be the biological trope for the
new phenomenon of mass behavior. The regression from youth to adolescence and childhood would thus be the narrative form for what liberal
Europe saw as an anthropological reversal from the individual as an autonomous entity to the individual as mere member of a mass. Given this
framework, the postwar political scenario could hardly encourage a rebirth of the bildungsroman: that mass movements may be constitutive of
individual identity—and not just destructive of it—was to remain an
unexplored possibility of Western narrative.

Homeless, narcissistic, regressive: the metamorphosis of the image of
youth in our century is by now a familiar fact. Less familiar is its rapidity:
only fifteen years before the war, Marlow's and Kröger's destiny had been
quite a different one. However problematical, their subjectivity had been
free to unfold in a world not yet enclosed and dominated by institutions.
"The school was over," reads the first page of *Tonio Kröger,* in perfect contrast to *Törless:* "Through the paved courtyard, and out of the iron gate,
flowed the liberated troops." In *Youth,* for its part, Marlow's ship—this
British Trinity of School, Army, and Factory all in one—is conveniently
burned and sunk so that the young second mate may enjoy the independence of "seeing the East first as a commander of a small boat." Yes,
institutions still have limited power here, and Marlow and Kröger will be
among the last novelistic heroes to grow up and achieve maturity. Which
is to say that Conrad's and Mann's bildungsromane are morphologically
closer to Goethe's than, say, to Kafka's or Joyce's: or also, turning the
matter around, that there were more structural novelties in a decade than
in an entire century. Surprising? Maybe—if one sees literature as a rest-

less, self-questioning discourse engaged in a sort of permanent revolution. Not really, if one accepts the idea that inertia rules literature just as many other things, and that the rhythm of literary evolution is thus necessarily uneven: long periods of stability "punctuated," as Gould and Eldredge would say, by bursts of sudden change like the one I am trying to describe. Why change should occur at all, and how, is something I shall return to after a short technical parenthesis.

Following Barthes and Chatman, contemporary narratology usually groups narrative episodes in two basic classes: "kernels," abrupt, irreversible choices among widely different options, and "satellites," slower, subordinate events that qualify and enrich the chosen course. In tune with their respective functions, satellites belong to the narrative "background" (to use Harald Weinrich's terms), embodying social regularity, whereas the "foreground" is occupied by kernels, which are typically the hero's doing, and have therefore enjoyed a structural centrality in most narrative forms, from epos to tragedies and short stories. From the eighteenth century onwards, though, at one with the growing regularity and interdependence of social life, novels started to bridge the gap between background and foreground, and in the narrative slowdown that followed, the role of kernels started to decline, and that of satellites to grow. The bildungsroman happened to come into being at the very moment when the new trend and the old conventions were balancing each other, and out of this unique historical conjuncture arose a narrative episode of unprecedented flexibility. An episode organized as an *opportunity:* as a satellite, hence with nothing frightening about it—yet a satellite so rich in potentialities that the hero may well want to transform it into a kernel. An opportunity in which the social background offers a choice to the hero: the ideal medium for a story of socialization and growth—of socialization *as* subjective growth. And also a beautiful way to rescue one of the key words of modernity—"experience"—from its metaphysical captivity, offering a visible form to its sense of discovery free from danger, of renewal without revolution, of homogeneity between the individual and his world. Would experience be such an important word for us, had not the novelistic episode taught us to recognize its features?

Growth, then, and experience. But the world of the late bildungsroman has solidified into impersonal institutions, while youth has become more vulnerable, and reluctant to grow. With a shift in narrative agency, opportunities turn into accidents: kernels are no longer produced *by* the hero as turning points of his free growth—but *against* him, by a world that is thoroughly indifferent to his personal development. In the abstract and often uselessly painful tests enforced by the school, the individualized socialization of Western modernity seems to collapse back into archaic initiation rituals; more informally, seemingly harmless episodes turn out to be, most strikingly in Kafka, all-encompassing trials.[2] Or, as we also say, "traumas": a metaphor which, according to the *OED,* crystallized in 1916. At the polar opposite from experience, in a trauma the external world proves too strong for the subject—too violent: and institutions (whether run by Irish Jesuits, Austro-Hungarian bureaucrats, or American managers) tend of course to be careless and shattering in their violence. And as the whole process of socialization becomes more violent, regression inevitably acquires its symbolic prominence: faced with an increasing probability of being wounded, it is quite reasonable for the subject to try and make himself, so to speak, smaller and smaller. Under artillery fire, the favorite position of World War I infantrymen was the fetal one.

    This centrality of traumas—and hence of kernels, which are their narrative equivalents—helps to throw some light on a feature of literary evolution that is often misunderstood. In most historical accounts, literature is taken to change not only at a constant rhythm, rather than in punctuated fashion, but also along a sort of straight line: one step after another, one genre after another. At first sight, the early twentieth century seems to support this view, suggesting a continuity between the bildungsroman, its "late" version, and modernism. After all, don't we have the biographical evidence of Musil and Rilke and Kafka and Joyce, who all inherited the bildungsroman, developed it, and then proceeded "from" it "to" modernism? Well, not quite. If the internal structure of the novelistic episode is a good test for literary evolution, and I think it is, then we have three data with which to work: first, the nineteenth-century episode, where the functions of a kernel and those of a satellite balance each other; second, the late bildungsroman episode, which is undoubtedly closer to a kernel; third, the modernist episode, best exemplified by *Ulysses,* which is an overgrown satellite and nothing else. Do these three forms constitute a continuum, with the late bildungsroman acting as the transitional form between the nineteenth century and modernism? Obviously not. We need a different geometrical pattern here—not a straight line but a tree, with plenty of bifurcations for genres to branch off from each other. What really happened when the nineteenth-century episode fell apart, then, was that narratives could concentrate *either* on kernels *or* on satellites: the late bildungsroman chose the former, and modernism the latter. From their common starting point they proceeded in opposite directions: there isn't the least morphological continuity here, biographical data notwithstanding. In fact, one is tempted to claim that—in its commitment to traumatic narratives—the late bildungsroman, far from preparing modernism, did, if anything, *delay* it. But of this, more at the end.

The prevalence of traumas and kernels also created a taxonomic paradox, since they were making it difficult for the late bildungsroman to be a novel at all. To use the terms of *Soul and Forms,* which Lukács was writing in those very years, "isolated events" and "fateful moments" characterize the short story, or the novella, making it a more "rigorous" form than the novel, but also preventing it from representing "the evolution of an entire life"—the *Bildung*—that is the novel's prerogative. But the zeitgeist must have been on the side of the short story, and in stark contrast to Goethe and Austen, to Stendhal and Eliot, and even to Balzac and Flaubert, who had shown little or no interest for short narratives, all the authors of the late bildungsroman were superb writers of short stories. So much so, in fact, that they even attempted an alchemic experiment—the "bildungsnovelle," so to speak, best represented by *Youth* and *Tonio Kröger* (and, in a less consistent way, by *Jakob von Gunten* and *Törless*). Interestingly enough, in order to blend novella and novel together, Conrad and Mann both had recourse to the same device of "variation": the repeated shipwrecks of *Youth* or the emotional frustrations of *Tonio Kröger.* Combining the symbolic clarity of the short story's "fateful moment" and the empirical variety of the novel's "entire life," a story constructed on the principle of variation seems indeed to embody the best of both forms: except that it isn't really a story, as its parts are not held together by chronological relations, but only by the semantic affinity perceived by the unifying gaze of conscious memory—by the adult wisdom of Conrad's "strong bond of the sea," or Mann's haut-bourgeois composure. And here, of course, was the rub: because this retrospective maturity, so close to the spirit of the classical bildungsroman, was unappealing, and even incomprehensible, to the younger generation of writers. As early as 1904 Joyce had rejected precisely the all-encompassing voice that had made *Youth* and *Tonio Kröger* possible: "So capricious are we," he wrote in the very first sketch for *Portrait,* "that we cannot or will not conceive the past in any other than its iron memorial aspect. Yet the past assuredly implies a fluid succession of presents."

A fluid succession of presents: "Yesterday Basini was still the same, just as Törless himself; but a trapdoor had opened, and Basini had precipitated." *Törless* is a veritable collection of such traumatic discoveries—imaginary numbers and moral duplicity, the infinity of the universe, homosexuality, the hero's "second sight." The novel's meaning is thus no longer to be found in the narrative, diachronic relation between events, but rather *within* each single "present," taken as a self-contained, discontinuous entity. Törless's adolescence is less a story than a string of lyrical moments; after all, his keenest perplexity has to do with finding the right words—better, the right *tropes* for his discoveries. After the bildungsnovelle, then, the crisis of the novelistic episode was generating another hybrid: the lyric novel. Unusual as it is for a great lyric poet to write a good novel, in these years Rainer Maria Rilke did it (he did it twice, if one considers the shorter text of 1898, *Ewald Tragy*), and in *Malte* he posed a kind of symbolic problem that only the later poetry of the *Elegies* would solve. As for Joyce, in *Stephen Hero* he had already mentioned Dante's *Vita Nuova*—where the story is literally a pre-text for the lyrics—as a possible model; later on, his hero's theory of epiphanies was another attempt to subordinate the narrative line to punctual poetic vision. Lyric novel then. But what are those privileged moments that set poetry in motion?

Predictably, they are traumas again—traumatic discoveries of sexual desires that are as a rule both socially illicit and psychically irresistible. After the collapse of Youth and Experience, this new, alien force (the Es, the Id) pulverizes the only remaining cornerstone of the bildungsroman: the unity of the Ego. Yet its disruptive violence also brings to light the hidden worlds and unexpected possibilities out of which will arise the "poetry" thematized in the late bildungsroman. What Tonio learns from his secret, unreciprocated love for Hans Hansen proves "more important than what he was forced to learn at school." It is in the bedroom of a prostitute that Törless has a first glimpse of that "second sight" that will be his major intellectual discovery. It is while approaching a prostitute that Stephen "awakes from a slumber of centuries" and feels the "dark presence" of his future poetry. All these episodes (which have no equivalent in the tradition of the bildungsroman) are announcing that new reality—the unconscious, taken in a broad sense—which will play a crucial

role in the constitution of twentieth-century subjects, and in their socialization, which will consist more and more in an attempt to address and
colonize, in a variety of ways, their prelogical, submerged selves. (Modernism, in fact, may well be seen as the aesthetic protagonist of this new
pattern of Western socialization, in which unconscious psychic materials
are no longer obstacles but instruments of social integration.) But in our
novels such long-term developments are not in sight yet; we have the
problem, not the solution, and the unconscious is still the spellbinding
discovery of an unforgettable page by Rilke, in which Malte, still a child,
finds himself trapped in alien clothes, and in front of a mirror: "For a
moment I felt an undescribable, painful, and useless longing for myself:
then there was 'he' alone, *der Unbekannte,* the Unknown; there was nothing but him. . . . He was the stronger of the two, and I was the mirror."
A child facing a mirror, and trying on some new clothes, like so many
young novelistic heroes. Two archetypal scenes in the construction of
Western identity but the emergence of the unconscious-unknown reverses
their meaning, and they appear now as the destructive trauma described
in *Beyond the Pleasure Principle,* against which, writes Freud, "all possible
means of defense will be mobilized." "God, all these thoughts, these
strange desires, this looking for and groping after a meaning! To be able
to dream, to be able to sleep! And what is to come—let it come." Thus
Jakob von Gunten, and Törless: " 'You used to be so gentle to me . . .'
'Shut up! It wasn't me! . . . It was a dream . . . A whim.' "—It wasn't
me! Törless's disavowal of his emotions sums up the strategy of the genre
as a whole: having always dealt with the growth of self-consciousness, it
was inevitable for the bildungsroman to recoil in front of an alien, unconscious reality. As is often the case in history, the very conditions of its
previous supremacy prevented the bildungsroman from playing a central
role in the new phase of Western socialization.

"I am in between two worlds, at home in neither, and as a consequence
everything is a bit difficult for me." Although Tonio Kröger's last letter
to his Russian friend seems to announce the emotional fissures to come,
his story suggests that the acclaimed artist and impeccable bourgeois is in
fact at home in *both* worlds. "But what had there been, in all that time in
which he had become what he now was? Waste; desert; chill; and spirit!
And art!" Waste—and art! The secret of Mann's narrative lies in the si-
multaneity of the two: the humiliations inflicted on the young Tonio always reshaped by the beautiful words of the mature Kröger. This isn't
just a *story* of traumas overcome: it is Mann's very style that is antitrau-

matic. To borrow another expression from *Beyond the Pleasure Principle*, it is a style that unfailingly brings those shocks "to the level of consciousness," ordering them as "lived experiences" within conscious memory that, for the younger generation, will aimlessly follow each other as so many unrelated presents. This is even truer of *Youth*, where Marlow defuses traumas by transforming them, so to speak, into instant memories: "We pumped watch and watch, for dear life, and it seemed to last for months, for years, for all eternity, as though we had been dead and gone to a hell for sailors. . . . And there was something in me that thought, By Jove! This is the deuce of an adventure—something you read about; and it is my first voyage as second mate—and I am only twenty—and here I am. . . . I was pleased. I would not have given up the experience for worlds." How remote is this "something" from Törless's "whim" and Malte's "*Unbekannte*"! It is a reflexive, friendly support to personal identity, not a threat to it: and whereas Rilke's hero will feel "a useless longing" for himself, Marlow still cries aloud his confident "here I am"!

Rilke on traumas: "If words did indeed exist for that event, I was still too much of a child to find them." In Benjamin's famous essay, traumas force Baudelaire's poet to cry out in pain; in Musil, they are encircled by a labyrinth of dubious tropes; in Kafka, hidden by a haze of qualifying clauses. In all these instances, the clearest sign that a trauma has occurred is the fact that language no longer works well: that it is impossible to find adequate words for the reality of war, as millions of veterans will put it. In Conrad and Mann, on the contrary, the proper words are always at hand. As Marlow's ship blows up, nearly killing him, "the sky and the serenity of the sea were distinctly surprising. I suppose I expected to see them convulsed with horror." In a single sentence Conrad combines here hyperbole and skepticism, danger and distance, youth and maturity: the trauma has been overcome because it has been *stylized*. And the style is, of course, irony: "Yet, on the other hand, Tonio himself could feel that the writing of verses was something excessive, something definitely unbecoming, and, to a certain extent, he had to concur with all those people who considered it a surprising occupation. Except that . . ." Tonio's poetic vocation has arisen out of a sequence of traumas, and its discovery was itself a trauma: but the words of "all those people"—the prosaic words of common opinion—are there, and are capable of counterbalancing all that. It is the antiradicalism of irony, which so much delighted the young Mann: irony as mediation, as the diplomatic device to keep crises under control. Irony as the style of good breeding, and of bourgeois decorum: "As an artist, Lisaweta, one is already enough of an adventurer in his heart. Outwardly, one has to wear proper clothes, for God's sake, and behave like a respectable person!" And also, why not, write in a sensible, civilized style.

And behave like a respectable person. According to Norbert Elias, this would imply first of all holding in check one's animal drives. This is why table manners are such a basic test of urbanity, and also why dinners have had such relevance in civilized and civilizing novels. But *Portrait* opens with a dinner's violent disruption, and *Amerika*'s first turning point is announced—at dinner again—by the violation of all bodily and linguistic etiquette. The hour of *Dinnerdämmerung* has come, and it is not (only) a joke, because dinners embody a vital social need—the need for *neutralized spaces:* for areas where people may meet without fear under the protection of clear, unchallenged rules. (The rules themselves, of course, cannot be socially neutral, but they apply impartially to everybody.) Moreover, when a world enjoys a Hundred Years' Peace (as Polanyi defined European history between 1815 and 1914) neutralized spaces tend inevitably to increase in number, and to occupy a growing portion of social existence: the bildungsroman, for instance, took place almost entirely within their boundaries—and understandably so, because in such areas individual growth is sheltered, and easier, and less painful. When Mr. Green's behavior at dinner makes Karl Rossmann feel that "their inevitable social and worldly relations were to bring total victory or total defeat to one of them," what Kafka implies is that the neutralized space par excellence has reverted to the state of a battlefield; so that, even from this side, the subject is no longer shielded from traumatic encounters.

Free, equal, homogeneous enclaves—within societies that are emphatically not so. There is something so unreal about neutralized spaces that their disruption, however threatening, has nonetheless a liberating quality. As in the tragic paradigm, the pain of trauma is the price for truth: for the discovery of a violent power behind the facade of an impartial civilization: for the epiphany of "Class relations," as Jean-Marie Straub retitled his lucid, pitiless version of *Amerika.* But something is missing from these social epiphanies: *claritas,* as Stephen would say. The moment of revelation turns out to be also the moment of maximum ambiguity— most notably in *Amerika,* where hesitant and contradictory formulations are the puzzling echoes of all narrative turning points (so much so that Straub, in order to establish his reading of the text, erased from it almost all of the dialogue). Despite Stephen's peroration on "radiance," then, the striking fact about epiphanies, in the late bildungsroman, is that they are indeed signs but signs belonging to an unknown language, "a language we cannot hear," as Törless puts it. "He was thinking of ancient paintings he had seen in museums without understanding them well. He was waiting for something, just as he always had when in front of those paintings—but nothing ever happened. What would it be? . . . Something extraordinary, never seen before . . . words could not say it." "My life here," writes Jakob von Gunten, "strikes me at times as an incomprehensible dream." And Malte: "If words did indeed exist for that event, I was still too much of a child to find them. . . . I obscurely foresaw that life would be full of strange things, meant for *one* only, and unspeakable."

What promised to be a painful knowledge turns out to be a painful enigma. Rilke again: "What did that old woman want from me, creeping out of that hole? . . . I understood that the old pencil was a sign, a sign for the initiated; a sign that drop-outs know well. . . . This was two weeks ago. But now not a single day goes by without one of these encounters. Not only at sunset, but at midday, in the most crowded streets, all of a sudden a short man appears, or an old woman, and they beckon, they show me something, and then they vanish." We are so used to grieving for the meaninglessness of life that, at first, it may be hard to realize that Malte's complaint, here, is that the world is too meaning*ful;* there are too many signs, and signs are threats, because in them lurks *der Unbekannte,* the Unknown. ("All / Is not itself," as the *Elegies* will say.) This veritable semiotic anxiety will then produce its own form of regression: the yearning for a world freed from the plurality, and hence the uncertainties, of signification: for a world of Un-signs, as it were. It is Tonio Kröger's longing for what is "irrelevant and simple." It is Kafka's impossible hope—so well described by Sartre—for a stretch of flat meaningless nature. It is Jakob's compulsive drive to hide all personal signs under a uniform. But the most revealing figure is Rilke's "mother": the *Erklärer,* the "light-thrower" of *Malte* and the *Elegies,* who turns signs into things; who de-semiotizes, so to say, what is "nightly-suspect," restoring in its place the solid reality of "those dear, usual objects which stay there, *ohne Hintersinn,* with no hidden meaning, good, simple, unequivocal."

"Till that moment he had not known how beautiful and peaceful life could be. The green square of paper pinned round the lamp cast down a tender shade. On the dresser was a plate of sausages and white pudding and on the shelf there were eggs. They would be for the breakfast in the morning after the communion in the college chapel. White pudding and eggs and sausages and cups of tea. How simple and beautiful was life after all!" It is the most obedient evening in Stephen's life, and his words echo Malte's delight in the lack of hidden meaning of good simple objects. But it is only a passing moment: in the struggle among signs and Un-signs *Portrait* sides resolutely with the former. "Many in our day" reads the 1904 sketch, "cannot avoid a choice between sensitiveness and dullness." Simplicity may be a form of dullness, after all: sensitiveness, the capacity to perceive and confront Rilke's unknown—to see "a winged form flying above the waves and slowly climbing the air." As *Portrait*'s great epiphanic passage begins, Stephen faces the same question—"What did it mean?"—that paralyzed his predecessors. But in his case the enigmatic meaningfulness of "a girl gazing out to sea" is "an instant of ecstasy," and his prompt mention of medieval illuminations—signs growing out of signs—shows that he is perfectly at home in the labyrinth of endless semiosis. In a Rimbaud-like episode of initiation and rebirth—a perfect kernel, in all possible respects—epiphany redeems the meaninglessness of the past, revealing that Stephen's youth had always had a secret aim— the discovery of an artist's "soul"—and that it has finally achieved it. One could not wish for a better closure for Joyce's ambitious *Künstlerroman*.

Except that, of course, *Portrait* goes on, and the following chapter, compared to all previous ones, is strikingly blank and pointless. Neither visions nor rebirths here, but idle conversations to kill the time; no menacing institutions, but a banal everydayness; the seer has turned into a young pedant, for whom epiphany is jut a tricky philological riddle. In every respect, this last chapter seems to have one possible function only: the merely negative one of invalidating what, up to then, had been constructed as the meaning of the novel. And here, of course, one may claim that all texts play this trick upon themselves, plunging happily into unreadability, with which the case is dismissed. But I happen to think that literature is not produced to multiply symbolic tensions out of control, but rather to reduce and contain them: and as the ending of *Portrait* seems to contradict this thesis, I have to provide an explanation for it. Why this slowdown, this anticlimax? Why should Joyce undo the meaningful irreversibility of chapter four? Indeed, why did Joyce write the fifth chapter at all?

Perhaps the last question is stupid, period. Or perhaps it would be stupid if novels were perfect beings, thoroughly inspired by one unitary design: in which case all that is there *has* to be there, and the idea of a useless element is simply inconceivable. Like most things human, however, novels may be closer to bricolage than to engineering: and in this case images, episodes, or whole chapters would be highly contingent products, which may, or may not, be where they are; and may, or may not, work well in the overall structure. Writers make literature, as the saying goes, but cannot chose the conditions, nor the materials with which they make it.

Let us think of Joyce as bricoleur, then, musing upon the materials put at his disposal by literary tradition. First of all, reasonably enough, the debris of the bildungsroman itself: Flaubert's flat prose of the world, where the very notions of experience and growth had disappeared. "It would be easier," wrote Pound in 1917, "to compare *Portrait* with *L'éducation sentimentale* than with anything else": true, but to revitalize the form of the bildungsroman Joyce also needed an antidote to Flaubert's insignificant everydayness. Why not the poetry of traumatic intensity originating in Baudelaire, and developed by Rimbaud, who was, after all, the archetypal "artist as a young man" of the late nineteenth century? In a somewhat similar vein to Benjamin's Baudelaire, Joyce's use of epiphany may thus be seen as a bold attempt to confront traumas and their linguistic turbulence: to master and "use" them as means for self-revelation, and growth (and even socialization: they point the road to adult work).

Flaubert and Rimbaud: a plausible matrix for *Portrait*'s well-known oscillation between "dullness" and "sensitiveness," between a meaningless everyday (preferably at the beginning of chapters), and meaningful revelations (preferably at the end). Flaubert and Rimbaud . . . Flaubert *or* Rimbaud, we should rather say. Their versions of experience were so utterly incompatible that, "in the end" no reconciliation or compromise was possible: Joyce had to choose between them. But what should be the criterion for his final choice? What made more sense in terms of the regeneration of the bildungsroman was clear enough: Rimbaud, kernels, epiphany, chapter four. But just as clear was what made more sense within the wider historical trend of Western narrative: Flaubert, satellites, pro saic dullness, chapter five. Joyce's double choice was, then, the sign of a double bind: of a contradiction that even the most scrupulous brico-leur in the world (which Joyce certainly was) could not hope to solve. The merit of *Portrait* lies precisely in not having solved its problem. Or in plainer words: the merit of *Portrait* lies in its being an unmistakable failure.

Portrait as bricolage; as bricolage manqué: as a structural failure. And fortunately so. Had it been otherwise—had *Portrait* been, say, as good as *Tonio Kröger*—we would have no *Ulysses*. Thomas Mann's bricolage—his essayistic mediation between the realistic novel and German tragic thought—proved so successful that he preserved its formula for half a century, thereby introducing no great novelty in the evolution of narra-tive. Inertia is the dominant force, even in the realm of literature, and as long as a form works well there is no reason to modify it: *it is only when it fails that the need for change arises.* Think of the internal articulation of the late bildungsroman: at one pole the smooth formal achievements of *Youth* and *Tonio Kröger;* at the opposite one, the increasingly unstable-unfinished mosaics of *Malte, Portrait,* and *Amerika* (with *Törless* and *Jakob von Gunten* somewhere in between). In terms of historical evolution on one side a well-functioning bildungsroman, and the Long Nineteenth Century of Conrad and Mann; on the opposite side, erratic and unsteady structures, and the modernism-to-come of Rilke, Kafka, and Joyce. Doesn't this sug-gest that the latter trio was literally *forced* into modernism by its failure with the previous form? Without failures, I insist, we would have no literary evolution, because we would have no *need* for it. Perhaps, then, we should stop pretending that failures are really masterpieces in disguise, and should learn to accept them as failures, appreciating their unique historical role.

To the inevitable question, "Would you mind explaining what exactly *is* a literary failure?" I would reply, although sketchily, that it is the sort of thing that occurs when a form deals with problems it is unable to solve. This definition presupposes in its turn the idea that symbolic forms are fundamentally problem-solving devices: that they are the means through which the cultural tensions and paradoxes produced by social conflict and historical change are disentangled (or at least reduced). Here lies the so-called social function of literature, with its so-called aesthetic pleasure: solving problems is useful and sweet. So much for my personal convic-tions, which I have tried to justify more at length elsewhere, and which are of course thoroughly questionable. But if they strike you as plausible, then a form that addresses problems it cannot solve is indeed a failure, socially and aesthetically. For the late bildungsroman—this most painfully intelligent and strangely short-lived episode of modern literature—this insoluble problem was the trauma. The trauma introduced discontinuity within novelistic temporality, generating centrifugal tendencies toward the short story and the lyric; it disrupted the unity of the Ego, putting the language of self-consciousness out of work; it dismantled neutralized spaces, originating a regressive semiotic anxiety. In the end, nothing was left of the form of the bildungsroman: a phase of Western socialization had come to an end, a phase the bildungsroman had both represented and contributed to. The strength of its pattern—the stubbornness, in a sense—can be seen nowhere as clearly as in Joyce, who devoted a first novel to Stephen Dedalus, and then a second novel, and then the beginning of a third novel. But the nineteenth-century individual—Stephen Hero—could hardly survive in the new context, and in an epoch-making change the decentered subjectivity of Leopold Bloom—this more adaptable, more "developed" form of bourgeois identity—set the pattern for twentieth-century socialization.

Just one final remark, on *Portrait* again. As we saw, we have here a Flaubertian field of repetition, satellites, and meaninglessness—and a Rimbaudian one of epiphanies, kernels, and meaningfulness. The first mention of epiphany though, in *Stephen Hero,* had established quite a different paradigm: "This triviality made him think of collecting many such moments together in a book of epiphanies. By epiphany he meant a sudden spiritual manifestation, whether in the vulgarity of speech or of gesture." As the narrator tells us, this is a "trivial incident," a banal satellite, not a visionary rebirth. Somehow, however, this everyday occurrence is also significant: and the "spiritual manifestation" of epiphany is to be found *in* "the vulgarity of speech or of gesture," not in mythic forms flying away from it. The significance of what is insignificant: what Stephen Dedalus had come across in 1906 "one misty evening, as he was passing—of all places—through Eccles St." was of course *Ulysses*. But the encounter had taken place too early, and the oxymoron of a meaningful meaninglessness was still too elusive: in that very same page of *Stephen Hero* Joyce veered away from "superficial" epiphanies, soon to replace them with the "deeply deep" ones of *Portrait*. Yet that early page had been written, and since Stanislaus Joyce was nice enough not to throw it away, it may teach us that literary change does not occur as a straight growth (*Stephen Hero,* then *Portrait,* then *Ulysses*), but as a branching process (*Stephen Hero,* and then either *Portrait* or *Ulysses*). Joyce chose the *Portrait* way, as we know, but it led nowhere. Far from preparing *Ulysses, Portrait* delayed it, and in order to invent Bloom, Joyce had to forget his *Künstlerroman* and retrace his steps all the way back to that initial bifurcation near Eccles St. It is an arabesque that may be taken as a miniature for the late bildungsroman as a whole: every tree has its dead branches, and this, alas, was one of them.

NOTES

1. The idea that youth would "naturally" develop into adulthood had apparently become so unconvincing that Joyce inverted Goethe's trajectory, abandoning the bildungsroman for the earlier form of the *Künstlerroman* (the artist's novel), where growth and independence are the prerogatives of an exceptionally gifted minority. As a consequence, the idea of "vocation," which the nineteenth century had brought down to bourgeois earth, reacquires the metaphysical halo of Stephen's final words ("Welcome, O life! I go to encounter for the millionth time the reality of experience, and to forge in the smithy of my soul the uncreated conscience of my race").

2. Karl accepts an invitation to dinner from his uncle's best friend. At midnight, a letter reaches him: "Beloved nephew! You have resolved tonight, against my will, to leave me: be therefore constant in your resolution all life long. Only thus yours will be a manly, mature decision." As a consequence, Karl is once more banished from his family.

3

TOWARD VARENNES

ટ**ે**

Ann Rigney

Here perhaps is the place to fix, a little more precisely, what
these two words, *French Revolution*, shall mean; for, strictly considered, they may have as many meanings as there are speakers
of them.
—Thomas Carlyle

NUMEROUS HISTORIES OF THE FRENCH REVOLUTION were
produced in the course of the nineteenth century, as France swung back
and forth between empire, monarchy, and republic. These histories were
written from different political perspectives by writers who were less often
professional historians than journalists, men of letters, or politicians.
Later commentators on this massive corpus have usually been themselves
professional historians, concerned, as historians of the Revolution, with
the work already done in the last century; concerned, as historians, with
the history of their own discipline and how it emerged from its nonprofes-
sional origins, or with the history of political thought and debate in the
nineteenth century as reflected in these monumental and, in certain cases,
best-selling works.[1]
    One might approach the historiography of the Revolution, however,
from yet another perspective, and study it as a discursive phenomenon.
Traditional academic divisions between historical and literary studies have
not been conducive to such an investigation and hitherto little work has
been carried out in the field. But recent theoretical developments in historiography, together with the extension of discursive studies beyond the

narrow realm of "literary" texts, have changed this situation.[2] As the historian Michel de Certeau writes in his *L'écriture de l'histoire* (1975): "One step more, and history will be regarded as *a text* which organizes units of meaning and carries out transformations of them according to certain definable rules. Indeed, just as historians can make use of semiotic procedures in order to revitalize their practice, historiography itself is a legitimate object of semiotic analysis to the extent that it is narrative or a distinct type of discourse."[3]

In taking the step proposed by de Certeau toward a textual study of French Revolution historiography, my purpose here is not to use the notion of verbal construct to demonstrate once again that no account of the Revolution can ever be objectively true; nor is it simply to prove or to contradict the well-known fact that Thiers was a liberal and Jaurès a socialist; that Michelet preferred Danton, and Louis Blanc, Robespierre, and that Lamartine took considerable liberties with Madame Roland. What is at issue here, rather, are the procedures through which any interpretation of the Revolution, whatever its color, is produced and conveyed in the form of a text. What is the nature of the transformation between history-as-event (*das Geschehene*) and history-as-narrative (*die Geschichte*)? How are historical data represented, and thereby reinterpreted, in these narratives? Questions like these involve an initial shift of emphasis away from the ideological and methodological differences between the various writers to the common ground which they share as narrative historians of the French Revolution in the century that followed it.

This brief paper can be no more than a preliminary investigation of what is a large, and as yet relatively unexplored, field; and I will limit my observations to a single episode in the Revolution—"Varennes"—as it has been represented in the histories of Mignet (1824), Thiers (1823–27), Carlyle (1837), Lamartine (1847), Michelet (1847–53), Blanc (1847–62), Aulard (1901), Jaurès (1901–4), and in two works devoted exclusively to this event: Alexandre Dumas's *La route de Varennes* (1860) and Victor Fournel's *L'événement de Varennes* (1890).[4] Limiting my material in this way, however, has the decided practical advantage of making it possible to study specific examples of the mediation between event, evidence, and representation—a subject left largely untouched by Hayden White, whose pioneering "tropical" approach to historical discourse has tended to neglect its specifically historiographical function: namely, to represent particular events that have actually happened.[5]

For, no matter how many possible points of comparison exist between
fictional and historical narrative (and undoubtedly there are many), it
remains an irreducible fact that history treats of real, not imaginary,
events. The French Revolution took place between 1789 and 1794; the
Bastille surrendered to the Parisian crowd on 14 July 1789; the king fled
with his family from the Tuileries on 20 June 1791, only to be captured
the following day at a place called Varennes. . . . These events predate
any account given of them, the French Revolution being both the prerequisite and the referent of any "History of the French Revolution." (In
contrast, the fictitious Jean Valjean has to struggle through the sewers of
Paris only when Hugo's pen sends him there; and, although there was
certainly a revolt in Paris in 1832, the particular barricade on the rue de
la Chanvrerie which brings together Marius, Valjean, Gavroche, and the
rest was only raised in 1862, together with *Les misérables.*) Starting from
the observation that historical discourse has a *referent,* the present paper
will explore further the nature of historical reference and how it influences
the actual composition of historical narratives.

Although historical discourse is referential, it differs from other forms
of referential discourse precisely because it is *historical.* Its object is past.
Louis XVI could only flee to Varennes once, and that was on 20 June
1791; even if Robespierre could be guillotined again, this would be for
the second time and would, therefore, be a different event. Chemical
reactions can be reproduced, and a geologist might always go back to the
actual rock specimens if he wishes to verify his findings or those of a
colleague. In contrast, historical events have become a function of the
discourse that refers to them. As Roland Barthes has put it: "This must
surely be the only type of discourse where the target-referent is external
to discourse, without it being ever possible to reach it, however, except
within discourse."[6]

The historian is dependent on (as well as indebted to) the testimony of
others: the traces left by the event in a variety of primary sources where
it has already been selectively represented, interpreted. The constitution
of its significance as an event was contemporary with the drama of Varennes—indeed inseparable from it. Each historian refers to the Assembly's action in immediately renaming the king's flight "the abduction
of the king"—a change of name that had practical effects on the events
that followed. Victor Fournel shows how the *procès-verbal* issued by the
municipal council of Varennes, and used as a source by subsequent histor-

ians, had actually been rewritten a number of times under the supervision of the departmental official in charge of printing it, who had found the original version too royalist in sentiment. But is the first, uncensored version of the *procès-verbal* really an authentic or unmediated account of the king's captivity *chez* Sauce, as Fournel seems to suggest?[7] "The nation felt abandoned, orphaned," writes Aulard (118), a reaction which suggests that even (perhaps especially?) eyewitnesses to the event experienced it through the filter of their political interests, beliefs, fears. In any case, it is clear that the schematization of events is not the private preserve of subsequent historians and that, in setting out to narrate, the writer enters well-charted, well-codified territory, not virgin forest.

That events become a function of the discourses which refer to them can be considered from another perspective also. Any representation of events—whether by witnesses or later historians—involves selecting those details considered representative of them, constitutive of their significance. Speaking about events is always a form of shorthand vis-à-vis the totality of "what happened." Nowhere is this more evident than with the use of a term like *the French Revolution* which by itself can be enough to refer unambiguously to a certain set of events that took place in France between 1789 and 1794. In certain cases, a nominal reference like this will be all that the occasion calls for. If, for example, I am writing a history of the English lyric in the first half of the nineteenth century, I may well refer to the impact of "the French Revolution" on the political ideas of Wordsworth, and presuppose that my reader knows *grosso modo* to which events I am referring.[8]

Which events indeed? If the context seems to call for a representation of the event "French Revolution," which events are to be selected as constitutive (i.e., representative) of it? Did it really end in 1794 and begin in 1789? An event, like the Hydra, is infinitely divisible into other events, there being no minimal event-units. Is a war, Louis O. Mink asks, the engagement between armies, between battalions, between companies, between individual soldiers?[9] A similar question might be asked of Varennes, divisible as it is into the preparations for the journey, the negotiations with foreign powers, the escape from the Tuileries, the journey toward the frontier, Drouet's cross-country chase, and so on. The escape from the Tuileries, for example, also involves a series of other events, such as the royal family leaving one by one through a side entrance, the queen getting lost in the environs of the rue du Bac, her encounter with Lafayette's coach, her reactions on seeing it—all of which might, of course, be summarized by the simple statement: "The royal family left the Tuileries in secret."

An event, be it the queen's encounter with Lafayette, the flight to Varennes, or the French Revolution, will be represented in greater or less detail (i.e., involving a greater or smaller number of other events) depending on its role within a particular discursive context. Thus, the first task of the historian, writes Paul Veyne in his *Comment on écrit l'histoire* (1971), is not to "treat" his subject, but to "invent" it. He must cut out from his primary sources the event "such as he has chosen to make it be": "Historians recount plots that are like so many routes which they map out at will across the highly objective evenemential field (which is infinitely divisible and is not made up of event-atoms); no historian describes the totality of this field, since a route is necessarily selective and cannot pass everywhere; none of these routes is the true one, is History. Finally, the evenemential field is not composed of particular sites, called events, which are to be visited: an event is not an entity, but the intersection of possible routes." [10] Varennes, France 1789–94, the Irish Famine, the first Crusades, the bombing of the Fabrique nationale in Liège—all are points on the open evenemential field of history; the historian, depending on his field of interest and the itinerary he wishes to plot out across it, will select certain points rather than others; the connections that he makes between these various points indicate the *sens,* the direction or tendency, of his route.

Theoretically, therefore, Varennes could be intersected in an infinite number of directions, as a crossroads of any number of itineraries. It could, for example, be treated as an episode in the "History of small towns in the French revolution," the "History of the Champagne," the "Life of Pétion," "Rural society in eighteenth-century France," "Kingship in Western thought," to name but a few. Depending on the subject chosen, the events of 20–21 June 1791 would be configured differently: in a history of rural communities in the eighteenth century, the swift response of the neighboring villages to the tocsin set ringing by Drouet and his patriotic colleagues would obviously figure more prominently than Pétion's *sans-façon* in eating his chicken dinner in the royal presence, an action more important, and more likely therefore to be represented, in a biography of the future mayor of Paris. In a history of Western kingship, however, the historian might consider it sufficient for his argument simply to refer to "Varennes" as an illustrative example of certain attitudes, without representing it in any detail.

If the historian decides to take in on his route the point that the king made secret preparations for his escape, he then has the option of also including certain other points: the various disguises adopted, the ruses devised in order to avert the suspicions of the attendants, the choice of couriers, the color of their livery, and so on. If he decides to include the point that the couriers wore bright yellow, he then has the further option of making the point that this was also the color of the prince de Condé, one of the leaders of the Emigration. However, this last point might also have been reached by an alternative route: the suspicions of the local inhabitants along the road to Varennes and their predictable reaction upon seeing the symbolic color yellow on a passing equipage; or again, through the character of Louis XVI, whose imprudence allowed such an indiscretion to be committed.

The accessibility of points on the evenemential field is theoretically a function of the primary record: a point must already have been made in discourse for it to be available as historical evidence (although there is no guarantee that this will always be the case in practice). Maintaining Veyne's agrarian or spatial metaphor, while developing more fully (and in a somewhat different direction) the rhetorical model that underlies it, I shall refer to the available points on the evenemential field as *topoi:* it is from the network of accessible topoi that the historian "invents" the historical events he sets out to represent.[11]

The set of topoi is not necessarily identical with the set of statements actually made in the ensemble of extant records; sometimes a topos is entailed by the evidence explicitly presented or can be inferred from it, and a historian's inventiveness may consist in large part in his ability to free himself from the particular perspective imposed on events by his sources. Topoi such as "the queen got lost in the rue du Bac," or "the king disguised himself in a gray suit," could not have become available without some explicit contemporary reference to that specific street or color, whereas Louis's royal imprudence may be inferred from his choice of equipage and the canary color of his couriers' livery. Similarly, it may not be necessary for the first *procès-verbal* produced by the municipal council of Varennes to contain any explicit statement to the effect that "the people

of Varennes are still loyal to the principle of monarchy" for their royalist
sympathies to constitute a topos, if these are evident from their account
of the incident. [12]

The accessibility of particular routes is also influenced, however, by the
writers' historical position vis-à-vis what has already been written in the
field; the connections previous historians have made between topoi open
up new evenemential areas, new areas of significance, which effectively
modify the set of topoi that later historians inherit. It is to be expected
that the mediating role played by the historiographical tradition in the
representation of events will be particularly important in the case of the
French Revolution: the set of data available to Jaurès is different from that
open to Thiers, not only because new sources have come to light, but also
because in the meantime Carlyle, Blanc, Michelet, and Lamartine (to
name but the most prominent) have written their histories of the same
event.

Although theoretically Varennes could be intersected in any number of
directions, in practice (as the royal runaways discovered to their dismay)
the number of routes passing through Varennes is limited and the best-
trodden one at this period is that linking Varennes to the French Revolution (the title of Lamartine's work masks what is in fact another history of
the Revolution). That Varennes should be configured as an episode in the
Revolution—indeed that so many writers should have chosen the Revolution as their field of interest—is not surprising, given the enormous
impact of this momentous event on French political life in the nineteenth
century. Yet it deserves explicit mention here because it illustrates how,
in practice, the representation of the past is mediated by ideological factors that give certain subjects more value, more interest, more topicality,
at particular periods and within a particular society. [13]

I

The historians considered here differ, sometimes appreciably, in the spa-
tiotemporal limits which they set to Varennes, and in the degree of detail
with which they represent it. Michelet, for instance, begins his account
with Van Dyck's portrait of the hapless Charles I, which used to hang in
Louis's bedroom as a warning to him not to get on the wrong side of
Parliament, while Carlyle includes the massacre of the Champs de Mars
(17 July 1791) as being the final stage in the king's flight. Moreover,
where Mignet devotes three pages to his account of the king's escape and

arrest, Thiers fifteen pages, and Carlyle thirty-eight, Michelet gives it more than fifty, and Fournel more than two hundred. Nevertheless, there is a striking degree of overlap between their various configurations of the event and their selection of relevant topoi: the comparatively minor detail of the color of the king's clothes recurs frequently, and almost every writer, even Mignet, refers to the (romantic?) rapprochement between Barnave and the queen in the course of the funereal return to Paris. The extent of the common ground between such different writers points to their exploitation of what, in practice, was only a limited corpus of texts, providing a finite amount of information about a select number of occur-rences. Furthermore, the unevenness with which events are portrayed in-dicates the arbitrary and inconsistent manner in which traces were left in the source texts. Carlyle, Michelet, and Blanc all mention the fact that Louis ate bread and cheese, and drank some wine, during his wait in Varennes; in contrast, none of these writers describes the actual depar-ture of the royal family from Paris. Instead, they shift abruptly—as does Mignet also—to the nocturnal doings of the marquis de Bouillé, leading up to his discovery, on his arrival at Varennes later in the morning, that the royal captives had already left for Paris under a heavy escort. Luckily, the same marquis de Bouillé left a set of memoirs behind him with which the historians could bridge the gap.[14]

That each account is composed from a set of ready-made building blocks is perhaps nowhere more apparent than where a writer chooses to quote statements that were made by those who actually participated in the drama of Varennes. A comparison of the various texts reveals that the same phrases are repeatedly selected for quotation; transported as discrete units from one text to the next, they remain basically unchanged in form, although they can be attributed to a different speaker. Alexandre Dumas has the crowd shout: "If it is the king you want, you will only get him dead" (147); this is followed up three pages later by Drouet's threat to Goguelat: "You want the king, he says; but, upon my oath, I tell you, you will only get him dead" (150). Blanc (705) and Michelet (604) use variants of the same phrase, ascribing it unanimously to Drouet, but lo-cating it at a different point in the proceedings.

Other examples of such fixed expressions are Drouet to Boniface Le-blanc—"Friend, are you a good patriot?"—in Blanc (706), Carlyle, in translation (26), Michelet (605), Lamartine (44), and Dumas (154); Bail-lon to Louis—"Sire, Paris has become a bloodbath. . . . Our wives, our children . . ."—in Michelet (606) and Blanc (706). By being repeated so often, these phrases acquire the value of historical clichés, not unlike "famous sayings" such as "We are not amused," "Alea jacta est" or, as in the example given by Vigny in his "Réflexions sur la vérité dans l'art" (1827), "Son of St. Louis, ascend to Heaven." [15] Although such sayings are almost invariably quoted out of context, their cachet comes precisely from the fact that they are reputedly authentic utterances, pronounced on specific historical occasions; indeed, it is the sense of the occasion that gives them their value. In the context of the representation of Varennes, "original" utterances are used to guarantee the authenticity of the account and to give a sense of local color, an illusion of dramatic immediacy. That they can be used in such a way, however, is at least in part due to the fact that, since these sayings are already so famous, they confirm the public's expectations about the event. Hence the paradox: the points where events are presented in dramatic form, using the direct speech of the partici- pants, may also be the most obviously mediated points in the narrative. This is highlighted in the works of Blanc and Michelet where many of these phrases are printed in italics.

The repetition of certain topoi may also play a role similar to that of the quotations discussed above: because they are already so well known, they provide the basis for the composition and the decoding of any new interpretation of the event. As such, they do not necessarily convey any new information about the event, information being always in inverse proportion to the degree to which it is expected. These commonplaces have, rather, a phatic function: namely, to reinforce the common ground already shared by the historian and his public so as to ensure the passage of new information. Moreover, the historian may select certain topoi— for example, the rapprochement between Barnave and Marie-Antoinette, or the mysterious stranger who passed on horseback—not because they are *significant* within his particular configuration of events, but because they enhance the interest, and hence the readability, of his account; in this indirect way, they serve to facilitate the adherence to the reader's version of the events being given. The prominent role played by the rep- etition of commonplaces in these texts (especially in those prior to Jaurès and Aulard) suggests, at the same time, that their sole function may be, not to inform, but to perform once again a story that is already known. In any case, it is apparent that historical narratives are perhaps more complex and heterogeneous in structure than has hitherto been realized;

that their role in configuring-representing events may be inseparable from other functions such as interesting their readers, explaining events to them, and persuading them of the truth of the representation given.

Once the basic elements of an event have become known—and, according to Aulard (118), Varennes, together with the Fourteenth of July, was one of the best and immediately known of the revolutionary events—the significance of a given version lies at least in part in its significant difference from the versions that have preceded it. Frequently, the historian's deviation from his predecessors is presented as a "correction" of their work in the light of a truth about the subject to which the writer claims to have access. This applies as much to the academic Aulard, who prides himself on living in an age where groups are more important than individuals, as it does to the adventurous Dumas, who retraced the king's path to Varennes in order to see for himself what the places were like and to consult with any remaining eyewitnesses; or to Lamartine, who claims to have based his account on his privileged access to private documents and memoirs, and on his personal interviews with the survivors. Asserting one's personal authority to correct the tradition is an inevitable feature of historiography: the historian, in presenting his version as the true one, enters into conflict with all other, rival versions. This "agonistic," or competitive, element will obviously be of particular importance in a politically charged context, where many versions of the same event are being produced, and where each new history must justify its existence accordingly. In certain cases, of course, claiming to "correct" the tradition may be a purely rhetorical strategy. Dumas and a later writer like Charles Aimond, for example, having in fact little new to say, are obliged to misrepresent the tradition in order to be able then to refute it: in his *L'énigme de Varennes* (1936), Aimond asks whether it is really true that the plans for escape were foolproof, as a prelude to showing, like almost every writer before him, that they were not.[16]

The intertextual relationship between the individual history and the tradition may take various forms, the work of predecessors being contradicted, supplemented, or simply exploited in the composition of the new text. Jaurès, for example, invokes Louis Blanc's account and then proceeds to "improve" upon the latter's work, by investigating Marat's prophecies of the royal flight with "greater precision than the great historian" had done (1030). It would be interesting, on another occasion, to study such explicit markers of intertextuality as expressions of the different alle-

giances established between individual writers in the tradition. What I
wish to concentrate on here, however, is the implicit intertextuality at
work in the selection of topoi—more precisely, in the regular inclusion of
certain topoi that have become key points of controversy in the course of
the different accounts. The interdependence of the individual text and the
tradition is such that a writer is obliged to show her hand on these disputed issues, even where they are not immediately pertinent to her argument, in support of her claim to be giving an adequate and veracious
account of Varennes. Thus, it can be said that the historian's subject is
not merely the event; it is also the truth or falsity of the ways in which it
has already been represented. Her task is not only to represent, but to
remedy, and at times she may even have to overstate or overload her case,
exaggerate certain elements, if she is to correct previous imbalances and
swing the scales back to "zero."

When Marie-Antoinette encountered Lafayette's coach outside the palace (if she did), did she in fact touch it out of spite or did she shy away,
even run away, in fear? Did Drouet act on is own initiative in sounding
the alarm or was he simply the representative of the municipal council of
Sainte-Menehould? Was the comte de Dampierre brutally dismembered
after being murdered by the hostile crowd?[17] While most of these questions present a choice between two alternative versions of an event, the
controversy as to why Latour-Maubourg sat in the attendants' coach,
rather than with the royal family, gives rise to a number of different interpretations. All writers mention the fact that, on the road back to Paris,
the royal party met up with the three Assembly representatives—Barnave, Pétion, and Latour-Maubourg—and with only a few exceptions,
each writer also mentions the fact that Latour-Maubourg did not join his
colleagues in the royal berline. Why not? Thiers (290), Blanc (708), and
Dumas (193) write that this was because he wanted to give Barnave an
opportunity to get to know the queen; Carlyle, however, tells us that, as
a "mere respectability," he was assigned to the second coach (31); Lamartine approaches the question more indirectly and, never mentioning the
presence of the third man on this occasion (although only two pages earlier he has related how the Assembly delegated *three* representatives), he
describes how Barnave and Pétion rushed gallantly into the royal coach to
protect the king and share his perils (45); Michelet claims that, as a former acquaintance of the queen, Latour-Maubourg was embarrassed to
meet her eye in his new capacity as Assembly representative (633); finally,

Aimond scrapes the bottom of the historical pot to come up with the suggestion that Latour-Maubourg's figure was simply too bulky to fit into the royal coach (176).

The work of Victor Fournel marks the limits of the innovation possible within the scheme inherited from Blanc, Michelet, and their predecessors. Fournel goes into great detail concerning the event, working through the repertoire of different topoi and comparing the different versions of each one. Saturation point is reached when all the variants have been accounted for as much as the available sources permit, and Aimond, writing more than forty years later, is hard put to justify his repetitive representation of events. In contrast, Aulard and Jaurès only actualize a minimum number of topoi relating to the king's flight. Presupposing that the basic facts concerning this event are already known, Jaurès can simply refer in passing to the "enormous berline" and to the yellow color of the livery (and therewith imply the commonplaces of the king's royal stupidity in his choice of vehicle and livery) on his way toward other topics of more immediate relevance to his account (1029). Similarly, Aulard gives only a brief synopsis of the escape and arrest, going on the explicit assumption that, since the event is so well known, it does not need to be represented again. Instead, he devotes his attention to the reaction among the various political groups in Paris and to the question whether republicanism was in fact the dominant opinion at this period. This very emphasis, however, can be seen as a refutation of a commonplace inherited from earlier writers like Michelet, who had portrayed Varennes as France's discovery that it could do without a king.

While theoretically the set of possible statements to be made about Varennes remains constant in accordance with the primary records extant, in practice, the set of choices actually open to any particular writer is effectively regulated by what previous historians have chosen to stress or ignore: What has been misrepresented? What has been left out? The evolution of the historiographical tradition cannot be understood, however, in isolation from developments in other discursive fields and in the sociopolitical arena. The presence of Marx between Louis Blanc and Jaurès influences the set of possibilities open to the latter. New, hitherto unrecognized topoi become apparent in the primary records when these are considered from the perspective of a Marxist theory of class struggle or in the light of events—such as the Commune—which have taken place in the meantime.

Some of the differences between the history written by the academic Aulard and, for example, that written half a century earlier by the poet-historian Lamartine, might also be accounted for by changes in literary fashion, and in the relations between history writing and other literary forms such as the novel. Just as contemporary taste allows Lamartine to actualize the maximum number of pathetic and *larmoyant* topoi in his account of Varennes, so too the contemporary taste for *narrative* history influences the degree to which his account is narrativized and the detail with which events—particularly events of an intimate or sentimental order—are represented: "At Varennes, the night had gone by for the king and for the people, palpitating between hope and terror" (43), and so on.

II

The historian's selection of significant evidence is inseparable from his articulation of that evidence in a new discourse: it is at the level of discourse that the significant connections between topoi are established and revealed.

Although events take place in a temporal order, there is no natural order to the set of possible things that could be said about Varennes. Of course, a narrator might choose to follow the king's activities in chronological sequence moving from his preparations for the journey, to the journey itself, to his arrest at Varennes, to his hopes and fears during the night, to his reception of the Assembly's decree ordering him back to Paris, and so on. Any such "natural" order can only be constructed, however, at the cost of disrupting other, equally "natural" orders: instead of entering the narrative at the moment of its reception by Louis, the Assembly's decree might also have been introduced in the context of the measures taken by the Assembly the previous day as soon as they heard that the bird had flown.[18]

The historian, unlike the novelist, starts from a multiplicity of agents, settings, actions, circumstances, which he has then to organize into a narrative: the *fil conducteur* of this narrative organization may be a person (e.g., the king), an institution (the Assembly), a place (Paris, Varennes), a topic (security at the palace, the reaction in Paris). Depending on which *fils conducteurs* are chosen, different hierarchies are established among topoi at the level of representation. As in a painting, some elements will be foregrounded and represented in detail, while others are relegated to a merely auxiliary or background role. The murder of Dampierre, for instance, could become the (foregrounded) subject of a separate article by Georges Lefebvre in 1941.[19]

Where Carlyle and Blanc cut briefly to the reaction in Paris as soon as they have put the king on the road to Varennes, and where Michelet follows the movements of the king until his departure from Varennes, Jaurès's narrative never leaves Paris, treating the king's flight, as well as his return, only in the context of the impression these make on the Assembly: "Then, as the Assembly is doggedly trying to reconcile the Revolution and the king, it is suddenly struck by the devastating news: the king has gone . . ." (1027). In Jaurès's text, the topos "the king fled" has been demoted or reclassified and forced to play an auxiliary role vis-à-vis the foregrounded subject, "the power struggle in the Assembly." It is this subject, rather than "what happened to Louis XVI and Marie-Antoinette," that governs the selection of topoi.

Since it is impossible to speak simultaneously of the king and of the Assembly, a narrator has to choose one or the other, or alternate strategically between the two. In the case of Jaurès, at least, it is clear that his choice implies a certain interpretation of where the locus of the action lies and who its protagonists are. But one must be wary of systematically attaching ideological significance to the formal organization of the narrative. (It has already been suggested that the focalization of events through Bouillé may be simply a consequence of the fact that he is the principal, if not the only, source for certain scenes in the drama of Varennes.) The alternation in Lamartine's account between events in Paris and what was taking place in Varennes may also have a purely rhetorical function: namely, to create suspense and narrative interest by leaving Louis's fate apparently undecided, much as an Eugène Sue will abandon his Goualeuse just as she falls into the hands of her would-be assassins.

The topos of the "patriotic chambermaid who discloses the royal plans" is a good example of the way in which a single element can enter into different relations with other topoi depending on the context in which it is placed within the framework of particular representations. What follows is a brief account of the eavesdropping chambermaid (or was she a laundress?) across the various histories from Thiers to Jaurès.

In his account of the preparations for flight, Thiers refers to the fact that "a scare" caused the journey to be postponed until a day later (280). Carlyle, in the context of his description of the various preparations to be observed at the Tuileries, mentions a "certain false Chambermaid of the

Palace" who betrays much to her lover Gouvion, commandant of the National Guard (9). Michelet begins his account of the royal escape with a discussion of the king's apparent lack of concern for the loyal servants he abandoned and the confidence he betrayed. As an illustration of this, he describes the case of Bailly: "having received a clear warning from one of the Queen's ladies-in-waiting, he had the reprehensible weakness to pass this denunciation on to the Queen" (592). Michelet later returns to our patriotic chambermaid in explaining why it was that the flight had to be postponed: the king waited until 20 June when the woman who had denounced them would go off duty (592). In Lamartine's account, the chambermaid first appears as a "fanatic democrat" in the context of the letter which Bouillé received from the king explaining why D day would have to be postponed (28); "this faithless woman" is mentioned again in the context of the queen's secret preparations and the fact that she has had to suffer "the perfidious vigilance of one of the women in her personal service" (29). In Blanc's account, the "patriotic chambermaid" is expanded into three different maids, each one introduced in the context of a different subject. The first is a laundrymaid who finds a compromising letter in a gown belonging to one of the queen's attendants and communicates this to her lover, who passes it on to Marat—an incident used to explain the background to the latter's prophecies concerning the imminent flight of the king (692). Secondly, there is Gouvion's mistress (cf. Carlyle), who writes a warning letter to Bailly (cf. Michelet)—an example in Blanc's text of the sort of leaks that had developed in the plot (692). Finally, he includes yet another maid as the cause of the twenty-four-hour delay (cf. Thiers, Michelet, Lamartine): "This twenty-four-hour delay was due to the fact that one of the dauphin's chambermaids (a very reliable person who was to have gone on duty the day originally chosen) had fallen ill, and that her colleague, strongly suspected of jacobinism, stayed on duty until the twentieth; since they dared neither to trust her nor to dismiss her, they preferred to wait" (693).

Jaurès, in contrast to Blanc, focuses on a single hypothetical chambermaid, an amalgam of all the others, and referred to simply in her capacity as "the invisible listener" (1034) or as "the ear of the people" (1033—compare Lamartine's "faithless woman"). This invisible listener tells her lover of what she believes was an attempt made to abduct the king; he passes on her story to Marat who publishes it, thereby paving the way for the Assembly's subsequent fiction that the king did not run away, but had been abducted. Jaurès not only reproduces the story as it was printed in *L'ami du peuple,* he also presents a hypothetical reconstruction of the eavesdropping incident, focalized through the anonymous listener, in order to show how easily such a fiction might have germinated in the popular imagination. By thus foregrounding a topos which in other accounts is used merely as an auxiliary detail illustrating a number of different subjects (in Lamartine's case, for example, the victimization of the royal family by the people), Jaurès manages to link up Marat's prophecies with the Assembly's reactionary fiction: a new line is drawn from our patriotic chambermaid to Marat's writings, to the fiction of the "abduction of the king," which ironically they prepared, and, ultimately, to the consolidation of bourgeois power in the Assembly which, in Jaurès's account of Varennes, is the principal subject. All of these topoi have been actualized before in earlier texts, but Jaurès combines, reclassifies, and thereby reinterprets them in an original way.

The revelation of significant links between topoi is not dependent, however, on the fact that these occur in the same discursive sequence or in the same narrative context. A link might be made between the fact that Louis asked Sauce for bread, cheese, and wine while a prisoner at his house in Varennes, and the fact that he also asked for refreshments before making his reentry into Paris. When presented together in this way, it is obvious that there is a similarity between these two topoi, and that together they point toward Louis's obedience to the commands of his own stomach. But when they are to occur in different parts of the narrative, and then only as auxiliary details, how might their similarity be foregrounded so that the link between them can be effectively made?

Michelet's work in particular illustrates how the similarities between topoi occurring in different places in the narrative can be foregrounded in such a way that the link between them becomes apparent. In what follows here, I shall consider briefly how he develops the subject "the foreignness of monarchy" in the course of his account of Varennes. The strategies that he uses exemplify the way in which the different levels of a historiographical text can be made to work together in order to transform diverse historical data into significant patterns.

Michelet prefaces his narrative account of Varennes with a chapter entitled "Précédents de la fuite du Roi," which is less a narrative representation of the different preparations for escape than a discursive account of the political and moral circumstances in which it could take place. Louis's preparations for the getaway are set in the context of his negotiations with the various foreign powers, although Michelet concentrates more on the "foreignness" of the courts with whom Louis is in contact than on the success or failure of his diplomacy. This peripheral element becomes fore-grounded even more prominently as these negotiations are set in the con-text of a variety of topoi relating to Louis's (voluntary and involuntary) foreign allegiances: he has family ties with most European monarchs; his own mother came from Saxony; as a king, he naturally identifies with other kings rather than with the French nation; as "le roi *très chrétien,*" his first allegiance must always be to Rome. A brief proleptic reference is also made to the future condemnation of Louis XVI on the charge of having betrayed France in asking for foreign aid (583). Michelet not only in-cludes this concentrated dose of topoi relating to Louis's foreignness, he also reidentifies familiar evidence concerning the flight to Varennes in the light of the same topic: the gallant Fersen is redescribed as a Swede; Choiseul is identified as a member of "a family dear to Austria" (589). Thus, the preparations for flight chez Michelet: "The affair became alto-gether foreign. M. de Bouillé admits that he needed German troops in order to *control* the few Frenchmen he had left. His son tells us that he *demanded* foreign help. In Paris, the escape was plotted in the home of a Portuguese and was directed by a Swede; the coach was hidden in an Englishman's house" (583). Placed in such a context, the flight to Var-ennes, as potentially a flight from France, becomes charged with a new significance. Varennes will be the testing ground of the Revolution, and of the judgment later passed on the king for being alien to the spirit of France—as a king, as a member of a foreign family, and as someone who tried to abandon, betray, the country.

In the narrative of Varennes that follows these "Précédents de la fuite du Roi," Michelet uses basically the same set of topoi as his contemporary Louis Blanc. But the preceding discussion casts a particular light over the narrative account, which highlights, and thereby links, all elements that are in any way marked by the opposition between "things foreign" and "things French." The familiar facts that Bouillé's regiment was called the *Royal Allemand,* and that the soldiers stationed at Varennes were German speakers, become indicative of the alien principles they stand for in sup-porting the king. The fact that the royal family travels under the passport of a Russian noblewoman ceases to be merely an incidental part of their disguise, and paradoxically reveals their true identity as foreigners; in this context, Drouet's question, on perusing their passport, becomes ironic: "Ladies, if you are foreigners, how is it that you have so much influence that at Sainte-Menehould fifty dragoons should be ready to escort you, and as many again at Clermont?" (600).

The route traced by Michelet across the evenemential field of Varennes includes, moreover, a number of topoi that do not often figure in other accounts: for instance, the fact that Choiseul (he of the "family dear to Austria") abandoned his post and set off in the direction of Luxemburg (597). The fact that Varennes is a frontier town is also stated explicitly so as to explain why the inhabitants should be so particularly sensitive to the threat of foreign invasion (601–2). In contrast, the young lieutenant Röhrig who rode off from Varennes so as to warn Bouillé is left nameless, being identified in this context simply as a young German who panicked in the crisis (599). Thus the manner in which an element is described or identified changes its capacity for combination with other topoi: because Varennes is a frontier town, Röhrig a German, and Fersen a Swede, they belong to the same pattern.

The revelation of this significant pattern in Michelet's text is above all an effect of the strategic conjunction of commentary and narrative; "revelation" is to be understood here both as "uncovering" and as "making apparent," for perhaps the most important point to be noted here is the rhetorical, indeed didactic, function of the way the account has been organized. In his Varennes, Michelet not only gives an account of "what happened," he also *makes clear*—unmistakably clear—what significant connections are to be made between the different features of the event: representing is inseparable from posting the significance of what is represented.[20] In choosing to place his commentary before his narrative account, in letting his "Précédents de la fuite du Roi" act as a key signature for the reading of the narrative that follows, Michelet manages to make these connections appear, moreover, as if they were intrinsic to the events themselves (Varennes "tel qu'en lui-même") and not simply the product of an ex posteriori interpretation imposed on them.

Michelet's Varennes seems both to exemplify Veyne's account of the way historians configure events by plotting out different itineraries across the field of what happened and to point to the limits of such a model. Whereas Veyne dismisses the question of the discursive *representation* of events with a brief reference to "established literary forms,"[21] Michelet's configuration-representation of Varennes in terms of the opposition foreign-French seems to point to the difference or gap between the event-as-sign and the historical-text-as-sign. It is certainly true that Fersen came from Sweden and that Varennes is near the border; but to what extent is the line that Michelet's text draws between them of a symbolic or of a historical order? And to what extent is it possible to dissociate Michelet's configuration of events from his didactic purpose in explaining events to the public, in interpreting events for the public, through the mediation of his discourse?

III

Thiers ends his Varennes with a comment on the account he has just given: "Such was this journey, the disastrous outcome of which cannot in fairness be attributed to any of the individuals who had prepared it" (292). Carlyle concludes also with a metacomment: "This was the Royal Flight. Thus was the Throne overturned thereby" (37); Blanc with the comment: "Thus did the tragedy of Varennes reach its conclusion. 25 June! fatal date for Louis XVI" (710); Lamartine with: "Such was this flight which, had it succeeded, would have changed all the phases of the Revolution" (49). Michelet ends his chapter on the flight to Varennes with a tableau and a commentary that sums up, and posts, the guiding theme of his account: "Yes, this was truly France. And those Germans who were running, and Bouillé who was leading them, and the King who was being led away, what was all that then? . . . It was rebellion" (608).

A number of points emerge at the end of this preliminary survey of the roads to Varennes, indicating possible directions for further research. First, the writers considered here differ in their style, in their method, and in their interpretation of the Revolution. Nevertheless, it can be said now of each historian—of Jaurès and Aulard, as much as of Michelet and Carlyle—that he selects historical topoi and combines them in a new discourse where he redescribes and reclassifies them so that they will represent Varennes such as he has chosen "to make it be" (to recall Veyne's phrase). In each case, representing Varennes is a creative activity, or *poiesis* in its root sense of "making" or "shaping": something new, something original—another Varennes—is produced out of inherited materials, through discourse. Seen from this perspective, the composition of a historical text is an integral part of the historian's task and not, as has sometimes been suggested, in contradiction with it or irrelevant to it. What is needed then is further study of the specific role of *discourse* in the configuration of historical events, and of the different signifying modes exploited by historians in particular instances. Such a study of historical discourse will have to take into full account, however, the complex set of constraints to which historical discourse is subject, precisely because it is *historical* and claims to be veracious: the historian is limited by "what happened"; each individual act of historiographical "invention" starts from inherited data; and each such act takes place in a sociohistorical context where other versions of the same events exist, and where certain conventions of historical representation are more acceptable than others.

Second, it has become apparent, at the same time, that writing the history of the French Revolution is not limited simply to the representation-configuration of events. Like all representations, these works are addressed to a reader, the narrator-historian fulfilling a hermeneutic, even didactic, role as a mediator (in Carlyle's case, literally as a translator) between events and the public. This is what happened, what does it mean? "Such was this flight which . . ." "Such was this journey, the disastrous outcome of which . . ." Once the public is admitted into historical discourse, once the public's importance is recognized, it becomes necessary to study the structure of that discourse in terms of its rhetorical, as well as its configurational, function.

Finally, the configurational function of these texts must be considered in the context of their undisguised self-referentiality as constructs, which forces us to recognize that perhaps these writers did not have to wait for Michel de Certeau (or for the present paper) to tell them that history "recounts its own work *and,* simultaneously, the work which can be read in the past." [22] What was all that then? This was the Royal Flight to Varennes. Thus was the Throne overturned thereby. Such was this flight . . .

NOTES

1. For the background to the production and reception of these works, see the following general studies: Alice Gérard, *La Révolution française, mythes et interprétations, 1789–1970* (Paris, 1970); Pieter Geyl, "French Historian For and Against the Revolution," in *Encounters in History* (New York, 1961), pp. 87–142; Jacques Godechot, *Un jury pour la Révolution* (Paris, 1974); J. McManners, "The Historiography of the French Revolution," in *The American and French Revolutions (1763–93),* ed. A. Goodwin, vol. 8 of *The New Cambridge Modern History* (Cambridge, 1965), pp. 618–52.

2. The following works can be cited as an indication of the ever-growing, if diverse, interest among historians and literary theorists in the nature of historical works as (discursive, epistemological) *constructs:* Roland Barthes, "Le discours de l'histoire," *Poétique* 49 (1982): 13–21; *The Writing of History: Literary Form and Historical Understanding,* ed. R. H. Canary and H. Kozicki (Madison, 1978); Michel de Certeau, *L'écriture de l'histoire* (Paris, 1975); Paul Ricoeur, *Temps et récit,* 3 vols. (Paris, 1983–85); Paule Veyne, *Comment on écrit l'histoire: essai d'épistémologie* (Paris, 1971); Hayden White, *Metahistory: The Historical Imagination in Nineteenth-Century Europe* (Baltimore, 1973); idem, "The Historical Text as Literary Artifact," in Canary and Kozicki, pp. 41–62; idem, "The Value of Narrativity in the Representation of Reality," *Critical Inquiry* 7 (1980): 5–27.

3. "Un pas de plus, et l'histoire sera envisagée comme *un texte* organisant des unités de sens et y opérant des transformations dont les règles sont déterminables. En effet, si l'historiographie peut avoir recours aux procédures sémiotiques pour renouveler ses pratiques, elle leur est elle-même offerte comme un objet, en tant qu'elle constitue un récit ou un discours propre," de Certeau, p. 53. The translation is my own, as are all other translations from the French in this study; in cases where the original text offers particular points of difficulty or interest, I have reproduced it in the notes.

4. François Mignet, *Histoire de la Révolution française, depuis 1789 jusqu'en 1814,* 19th ed. (Paris, 1905), vol. 1; Adolphe Thiers, *Histoire de la Révolution française,* 10th ed. (Paris, 1841), vol. 1; Thomas Carlyle, *The French Revolution* (1906; rpt. London, 1973), vol. 2; Alphonse de Lamartine, *Histoire des Girondins* (Brussels, 1847), vol. 1; Jules Michelet, *Histoire de la Révolution française,* ed. Gérard Walter (Paris, 1952), vol. 1; Louis Blanc, *Histoire de la Révolution française* (Brussels, 1847–62), vol. 1; Alphonse Aulard, *Histoire politique de la Révolution française: Origines et développement de la démocratie et de la république 1789–1804* (Paris, 1901); Jean Jaurès, *Histoire socialiste de la Révolution française,* ed. Albert Soboul (Paris, 1969–73), vol. 1; Alexandre Dumas, *La route de Varennes,* 14th ed. (Paris, 1978); Victor Fournel, *L'événement de Varennes* (Paris, 1890). Further references to the works cited above will be given in the text. The works studied here represent only a selection from all the writings produced on Varennes and the Revolution; with the exception of Dumas and Fournel, my choice has been restricted to writers in the canon or jury defined by Godechot (see n. 1). In his *L'énigme de Varennes: le dernier voyage de Louis XVI (juin 1791)* (Paris, 1936), Charles Aimond gives a bibliography which, apart from the works by Dumas and Fournel, lists ten other works devoted exclusively to this event (p. xii).

5. In *Metahistory,* Hayden White considers the elements or structures common to the works of various nineteenth-century historians concerned in each case with a different set of events (his analysis treats, moreover, both historical narratives and works in the philosophy of history). The present study is an attempt

to approach historical discourse from the opposite starting point: namely, the same event as it will be represented in a number of different texts.

6. "Ce discours est sans doute le seul où le référent soit visé comme extérieur au discours, sans qu'il soit pourtant jamais possible de l'atteindre hors de ce discours." Barthes, "Le discours de l'histoire," p. 20.

7. Fournel discusses the different versions of the *procès-verbal* in an appendix to *L'événement de Varennes*, pp. 309 f. That he believes the first version to be more original or authentic is suggested by the fact that he bases his own account of the recognition of the king at Varennes on the censored passages in the published version. For a discussion of the various ways in which the re-presentation of the Revolution played a role in the Revolution itself, see Mona Ozouf's study of the role of commemorative feast days and of the discussion surrounding the choice of event to be commemorated: "De thermidor à brumaire: le discours de la Révolution sur elle-même," *Revue historique* 243 (1970): 31–66. For a modern parallel, see Barthes's description of the way in which the participants in May 1968 both adopted the symbols of previous revolutions and self-consciously created their own in his "L'écriture de l'événement," *Communications* 12 (1969): 108–12.

8. In his study "Events, Periods, and Institutions in Historians' Language," *History and Theory* 6 (1967): 159–79, Robert C. Stalnaker shows how the term *Renaissance* can be used to refer unambiguously to an event about whose parameters there is rough agreement, but whose particular configuration is constantly open to redefinition.

9. Louis O. Mink, "Narrative Form as Cognitive Instrument," in Canary and Kozicki, pp. 129–49.

10. "Le premier devoir d'un historien n'est pas de traiter son sujet, mais de l'inventer" (p. 339). "L'historien découpe dans les témoignages et documents l'événement tel qu'il a choisi de le faire être" (p. 55). "Les historiens racontent des intrigues, qui sont comme autant d'itinéraires qu'ils tracent à leur guise à travers le très objectif champ événementiel (lequel est divisible à l'infini et n'est pas composé d'atomes événementiels); aucun historien ne décrit la totalité de ce champ, car un itinéraire doit choisir et ne peut passer partout: aucun de ces itinéraires n'est le vrai, n'est l'Histoire. Enfin, le champ événementiel ne comprend pas des sites qu'on irait visiter et qui s'appelleraient événements: un événement n'est pas un être, mais un croisement d'itinéraires possibles" (p. 51).

11. Veyne describes historiography as progressing through the extension of the repertoire of questions—topics—that can be put to the historical record, thereby opening up new fields in what has hitherto been considered "non-evenemential" (i.e., nonsignificant, irrelevant)—fields such as climate, poverty, food, etc. (see pp. 258 f.). Although the rhetorical model underlies Veyne's notion of "invention" and "topics," and of the procedures by which historical "intrigues" are constructed, he himself, as an epistemologist-historian, is not

interested in the forms of rhetorical mediation between the evenemential and the narrative representation of events, which is the topic of the present study. In contrast to the present study, moreover, Veyne is concerned with the theory of historiography, the proper task of the historian, rather than with the analysis of actual texts—texts which may fall far short of his ideal, or which may have been written at another period when history writing played a different role within the discursive economy, as is the case particularly with the earlier works considered here.

12. My treatment of the problem of "documentation" (so central to historical research) has inevitably oversimplified the critical work of the historian in assessing the authenticity and veracity of particular testimonies, in collating different testimonies, and in drawing conclusions from the established evidence—in short, the methods of "historical criticism" as these have been succinctly set out by Léon E. Halkin in his *Initiation à la critique historique,* 4th ed., Cahiers des Annales 6 (Paris, 1973). There is never any guarantee, however, that in practice historians will actually have followed these critical procedures, or that their deviation from them will be apparent in their texts (see n. 14).

13. Consider the following comment made by the critic Henri Baudrillart in his review "Les historiens de la Révolution française et la Révolution de février," in the *Revue des deux mondes,* n.s. 6, vol. 8 (1 Oct. 1850): 808–31: "Indeed, let it be said in passing, that if anything does away with the need to demonstrate yet again that the Revolution is not an accidental fact . . . it is its very fecundity, even today, both in the realm of ideas and in that of positive realities. . . . Like a religion, it has had, and continues to have, its apostles, its visionaries, its martyrs, its inquisitors, its schisms, its heresies, its innumerable sects. Now that pious stories have almost ceased entirely to delight and inflame the people's nights, it is most often to the Revolution they turn to get drunk on memories and to find objects to emulate and venerate" (p. 812).

14. In contrast, both Dumas (p. 159) and Lamartine (p. 41) describe the moment of departure. Have these writers access to another source, or do they simply fill in the gap according to what they believed probably happened, given common sense and the known circumstances? Can the reader always tell the difference between the *vraisemblable* and the *véridique?* In this context, consider also Michelet's lament for the lack of sources with which to describe the precise moment at which Louis was arrested: "The history of the tragic moment when the King was arrested is, and will always be, imperfectly known" (p. 598).

15. Alfred de Vigny, "Réflexions sur la vérité dans l'art" (1827), preface to his *Cinq-mars ou Une conjuration sous Louis XIII* (Paris, n.d.): "Study closely the origin of certain actions, of certain heroic cries which have mysteriously come into being: you will see them emerge ready-made from hearsay and from the

murmurs of the crowd without containing in themselves more than a shadow of truth; and, nevertheless, they remain forever historical" (p. 12).

16. Aimond, p. 7.

17. For an account of the widely different versions of the murder of Dampierre, see Fournel, pp. 228–29.

18. A similar point might also be made concerning the king's "Proclamation à tous les Français." Where Blanc includes this at the moment of its reception by the Assembly to whom it was addressed (p. 696), it is later presented by Sagnac as part of Louis's preparations for departure. See Philippe Sagnac, *La Révolution (1789–1792)*, vol. 1 of *Histoire de France contemporaine depuis la Révolution jusqu'à la paix de 1919*, ed. Ernest Lavisse (Paris, 1920), p. 295.

19. Georges Lefebvre, "Le meurtre du comte de Dampierre (22 Juin 1791)," *Revue historique* 192 (1941): 241–52.

20. The hermeneutic or didactic concern with both representing and posting the significance of what has been represented is by no means restricted to earlier writers like Carlyle and Michelet. Jaurès, for example, gives a lengthy quotation from Barnave's speech to the Assembly on 21 June, which he then proceeds to "translate" step by step into the following description: "This was to concentrate the entire direction of events in the hands of the Assembly; to cast suspicion on anyone who would attempt to arouse the people to the point of overthrowing the monarchy. This was to proclaim that the leadership of the new world belonged to the *proprietary* elite which was held to be the only thinking body" (p. 1040). Similarly, after quoting from the king's proclamation to the Assembly, he identifies it with the comment: "This was counter-revolution" (p. 1041).

21. "Récapitulons: l'histoire est une activité intellectuelle qui, à travers des formes littéraires consacrées, sert à des fins de simple curiosité" (p. 103).

22. "[L'histoire] raconte son propre travail *et*, simultanément, le travail lisible dans un passé" (p. 56).

4

THE REVENGE

OF LITERATURE:

A HISTORY OF HISTORY

Linda Orr

> This human mind wrote history, and this must read it. The
> Sphinx must solve her own riddle.
>
> —Emerson

MODERN HISTORY APPEARS to detach itself from literature in order to associate with the social sciences and, more precisely, with their quantitative sectors. If literature is understood in a limited generic sense, this historical perception makes sense; in fact, it is in the interest of history, transformed into a science, to construct a periodization around such an epistemological break. But "literature" does not retreat so easily; it remains implicated in history, where it assumes various guises as writing, language, text, rhetoric, fiction, reading, and so forth. What if we were to express logically, theoretically, or even "symbolically," as Michelet would say, Voltaire's ostensibly historical observation "that Fable is the elder sister of History"?[1] We would come up with something like "Fable is always the double or other of History."

I. A HISTORY OF HISTORY'S ESCAPE
Many histories of history in our present tradition (Ritter, Fueter, Shotwell, Thompson, Barnes, Lefebvre) agree in locating the epistemological break between rhetorical, narrative, or philosophical history—that is, literature—and analytic, critical, scientific history at the influential time

of Leopold von Ranke (1795–1886) and his students. But the cumulative effect of reading these works, especially as a literary historian, is curious: one becomes aware of a repetition in form and strategy, despite diverse content; an eerie feeling of having heard the same claims over and over, only expressed in different ways, creeps in. At each stage a new, improved history, if not the "real" history, seems to emerge from the old errors (fables or primitive attempts at science). Might not this version qualify as another kind of history of history? What are its implications? We might invert and rewrite Stephen Dedalus's much-quoted aphorism from James Joyce's *Ulysses*—"History . . . is a nightmare from which I am trying to awake"[2]—by saying that literature is the nightmare from which history is continually trying to wake.

In order to serve as the distinctive myth of modern historical writing, the epistemological break between history and literature needs to appear as clean as possible. Historical material "before the break" is ever and again reorganized so as to prepare, to anticipate, even to prophesy that switch. In this way, the arbitrary location of the break and especially competing ways of reading the same history are covered over. "After the break" the question emerges as to whether future developments simply modify the restructured tradition or split, in turn, from it. Discomfort with Ranke the father begins to show.

A dramatic schism punctuates the article "History and Literature" in the *Larousse Encyclopedia:* "In the course of the nineteenth century, as a consequence of the progress of erudition and of a concern for critical rigor; there happens a reversal which is confirmed in the twentieth century: the solicitations of knowledge win out over aesthetic preoccupations, and history leaves literature in order to become an autonomous discipline."[3] Before the "reversal," history and literature are mixed together, interdependent, perhaps even inseparable. An opposition struggles, however, within the strained identity, and knowledge, having grown stronger, overthrows aesthetics and wins. Or rather history abandons one mistress (or mother?) in favor of another's solicitations.

It may be true that historians before the eighteenth or nineteenth century saw no contradiction, as did neither Aristotle nor Cicero, in the fact that history functions as both a system of poetics and truth ("Historia vero testis temporum"). Prescientific historians might wonder why their successors frantically invented a problem where none (or a different one) existed, just as the latter are shocked by the apparently thoughtless mixture

of fable and truth in the writings of the former. Macaulay was more dis-
appointed by Thucydides than the more understandably "childlike" ancestor Herodotus, since the former abandons conscientious analysis without
warning for totally fabricated speeches. Such an incongruous practice
"violates, not only the accuracy of history, but the decencies of fiction."[4]

History wanted out of literature just as literature was finally going to
let it in. *English Literature* (1897) by Stopford Brooke allows that "History
. . . was raised into the rank of literature by three of Johnson's contemporaries" (Hume, Robertson, Gibbon).[5] Oddly enough, critical, or scientific, history wanted nothing to do with the products of what will come
to be called the Age of History, spanning from Voltaire and Gibbon to
Macaulay, Michelet, and Carlyle. By the nineteenth century, everyone,
and no one, was a historian: history came to provide the main common
denominator for the many hybrid genres that characterized the (Romantic) period, combining epic, utopia, political economy, political philosophy, religion, fiction, and lyricism. Poets wrote history literally (Schiller,
Lamartine) and figuratively (Hugo, "La Légende des siècles"). And certain
historians (especially Barante and Thierry) were heavily influenced by the
novels of Walter Scott or Chateaubriand, even though history maintained
the prestige of a more traditional, classical genre in comparison to the
novel. Coveting such status, Balzac could make the case that his "history
of social customs" filled Voltaire's legacy better than the "dry and tedious
nomenclatures of facts called Histories."[6] Even Whitman defined his
Leaves of Grass (1855), inscribed "To a Historian," as the "history of the
future."

It is as if history awakes in the nineteenth century surprised and even
horrified to see how closely it is coupled with fiction. It seeks thereafter
to widen a difference within its very self, in order not to be engulfed by
that other self—and the effect is to invent the modern definition of history, to inaugurate a tradition by rewriting the history of history, and in
so doing to institute that difference as science.

Ranke stood, then, as the useful hero of the "reversal" to whom the
past would have to accommodate itself and from whom the present might
be derived. Although such is not the issue here, it would be interesting
to understand the international conditions that permitted such a consensus around German critical historical scholarship. It is no accident that
such a revision of history managed to prevail at a time when histories of
history themselves were an important production of the scholarship they,

in turn, so admired. It should, therefore, have been simple for historians of history to find suitable ancestors for Ranke, but such was hardly the case. Thucydides is almost universally acclaimed as the forefather of Western history, but his infamous speeches make him an ambiguous beginning. Shotwell, for one, prefers Polybius (after whom we must wait until Ranke for critical history). And recent developments in social history, the search for a social "imaginary," have promoted the cause of Herodotus.[7]

Between the Greeks and Germans an abyss appears to yawn in which there were more examples to avoid than to imitate. The "realistic" narratives of Caesar made him a positive candidate, but, as Macaulay insisted, they could also be considered as mere "military dispatches." Machiavelli and Guicciardini also meet a curious fate in the history of history since their "pragmatic" and "political" point of view allows them to anticipate modern history in spite of themselves—if, of course, one refuses to take into account their own rhetorical heritage.[8] In brief, the "didactic" (Dionysius of Halicarnassus) or "rhetorical" (Isocrates) traditions of Greek culture won out. Literature traces the larger circle around history: Tacitus and Livy are considered writers instead of historians. Then, later, Christian history, from the Middle Ages to Bossuet, adapted the practices of classical didacticism to its theory of Divine Providence. Although Lanson is only surveying three centuries of specifically French "history," the literary historian surprises himself by confessing to having found none before Voltaire's.

Ranke's status itself is not as secure as it may appear. Fueter's *Histoire de l'historiographie moderne* (1914) calls Voltaire's *Siècle de Louis XIV* (1751) "the first modern historical work."[9] Taking Ranke as too literal a turning point obscures, as Lefebvre pointed out in *La Naissance de l'historiographie moderne* (1971), what led up to him: the work of the seventeenth-century Benedictines of Saint-Maur and, in particular, Jean Mabillon (1632–1707), which makes the *Monumenta Germaniae* and thus B. G. Niebuhr and finally Ranke possible.[10] The English could, on their side, mention that Gibbon was the first historian to train himself as a self-conscious professional from an early age. The motley crew of statesmen, politicians, poets, dramatists, philosophers, and journalists who write "history" (Caesar, Petrarch, Boccaccio, d'Aubigné, Racine, Hume, Thiers, Voltaire himself) finally did not a discipline make. Even today, if read at all, the works of these writers survive either as a marginal class of literary history or they are subsumed into the status of (subjective) documents serving a history of mentalities. The prehistory of history reveals itself as a history of literature within which is embedded an almost invisible prediction of scientific history.

If we put aside the history constructed from an epistemological break, another history of history emerges in which each succeeding wave claims to abandon fable in order to practice, at last, "history proper" (to use Macaulay's term). Voltaire predicted that the invention of printing (under Charles VII) and then the emergence of the modern political system (under Louis XIV) would contribute to conditions culminating in the possibility of a "rationalist" philosopher and historian—that is, himself. But he was foiled by underestimating that readers would see him implicated in his own regressive, historical objects: Louis's court or the fable of popular customs (*moeurs*).[11] If Gibbon, in turn, tried to elaborate the philosophic history that Voltaire heralded without fulfilling himself, the next wave, Ranke and his admirers, would simply change the nature of history and pass Voltaire and Gibbon by. Previous historiography, wrote Meinecke in his introduction to *Historicism: The Rise of a New Historical Outlook (Die Entstehung des Historismus* [1936]), missed the "profounder background" of "the world and all its life" which "historism" captured by reorienting history around problems of the individual and temporal development (thus helping to constitute the existence, in the nineteenth century, of both).[12] Positivist history arose, at the end of the nineteenth century, in opposition to Romanticism, but the Romantics, who never called themselves that, thought they were already positivists. It gives one pause to read a description of the new scientific French historical practice in *La Revue des deux mondes* (1847) with which Michelet, as well as Guizot, Thierry, Barante, Mignet, and Sismondi, are identified: "For the past fifty years, in fact, the domain of history has expanded singularly. This science, lost for a long time in systems, has grown closer to the positive sciences through the strict observation of facts."[13] We might again interpret another one of Voltaire's statements as both historical and proverbial: "All history is recent" (III, 350). He might have meant recent in terms of his own time, but history is always "recent" in that otherwise it turns back into literature.

Recent history feels ambivalent about Ranke and the institution of the end of the nineteenth century that made its own advent possible. While it has kept the experimental, positive side of historicism, it has gone beyond political event-history (which, however, seemed expansionist when it came along, in relation to the history of kings). On the one hand, Guy Palmade writes that Lefebvre's "immediate history" "only tends to ask Ranke's old question . . . even if this 'how things truly came about' is enlarged."[14] The *Larousse Encyclopedia* article "History" judged that the old "fixed rules" are still respected, though "in the service of a new conception of history."[15] On the other hand, the Annales school, Lucien Febvre for one, defined itself in opposition to Ranke. Braudel, too, in his *Ecrits sur l'histoire* (1969) does not hesitate to mark a break between himself and the German historian, "a stranger to our thought," for he spoke "'of the solid terrain of history.'"[16] Must we always read recent history (history itself) as both expansion and break? The controversial "total history" of the first half of the twentieth century, associated first with Henri Berr and later with Lucien Febvre and Marc Bloch, emphasized the theme of open collaboration with a plethora of allied sciences (first geography, anthropology, sociology, and philosophy, then demography, ethnology, collective psychology, psychoanalysis, and especially economics, mathematics, statistics, and computer science). The historical object has multiplied spatially and temporally.[17] It has proliferated culturally and socially, entering into previously invisible realms like death, childhood, and the imaginary. The territory of history has in fact grown enormous and vertiginous, that is, "universal."[18] Whether in *La revue des deux mondes* (1847) or in the *Annales E.S.C.* (1946) a century later,[19] it seems inconceivable that history should continue each time to explode in such quantum leaps. But does it?

Is it paradoxical or natural that such an ambition should accompany an equally forceful moment of self-critique? Is the critique always simultaneous with the appearance of progress, or do they alternate in cycles (Saint-Simon's binary theory of organic and critical history)? Carl Becker deconstructed the notion of "hard, cold" facts in the 1920s. Nor can these growing challenges perhaps be separated from a larger pervading sense of modern uncertainty, whether associated with Heisenberg's principle of physics or the mood of "suspicion," as Hannah Arendt called it, surrounding the Second World War. But has uncertainty truly undermined the nineteenth-century rules of positive knowledge or has it simply prompted a rhetoric of caution, usually dispensed with in the preface, while the truth-teleology resurrects itself in the body of the monograph? An American collection of "quantitative research in history" repeats the now clichéd expressions. The contributing scientists did not expect a "full

knowledge of reality but an increasingly closer approximation to it . . .
the asymptotic approach to truth." The "highly effective deployment of
our limited information" should procure "a certain amount of assurance."[20] And a sentence from Le Roy Ladurie's *The Territory of the Historian*
(1973), which capitalizes upon the continued expansion of history's empire, reveals what is perhaps a double bind (let's call it the "scientific
imaginary") within which historians must work: "To put it in its most
extreme form (and it is an extreme so remote and in some cases so beyond
the scope of present research as to be perhaps only imaginary), history
that is not quantifiable cannot claim to be scientific."[21]

II. THE RETURN OF LITERATURE

Whether this is a paradoxical side effect or a law, it appears that the more
history presses toward science, the more literature, or a has-been history,
is produced. Michelet, in particular, was obsessed by the question dramatized in *La Sorcière:* the Inquisition only multiplied its weighty tomes of
talk without ever seizing the reality of the witch—*"Parole!"* ("Talkmon-
gers!").[22] Was he too, in reality, just another priest-scribe, a propagator
of hyperbole, a member of that race he most hated and against which his
entire work was written?

Despite continual self-critique, certain almost mythical images of defense underlie history's attempt to repel the ever-imminent, total invasion
of fiction. They include what might be called the historian's hermeneutic
circle (the ideal figure behind the asymptote), or playing two ends against
a middle. Such a strategy echoes, in fact, the shape of the history of
history in which the latest scientific developments link up with the most
distant beginnings, instead of the intervening mishaps.

The two ends of the historical process appear, separately and sometimes
together, to escape a fiction machine in the middle, often compared with
the children's game of "gossip" or "telephone." One can imagine that this
kind of observation would feed Voltaire's vigilant critique of history—
which it does: "The first foundations of every history are the narratives,
of fathers to their children, transmitted then from one generation to another; they are at the most only probable at their origin, when they do
not shock common sense, and they lose a degree of probability at each
generation" (3:347–48). In this view the last or latest historian seems
simply to augment the progressive snowballing fiction instead of reducing
it to a "minimum," or a probability of truth. Such an argument fuels the

facile aphorisms of history defined as "masses of worthless gossip" (Herbert Spencer), "a shallow village tale" (Emerson), or "the distillation of Rumor" (Carlyle).[23] And yet we may not want to jettison such an interpretation entirely, for important issues are raised: the effect of popular and professional transmission on the making of historical truth, that is, the way in which traditions are formed; and even the role of "common sense" in such a process or, in other words, the role of a common consensus. Voltaire allows for the probability of truth, but he qualifies this minimum promise by bringing in the most slippery of notions, common sense, as its grounding.

If the first foundations of history, albeit only probable, come as close to reality as the asymptote comes to the perpendicular, it is important to coincide with those foundations. The eyewitness conventionally represents such a privileged point of view, and, again, despite warnings, even the most wary, like Montaigne, fall into the typical traps. In his essay "On Books," the French writer states his preference for "historians either very simple or excellent"[24] but finds that most fall in between: "they want to chew the morsels for us; they give themselves authority to judge, and, consequently, incline History to their fantasy. . . . Thus, by many lovely words, they go about mixing a fine contexture of rumors that they amass at the crossroads of towns" (1:459). Montaigne suggests that only an eyewitness would protect history from rumor. In the essay "Cannibals," Montaigne refines this already strict condition, specifying the advantage of a "simple and crude" (*grossier*) eyewitness for the same reasons that explained his preference for a simple historian: clever persons gloss what they see, "in order to make their interpretation all the more worthy" (1:233). Is, then, such a person as an "excellent" historian even imaginable—that is, one who does not fall victim to the temptation of the gloss? And is the gloss-free account any more feasible than the historian who would accomplish it? Moreover, what is Montaigne's own status in this context? (He admits that his choice of eyewitness saves him from the boring task of sifting through all the cosmographies.) Is Montaigne a "clever man" who already deforms the "simple and crude" testimony, or another "simple and crude" observer himself? And should we be flattered to be conversing with so many simpletons, or distrustful of the sophisticated speaker who not only glosses but flatters us by saying we need no gloss?

Inconsistency is just as prevalent if one reverses preferences and rejects the testimony of eyewitnesses as being too involved in the event in favor of the progressive detachment or objectivity of future historians. Instead of widening the distance, that is gossip, between itself and probable truth as in the example from Voltaire, the distance of objectivity should, paradoxically, diminish that gap and make the outcome of truth more likely. But Tocqueville asks the next, appropriate question: What happens if objectivity leads to indifference and oblivion? Instead of becoming more possible, that history will simply be lost. In his *L'Ancien Régime et la Révolution,* he settles on the perfect moment for expressing the "true sense" of the Revolution as the one that just happens to coincide with his own writing. "It seems that the moment to research and say it has come, and that we are placed today at that precise point from which one can best perceive and judge this great object." [25] That precise moment appears to come once in the lifetime of an object of study; at least the historian, like Tocqueville, must advance this argument. A special crossing like the Greek *kairos* occurs so that the right archives are available to the right historian practicing the proper historical method. But, since each historian makes the same case, that precise moment located in a mythical timespan between passion and oblivion, at the nexus of method and research, hardly a rigorous criterion, gives the effect of floating through time with the persons who make use of it.

When the two ends take a next step and join together against the middle, the result is a (hermeneutic) circle. The historian traditionally desires to cut through the intervening interference, or to bypass and ignore it, in order to encounter the object afresh as if for the first time, in order to make history live. Michelet is again the model: his literal desire to reunite with the *body* of France expresses most radically the archetypal project. Is there a connection between this phenomenon and the fact that historians privilege, on the one hand, archives, and, on the other, the latest articles, monographs, or books to the neglect of the dusty tomes in between or even the not so dusty thesis fallen from fashion? One wonders if historians have not dropped history from among their interests.

The more complex image of the asymptote refines the implications of the circle, incorporating theoretical difficulties without giving up the mythical attraction of that round shape. As error heaps up its hyperboles, the bell curve of the hyperbola swells between the two opposite ends which keep approaching the perpendicular line, from which they remain separate. But the line also connects them by the consistency of its refusal to connect.

The edges that historians keep throwing out beyond the grasp of fiction continue, however, to fray, and the effort to fight fiction seems more futile if not doomed. Everywhere the historian looks, language encroaches, both on the side of the archive and on the side of transposing that archive through analysis into a written interpretation. Of course it is nothing new to suggest to historians that they are aways dealing with *texts,* that ubiquitous word superseded at times by *discourse.* But even in Lucien Febvre's moving litany there remains, along with the impatience, a desire, after all, to reserve still a small space outside of literature: "Texts, yes: but there are *human* texts. Texts, undoubtedly: but all texts. . . . Texts, of course: but *not nothing* but texts."[26] Febvre exposes his passage to the rhetorical question: What, after all, is this *not-nothing?* Again it is no news to suggest that models, that is, frames of analysis, are not neutral. Narrative or story has also emerged once more as not only a primary mode of historical persuasion but as an instrument of cognition. Finally writing itself, whether filed under the old category of "rhetoric" as ornament, or, using the eighteenth- and nineteenth-century word *style,* has also become problematic. It no longer simply serves as the historian's secret torture or joy.

The story of the ambiguous relationship between language and historical research runs through our tradition like a negative ground, an antistory that is as important to the survival of that tradition as its more publicized truth claims. In fact, the force of this tradition depends as much on the continually renewed opposition between literature and history as on the inventory of scientific gains. It is true that we no longer seem to place the emphasis on "a style serious, pure, varied, agreeable" (3:367) that Voltaire thought necessary in his day. At the height of narrative history, Sainte-Beuve already asked whether good writing does not go counter to good research: "Where is the historian who can unite the beauty and purity of form that belongs in every genre to the Ancients, with the depth of research imposed on the moderns, and should we hope for him in the future?"[27] The form of his rhetorical question suggests, moreover, that the two aspects of the historical practice are not only in tension at certain periods of history but are perhaps by nature antagonistic. Today's Parkman Prize assumes not only that the best history manages to combine both qualities but that it must be very difficult to do so if it merits a prize. In our day, as before too, the evaluation of style often substitutes for a discussion of ideology on one side or the other: either a smooth narrative style is incompatible with professional specialization and associated with a vulgarizing commercialism, or a professional style (jargon) supposedly disguises the absence of lucid thought.

The antilanguage bias that cuts through the history of history is charged with emotional content; besides hostility or defensiveness, a tone of disgust suggests a more underlying fear. In Harry Elmer Barnes's classical *History of Historical Writing*, a first sentence praises Polybius because he "carefully considered the matter of the reliability of the sources which a historian must use." Then a second sentence, immediately following the first, reveals the other reason for praise which is equally important: "He . . . was a relentless foe of rhetoric, which was already beginning to debauch Greek and Roman historical writing."[28] In this antistory of our Western origins, the fourth-century rhetoricians (Isocrates with whom the historians Ephorus and Theopompus [!] were associated) encouraged the corruption and "debauchery" that spread and caused the "decline and stagnation" of Roman imitators. Because of my own interest in reappraising the French Romantics, I have to applaud Barnes when he goes out of his way to signal the French representatives of the scandalous tradition (including its most flamboyant Romantic) while quoting Hermann Peter on the Greeks: "With their tendency to insipid moralizing, the interpolation of florid and fictitious speeches, and their 'passion for panegyrics,' the historical works of the rhetorical school, like those of Froissart and Lamartine in later days, 'exhibited artistic but not historical genius'" (35).

If social scientists acknowledge that language is a tar baby (the more you fight it, the more you stick to it), why does it appear that they do everything in their power to deny its role? They pride themselves on getting out of narrative, while they continue to parallel narrative's own attempt to subvert if not overcome itself in new or antinovels. The relationship between the two systems is almost symbiotic.[29] And narrative or language reappears in ever more disguised forms. Giving the impression of purifying their prose of metaphor, of almost getting out of language, historians work their arguments, instead, around "figures" and "graphs." It is not only in isolated metaphors that historians keep returning to rhetorical "figures" and "writing" (*graphein*).

Are we still the heirs of the empirical paradox in which we must study history (or nature) itself, not books, but communicate with it, and communicate our findings in a language that is ours and perhaps not its? To deny the issues behind that paradox is to reinforce what Roland Barthes calls the referential illusion or the "effect of the real" which he associates in particular with nineteenth-century history. Thiers, one of its foremost exemplars, promoted the following ideal: "to be what things themselves are, nothing more, to be nothing except through them, like them, as much as they are." [30] History was, therefore, supposed to speak itself. But the implicit paradox resulted in a kind of conceptual monster behind the ideal, such as the Talking Event or the Writing Hand of History. In my own work, the figure of stenography best incarnates the oxymoronic, even mythical, impulse: shorthand attempted to close the gap between speech and writing so that the (revolutionary) acts of the people would correspond with the (legislative) acts of the people's representatives. Or, in twentieth-century terms: such a history desires to realize and perpetuate the speech act. But the failure of such an aspiration has led historians to ask whether language only sticks to history in order to separate history from its truth. They wonder if language does not represent the infinite gap between the asymptote and the perpendicular.

An arbitrary line toward which the asymptote can eternally travel is better than erasing the line altogether and leaving the trajectory of the search in suspended suspension. Without philosophic pretense, the article "History" in the nineteenth-century *Larousse Encyclopedia* states this condition: "History changes its aspect with each generation. . . . it was right for painting to vary with the model." [31] But do we allow the consequences of this statement to sink in? This would mean that the observer and the observed are mutually self-constituted with no other reference point besides that which they work out within themselves in and as their history.

We might say that the two terms, both inseparable and opposing, the one by definition excluding the second, mutually constitute each other so that neither is the cause in relation to the other as effect, but both function as effects of the effect in a system neither and both control. Moreover, we should qualify this system of mutual self-constitution as ironic or at least as subject to coming undone while constantly reproducing itself. It functions for us, which is what matters: in fact, it seems to function, if not perfectly, so rationally or naturally that we forget and take it for granted. To think otherwise about our reality is to exercise a kind of "counterintuitive" knowledge—which should be the very definition of the historical imagination.

The word *history* itself makes the comparison with the linguistic sign almost inevitable. Hegel, in his *Lectures on the Philosophy of World History* (*Vernunft in der Geschichte*), knew that the ambiguity or double meaning of *history* (*historia rerum gestarum* and *res gestae; énonciation* and *énoncé;* study of the object and object of study), which was probably no coincidence, located both the word's power and weakness.[32] This outrageous pun is a kind of archetypal linguistic sign itself, both fusing and distinguishing within it word and thing, word and deed, text and event (signifier and signified).

Neither language nor history is self-constituted once and for all, but in the "necessary illusion," in Nietzsche's phrase, of that referential aspiration they continue to function, or misfunction, or both, ironically, at the same time. The process of differentiation that appears permanently fixed and constantly changing is arbitrary, and there is no uncontaminated reference from which to begin or toward which to travel. Always in medias res, driven and desiring to make both social and personal sense, we de- and recode (to use Hayden White's semiotic vocabulary) what is already encoded or what resists coding (which, I read, we encode as such). Although theoretically we can put forth the paradox of "mutability" and "immutability," to use Saussure's terms, they are mutually exclusive: the arbitrary order of language is broken by no one, and yet the free signifier respects nothing. They should not be able to coexist. In our current debates it is hard to say whether we are always under the eternally resistant power of one self-sustaining institution (and which is it—history or literature?), just as persistently undermined by its fleeting, unreadable Other (history or literature?), or whether nothing can even stand long enough to claim the name of institution. At times our frustration is so great that we think we can never make sense, and at other times communication is ecstatic. At times history is the maddening repetition of repressive violence, and at other times an undeniable wind of possibility sweeps the streets. At times the stories we have heard and read make such absolute sense that "we disregard whatever others might be imagined,"[33] and at other times we see those stories riddled with lies and try to imagine everything otherwise.

The ironic system we live in, or that lives in us, keeps us moving, if not in place, then in displacements. It might even be said that the excess, gap, aporia, or whatever metaphor we use for the inability of self-constituted terms to coincide with themselves or with their opposite—that the overlap and undermining make history possible, make it conceivable. Otherwise we would be mobile statues of the dead. That is, in a more theoretical sense, the linguistic "leftover" comes back to us as our notion of time to which we give a reality and measure as history. Time or history enables us to represent the linguistic slippage that otherwise escapes us, without which we might have no sense of time. On the other hand, this very phenomenon of rhetorical imprecision which makes history possible, if not necessary, also dooms it to failure. We seem to be moving but we can never arrive. We have to tell histories to explain ourselves although we can never, in however many tellings, get it right. If linguistics (the sign), or literature as the rhetorical working out of that linguistic effect, comes to name our system as I have described it, then literature, ever absent and unreadable except as a condition for history, would indeed paradoxically trace a last, large circle around history. But this only reverses the old order, putting literature over history, and we have once more lost the delicacy of meaning's juggling act, the tension of counterintuitive knowledge—the secret of a working, nontotalizing democracy. If history, even the word itself, cannot help but speak to us of linguistics (or discourse),[34] linguistics bears within its own debates a course in the historical problems of modern political philosophy: how "arbitrary order" and the "free" signifier challenge each other.

III. THE ENIGMA OF HISTORY

Neither honesty nor deception, neither truth nor error, an errancy—not necessarily terror—circulates within language and history. So what status should we attribute to the truth claims or accusations of lies in history? Is it as Byron suggests in *Lara* that History "lies like truth, and still most truly lies"? Should we read the prefaces of history books as we would read the preface of Balzac's *Père Goriot,* for instance, where he writes that "all was true," that is, with irony? Histories look like novels (especially novels published in the eighteenth century) in which authors go to great lengths to describe where they found the manuscripts that they have transcribed as accurately as possible or where they listened to the oral account. Is the difference—no less important—between the two genres that historians and their readers believe in their prefaces whereas in fiction we suspend disbelief? (Do we need, then, both a history of our belief in our own historical and linguistic representations—for example, Foucault's *Les Mots et les choses*, Genette's *Mimologiques*—and more *Rezeptionsgeschichte* or sociology of literature?) Hannah Arendt impertinently reflects upon the question of why historians continued to hold down the fort of determinable truth, while, she maintains, philosophers and natural scientists had long abandoned it. Her hypothesis is paradoxically very historicist itself: she suggests that historians became fixed in the now ancient practices of science. The positivist historian still regards his object, according to Arendt, with "that quiet, actionless, and selfless contemplation" common to "Aristotelian and medieval natural science."[35]

We readers and teachers of literature might retrain our students in the conventions of truth claims, especially evident in prefaces. We should go back even before the eighteenth century, to the seventeenth-century theory of verisimilitude (*le vraisemblable*). As La Calprenède noted in his preface to *Faramond* (1661), his novels contain "nothing against truth, things beyond truth."[36] In this vein, "vraisemblable" seems truer than truth which, as Bayle remarked, would be taken for satire if it was really revealed. L'abbé Bordelon quipped in his preface of 1711 that he might have, like Cervantes, recounted that he "paid for the manuscript in Greek or Arab through the nose": "it wouldn't occur to me . . . to force myself to deceive the public so crudely."[37] But the public catches on too quickly and realizes that even this ingeniousness is yet another form of ingenuity to make us believe.

The writer who wishes to be believed as a teller of truth must stay a step ahead of (or perhaps, even better, behind) current literary practices. One of the most beguiling strategies would, then, consist in anticipating the reader's suspicions and appearing above any tricks. (Is this the effect today of such a demystifying book of history as Paul Veyne's *Comment écrire l'histoire* or *Les grecs ont-ils cru à leurs mythes?*) Lucian and Cervantes went as far in that cycle of one-upsmanship as anyone can. Lucian prefaces *A True Story* (or *History,* depending on the translation) with a step-by-step deconstruction of each spiral of the "vraisemblable." Not only does he warn the reader that the pages to follow are fiction even though they are told as if every event happened in reality, but he goes further by making the strategy behind this confession explicit. By admitting that his truth is a lie, he expects his lies to be more "honest" than the truth. "But my lying is far more honest than theirs, for though I tell the truth in nothing else, I shall at least be truthful in saying that I am a liar."[38] Cervantes, who adds still another twist to Lucian's maneuvers, outmaneuvers them all, including the brave abbé Bordelon who thought he had called Cervantes's game. Cervantes, forgetting or omitting the subtitle which would explain the genre of his work, seems to have meant his *historia* in the sense of a narration of actual, past events.[39] His procedure is complicated in that he absorbs the truth-oath preface into the body of his work, in which the narrator explains that he bought, for a steal, the valuable manuscript *History of Don Quixote de la Mancha, Written by Cid Hamete Benegeli, Arabic Historian.* His real preface, of the Lucian variety, should then demand that the reader not believe any of Benegeli's history. But it contains in fact another mini-novel, reinforcing the truth of fiction and undermining it at the same time. The "author" asks his friend what he can do to make readers believe that *The History of Don Quixote* is really true. The friend trains him to be a historian: add quotes, footnotes. Or rather trains him to fake being a historian. That means that the reader, trained to make the next step, wonders if the claims to historical truth she or he will find throughout the novel are not equally artificial? Or do we, rather, compare by now this "author" figure encouraged by his Sancho Panza realistic friend to Don Quixote himself? And at first we find him likeable, that is, believable, but then become suspicious of that author of the "author" who exploits the double entendre of the word *history* which lies at the source of his protagonist's madness.

History requires, then, an edgy capacity for sustaining the enigma of irony. Professional limitations have often been associated with notions of psychological subjectivity, cultural bias, or political attitudes, all of which are believed to be correctable—or at least subject to investigation. The implications of a linguistic system or representation make these limitations more than temporary obstacles. The paradoxical effects produced by the self-reconstituting system are integral to the practice of history and need not, therefore, elicit either a priori positive or negative judgment. They do point up occupational hazards which are themselves ambiguous, such as history's double-time, or duplicity, and its ruse.

We often consider that we can only read the past in terms of the present—which is also already a particular desire for the future. Whether we remind ourselves at this point of that complex triangle of the sign, we can again bring up the problem in the context of history in which it is difficult, if not impossible, to tell which of the two, or three, terms is determinate. It is not as simple to say, as we used to even in terms of metaphor, that the present is a mere neutral vehicle for the content or tenor of the past. Or that the past will stay in its place.

The "focalization" (point of view) of history in terms of the present or a desired present produces an automatic internal teleology, the "optical illusion" of history. François Furet studies a notable example of this effect in his *Interpreting the French Revolution*. He would like, however, to isolate the dangers of such an illusion in the practice of Jacobin historiography: the past culminates in the Jacobin view of the world which asks only to work out the logic of its desire transformed into prediction, if not imperative. The function of Jacobin historiography is mainly to revitalize that desire, not analyze or put it into question. In this supposedly extreme case Furet suggests that the Jacobin double-time ("a double-action mechanism")[40] borders on duplicity. In the English tradition Whig history incarnates the same phenomenon to which Herbert Butterfield in his preface to *The Whig Interpretation of History* gives an extended sense: ". . . to praise revolutions provided they have been successful . . . to produce a story which is the ratification if not the glorification of the present."[41]

A past so deformed appears to some as no better than a mirror image of the present, and history, like the restructuring of free signifiers, becomes the play of its own reflections. Again this need not evoke a negative evaluation. Burckhardt, for instance (one of Nietzsche's most important mentors on this subject), was not daunted by recognizing history's unavoidable mirrors: "After all, our historical pictures are, for the most part, pure constructions. . . . Indeed, they are mere reflections of ourselves."[42] Like some of our ambiguous (or duplicitous?) contemporary historians, Burckhardt did not, however, hesitate, whether in irony or innocence, to continue speaking of "our pursuit of true knowledge." For Croce the "subjectivity," or subjective identification that might be a nuisance to some historians not only provided the only possibility of understanding the past, but that secret of creating "living history" in which the historian's daily business, even his love affairs, works to his advantage. In such a context, Croce reasons, "certainty" is no longer a problem, much less an issue.[43] Hannah Arendt, historicizing again, implies that the mirror now dominates our modes of perception: "The modern age, with its growing world-alienation, has led to a situation where man, wherever he goes, encounters only himself."[44]

The history we read, whether by deforming or blocking out the past, has already done enough damage to our understanding, but what if history's only purpose is to mark the place where each time it destroys over again the past it intends to save? Tocqueville, meditating on the French Revolution, recognized that history has no choice but to praise successful revolutions, since the others leave no trace, or each "succeeding" revolution recasts a past more appropriate to its own design, that is, erases the past it has come to replace. By so doing revolutions end up paradoxically undermining their own capacity for historical explanation and justification because "the great revolutions that succeed, making the causes which produced them disappear, become therefore incomprehensible by their very success" (2:83). Not only would a history of the period before the Revolution be impossible (except as the optical illusion of the revolutionaries) but history, always so manipulated, could no longer even be comprehensible. Historiographical practice is, therefore, by definition, violent or revolutionary: the mirror phenomenon cleverly covers up a murder. We ask if theory produces the practices which, in turn, legitimate the theory, but what are the implications for the historical object? Collingwood in his *The Idea of History* (1946), continuing the preoccupation of Michelet in *La Sorcière,* describes the historical method as "torture." The inquisitioner gets the answer he wants and the witch forever escapes as she is burned. The historian kills the past he claims to resurrect; he is the detective of the crime he himself commits.[45] In *L'Ecriture de l'histoire* (1975), Michel de Certeau seizes the ritual aspect of this irreducible double bind in which history "reiterates . . . the myths that are built on a murder or an originating death [*mort originaire*], and make language the trace, always the after-image, of a beginning as impossible to recapture as to forget."[46]

The mirror phenomenon reversed gives the invasion of the zombies, life as a history that won't be killed and die. Michelet's *History of the Nineteenth Century* is populated by *revenants,*[47] and Marx in his *Eighteenth Brumaire of Louis Bonaparte* sees too only the ghosts of the old revolution. He made the famous analogy with language saying a beginner can only "freely express himself . . . when he . . . forgets his native tongue in the use of the new."[48] The proletariat must invent a new language, but how is that possible without reference to the old? We might go a step further as well and say that we can also only express ourselves when we forget the constant instability of meaning, or act when we forget the inescapable resistance of ideology. Nietzsche in *On the Advantage and Disadvantage of History for Life* complains of the excess of history, its status as the malady of our time. We are always late arrivals, "congenitally gray haired." "History *must* itself dissolve the problem of history."[49] Or, in order to study and use it properly again, we must undo all that we have learned from it.

One is left with the double bind imperative: you cannot ignore the past (or it will return to haunt you), and you must ignore the past if you want to live. Such a predicament sounds like that of the general will that cannot err and has to err. Implied in our dismay before such a paradox is the large question of historical determinism. Is history open, is the present really open to the future, is there such a thing as the new? The new language that Marx's proletariat had to learn would also turn out to deliver its *"own original* name."[50] Is history open or closed, circular or spiral, ocean or prison? (And which is language?) Can it inconceivably be both radically open and closed at the same time? Before a revolution occurs—and this prerevolutionary moment is the metaphor for unreadable historical contradiction at its greatest intensity—the institution that appears at its most impregnable moment is about to fall, but how do we know? We say in a variety of clichés that history knows, that history in fact always knows best, that justice (*justesse*) or right will out in history. And yet from our vantage point it seems always to be going wrong. The ruse of history is, first of all, that impression it gives, like language, of always being logical or natural, making ultimate, even intimate sense. But since, again like language, the "free" signifier is constantly realigning the whole slippery system, everything can change from one day to the next. And we are each time encouraged to begin again no matter how burned, like the French people who each time believed the sun (king) would help them prosper. We can both be engaged in the larger wheels of modes of production and *longue durée* and create our own historical destiny. Or as Michelet said: Man is his own Prometheus. History is determined or rather both overdetermined and undeterminable. The aphorism from Marx can make more sense without resolving our dismay: Man makes the history he cannot know.

Those who would make the history they desire must make it perform an (impossible?) correspondence with itself, with its own, original meaning, and this involves reading, what Trotsky called, "an irony deep laid in the very relations of life." And from "a failure of correspondence" springs "the comic, as also the tragic"[51]—unless we would also prefer to speak of a history ironically comic, that is, always and never coming out right, in which farce and tragedy flip back and forth over the same objects. Tocqueville (in horror or amusement?) observed the reaction of those on the brink of a revolution that would retrospectively appear so obvious: "There is almost nothing for which they are not prepared, except what happens" (2:280). If any provisional definition of history emerges, it sounds again like an aphorism or enigma: history must always come out right by coming out differently than expected, what appears to us as wrong, for we keep reading ourselves in it as Other and the Other as ourselves.

What kind of historiography does the history of errancy and missed correspondence call for? As a literary critic, I might argue that the historian talks about expanding, exploding historical objects, to avoid reading the symptoms that might deter history from ever reaching that object no matter how infinitely displaced: problems of language and form, reading and writing. For instance, what is the status of the supposedly nonnarrative material in the contemporary historian's account, the *graphs* and *figures?* These are the places in which the narrative represents the outside authority of its reference, a new form replacing the old quotations, but with the same function: that space is not so much outside of the narrative as the outside which the narrative posits, the fiction in relation to which history constructs its field of operations. Or what provokes, to take another example, the self-consciousness of Le Roy Ladurie who places the verb "read" in quotes? He suggests that we might begin at the end of Chaunu's *Seville* "by 'reading' the magnificent collection of graphs" (22). And yet would such proddings not function, in the end, as the revenge of the literary critic, so long a handmaiden of history? They would translate into the not so subtle recommendation that historians train themselves in theories of literature, along with their courses in statistics. This counter-imperialistic design of a literary critic comes, of course, at a time when critics are still unsure of their own independence from "literary history." What is recent criticism but the continued investigation of history (de Man, Jameson, Genette)? Louis Blanc had a vision of a similar "new history" that would begin by enumerating the misreadings of past historiography, especially those "chance suppositions" of Michelet, but he confessed that in some cases (Lamartine!), one would have to discuss every word.[52] Consequently, he wrote his twelve narrative volumes of the *Histoire de la Révolution française* (1847–62)—a much more manageable task.

Perhaps, though, the answer to my question is that the shifting of an empirical ground to a literary undermining in history will change nothing for the working historian except at most what Wallace Stevens called an "appreciation of a reality," unless a complete and radical change has already occurred but we are not yet able to read it.

Instead of coming from literary criticism or even history itself, the most consistent critique of history is still performed by the novel: fiction evokes the other history that history refuses to write, preferring its traditional fictions. But fiction is no more off the hook than history. On the one hand, history does the dirty work of establishing the baseline of verisimilitude so that fiction can take flight with a protective netting underneath. On the other hand, does not fiction resent being so dependent on history for fixing a dividing line which gives fiction the effect of a fantastical freedom while actually tying it down more deviously? Is that why we find antihistory passages in literature as violent as the antilanguage passages in history? Perhaps one of the best examples is still the scene in Hugo's *Quatrevingt-Treize* in which the three children destroy yet again the (text of the) martyr Saint Bartholomew, infinitely resurrectable: "Tear history to pieces." [53] No more or less subtle is the struggle in Flaubert's novels between the constant fascination and power of historiography and the equally persistent disclosure of its strategies (e.g., Bouvard and Pécuchet's methods of writing the history of the duc d'Angoulême).

Proust, especially, produced an entire novel from the side effects of the obsession to write history. The issue is easier to see on a thematic level where it constantly reappears; not only is Swann himself compared to a historian, but the narrator's jealousy gives him the obsessive desire to know its object, the *fugitive* Albertine. This jealousy is compared to the parallel of history writing and *corrida*: "always retrospective, it [jealousy] is like a historian who has to write the history of a period for which he has no documents; always belated, it dashes like an enraged bull to the spot where it will not find the dazzling, arrogant creature who is tormenting it and whom the crowd admire for his splendour and cunning [*ruse*]." [54] Blinded by its rage to know at least from where comes its pain, the bull keeps missing the arrogant toreador it strikes out against, having no proof even of the existence of that other creature except in the wounds inscribed on its own body. Proust leaves some ambiguity as to whether, first, there is ever a document that decides the issues once and for all (what Michelet called the "inestimable piece")[55] or, second, whether history could ever conceivably arrive on time—and kill the matador. Without worrying about these ultimates, the effect is still the same; all that is visible (intelligible, readable) is the turning and twisting of the bull. One is not sure if the crowd sees history or if it simply admires the ruse of its elusiveness. Although we rarely think of Proust as having a theory of democracy, this ambiguous relationship of the crowd with that element that alludes not coincidentally to Hegel's ruse sets up the problem of modern society.

A new history would take them a step back from the last new history to say only that it missed again. No. That is no more than a reversal of the old history. The new history would take a step back from itself to say that it missed again what the old history did so well without knowing. . . . It might be interesting to see a historical narrative that raveled a series of questions concerning what it would be necessary to know in order to pose the main question, which itself would have to be postponed, as would the answer; or that would detail what is always eliminated; or the back and forth between question and document which rephrases the question which requires a rereading of the documents, and so forth, allowing that figure of zigzag to act as the history itself. Would such stories be remarketed as novels? It is only fair to say, as well, that fiction, even when it undermines the arbitrary baseline of history, has no other dynamic to move it along than that story of history's failure: that is, another kind of history.

NOTES

1. Voltaire, *Dictionnaire philosophique,* in *Oeuvres complètes* (Paris, 1879), 4:619; hereafter cited in text.

2. James Joyce, *Ulysses* (New York, 1961), p. 34.

3. Alain Melchior-Bonnet, "Histoire et Littérature," in *La Grande Encyclopédie* (Paris, 1974), 10:5939.

4. Thomas Babington Macaulay, "History" (1828), in *Critical and Miscellaneous Essays* (Philadelphia, 1879), pp. 145–87, 154.

5. Stopford A. Brooke, *English Literature* (New York, 1897), p. 202.

6. Honoré de Balzac, "Avant Propos," in *La Comédie Humaine* (Paris, 1976), 1:19.

7. See François Hartog, *Le Miroir d'Hérodote* (Paris, 1980).

8. For a revision, see Nancy Struever, *The Language of History in the Renaissance: Rhetoric and Consciousness in Florentine Humanism* (Princeton, 1970).

9. Eduard Fueter, *Geschichte der Neueren Historiographie* (Munich, 1925), p. 354.

10. Georges Lefebvre, *La Naissance de l'historiographie moderne* (Paris, 1971), pp. 102–3.

11. See Suzanne Gearhart, "Rationality and the Text: A Study of Voltaire's Historiography," *Studies on Voltaire and the Eighteenth Century* 140 (1975): 21–43, also her *The Open Boundary of History and Fiction: A Critical Approach to the French Enlightenment* (Princeton, 1984).

12. Friedrich Meinecke, "Preliminary Remarks," *Historism: The Rise of a New Historical Outlook,* tr. J. E. Anderson (London, 1972), p. lv.

13. Charles Louandre, "Statistique littéraire de la production intellectuelle en France depuis quinze ans," *La Revue des deux mondes* 20 (1847): 426.

14. Guy Palmade, "Préface," in Lefebvre, *La Naissance de l'historiographie moderne,* p. 6.

15. Pierre Thibault, "Histoire," in *La Grande Encyclopédie, 10:5938.*

16. Fernand Braudel, *Ecrits sur l'histoire* (Paris, 1969), p. 18.

17. See *Faire de l'histoire,* ed. Jacques Le Goff and Nora Pierre (Paris, 1974), 1.

18. See Michel Serres, "L'univers et le lieu," *L'Arc* 72 (n.d.): 62–66.

19. First entitled *Annales d'histoire économique et sociale* in 1929, "Civilisations" was added to make the new title in 1946: *Annales: Economies, Sociétés, Civilisations.*

20. *The Dimensions of Quantitative Research in History,* ed. W. O. Aydelotte et al. (Princeton, 1972), p. 11.

21. Emmanuel Le Roy Ladurie, *Le territoire de l'historien* (Paris, 1973), p. 22; hereafter cited in text. In English as *The Territory of the Historian,* tr. Ben and Sian Reynolds (Chicago, 1979), p. 15.

22. Jules Michelet, *La Sorcière,* ed. Paul Viallaneix (Paris, 1966), p. 301; in English as *Satanism and Witchcraft: A Study in Medieval Superstition,* tr. A. R. Allinson (New York, 1971), p. 323.

23. Burton Stevenson, *The Home Book of Quotations* (New York, 1967), p. 901 and H. L. Mencken, *A New Dictionary of Quotations* (New York, 1942), pp. 538–39.

24. Michel de Montaigne, *Essais,* ed. Maurice Rat (Paris, 1962), 1:458; hereafter cited in text.

25. Alexis de Tocqueville, *L'Ancien Régime et la Révolution,* ed. J.-P. Mayer, in *Oeuvres complètes* (Paris, 1952), 2:81; hereafter cited in text.

26. Lucien Febvre, *Combats pour l'histoire* (Paris, 1953), p. 12. See also Denis Hollier, ed. "Histoire," *Panorama des sciences humaines* (Paris, 1973), pp. 593–645.

27. Sainte-Beuve, "Réflexions sur les lettres," in *Dictionnaire alphabétique et analogique de la langue française* (Maroc, 1957), 3:516.

28. Harry Elmer Barnes, *A History of Historical Writing* (Norman, Okla., 1937), p. 34; hereafter cited in text.

29. See Hans Kellner, "Disorderly Conduct: Braudel's Mediterranean Satire," *History and Theory* 18, no. 2 (1979): 197–222.

30. Quoted in Roland Barthes, "Le discours de l'histoire," *Poetique* 49 (1982): 20.

31. Pierre Larousse, "Histoire," *Grand dictionnaire universel du XIXᵉ siècle: français, historique, géographique . . .* (Paris, 1873), 9:300.

32. Georg Wilhelm Friedrich Hegel, *Lectures on the Philosophy of World History: Introduction: Reason in History,* ed. Johannes Hoffmeister, tr. H. B. Nisbet (Cambridge, 1975), p. 135.

33. Ferdinand de Saussure, *Course in General Linguistics,* tr. Wade Baskin (New York, 1966), p. 67.

34. See Hayden White, *Tropics of Discourse* (Baltimore, 1978), p. 4.

35. Hannah Arendt, "The Concept of History," in *Between Past and Future: Eight Exercises in Political Thought* (New York, 1954), p. 50.

36. Gaultier de Coste La Calprenède, *Faramond, ou l'histoire de France* (Paris, 1661), 1, sig. E3.

37. Abbé Laurent Bordelon, "Preface," *Gongam, l'homme prodigieux . . .* (Paris, 1711).

38. Lucian, *A True Story,* tr. A. M. Harmon (London and New York, 1913), 1:253.

39. See Bruce W. Wardropper, "Don Quixote: Story or History?" *Modern Philology* 63, no. 1 (Aug. 1965): 1–11.

40. My translation of *mécanisme à double détente.* François Furet, *Penser la Révolution française* (Paris, 1978), p. 18; in English as *Interpreting the French Revolution,* tr. Elborg Forster (Cambridge, 1981), p. 5.

41. Herbert Butterfield, *The Whig Interpretation of History* (London, 1931), p. v.

42. Jacob Burckhardt, *Reflections on History* (Indianapolis, 1979), p. 35.

43. Benedetto Croce, *History: Its Theory and Practice,* tr. Douglas Ainslie (New York, 1960), p. 15.

44. Arendt, "The Concept of History," p. 89.

45. R. G. Collingwood, *The Idea of History* (Oxford, 1946), p. 269.

46. Michel de Certeau, *L'Ecriture de l'histoire* (Paris, 1975), p. 61.

47. Jules Michelet, *Histoire du dix-neuvième siècle,* ed. Bernard Leuilliot, vol. 21 of *Oeuvres complètes,* ed. Paul Viallaneix (Paris, 1982); see, e.g., p. 89.

48. Karl Marx, *The Eighteenth Brumaire of Louis Bonaparte* (1963; rpt. New York, 1972), pp. 15–16.

49. Friedrich Nietzsche, *On the Advantage and Disadvantage of History for Life*, tr. Peter Preuss (Indianapolis, 1980), p. 45.

50. Karl Marx, "The Class Struggles in France: 1848 to 1850," in *Surveys from Exile*, ed. David Fernbach (New York, 1974), p. 74.

51. Leon Trotsky, *The Russian Revolution: The Overthrow of Tzarism and the Triumph of the Soviets*, ed. F. W. Dupee, tr. Max Eastman (Garden City, N.Y., 1959), p. 250.

52. Louis Blanc, *Histoire de la Révolution française* (Paris, 1847–62), 11:402.

53. Victor Hugo, *Quatrevingt-treize* (Paris, 1965), p. 270. See also Jeffrey Mehlman, *Revolution and Repetition: Marx / Hugo / Balzac* (Berkeley, 1977).

54. Marcel Proust, *A la Recherche du temps perdu* (Paris, 1954), 3:147; in English as *Remembrance of Things Past*, tr. C. K. Scott Moncrieff et al. (New York, 1981), 3:143.

55. Jules Michelet, *Histoire de la Révolution française* (Paris, 1952), 1:187.

5

CONVERSATION AND
POLITICAL THOUGHT

ào

David Boucher

THE IRONY OF PRESENT REVISIONIST PRESCRIPTIONS for studying the history of political thought is that they at once deny and affirm a conversational relation between the historian and the authors of past political texts. What does this mean? Many historians of political thought imagined themselves to be engaged in a dialogue with political thinkers and considered it to be their imperative duty to expose the incoherencies in pernicious and dangerous doctrines. The pedigree of this predilection is long established and needs no further illustration here. This ahistorical enterprise reflected the Machiavellian predisposition to "converse" with the ancients." This tendency toward conversation implicitly postulated the idea that texts can be brought to life in the present world of the historian and made to contribute, if not directly, then incidentally, to pertinent and pressing problems.

Revisionist historians of political thought—I have in mind Skinner, Pocock, Dunn, and their followers—pronounced the conversational technique to be spurious on the grounds of anachronism and because it broke the bounds of the proper limits of historical inquiry.[1] It suffices to point out here that the revisionists, as I understand it, wanted to change the relationship between the historian and the texts. Instead of the texts forming part of the present world of the historian, the historian has to intrude himself into the then present world of the texts. Instead of the conversation being conducted in terms dictated by the historian, the authors of the texts, and, more broadly, the linguistic conventions that constrained their thoughts are to set the conditions of the conversation. Understanding a text, the revisionists believe, is similar, perhaps even identical, to understanding the meaning of discourse in a dialogical context. The historian makes an imaginative leap back to a past where he becomes privy to the conversations of others. However, the historian is not an interlocutor in the dialogue, nor a participant in the sense that he contributes to the substantive details. The historian in this respect appears to have a different role, and that is as a custodian of the then current meaning of what was said. Nevertheless, although the historian does not contribute to the conversation, he imagines himself to be a spectator who is familiar with the prevailing linguistic conventions and can detect nuances of meaning because of this familiarity.

In this essay I want to demonstrate, by citing representatives, that the revisionists do closely identify understanding spoken discourse with the activity of understanding written texts. They assume that the same criteria of understanding are applicable to both. I want to cast some doubt upon this identification and deny that understanding the texts of past political thinkers can fruitfully be conceived in terms of a conversational or dialogical relationship. Further, I will offer my own view on the nature of the relationship between the interpreter and the texts interpreted, and between histories of political thought and the pasts they purport to recover.

For Skinner, Pocock, and Dunn oral and written discourse are forms of social action. Articulate people, who have been constrained by the vocabularies available to them and who have spoken or written their thoughts down in words, have been engaged in the performance of linguistic actions. These people have in essence been doing things with words. Understanding what they have done entails an awareness of the limits of what they reasonably could have been expected to have done given the linguistic and other social constraints operative upon them. Understanding is contextual; it is a matter of reunifying the text with its context. Although the three methodologists differ in their theoretical pronouncements and prescribe different ways of achieving a historically credible understanding of a text, they are at one in assuming that the principles which apply to understanding spoken utterances also apply to understanding written texts. When they discuss the problems of historical inquiry they use the terms *speaker* and *writer* interchangeably. Hearers and readers appear to exhibit no significant differences, and the range of things that can be done with oral discourse also appears to be able to be performed with written discourse.

Let me illustrate briefly the point I am trying to make. John Dunn, in his "The Identity of the History of Ideas," constantly portrays the activity of being a historian as that of listening to conversations between speakers. Historians of ideas are to regard "talking and thinking" as "social activities," and the men who appear in their stories must "appear as speakers." Political writers are acting the "role of the speaker" when they enter into arguments, and the historian must attempt "to grasp what the speaker was doing in saying" what was said. In order to do this the limits of the context have to be circumscribed, and "what closes the context in actuality is the intention (and, much more broadly, the experiences) of the speaker." Indeed, in what is a self-evident association of oral and written discourse, Dunn suggests that "Locke, in talking, talks about what he talks about." [2] This clearly indicates that Dunn regards political theorists as participants in a conversation in which it does not really matter whether their contributions were oral or written because the same procedures have to be invoked to attain a historical understanding of the meanings they hoped to convey.

Skinner's arguments are well known and there is no need to rehearse them here. All I want to highlight is the fact that he makes extensive use of a theory that was explicitly formulated to illustrate the existence and operation of illocutionary forces in the speech acts of individuals. These individuals invoke the prevailing linguistic conventions that circumscribe the limits of what they are able to do with words. J. L. Austin's theory is meant to demonstrate that when people talk to one another, and are aware of the conventions pertaining to spoken discourse, they can do more things with words than merely use them to describe. [3] Skinner wants to make the notion of an illocutionary force, that is, what a person is doing in saying something, equivalent to the intention that authors had in writing texts. Skinner's identification of intentions with illocutionary forces constitutes a departure from Austin's own views. Austin certainly believed that it is possible to perform illocutionary acts unintentionally. He says, for example, "I may order someone to do something, when I did not intend to order him to do so" (106, n. 1). Skinner, however, never attempts to establish the point why illocutionary forces must be intentional. His identification is merely a stipulative definition to demonstrate that authors as well as speakers do things with words, and that therefore it is necessary to recover the intentions of those who wrote texts before we can understand the meanings they intended to convey. In order to show that it is imperative that we know the intentions that people had in making certain utterances, he often uses the example of a policeman uttering the words "the ice over there is very thin." Without knowing that the addressee is a skater we would not be able to infer the policeman's intended illocutionary force in using the words he used; that is, he intended to issue a warning. Skinner then assumes that the same process of understanding must apply to the reading of texts.[4]

Pocock, although initially committed to Thomas Kuhn's idea of paradigms, has tended, in later writings, to lean more heavily toward Austin's theory of speech acts. Again, like Skinner, Pocock links written and oral discourse, and uses examples from both to illustrate the activity that the intellectual historian has to undertake in reconstructing the political discourse of the past. I need cite only one example to substantiate my point. Pocock suggests "that the student of political discourse is generally engaged in the study of dialogues between speakers, hearers and respondents, each of whom is in some degree capable of exploiting the resources of language and performing acts of speech within the patterns imposed and permitted by the dialogue."[5]

It is appropriate at this point to distinguish the conversational relationship Skinner, Pocock, and Dunn have in mind from that espoused by Richard Rorty. I will reserve my comments on the bearing that the intentionalist debate has on my argument until the conclusion.

Rorty is addressing himself to a different question from that which preoccupies the three methodologists. The fundamental question implicit throughout Rorty's *Philosophy and the Mirror of Nature* is "What is it that philosophers do?"[6] His answer to the question is that philosophers have generally been doing one of two things. They have misguidedly searched for the epistemological foundations upon which the whole of knowledge must rest, or they have reacted against this enterprise by expressing a distaste for adversary confrontation in philosophy. They abjure the idea that we can ever attain "epistemological commensuration." Philosophers who address themselves to epistemology are "systematic" philosophers, and those who react against them and deny the efficacy of constructing epistemologies as foundations upon which commensurable discourses rest are "edifying" philosophers. The edifying philosophers—Rorty has in mind Goethe, Kierkegaard, Santayana, William James, Dewey, the later Wittgenstein and the later Heidegger (366–67)—"are *intentionally* peripheral . . . [they] destroy for the sake of their own generation" (369). They deny absolutism and wish to keep the path of inquiry perpetually open. "Edifying" philosophers as opposed to "systematic" philosophers do not see their enterprise as one of confrontation and their relation to other philosophers as adversarial. Instead, in Rorty's view, they are engaged in "conversation." Their aim is to facilitate the continuance of the conversation "rather than to find objective truth." Indeed, "to see keeping a conversation going as a sufficient aim of philosophy, to see wisdom as consisting in the ability to sustain a conversation, is to see human beings as generators of new descriptions rather than beings one hopes to be able to describe accurately" (377–78).

The conversation to which Rorty refers is a much more grandiose conception than that held by Skinner, Pocock, and Dunn. It is not a relationship that pertains between individuals in a temporal circumstantial situation where speaker and interlocutor meet face-to-face, and where thoughts are exchanged directly between identifiable spatially located participants. Rorty's use of the idea of conversation is an invocation of Michael Oakeshott's alluring description of human intercourse. For Oakeshott the "conversation of mankind" comprises a number of modes, or idioms. Poetry, science, practice, and history are the significant and idiomatically distinct contributory voices in this transhistorical conversation. The notion of a conversational relationship pertaining between the different voices is not offered as a proposition about the exact identity of the terms on which each voice tolerates the others. It is offered instead as an "appropriate image" in terms of which to comprehend the "manifold" which constitutes the "meeting-place" of "diverse idioms of utterance which make up current human intercourse."[7] Philosophy is one voice in the conversation, reflecting upon the other voices and their relation to one another, but having no "specific contribution" to make.

Rorty finds Oakeshott's imagery conducive to his own views on human intellectual activity. Indeed, he uses the notion of conversation, like Oakeshott, in a special sense. Rorty explicitly affirms this when he says,

"I want to give a very high-toned sense to 'conversation.'" The notion of a conversation is a shorthand account of what stands for "the whole human enterprise—culture."[8] Rorty's view is that "it is pictures rather than propositions, metaphors rather than statements, which determine most of our philosophical convictions."[9] In this respect the idea of a conversation must be understood to be a metaphor meant to be evocative of an image of human endeavor as a civilized, congenial, good-humored, and polite relationship of mutual toleration rather than one of hostile confrontation and provocation.

The "high-toned" sense endowed by Rorty upon the notion of conversation is different from that which I have attributed to Pocock, Skinner, and Dunn. Although ostensibly they appear to be asking a similar question to that posed by Rorty, it is in fact very different. The question "What is it that philosophers do?" is addressed by Rorty to the whole of the activity of philosophizing. In other words, he is attempting to discern the character of the philosophic enterprise. When Pocock, Skinner, and Dunn pose the question they are addressing it to particular statements that certain philosophers have made. They want to know what speech acts were being performed in the use of certain words by specific philosophers on specific occasions. To put the matter in Collingwoodian terms, Rorty and the three methodologists are concerned with different question-and-answer complexes. My comments in this paper are addressed to the conversational relationship which Pocock, Skinner, and Dunn implicitly assume. My remarks have very little bearing upon the special sense which Rorty gives to the notion of conversation. Indeed, my own conclusions may be taken to be an indirect affirmation of the type of relationship Rorty wants to sustain in respect of the whole of intellectual history.

I now want to cast some doubt upon the utility of believing that the historian's act of understanding is similar to that of an eyewitness to conversations, or arguments, between speakers. In doing so I will attempt to solicit the aid of others who want to maintain a distinction between spoken and inscribed discourse.

As a means of communicating knowledge, Socrates argues in the *Phaedrus,* the written word is far inferior to the spoken. The written word is not capable of making a distinction between readers who are ignorant and unresponsive, and those who are intelligent and receptive to what the author wants to convey. Further, it is inferior to speech in that "if it is ill-treated or unfairly abused it always needs its parent to come to its rescue;

it is quite incapable of defending or helping itself." [10] As I see it, such writers as Pocock, Skinner, and Dunn, albeit implicitly, want to eliminate this distinction and take on the role of the defenders of the meaning of discourse. In this respect they are self-appointed surrogates of the authors of texts; they defend the meanings of texts as if these meanings were conveyed in the medium of spoken discourse. These methodologists of the study of the history of political thought want to present themselves as the legitimate guardians of the textual children whose parents are no longer in a position to exercise responsibility. These methodologists are implying that our attempts to understand written texts must be conducted as if these texts were composed in the medium of spoken discourse. This endows them with the same properties as spoken utterances, namely, the possibility of being defended in the give and take of a dialogical setting. In the absence of the author, the interpreter is transformed into the speaker defending authorial meaning, while being in the invidious position of conducting the role of speaker through the medium of inscribed discourse.

How can we begin to untangle the conflation of spoken and written discourse? Let me state a few obvious points. A great deal of political activity takes the form of spoken dialogues between interlocutors. However, the type of political activity we encounter, as historians of political thought, is in the form of written discourse, and the responses made, in writing, by the readers of written discourse. The artifacts we seek to understand are the premeditated constructed works of literate and articulate people. Their works were primarily meant for a reading audience. Indeed, if they were not iterable they would not have the character of inscribed discourse. In essence, the books and pamphlets which form the core of the subject matter of the history of political thought are the inscribed relics of literate people who once lived, but are no longer living. When a historian attempts to understand a written text, deliberately composed in the medium of inscribed discourse, he is reading an argument in the medium through which the author intended to convey a certain meaning. But when a historian attempts to understand evidence of spoken discourse he is no longer dealing in the same medium as the persons whom he seeks to understand. The translation of the spoken into the written can easily lose the prosodic features, such as tone, rhythm, and physical gesture, that were ineluctably tied to the meaning of what was said. But the writer who is already constrained by the medium of

inscribed discourse is from the outset forced to work within the limitations of its constraints. Thus the stress of the methodologists discussed
here upon the features of spoken discourse would seem to be misplaced
because it is the features of the written medium that are important for
our understanding of texts. What these writers need to explore is whether
the range of things that can be done with written discourse is broader,
narrower, or fundamentally different from the range available in spoken
discourse.

To utter certain words in face-to-face conversation definitely has physical characteristics different from the act of inscribing language. Austin,
for example, identifies a number of features which are always present in
the act of saying something. First, certain noises are uttered. This is the
"phonetic" act, and the utterance is described as a "phone." Secondly,
these noises are words which belong to a vocabulary, have a grammatical
form, and are uttered with a range of intonations. This is the "phatic"
act, and the utterance is a "pheme." And, thirdly, the act of saying involves using a pheme to express a more or less definite sense and reference
(92–93). Whereas these acts may have similar counterparts in the act of
writing, we cannot assume that they will have exact equivalents. Their
equivalence is something to be demonstrated rather than presupposed.

A difficulty occurs when speech does not have the character of spontaneous conversation. A prepared text can be spoken, and this is the act of
vocalizing an inscription. A typical instance is the performance of a play.
The inscribed language is not merely read. The written discourse has to
be translated into the medium of speech. The aim of translation from one
medium to the other is to breathe life into the relics of life. The director
has to interpret the text and attempt to project meaning by using the
skills of the actors. Thus a poorly presented tragedy can readily take on
the character of a comedy. The translation from written to spoken discourse is, then, constrained by the text and must remain within certain
limits if it is to be accepted by theater audiences as an interpretation,
rather than a misinterpretation of a particular play.

A further step on the road to distinguishing the written and the spoken
word can be taken if we look at some of the ideas of Hans-Georg Gadamer
and Paul Ricoeur. Plato had intimated a distinction by suggesting that
the written word distances itself from the speaker. Whereas in spoken
dialogue the close proximity of the interlocutors is a desirable and necessary condition of attaining adequate understanding, Gadamer points to

the idea of distance as a condition of achieving a genuine understanding of a written text. The traditional hermeneutic theorists who concerned themselves with the epistemology of interpreting texts[11] formulated theories with the express intention of building a bridge between the past and the present. Like the methodologists with whom I have been concerned, they want to anchor firmly the meaning of a text to the consciousness of the author. In other words, they want to formulate a method for reaching behind the text and discovering the psychology of the author who composed it. Hermeneutic principles and procedures, they believe, would provide the means for overcoming temporal distance, and for the achievement of the meaning the author hoped to convey.

Gadamer, however, shifting the emphasis away from epistemology and toward ontology, denies that we can transcend temporal distance. The desire to bridge the gap between now and then is a forlorn hope, doomed to failure before it even begins. Distance, far from being an obstacle to interpretation, is the positive and productive possibility of understanding.[12] There is no "yawning abyss" to be transcended because the temporal distance between then and now "is filled with the continuity of custom and tradition, in the light of which all that is handed down presents itself to us" (204–5). Distance is a necessary condition of coming to know the "true content" and "true significance" of a text. This is because of the "curious impotence of our judgment" in circumstances where the distance in time is not sufficient enough to have afforded us sure criteria for understanding its true worth or significance. Once a text has severed its connection with the historical contingencies that surrounded its appearance, it takes on the character of a self-contained entity that presents itself to us in its entirety. It is the "the matter of the text" that projects itself to us and takes on an autonomous existence. Distance provides us with the possibility of discovering the "true meaning" of a text, but this discovery is never fixed and final, it is an "infinite process" (265).

This is a firm denial of equating the meaning of a written text with the consciousness, or psychology, of its author, whereas spoken discourse, in a conversational setting, is always and everywhere the attempt to understand what the speaker wants his or her words to mean. This is the point where the distinction can be developed even further. Ricoeur takes Gadamer's notion of distance and uses it to create an even greater divide between speech and writing. Discourse, for Ricoeur, "is always about something," and has reference to a speaker.[13] In addition to having a world, that is, its contextual referents, discourse is addressed to someone, namely, an interlocutor. However, written and spoken discourse differ from each other in respect to the degree to which distanciation has taken place. The distinction between oral and written discourse is reinforced by means of the extension of the idea of distanciation. In oral discourse we find a rudimentary form of distanciation. Language realizes itself in the event of discourse, but the transitory and fleeting event of saying is itself surpassed by what is said. In other words, what endures is not the event of saying but the meaning of what is said (134). Here the meaning of what is said is closely related to the intentions of the speaker and to the ostensive reference of the sentence. In written discourse, however, three further stages of distanciation appear.

The meaning of an inscribed text and the author's intentions cease to coincide in the second moment of distanciation. At this point the meaning of a text escapes the restricted horizons of its author, and the prosodic features which support oral discourse cannot be invoked to rescue authorial meaning. Thus meaning breaks "its moorings to the psychology of the author" (201, 139). What Ricoeur is doing at this point is denying that the principles of understanding applicable to a dialogical situation can be translated into criteria for interpreting texts. A third moment of distanciation occurs in the process of the "decontextualization" of the text from its context. As Ricoeur puts it, "from the moment that the text escapes from its author and from his situation, it also escapes from its original audience. Hence it can procure new readers for itself" (192). Unlike spoken discourse in the dialogical situation, the text is not addressed to an interlocutor; its addressee is potentially anyone who can read. The fourth moment of distanciation emancipates the text from its ostensive reference. In spoken discourse the reference of what is said is circumscribed by the dialogical situation, whereas a text distances itself from its circumstantial referents. Its reference now becomes what Gadamer called "the matter of the text," and what Ricoeur describes as its "world." This world is what the text projects in front of itself. It is the world conjured up by the text. The sense of the work can be gleaned from its internal features, "whereas the reference is the mode of being unfolded in front of the text." This is the "referential moment," or the "referential dimension," of the text (93, 112).

In spoken discourse we look behind what is said to the intentions of the author in saying it, but in understanding written discourse this connection between the author and the meaning of the text has been severed through the process of distanciation. The text projects its own world in front of itself, and the enterprise of seeking to get behind the text and recover the meaning the author wanted to convey is a futile aspiration doomed to failure because distanciation prevents its attainment.

The arguments I have presented here do not prove that the identification of written and spoken discourse is fundamentally mistaken; indeed the idea of proof appears to me to be redundant in such matters. What I have done, by calling upon the aid of some writers to strengthen my case, is to cast considerable doubt upon the efficacy of attempting to understand written discourse as if it were identical to understanding spoken discourse in the circumstantial speech situation. But to stop at this point would be to arrest prematurely an exercise that has not yet reached its destination. Having suggested that the prescriptions of such people as Skinner, Pocock, and Dunn, along with those of their increasing band of followers, are mistaken in imagining that the retrieval of meaning involves reconstructing a context in which texts are treated as if they are contributions to face-to-face conversational encounters, I am obliged to put forward what, for me, on the basis of what I have argued, is a plausible alternative.

The alternative I present, albeit briefly, is not an attempt to tell historians of political thought what they ought to be doing. It is an attempt, irrespective of what they think they are doing, to circumscribe the limits of what they are in fact doing. It is the old philosophical enterprise of attempting to understand differently something that is already understood.[14]

Let us begin at the beginning. In writing a history of political thought we have before us inscribed relics, all composed by someone somewhere in the past, which stand as evidence of something that happened, namely, the act of composition. But the act of composition has not itself survived the ravages of time. We do not have before us the author sitting down writing and committing those thoughts to paper. Instead, all that remains is the result or conclusion of the act of composition. The inscribed text is the evidence we have of the act of composition, and what survives is the author's attempted embodiment in written discourse of the meaning then present in his or her head. The unfortunate thing about meaning is that it does not itself survive. All that survives is more or less imperfect evidence of meaning in the form of inscribed discourse. The meaning that the author wanted to convey is not frozen into the text; it simply did not survive the passage from the past to the present. All we have in the present are survivals of past acts of composition. I am willing to concede that in spoken discourse, involving as it does certain prosodic features not available to the inscriber of discourse, there may be a case for suggesting that meaning is embodied in the total speech situation. The speaker in conversation with others is available to defend himself and ensure that the intended meaning corresponds to the received meaning. However, if this is the case, it differs from inscribed discourse.

Inscribed discourse is not the receptacle of meaning; it has an entirely different character. It is the evidence from which we infer meaning. In intellectual histories in general what we find is the presentation of meaning in the form of a history book. This meaning is substantiated with, or supported by, illustrations from the works of past writers, and their texts are taken to be evidence for interpreting their meaning in one way rather than in another. Each interpretation is different, even though the text interpreted notionally remains the same. This is because, in some part, at least, the interpreter inherits the texts as interpretation and not as virgin soil uncontaminated by human interest. The interpreter uses interpretations as points of entry into the text and will periodically feel the need to refute one view and sustain or modify another, often by using the same textual evidence differently and in support of the new inferred preferred meaning. In interpretation the words, sentences, and statements contained in an inscribed text are used by the interpreter to illustrate an argument. Often they are presented out of sequence, set side by side with statements abstracted from different parts of the text, and drastically foreshortened to fit the requirements of the enterprise. Those aspects of a text presented by the interpreter are not themselves the argument of the interpreter, they are his evidence, and this evidence is offered as an invitation to concur with the meaning inferred from it.

The interpreter is offering us a meaning, inferred from the textual evidence, in lieu of the meaning that has not survived, and if by coincidence or chance the meaning offered duplicates the original, I can think of no means by which we could ever know. Intellectual history is the art of inviting the reader to imagine the possible configurations of meaning a text can bear. The history of political thought, for example, is not about the recovery of meaning, it is about the inference of meaning from the relics of what was once meant. In other words, we construct a meaning;

not any fanciful configuration, but one that the evidence obliges us to believe. However, it is not the textual evidence alone that stands as the criterion of the truth of interpretations. Indeed, the procedures and rules of scholarship that govern the manner of inference have as much, if not more, bearing upon whether an interpretation is to be acknowledged as an instance of the historical mode of inquiry. But it must be remembered that present subscriptions to contemporary manners of historical inquiry and intellectual etiquette betray the historicity of interpretations just as much as the language of a text betrays the historicity of its time of composition. Thus, as far as I can see, there are two constraints upon the meanings achieved in the history of political thought. First, there is textual evidence, and by this I mean both the inscriptions of political thinkers and the evidence we have of the times in which they lived. And, secondly, we have the manner or mode of inquiry in terms of which the interpretation is formulated. Texts, indeed, are the bedrock to which interpretations must be anchored, but they point to nothing more beyond themselves than a possible world of meanings achievable through subscription to the current standards of scholarship and procedures of inquiry governing the mode of inference employed.

I have suggested that original meanings are lost and irrecoverable. The historical interpretation of texts is a present activity concerned with present survivals understood in terms of the category of the past. The act of composition has not survived; only the imperfect result of something that once happened, but is no longer happening, stands before us as evidence of possible meanings, none of which can be compared to the original. The authenticity of the meaning offered to interpretation is not, and cannot, be substantiated with reference to the unknowable original, but by means of the extent to which the interpreter has been faithful to acceptable procedures of inquiry in placing together the evidence and inviting us to accept the meaning inferred from this configuration, rather than a meaning inferred from another. What I am suggesting is this: given that original meanings are unattainable, the refinement of the procedures of inquiry has to acknowledge this and aim for what is attainable. It is not my business here to suggest what these methods should be. I have merely attempted to show what it is we do, and what in fact we attain, in the history of political thought and, by implication, in intellectual history in general.

So far I have directed my attention to the inference of meaning from inscribed texts, distanced from their authors and from the acts of their composition. I now want to say something about the implications this view has for books in which we find histories of political thought. The placing together of configurations of meaning in a continuous sequence through time, whether it be chronological or thematic, or perhaps both, is not the presentation of something, to put it in Rankean terms, that actually happened. It is the creation of a new world, in place of the one that is lost. Histories are substitutes for, and not reconstructions of, the past. And what counts as a substitute is determined by what is currently acceptable within the historical mode of inquiry. Indeed, had we lived in earlier times we could have composed speeches and imputed them to famous leaders, reiterated myths such as the division of the world between Japheth, Ham, and Shem, or written about the past as if it contained only the deeds of kings and their courts, or the theories of great philosophers. All these preoccupations were, but are no longer, acceptable substitutes for the past that has not and could not have survived.

In a very real sense, then, the present influences the past,[15] and not because we can change it, but because we can change the substitutes acceptable in place of it. The past is at our mercy, not because we can alter what happened, but because it is we who decide, as collective members of an academic discipline, who and what will figure as significant in our substitutes. For whatever reasons, scholars elevate some thinkers above others. These "greats" are regarded as being in some way significant, but the patterns in which these thinkers are woven will differ from one commentator to another. In addition to the broad constraints of the expectations of one's audience, and what will be tolerated as a statement falling within the ambit of the historical mode of inquiry, decisions have to be made about the scale upon which a history of political thought will be written. By the term *scale* I mean the degree of comprehensiveness and the allocation of differing degrees of space to those authors lucky enough to be included. The historian cannot include everything, therefore he has to scale down his account while attempting to maintain or achieve a balance in what Hexter calls its tempo. This will involve judgments about the significance of various writers in the story one wishes to convey. Personal preference, a certain sympathy for a manner of thinking, or the discovery that someone said something that was subsequently said by a greater political philosopher, might elevate the status of any one of a number of aspiring candidates and merit his or her inclusion in a history of political thought. Thus lesser thinkers become promoted, relegated, and even disappear from the list of significant thinkers in the history of political thought. Take, for example, the case of Pierre Dubois, the fourteenth-century thinker who wrote *De Recuperations Terrae Sanctae.* In two substantial histories of political thought Dubois merits little attention. Sabine devotes half a page and two short references to him, while Bowle apologizes for not discussing his work at all.[16] However, the author of a less ambitious general history of political thought outlines Dubois's work in five pages and refers to him on six other separate occasions. The reason for the greater allocation of space to Dubois is that the author considers him to be significant in bridging the gap between the ideas of Dante and Marsilius and in having anticipated the thinking of Bodin, Montesquieu, and Rousseau.[17] Indeed, Dubois seems to be one of those unfortunate thinkers who is completely at the mercy of historians. In 1899 he was rediscovered after a considerable period in obscurity, congratulated for saying something in support of feminism, and described as a "forgotten radical."[18] However, his bad fortune is such that he has once again become forgotten. R. N. Berki, for example, in a recent history of political thought, makes no mention at all of Dubois.[19]

Why does this sort of thing happen? The obvious answer is that those writers who are no longer with us cannot make out their own cases for inclusion in the substitutes we create for the past. Consequently, it is we who look for apparent connections and identities in the evidence, and it is our evaluation of their significance that determines the candidates we will support. The decisions about what aspects of significance to employ as criteria of selection are conditional upon the assumptions the historian has about the nature, scope, and purpose of history.

All historical inquiry proceeds by means of evidence that supports inference. If the evidence appears to point strongly in one direction rather than in another, then that is the path we must follow. When the intentionalist tells us that a certain author wrote a particular sentence with the intention of conveying a precise meaning, we are asked to accept the argument on the grounds that the evidence leads us to believe that the intention inferred is more probable than any other. The juxtaposition of evidence from which an intention is inferred is no different from the process of historical creation I have been describing. The selection of intentions as the criterion of meaning, as opposed, for instance, to social or economic circumstances, is a decision about the sort of evidence that is admissible in a historical inquiry. To suggest that intentions or economic considerations must be preeminent in historical inquiry has no direct bearing on my argument. Indeed, my argument and the arguments of the intentionalists belong to two different universes of discourse, or logically distinct spheres of inquiry. I am trying to portray what it is we actually do, as opposed to what we think we do, when we engage in historical inquiry. We create a quasi world of texts, the elements of which appear differently in each and every story that is told. The argument about intentions is not a question about what happens, or what it is we do when we interpret texts. It is a question of limiting, or even of weighting certain evidence in an attempt to give it more significance, or more preeminence, in the business of juxtaposition. It is only when the imagined imperative to retrieve intentions is justified in terms of objectivist arguments that the paths of the intentionalist and my own actually cross. Then the issue becomes not one of the retrieval of intentions versus some other desirable focus of attention, but the more fundamental question of whether there is a past or not. My answer to this question is that there is not, or that if there is, it is not recoverable. All we have is more or less acceptable arrangements of evidence that act as a substitute for what is irretrievable. Many intentionalists simply assume that the aim of history is to emulate the Rankean ideal of understanding the past as it really was. They then proceed to show that the retrieval of authorial intentions holds out the best hope of attaining this ideal. A number of intentionalists have implicitly accepted that the justification of the retrieval of intentions may not have the philosophical force that they had hoped, and they resort instead to moral persuasion. E. D. Hirsch, Jr., maintains that we are morally obliged to abide by the "ethics of language" and respect the intentions of past authors. In "ordinary discourse" we are careful to "conjoin a man's intentions to his words," and Hirsch professes himself not to be impressed with the view that this "ethical imperative of speech, to which we all submit in ordinary discourse, is not applicable to written speech or, in particular, to literary texts."[20] John Dunn says something similar when he suggests that "if we claim to *know* about other men, we must try as best we can to give them what is their due, their right. This is a simple moral duty, not a guarantee of epistemological prowess."[21]

The argument concerning intentions is, in my view, internal to the activity of interpretation and pertains to the question of what is and what is not a desirable form of inference to be tolerated within the ambit of a particular mode of inquiry. My conclusions, like those of Rorty, suggest that no ultimate, or objectivist, justification can be given to establish the case for the retrieval of intentions to the exclusion of other interpretative pursuits. Peaceful coexistence, playful persuasion, mutual toleration, and the recognition that confrontation leads to entrenchment rather than to the changing of intellectual commitments should lead us to accept methodological pluralism in preference to the absolutist claims of any one mode of inference.

I have tried to show how we need to make a distinction between the procedure and manner of understanding written and spoken discourse. In addition, I attempted to apply this to what historians actually do when they write histories, and I suggested that the refinement of methods must work within the limitations of what it is possible to attain. Finally, I maintained that histories of political thought, far from recovering the past, offer more or less acceptable substitutes for a world that has not survived. I am aware that some of what I have said is highly contentious, and no doubt much of it may be mistaken. But if what I have said provokes a more considered examination of what historians of political thought can reasonably be expected to attain, rather than the formulation of laudable, yet impractical ideals, then I will have achieved my objective in writing this paper.

NOTES

1. See my "New Histories of Political Thought for Old," *Political Studies* 31 (1983): 112–21; "The Denial of Perennial Problems: The Negative Side of Quentin Skinner's Theory," *Interpretation: A Journal of Political Philosophy* 12 (1984); "Language, Politics and Paradigms: J. G. A. Pocock and the Study of the History of Political Thought," *Polity* 17 (1985). It is appropriate here to express my long-standing debt to Dr. Joseph Femia who read and commented upon earlier drafts of this paper.

2. John Dunn, "The Identity of the History of Ideas," *Philosophy* 43 (1968): 88, 92, 93, 94, 98.

3. J. L. Austin, *How to Do Things with Words,* 2d ed., ed. J. O. Urmson and Marina Sbisa (Oxford, 1976); hereafter cited in text. Austin does concede that conventional nonverbal acts may have illocutionary equivalents, but even here he is discussing face-to-face social action; see p. 121.

4. See, e.g., Quentin Skinner, "Meaning and Understanding in the History of Ideas," *History and Theory* 8 (1969): 3–53; idem, "Conventions and the Understanding of Speech Acts," *Philosophical Quarterly* 20 (1970): 118–38; idem, "On Performing and Explaining Linguistic Actions," *Philosophical Quarterly* 21 (1971): 1–21; idem, "Motives, Intentions and the Interpretation of Texts," *New Literary History* 3 (1972): 393–408; idem, " 'Social Meaning' and the Explanation of Social Action," in *Philosophy, Politics and Society,* ed. Peter Laslett, W. G. Runciman, and Quentin Skinner (Oxford, 1972), pp. 136–57.

5. J. G. A. Pocock, "The Reconstruction of Discourse: Towards the Historiography of Political Thought," *Modern Language Notes* 96 (1981): 963.

6. Richard Rorty, *Philosophy and the Mirror of Nature* (Oxford, 1980); hereafter cited in text.

7. Michael Oakeshott, "The Voice of Poetry in the Conversation of Mankind," in *Rationalism in Politics and Other Essays* (London, 1974), pp. 198–99. For a discussion of "History" as one of the idiomatically distinct contributions to the conversation, see my "The Creation of the Past: British Idealism and Michael Oakeshott's Philosophy of History," *History and Theory* 23 (1984): 193–214.

8. Richard Rorty, Charles Taylor, and Hubert L. Dreyfus, "A Discussion," *Review of Metaphysics* 34 (1980): 52.

9. Rorty, *Philosophy and the Mirror of Nature*, p. 12; cf. p. 163.

10. Plato, *Phaedrus and Letters VII and VIII,* tr. Walter Hamilton (Harmondsworth, 1973), par. 275, p. 97.

11. Here I have in mind Dilthey and certain modern theorists who follow this tradition, namely, E. D. Hirsch, Jr., and Emilio Betti.

12. Hans-Georg Gadamer, *Truth and Method* (London, 1975), pp. 8, 115, 263 f., 411; hereafter cited in text.

13. Paul Ricoeur, *Hermeneutics and the Human Sciences,* ed. John B. Thompson (Cambridge, 1981), p. 198; hereafter cited in text.

14. In what follows I confess that I have learned most from Dilthey, Bradley, Collingwood, Oakeshott, Gadamer, and Ricoeur, without finding myself able to subscribe to all that they argue.

15. For an imaginative and contentious theory about how the present influences the past see Harold Bloom, *The Anxiety of Influence* (New York, 1973).

16. George Sabine, *A History of Political Theory* (London, 1968), pp. 267, 291, 299; John Bowle, *Western Political Thought: An Introduction from the Origins to Rousseau* (London, 1947), p. 242.

17. Phyllis Doyle, *A History of Political Thought* (London, 1937), p. 155; see also pp. 88, 93, 112, 122.

18. John Neville Figgis, "A Forgotten Radical," *Cambridge Review* 13 (June 1900): 373–74.

19. R. N. Berki, *The History of Political Thought* (London, 1977).

20. E. D. Hirsch, Jr., *The Aims of Interpretation* (Chicago, 1976), p. 90.

21. John Dunn, "Practising History and Social Science on 'Realist' Assumptions," in *Action and Interpretation*, ed. Christopher Hookway and Philip Pettit (Cambridge, 1978), p. 174.

6

NOTES TOWARD

(AN UNDERSTANDING OF)

SUPREME FICTIONS

&

Dell Hymes

MY TOPIC IS CHANGE IN ORAL NARRATIVE, and more particularly, in those serious oral narratives we commonly call myths. My examples will come from the Indians of North America, and mostly from the North Pacific Coast. My theme is that understanding change, and whatever else one may wish to understand about these narratives, involves the fact that they are literature. Not in the sense of being "literate," of course, but in the sense of being literary, of having characteristics in common with what we accept as literary art. Three authors afford a useful framework for establishing this: Robert Alter, on biblical narrative; Michael Riffaterre, on nineteenth-century novels; and A. J. Greimas, on narratology.

I take a title from Wallace Stevens, because, when asked to write, it struck me that if the tellers of the myths I have most studied had had the chance to reflect on their art, to look at it, as it were, with sympathy and distance, they might well agree that Stevens got it right: it must be abstract; it must change; it must give pleasure. After considering the three authors, I will turn to these three "musts." Much of what is said in regard to literary art has to do with change, but my view of it will be put forward under the Stevens rubrics.[1]

I

Literature that is oral is often set apart. One may read, for example, that orality implies oral-formulaic composition. For hundreds of oral traditions in the world, that is not so. In particular, it is not so for the traditions of the North Pacific Coast of the New World, which I have studied for forty years. The oral-formulaic approach, while it has usefulness for many traditions of the Old World, does not easily fit all of them, and a recent survey, although it tends to identify the approach with "orality" itself, mentions not a single New World case. Work of the kind I draw on here, done under the heading of "ethnopoetics," goes unmentioned.[2] In sum, who says "oral" need not say "formulaic."

Another writer with a conception of what orality must be, Walter Ong, describes oral narratives as necessarily "prolix."[3] But the narratives of the North Pacific Coast are remarkably terse.[4]

A terse style is illuminatingly discussed by Robert Alter, who speaks of "the reticence of the biblical narrator,"[5] and credits Erich Auerbach (*Mimesis*) with having shown more clearly than anyone before him "how the cryptic conciseness of biblical narrative is a reflection of profound art, not primitiveness" (17). It is therefore disappointing that Alter considers such art to begin with the Hebrew Bible, as against not only the verse epics of neighboring societies but also folklore generally. Folktale serves as a foil in his account, a genre where one would not expect morally problematic interiority, where one finds fixed figures, where a pattern of repeated actions is of course mechanical (28–29, 32, 106). Others may share similar assumptions. Yet features that Alter singles out are features of oral narrative among Indian people of the North Pacific Coast.

Let me show respect for Alter's work by using it to suggest what one might call a Noachic covenant of narrative. Biblical narrative always will have a special place, but other traditions know something of the art it discloses.

II

Alter provides two overviews (95–97, 179–85). Let me first consider features brought out only in the concluding overview, then take up the features of the first (having to do with kinds of repetition).

(a) "Everything in the world of biblical narrative ultimately gravitates toward dialogue" (182). So also in oral narrative generally. In Indian narrative, when activity and quoted speech are combined, what is said is almost invariably the culmination of the series, the endpoint of a formal unit. (See scenes i, ii, iii of the appended text).[6]

(b) Alter calls attention (187) to alteration of a single term across turns of speech as often finely significant, and part of a larger pattern of defini-tion of character through contrastive dialogue. A favorite set form in Indian narratives is one in which a series of questions is pursued, all answers being rejected but the desired last. Two girls bathe, only to find their clothes taken by two men. They address the men through the range of kin terms, beginning with courtesy kinship, but at last give in and address them as "my husband."[7] A girl comes seeking a great hunter as husband, but he is not at home, and his unworthy partner pretends to be he. In bed at night he touches the girl on her head, asking "What is this?" "My head." "No, our head." (The effect is particularly nice in Chi-nookan, where "our" can be expressed not only as plural, but as dual ["just you and I"].) And so on down to private parts.[8] In the Kathlamet "Sun's myth," the chief who has found the house of the Sun asks a young girl about each of the kinds of valuable goods on the walls of the house. Each time she answers "whose" with "ours": they belong to her grandmother and herself, and will be given away at her puberty rite. The contrast is both local and cumulative: each time, there is a contrast between men's wealth and the amazing answer that women own it and ultimately, ac-ceptance.[9]

(c) "In the Bible . . . the narrator's work is almost all *récit,* straight narration of actions and speech, and only exceptionally and very briefly *discours,* disquisition on and around the narrated facts and their implica-tions." So with Indian narratives. Tellings to outsiders, especially in English, may be more elaborate, because they make explicit motives and details a native audience could be expected to know. Sometimes a practiced source may even take on the role of collaborator, carefully inter-spersing ethnographic and linguistic explanation.[10] A revitalization move-ment, such as the Feather religion, and long solitary pondering, may in old age produce a Coyote cycle in which Coyote inveterately intervenes to foretell and so explain. But these respond to the presence of anthropology and Christianity, and other narrators regard them as poorly told. Alter's words can stand as a criterion of traditional form.

(d) Alter calls attention to repetition of single words or phrases that often exhibits a frequency, saliency, and thematic significance not found in other narrative traditions. Exploration of the semantic range of a root and play with phonetic relatives is indeed distinctive. Its prevalence in

the Hebrew Bible is not matched in Indian narrative.[11] Significant repetition of words and stems as such, however, is common. Word repetition
is often a key to the boundaries and coherence of a formal unit. Repetition
across units may be thematic, something that can be called a keyword
(*Leitwort*). In the appended text, each of the first two scenes has the
mother twice respond to the daughter with "Shush!" (*Ak'washka*); the
second response ends each scene. In the third, final scene, the daughter
remonstrates, throwing back the very word. The point of the story, indeed, signaled by a title in which the mother (Seal) is named first, is the
consequence of acting as does the mother, insisting on what is proper at
the expense of what is apparent, something her "Shush!" sums up.

(e) Alter writes: "Where the narration so abundantly encourages us to
expect this sort of repetition, on occasion the avoidance of repetition,
whether through substitution of a synonym or of a wholly divergent word
or phrase for the anticipated recurrence, may also be particularly revealing" (180; see 97–103 on varied repetition). In the appended text, it is in
the moment of transformation and remonstrance, when the daughter assumes responsibility, that the explicit word "urination" is first used, as
against the recurrent euphemism in the preceding scenes, "go out."
Again, each speech by daughter and mother in the first two scenes and
the beginning of the third is framed by a transitive verb, here translated
"told" (*-lxam*). But the mother responds to the first remonstrance by
a formal lament, addressed, not to her daughter, but as if to the world
at large, framed by the intransitive verb of speech that is not directly
addressed, but broadcast (*-kim*). Though the daughter's final remonstrance cites the "told" of earlier exchanges, it is itself framed with
the same intransitive word. This simple substitution defines the two as
separate.

(f) Alter observes that a relational epithet generally tells us something
substantive without recourse to explicit commentary (180). In the appended text the man to be murdered offstage is introduced in relation to
the mother, "her younger brother," but throughout the action of the story
both daughter and mother refer to him in relation to the girl, as "uncle."
Therein is one indication that there is a second focus—not only the consequences of acting as the mother does, but also the experience of the girl.

(g) The term *motif* is used by Alter to indicate a recurrent "concrete
image, sensory quality, action, or object," one without meaning in itself
without the defining context of the narrative, that may be incipiently
symbolic or primarily a means of effecting formal coherence (95). In the

appended text there are two sequences of imagery and sensory quality. One is of darkness to light. Although the narrator says that the action of the first scene happened throughout a long long time, the scenes together have implicitly the unity of a single evening and night. Families go outside to relieve themselves before retiring for the night (i); they go to bed, mother and daughter below close to a (presumably smoldering) fire (ii); the daughter rises and raises a torch. A second sequence is of perceived wetness, from without to within. The daughter hears urination (i), feels dripping upon her (ii), which proves to be not semen but blood, and ends in weeping (iii). The two sequences are interwoven around the story's second theme, that of the emergence into maturity, through her own initiative, of a girl whom customary guides and values have failed. The sequences, together with that of speaking, converge on her maturation and apartness. The evening and urination are outside; the low fire and dripping are within; she herself makes and raises the torch, she herself weeps.

(h) Alter uses *theme* for an idea that is part of the value system of the narrative, and made evident in some recurring pattern (95). This is the common device of Indian oral narrative. Again and again, a theme is not stated, but shown by its place in a pattern. Thus, a spontaneous illustration of the speech of a man who would go about the camp in the old days has five stanzas (of three, three, three, five, and five verses, respectively), and the ending point of each stanza has to do with the theme of continuity of tradition.[12] Indeed, it is often by noticing the recurrence of an ending point that one recognizes in the prose paragraphs of published myths the formal relationships concealed within them.

A moving example, associated with repeated words, is found in a Takelma myth just mentioned (n. 9). The narrator, Frances Johnson, did not much remember the second part, in which the two men go upriver, question two women, find out what the women do when they return to their village across the river, kill them, don their skins, and act as them (so as to gain access to the village and the chief's lodge in which their father is prisoner, his body hung above a smoking fire for which the girls have been gathering pitch). What Mrs. Johnson remembered clearly was what the girls say in fearful anticipation, "Paddle a canoe over here, Strong-digging-dog / We fear Otter's children." We are told what the girls say, the first line or both, seven times: twice that the girls say it, twice that the brothers are advised on their way that the girls say it, so that they should too, once when the brothers, disguised as girls, do say it, again that the girls would say it, again that the brothers now say it.

Why did Mrs. Johnson remember just this so well? Perhaps because people often remember a memorable song or set of words from a myth, but here, I think, because the words sum up a theme. In the first part, two young men have an unreliable caretaker, their grandmother, but overcome her. In the second part, two girls have an unreliable caretaker, but are overcome. Whatever the point of the myth in earlier times, for Mrs. Johnson it is remembered in terms of caretakers who fail children, and, in the doubling of the theme, especially fail girls. Narrative falters, but not their cry.

(i) Alter notes patterning of sequence of actions, most notably in "the folktale form of three consecutive repetitions, or three plus one . . . usually concluding either in a climax or reversal" (95–96). Of course this is worldwide. Still, it can be important to recognize its relation to theme. In Victoria Howard's "Seal Took Them to the Ocean," a band of men engage in a series of contests underwater. One would expect the Chinookan pattern numbers, three, five, or ten, but there are eight. The collector, Jacobs, considers that the next two scenes, in which Sturgeon is observed in quite different behavior, must be intrusive from some other unknown story. But if one considers the structural signals of the theme of the story, the two scenes are a culmination of a series of ten. The story is a woman's elaboration of a male adventure into a parable of the fundamental value of reciprocity. In this version (but not others) the adventure is launched when one brother refuses any longer to supply another. The older brother then causes the seal to attract them, and, when harpooned, to take them ineluctably to the bottom of the sea. They survive the series of trials, with advice from a sister-in-law living there, and return despite a harrowing test (Symplegades). But then the narrator says that the younger brother and his people remained poor. Why, and why say it? Because the opening scene has shown him as one who violates reciprocity. Such indications at the opening of a story of moral worth or lack of it always correlate with outcome.

Together, the opening and close point to reciprocity as theme. So do the ninth and tenth encounters underwater. In one Sturgeon kills and bakes his wife to provide food, but she is magically restored. In the other Sturgeon steals a comb and spoon from a woman and puts them in his head. The first is an instance of the continentwide story of the benevolent

host, an expression of an underlying value, that of participant maintenance.[13] Nature, or better, the controlling powers and persons of the
world, are benevolent and provide of themselves to human beings so long
as human beings respond with respect and proper behavior themselves.
Human beings participate in the maintenance of this world. This fundamental reciprocity is shown to one of the younger brother's partners, Blue
Jay. Sturgeon is the greatest fish in the river and shows that as he offers
himself as food. The objects put in his head are, as it were, "stigmata,"
by which he will be recognized. But Blue Jay does not report and accept
this mutual dependence. Rather, he seeks to emulate it, and kills his own
wife, who, of course, does not revive. The younger brother and his men
have survived a great adventure, then, but nothing is said to show that
he has learned the lesson of personal reciprocity, and one of his men is
shown to have been offered the lesson of fundamental reciprocity and
failed to understand. The scenes with Sturgeon are not intrusive from
another (unknown) story, but, numerically and morally, the final test.

(j) Alter defines *type-scene* as "an episode occurring at a portentous moment in the career of the hero which is composed of a fixed sequence of
motifs" (96). There are striking examples in the oral traditions of the
North Pacific Coast. In each case a standard frame integrates an extended
sequence in a different way.

A trickster myth in the Kalapuya language of the Willamette Valley is
integrated by recurrent motifs of a generic kind (appetite or need, deception, trade, and so on) in each act.[14] It is further integrated by the fact
that the deceptions that begin and complete its dramatic events have five
elements, three of them in specific detail, in almost the same order. The
first act is a version of a major story of the region. To break a dam and
free water and fish kept from people by sisters, Coyote digs with one hand
while pretending only to drink with the other. In the last dramatic act,
he inserts his penis in a chief's daughter while pretending only to sing to
cure her. In both, he reaches and removes an obstruction (a penis tip in
the case of the chief's daughter); in both, stopped-up water is released; in
both he is detected; in both he goes in flight.

A stock opening is turned into dramatic suspense in the middle of a
Clackamas Chinook myth told by Victoria Howard. Some of these myths
start with a dangerous being, Grizzly Woman, arriving at a village, seeking out its chief, and making herself his wife. Indeed, Mrs. Howard

comments upon this as a characteristic of Grizzly Woman. Many die before Grizzly Woman is overcome.

Now, in the myth that begins with two men (bears) forcing two young
women bathers to become their wives, the one who becomes Grizzly
Bear's wife has a son and daughter. The son is all bear, like his father, the
daughter half human. While the mother and daughter are out digging for
roots, one by one four uncles come in search of the woman, and are killed
by the bears at home. Only then does the mother understand why the
daughter has asked that they go back early. Together they burn up both
bears.

The daughter now says they should go to her mother's people, but,
ashamed of her mother for having lost one eye, throws her off a cliff and
goes alone. The old woman nonetheless follows her, and the girl throws
her into a fire. She comes to a village, asks for its chief, and goes to his
house to be a wife, but the old woman arrives again, calls her by a name
that alludes to her part-bear nature (her feet), and warns people. The girl
goes on to another village, the old woman comes, the girl kills her and
throws her in the fire. The fourth time the old woman comes and names
her, the girl gains advice from Meadow Lark that her mother's heart is
not in her body but in her hat. When the old woman comes again, the
girl throws the hat in the fire as well. At the fifth village, no old woman
comes. The girl marries the headman, raises two sons, then in the men-
strual hut sharpens claws, turns into a dangerous being, and eats everyone, both there and in the villages she had passed through.

This last is told briefly. What the central part does is to use the arrival
of Grizzly Woman at a village to marry its chief, otherwise an opening
frame, as an instrument of suspense. The male bears had killed the uncles.
Will the bear's daughter now kill their people? Four times the mother
keeps such a story from starting. Conversely, in the appended text such a
story has already started. The bare beginning, that a woman comes to a
chiefly man to be his wife, echoes this same frame, casting an expectation
of horror over what ensues.

This central sequence is complex in its use of the type-scene, inter-
weaving, but not in lockstep, several strands of recurrent elements. And
although one would think one would want the mother to succeed, Mrs.
Howard deploys significant detail to another end. To have the mother's
heart separate in her hat is to identify her with the pursuing old women

in hundreds of stories across the continent (among them, Grizzly Women). To have Meadow Lark help the girl is to treat the girl as favored protagonist. In the first part mother joined girl to destroy Grizzly males. When the two separate, it is because of the girl. And it is not the pursuing mother, but the escaping girl, who will become Grizzly Woman and eat other people. There is indeed a cultural logic here: Grizzly nature, even partial, will out. Yet that eventuality did not deter Mrs. Howard from casting the mother as pursuing ogress, the daughter as one pursued and in need of help. This much, it seems, she identified with a daughter whose mother failed to respond to the danger of an uncle's death. (See also the appended text.)[15]

A third dramatic use of a type-scene is what I have called "extraposition." A series establishes that something will happen a certain number of times. When the last time is reached, the last outcome is not given. Something holds its place, and the outcome is given an entire scene of its own. In Louis Simpson's telling of "The Deserted Boy" in Wishram Chinook, the rhetorical number is five, and in one scene it is incrementally accumulated and divided with exactitude—almost to the end. The boy makes a line for fish from sinew left him by his grandmothers. The first day he catches one fish, eats half, saves half for morning. The second day, two, eats one, saves one. The third day, catches three, eats one and a half, saves one and a half; the fourth day, four (two and two); the fifth day—he has become a grown man. It is in the next scene that he examines his line, and finds, not fish, but a delicacy, a mixture of huckleberries and salmon. The daughter of the power in the river has taken pity on him; he stands and sings.[16]

In the Zuni language of New Mexico the rhetorical number is four. In Andrew Peynetsa's telling of "Coyote and Junco," Coyote has Old Lady Junco teach him her song, runs off, forgets it, and comes back to learn it again. The fourth time ends, not with his learning it again, but with Old Lady Junco putting a rock inside her blouse and saying, "He may come, but I won't sing." What happens becomes the fourth and final scene, and the expected four verses are doubled. Two times Coyote asks, but gets no response. Then he says he will give her four chances. When there is no response, he leaps to bite her, and cracks his back teeth on the rock (stanza 7). The final stanza (8) wraps up.[17]

A close-knit pattern can be deployed with telling effect. Chinookan narrators often enough present an action as a triplet, a sequence of three steps. Not "Coyote went to X," but "Coyote went, he kept on going, he arrived." In "The Deserted Boy," the first acts ends, hammering in three times that there are no people. The second act begins with the boy alone. In the first stanza he weeps, he hears a sound, he dries his tears.[18] This triplet marks a turning point. In the second act he will survive, step by step, with what his grandmothers have left him, and, rewarded, prosper. In the third act the tables are turned. It is the people who lack food. His grandmothers come to him and he repays them. When the rest of the people come, he turns, he looks, he sees them; he thinks how they abandoned him, he raises an east wind in which they drown. The triplet marks the turn to revenge.

Other oral traditions would provide other examples of this kind of literariness, showing that its characteristics are not limited to the Hebrew Bible, or to written compositions of literate cultures, or to the North Pacific Coast. Alter does at one point qualify the uniqueness of the traits in his first synopsis. He observes that motifs, themes, and sequences of actions abound in other narrative traditions, and that while keywords and type-scenes are distinctively biblical literary conventions, one can find approximate analogues of these in other traditions as well. He goes on to say: "What most distinguishes repetition in biblical narrative is the explicitness and formality with which it is generally employed, qualities that . . . support an unusual proportion of verbatim restatement." In traditions in which there is great density of data, repetition may be partly camouflaged, something we are expected to detect. "When on the other hand, you are confronted with an extremely spare narrative, marked by formal symmetries, which exhibits a high degree of literal repetition, what you have to look for more frequently is the small but revealing differences in the seeming similarities, the nodes of emergent new meanings in the pattern of regular expectations crated by explicit repetition" (96–97). Just so must American Indian and many other oral narratives be heard and read. (And for just this reason, interpretation without access to the language of the original, interpretation dependent on translation, that is to say, most published interpretation, must fall short.)

At another point Alter suggests that these ways of using repetition may have their origin in biblical poetry, "which, as in most cultures, antedates prose as a vehicle of literary expression" (97). Whatever the role of poetic parallelism in the specific case, we see that societies without it yet have ways of using repetition. Such literary expression probably is ancient in the world, a potential concomitant of narrative in any language.

Alter also suggests that such use of repetition, individuating characters, has its roots in the biblical view of man (115, 189). This may be true. And an Indian view of the world in terms of participant maintenance, of mutual obligation between human beings and other powers, is not so far from that of the Bible. Still, I would suggest that individuation through repetition is a potential resource generally in oral narrative. Some tales and myths of course are rather stereotypical (as are some segments of the Bible), but many are rich in implication of motive and feeling. It is perhaps a matter of the extent to which a narrative has been fed on, lived with, in the mind. Thinking narratives through in the light of the fate of one's community and self is human.

III

One might accept the evidence just given and conclude, not that American Indian narratives are literary, like the Hebrew Bible, but that the Hebrew Bible in origin is oral, like American Indian narratives. Let me consider a theorist with no intention of addressing anything oral. The narratives he treats are nineteenth-century novels, and narrative is discussed entirely in terms of reading.

In his concise and penetrating book *Fictional Truth,* Michael Riffaterre holds that fiction is truthful, not by reference to reality, but through verisimilitude based in language. Not information, but form, provides a sense of truthfulness, and form does so by means that often call attention to themselves as form, as artifice. Riffaterre locates verisimilitude in devices that repeat and presuppose a given. In particular, "any verbal given will seem to be true when it generates tautological derivations that repeat it in successive synonymous forms."[19] The given, the situational and linguistic starting point of a narrative, has a semantic structure. Its components may be implicit or only incompletely explicit. The text substitutes explicit and developed descriptions. These must conform to a consensus about reality already encoded in language (be "grammatical"). The combination of multiple references to the given, of the verifiability of each against the accepted idea of reality, of the bulk of detailed translations of each into actual descriptions, of convergence on one initial lexical or phrasal expression, conveys the impression of truth. At the same time fiction relies on codes, arbitrary conventions, that can be identified independently of the narrative, assigned to a viewpoint exterior to it, or perceived as irrelevant to the motivation of the narrative events. Fiction therefore emphasizes the fictionality of a story at the same time that it conveys the story as true: "Narrative verisimilitude tends to flaunt rather than mask its fictitious nature" (21). In fact, "more can be learned about fiction from those indices that point to narrative truth by seeming to flout it. Far from being the exception, these signs are much used, an indication of their importance. Indeed, they differentiate between literary and nonliterary narratives, and may even be a locus of fiction's literariness since all of them are tropes" (xv).

Three chapters develop three aspects of the argument: (1) the veridictory effect of multiplying representations; (2) commentary or gloss that presupposes the reality of the language in which the topics are broached, and thus functions as if it presupposed the reality of what it glosses (metalanguage); (3) two kinds of clues to truth suppressed in subtexts—constants perceived through comparison of versions of a subtext, and "ungrammaticalities" (things that do not fit), indicating an intertext as their source.

The richness of fiction, of nineteenth-century novels, affords many interesting examples and interpretations. In their spareness, the narratives of concern here are another world. Yet the dimensions addressed by Riffaterre are present, as I shall indicate. Whether or not Riffaterre's thesis can be sustained for fiction generally, I do not know. He cites interesting examples, but of course they are few in relation to the universe of novels. It will be enough for my purpose if his argument holds for what he does cite.

(1a) To multiply representations is a kind of repetition, as Riffaterre himself points out (45), and examples of repetition offered in connection with Alter could be offered again. Indeed it is very Chinookan to say that "repetition does not become a trope before the third time" (21). There is a further important respect in which Indian narratives employ repetition as a meaningful trope, one which is both explicit and persuasive.

In brief, Indian myths, and perhaps oral narratives generally, are found to consist of lines, marked by intonation contours, and secondly of units (one or more lines) marked in speech by particular contours, notably in English by a sentence-final fall.[20] It is by virtue of being an organization of lines that one can consider them, not prose, but a kind of poetry, and the units that enter into relation can be called "verses." Lines and verses need not be equivalent internally (in terms of numbers of syllables, stresses, alliterations, or the like). Their equivalence is external, in terms of relations they enter into with other lines according to a few types of pattern. One can say that this is a kind of verse that is "measured," rather than metrical.

The units that enter into relation are often marked in other ways as well as intonation, notably by initial words and phrases, such as particles translatable by "Now," "Then," "So," "Well," and expressions of temporal change. Turns at talk count as units of this kind. In the appended text the verses are shown flush left.

A particular oral tradition has conventions as to the grouping of such verses. In Chinookan there are two unmarked, or "default," options, a set of three, a set of five. Three or five verses, then, may form a "stanza" (two in an introduction); three or five "stanzas" may form a scene. In the appended text there are three scenes. The first two have three stanzas, the third has five. In the appended text, stanzas are shown by marginal (parenthetic) capital letters. (The two sets of five lines that open the third scene seem each to have the weight of a stanza.) In many traditions the unmarked relations have to do with two and four. Combined possibilities occur also, as in the Algonquian language Ojibwe, where sets of three pairs are prevalent. The possibilities of such organization are more diverse than can be considered here. Suffice it to say that there is meaning that covaries with the form, is one of "this, then that; this, then that." When Chinookan narratives have three units in a series, the pattern is one of "onset, ongoing, outcome." This sense obtains, from three verbs in a row ("he was going, he kept going, he arrived") to three major units in a row. Where there are five units, the convention is that the third is pivotal, completing one series, and beginning another, the two interlocking in it.

That lines and groups of lines are conveyed in terms of intonation contours (and, but only secondarily, pauses), and that the lexical and syntactic matters are often at the beginning of lines, can be taken as aspects of orality (although end-rhyme oral epics, as in Egyptian Arabic, are not unknown). That the traditions analyzed so far make use of just a few types of pattern may suggest an innate basis, along the lines of Chomsky's view of language. Perhaps human beings are "wired" in terms of a few alternatives, and, hearing narrative around them, select the option present in it. But an adaptive, functional explanation cannot be ruled out. An art that is to disclose itself in perceptible relations, that maintains interest for those who already know its story by news of form, not information,[21] is likely to build from the minimal possibilities of two or three. Two with four, or three with five, give consistency and options. Larger numbers would be multiples or harder to perceive.

Some narrators mark the verse units boldly and without exception. One such is Louis Simpson, whose Wishram narratives begin every verse with the double pair, "Now then," or an occasional substitute ("Now again," "Indeed"). Other narrators are less explicit. In either case the effect is both to frame what is narrated and to lend it a sense of necessary consequence. Such narration continuously arouses and satisfies expectation (to use the apt phrase of Kenneth Burke for the persuading work of literary form).[22]

Such conjunction of artifice and verisimilitude may be specific to oral narrative (and to writing derived from it), and may show that Riffaterre's argument extends beyond the fiction he addresses. The myths are indeed preeminently "fictional truths," conveying truths important to life, yet fictional to us, and sometimes to Indians. The Santa Clara Tewa of New Mexico introduce some stories with words like these: "In a place that never was, in a time that never was, this did not happen." The Nootka of Vancouver Island insist upon the literal truth of stories of how the founder of a kinship group obtained its prerogatives. Those are true because the initial adventure did happen and the story has been transmitted ever since in a known chain of succession. But myths can be referred to in English as "fairy stories." Inheritance, in short, is historical fact; the truths of myths may be of other kinds.

(1b) Riffaterre himself singles out humor as primary trope of his first kind. It is said to betray a narrator's viewpoint, while presupposing the existence of that about which it speaks humorously (xv–xvi, 41). On the one hand, repetition, in the sense of the maintenance of a uniformly humorous slant from one moment in a narrative sequence to the next—"this is the index of fictionality." On the other hand, verisimilitude requires adjustment to each successive context. And although humor as an index of fictionality is not necessarily repetitive, this type is the most important in narrative, says Riffaterre, for the intertwining of the two linear developments highlights the contrast between the adjustments of verisimilitude and the fictionality of repetition (45).

The thesis fits the examples Riffaterre advances, and certainly it fits some sequences in Indian myths. A favorite scene in stories of the trickster-transformer Coyote, sometimes repeated in the course of a cycle of his coming upriver, or the like, is one in which he has "died" or otherwise completely failed in an effort. He slaps his buttocks, or defecates, for his "sisters" (or "nieces") to come out, and asks them what to do. They refuse, saying he will just say that he knew already. He threatens to make it rain and wash them away. They tell him then the truth of his situation, and he says, "Ah, that is just what I was thinking." The scene doubly presupposes what has happened, viewing it with a repeated form of humor and embedding a partial replay in its explanation.

(1c) Riffaterre's second case in point is that of emblematic names for characters (xvi, 33 ff.): the faithful father of many, Mr. Quiverful (Trollope), the Barnacle family encrusted on the ship of state (Dickens). Such names are blatantly conventional yet function as givens repeatedly verified, at least in the stories addressed. Such imitative naming is hardly to be found in the Indian narratives considered here. Chinookan personal names, indeed, have the look of ordinary words, but are not; they are titlelike, their significance accruing through a line of bearers, confirmed with each new conferral.[23] Yet the names of actors in myths do what Riffaterre says emblematic names do. They posit a truth, because they designate not a person but a type (35). Such names may indeed be considered emblematic, accruing through stories, as personal names through lives, features of expectation. They are the aspect of myths that fits Riffaterre's notion of stories traceable to a single expression (sememe) as germinating source.

Not always quite the same type, to be sure. The type, and name, may be contested. Where native titles are known (they seldom are), they point in the languages I know best, those that once prevailed along the Columbia River from its Pacific mouth past the Cascades into treeless plateau, to exploration as well as elaboration. The term for "myth" itself, -k'ani, means "nature." To refer to a myth as "I-gunat i-ya-k'ani" is to say "Salmon his-nature." That indicates that the point is to show the consequences of having that nature, of acting as does Salmon in the story in question.

As a named figure, Salmon is constant in being chiefly, proud, and tense in relation to women. His enacted nature varies. A myth known from all the Chinookan peoples along the river shows him avenging the killing of his father by Wolves, aided by Coyote. One egg floats in the river from his father's death, found by Crow, nurtured by her. (The myth imagines a birth without need of women.) He finds his mother wife to the Wolves, dries up all water but a spring beneath her feet, and when each in thirst comes to it, kills them. He takes the woman as his own wife, but, going upriver, she exclaims when she sees maggots on his sleeping body. (Spring Salmon are prone to spoil.) Angered, he throws her up on a cliff and goes on. Later, he hears birds squabbling as to who will get what body part, sends them to carry her back, restores her, and they live on.

When Franz Boas revisited Charles Cultee in 1894, he asked him to tell again a Salmon myth he had told in 1891. The first act is a ritual journey upriver. Five times the returning Spring Salmon is hailed from the shore: "At last you come, you with maggots on your buttocks; if it had not been for me, your people would have died." Salmon asks who it is, is told it is an uncle or an aunt, and goes ashore with gifts. Plants are a domain of women, fish of men. The culture rightly heralds the return of salmon in the spring as life-giving, but in this myth the claims of women as food-providers are asserted; even Salmon accepts insult and shows respect. But in the second part, encountering another canoe coming downriver, whose trio claim to have gone even further in just one day, he refutes their claim and wrings their necks: Flounder, then Crow, then Blue Jay, the one who makes chiefs unhappy. In 1891 Cultee rushes to the second act, not pausing to correct an omitted line. The second act begins with Salmon in command, and the grouping of verses is not unmarked three or five, but intensifying pairs. Salmon uses sardonic, metalinguistic questions. In 1894 Cultee pauses to insert an omitted line of the last insult at the end of the first act, and begins the second act in ordinary three and five part sequences. Sardonic, metalinguistic questions are absent. When he disposes of the trio in the canoe, he does so in opposite order, Blue Jay briefly, then Crow (she is forbidden the river) then Flounder. She is told to go downriver. No need to rush to reassert the authority of Salmon, once past the plants. The story now ends with the claim of the plants (and women) ("Without me, your people would have died") forever falsified. In the winter there will be fish in the river as well as roots on the banks. (To be sure, the fish is feminine in gender.)[24]

Victoria Howard told this story in Clackamas, recognizable as such through the frozen formula "Without me your people would have died," but transformed. Travel upriver becomes a rehearsal in season of the appearance of plants and other foods, birds and fish as well, a pedagogic exercise. Question and answer identify the appearance and name of the food, and then its use is explained. The one who pronounces on such things is taken to be a fish person (that is, Salmon), as the telling proceeds in threes, plants, more plants, birds, fish, more fish. But when the third of the second trio of fish is reached, evidently the most important, Mrs. Howard breaks off the narrative. My mother's mother said, she says, it was Coyote (the coyote called Shtank'iya) who ordained the foods. Salmon loses his ritual journey, then even his place in the story.

Another of her myths, "Tongue," is known from independent versions to be about Salmon, explaining at the end why salmon come to some tributaries of the Willamette River and not others. Not so in Mrs. Howard's poignant story. The foolish Clackamas people allow themselves to be eaten by Tongue. One chief's wife, out gathering roots, survives to bear and rear her late husband's son. He grows rapidly, gains spiritual power in the mountains, stupefies Tongue by gorging him with deer created from rotten wood, and, with his mother's help, burns him up. Then he goes to the mountains to recreate the people ritually out of bones. When all have returned to the river, and his restored father is teaching the people to fish, he watches; some insult him as not working; he walks into the river forever. The pride, the river, echo Salmon. But he goes unnamed; the motherless avenger of another myth has become the type of a mother's precocious, chiefly son.

Similar analyses can be made of other major figures, notably the trickster-transformer Coyote. Coyote is popular among many writers and artists, for his countercultural ways and picaresque indestructibility, but just as he is not a god (as early Whites sometimes said), neither is he necessarily a hero. In the serious business of guardian spirit power and headmanship, Coyote was marginal, a figure through whom to mock such things, but not to obtain them. And within the limits of his germinating features, stories make him what he is. It is rather like the complexity inherent in a deity all powerful and all good, or a deity both one and three. One narrator may emphasize and punish Coyote's irresponsible acts, as does Louis Simpson, who has Coyote himself state that Eagle and Salmon are chiefs, but he is not. Simpson's version of the news about Coyote (who has performed fellatio on himself and tried to keep the news from coming out) ends with punishment: the people, having heard, twice refuse him food. Victoria Howard's version has Coyote embarrassed but

quick to learn, and end as pronouncer of things to come, saying that even
he could not keep such news quiet and it will always be that way. Hiram
Smith sympathizes: the sun was hot, he'd just awoken from falling asleep;
the power with which he throws up a wall or rimrock to keep in the news
is dramatized with gesture; and at the end, Coyote just runs off.[25]

A narrator may integrate several myths to explore the nature of Coyote,
and, through him, of the world. William Hartless does that in the Kalapuya myth mentioned earlier. Twice Coyote meets needs of his own (for
water, for eyes) in a way that serves others and the way things are to be
(water and fish are to be freely available, Snail is to have weak eyes).
Perhaps out of hubris, he then trades for body parts from vanity and lust
(for Nightingale's anus because its sound will make him the cynosure of
gatherings, for an old man's lengthy penis so as to reach girls bathing
across the river). In the first two adventures, he succeeds and goes on; in
the second two he fails and has to trade back. He goes hungry because the
birds he stalks always hear him farting; the penis gets stuck in the girl
and he has to call to the other girls to cut it off. The tip stays in. The
girl's father, a chief, seeks a shaman to cure her. Coyote pretends to be an
old, powerful, reluctant shaman, who knows about cases like this. At last
he arrives, gets raucous birds outside the house to help him sing his
curing song, goes in and copulates with the girl. The parts unite. Although when the people find out what he does, they kill his helpers, he
himself escapes, intact, the girl cured. He and the audience have had the
fun of embarrassing a chiefly family, and have presumably learned that
the balance of things has to do with what Martin Luther King would call
a double victory. The last act is a few lines, undramatized, reporting that
Coyote went on, made a fish trap (alluding to a story in which he makes
it possible for people who have no fish to catch them), has children (this
the one who ordinarily is always traveling and leaving children and wife
behind).[26]

Like Coyote, Blue Jay can be the focus of humorous repetition and at
the same time diverse viewpoint and exploration. He is never clever, unlike Coyote, but may range from boastful and troublemaking to sympa-
thetic and suffering, from comic insert to protagonist. There is a
remarkable example in which the type-scene, or pair of scenes, is that of
"Benevolent Host, Bungling Host." In one scene, someone comes to a
host who has power to provide food by cutting his own body or killing a
family member, either then being magically restored. In the second scene

he is invited in turn by his guest (reciprocity), who tries to emulate him, and fails. Repeated versions of the type show it to have been a favorite among peoples of the northwestern corner of Washington, and among the Quinault, remarkably, a series of nine such episodes opens a cycle integrated around Blue Jay.[27] Interest is sustained by varying (exploring) possibilities of motivation and response, usually humorous, and on the visit by Blue Jay and his wife to the Shadows, there is only a first part. No emulation follows; unable to perceive the Shadows, the couple have to give up and come back. In these nine episodes the attempt at emulation implicitly confirms the existence of the powers displayed in the first part. The set comes to a motivated end, when Blue Jay's child dies, unrevived, at the end of the ninth. He can no longer bear to stay there, and sets out. The narrator then has him join with others in otherwise separate cycles, first of a pair traveling to name rivers and creeks, then of transformers traveling to set the world right. There follow other kinds of Blue Jay story, including a journey to the land of the dead. The matrix is in effect a treatise on the name and nature "Blue Jay." The emblematic name generates almost certainly some of the stories of the initial nine, together with an architecture that first establishes, with repetition and humor, a family man who wishes to be chiefly with magical power, but fails, and because of the death of a child goes away to become part of the establishment of the world as companion to others.

If generation from emblematic names of comic repetition and exploration of character are features of literature, these stories are that.

(2a) Riffaterre devotes his third chapter to commentary or gloss that presupposes the reality of the language in which the topics are broached, and thus functions as if it presupposed the reality of what it glosses (metalanguage).

A verbal device of just this sort occurs often in Chinookan myths, and in each of the first two scenes of the appended text (lines 2, 19).[28] The idiom is "definite indefinite." To say one does not know is to presuppose there was a time to be known, to indicate that the narrator would tell you that as well, if only she could. A touch of ignorance makes the rest true.

The end of the appended text is a telling instance. In the daughter's remonstrance to her mother the third scene rehearses the events of the first and second. As metanarrative, it presupposes them. At the same time it treats what has happened as something that might not have: there was another possibility. As remonstrance, the daughter's speeches state two truths: the consequence of having acted as did the mother, and that there might have been another story.[29]

Conversely, when foreknowledge is fulfilled, the fulfillment confirms the prior language and event. There is indeed a general circle here familiar in the culture. A myth, set in the world before the people have come, may end with a pronouncement of what will be when they do. The sisters, for example, will not hoard salmon for themselves but be frogs on the bank or swallows that come upriver when the salmon do. In the world in which the myth is told, frogs are on the bank, swallows do herald salmon. Experience confirms story, story explains experience. The circle obtains within stories. In each of two parts of the Clackamas myth, "Gitskux and His Older Brother," Grizzly Woman comes while the brothers are hunting, kills the elder's wife, and dons her skin. The brothers know how to test her, and what to do to overcome her, because each of the wives has foreseen it all and told them what to do.

Remonstrance, prediction and pronouncement, and post hoc explanation (recall Coyote's fecal advisors in [1b]) are frequent metalinguistic instruments of fictional truth in myths.

(2a) For Riffaterre, metalanguage is connected to symbolism. His dimensions do indeed intersect and mingle across chapters, and symbolism especially links dimensions (2) and (3) (symbolism, subtext, intertext). There is a gap, he writes, between the metalinguistic structure that enters into referentiality, the sequential telling of the story, and the hierarchy of aesthetic values that makes the novel into an artifact. The gap is bridged, so it seems to him, by subtexts, texts that are neither subplots nor themes but concrete actualizations whose sole function is to be vehicles of symbolism. "They offer a rereading of the plot that points to its significance in a discourse closer to poetry than to narrative." The connection between the two types of discourse comes through verbal overdetermination, welding narrative text and symbolic subtext by either or both of two intermediaries, sustained metaphors, "as an imagistically motivated consecution," or phonetically motivated syllepses (words with two possible meanings) (xvii). Let me identify this as (2b).

Whether or not such relations hold for all myths, I doubt, but that some myths answer to what Riffaterre delineates, I feel certain. There might be syllepses, and associated pieces of actualization, if emblematic names are taken to embody conflicting possibilities, natures realizable in more than one way. Sustained metaphors, imagistically motivated consecutions, do exist.

One example has been described with regard to the appended text. The public consequence, and moral, is to act as does Seal, first named in the title of the myth. Two ethical dimensions inform Chinookan stories: to maintain social norms, and to respond to empirical realities (to be proper, to be smart). Heroes show both, numskulls neither. This myth has a tragic outcome because the mother does the first at the expense of the second. But in the story is an alternative account, of a daughter who responds to reality at the expense of norms. She is not named in the title, and she does not shape the outcome, but she shapes the words. The way of referring to the man as uncle, not brother, and the consecutive imagery of darkness to light, external to internal wetness, focus on her. I find it hard to deny to this aspect of the story terms such as *subtext* and *theme,* but to use Riffaterre's words, there is here "a discourse closer to poetry."

The "Sun's myth," as told by Charles Cultee to Franz Boas, is a striking parallel.[30] A great chief (he has five towns of relatives) rises each morning to see the sun, but it does not quite come out. He tells his wife he will go to find it; she asks ironically, "Is it nearby?" but he persists. After wearing out ten sets of moccasins, he finds a house, enters, and finds a girl. Questioning her, he learns that the wealth of the house will be given away when she matures (has a puberty rite and is ready to marry). He stays. For a few idyllic lines, they are together while the old woman goes out each morning to carry the sun across the world and comes back, always bringing gifts. But he cannot forget the shining thing that caught his eyes, and when, homesick, he wants to return, again and again rejects all other gifts and insists on that. "It is you who choose," the old woman says, as she hands him that and an ax. When he nears the first town of his relatives, the ax sings, he loses consciousness, he awakes to find the town and its people destroyed, he tries to get rid of the ax but cannot. This happens at each town, though he tries to hold back his feet at the last, his own town. Then the old woman appears, saying, "I tried to love you and I do love you. It is you who chose. You took that 'blanket' of mine." She takes back what he had taken. He goes a little distance, there he builds a house, a small house.

The title indicates that the public meaning of the myth is the nature of the sun. It is in the nature of the powers of the world to enter into reciprocity with men, to provide them wealth. She observes the norms of this relationship and responds to reality. As a relative, she cannot finally refuse to give him what he asks. Only there are powers too great for men. That the chief could not see the sun when he looked, and had to close his eyes when he looked at the shining thing in the house of the sun, was indication enough that he did not have knowledge of it, and therefore could not control it. Sensory detail is concentrated on him. It is he who sees or does not see, who wears out moccasins, and who, in graphic, varied detail, tries five times to get rid of the ax, to throw it, to scrape it off in the crotch of a tree, to burn it, but always it would stick to his fingers. Successive images of not seeing, and of taking what cannot be released, and failure twice to heed the warning of a wife, point to hubris in relation to the reality of the sun. She and her power remain. His people are destroyed and he is released to live alone.

It would be going too far to use Riffaterre's words and speak of a re-reading of the plot (xvii). The narrative tells both stories at once; there is here as with Seal a dialogic, dialectic interrelation. But both the sensory detail and images of the secondary story can indeed be said, as Riffaterre says is usually true of a subtext, to be "strung along the main narrative line in separate successive variants" (131). The detail and images would, I think, evoke identification, and in both myths remonstrance points to responsibility and the foregone possibility of another ending. That seems close to Riffaterre's next statement: "The story it tells and the objects it describes refer symbolically and metalinguistically to the 'novel' as a whole or to some aspect of its significance."

It seems reasonable to generalize a bit, and to take the essence of Riffaterre's notion to be the welding together of two trajectories, one primary and one secondary, what is secondary being dramatically foregrounded through sensory detail (what a body experiences) and imagery (of darkness and light in both).

(3) Riffaterre remarks on the unconscious of a text as represented by the symbolism of a subtext and by the intertext the symbolism mobilizes. He points to two kinds of clues, perception of constants in subtexts, and of "ungrammaticalities," inappropriatenesses that derive from reference to an intertext that is not part of the temporal dimension of the text in question. They give a narrative the authority of the real paradoxically by eliminating or suspending its most basic feature, time.

Perhaps the cumulation of the sensory detail in the appended text and the sun's myth can be taken as perception of constants, dimensions with symbolic significance. True "ungrammaticalities" are rare, but there is one that is striking in Louis Simpson's version of a Benevolent Host, Bungling Host myth involving Coyote and Deer. Deer has offered both meat and blood from his own body. Invited in return, he sees Coyote raise a knife to his wife, and stops him, offering meat and blood again, and repeating that they should come to him. In the course of the text choice of verb forms and initiation of address associates Deer and Coyote's wife, but isolates Coyote. Strikingly, what Deer says is accompanied by transitive verbs of speaking, what Coyote says with intransitive verbs. When he raises a knife to his wife, the word is without a relational prefix. All nouns of kinship and other relationship require such a "possessive" prefix—one does not say "son," but "his son," "her son," "my son," and the like. But here the word is not "his wife," but, ungrammatically, "wife." It is the culmination of verbal detail that isolates Coyote, and begins the peripety of the story. Coyote does not fail in an attempt to be a host; he is not allowed to make the attempt. (Contrast stories in which Blue Jay makes such an attempt and his wife or child dies.)

The same text involves, not an ungrammaticality, but the unique pro-motion of the usual word for "and" into a marker of verse units. It marks just those units in which Deer offers blood. No other version of this kind of story in the region involves blood as well as meat, and this, together with the tone of Deer's words, suggests that the Methodism Louis Simp-son had been taught has introduced the symbolism of the eucharist. Not to a Christian purpose, for it is Deer who offers both, and not in sacrifice, but as participant in an order in which he can restore himself. I think that Mr. Simpson here does two things: he reduces to its nadir his negative conception of Coyote, a conception reinforced in the remonstrance by the wife that concludes the text, telling Coyote no one would want to eat coyote (not to be useful to people being a punishment, and for the pun-ishment to be applied to Coyote a double degradation); and he finds in his own tradition an equivalent to the appeal of the outstretched hands of the host of the Lord's Table.[31]

An element that suspends time is built into Chinookan myth. The second element of a text is commonly an evaluation of one of the actors, phrased, not in a narrative tense, but in the "future." Not he or she did something, but he or she will do something, that is, will always, char-acteristically do something. But this element does not point beyond the text to an intertext. Rather, it implies a constant. The outcome for the actor in question will fit the goodness or badness of the conduct described. (Recall discussion with regard to Alter (i) of the outcome of "Seal Took Them to the Ocean.")

Certainly inappropriateness can recur as a frame for myths, a frame independent of time. The coming of a woman to a headman as his wife is one. No relationship began that way in actual life. Again, the domestic group in Victoria Howard's telling of "Seal and Her Younger Brother Lived There"—a consanguineal trio of Elder sister-mother : Younger brother-uncle : niece-daughter—is not a normal one, yet it recurs in four of the myths we have from her, each distinct, each working out the relation in a different way. In each a different one of the trio dies (in one, none do).[32]

But a search for "ungrammaticality," even for "inappropriateness," yields little in these myths. The spirit of Riffaterre's approach is better served by generalizing its concern with suspension of time. Suppressed or implicit meanings, connected with symbolism, and associated with suspension of narrative time, do appear if one attends to what may be called *set pieces and inserts.*

In Louis Simpson's "The Deserted Boy," the extrapolated scene in which the boy celebrates success is in principle indeterminate in length. The boy sings, and the song can be repeated as often as desired (in the text we have, three times, but it could have been five). Nothing further happens. It is like an aria in opera. And the scene with the song is followed by a stanza whose first verse repeats that the boy had camped overnight five times, whose second describes him as waking to find a woman beside him, followed by a number of lines (for Chinookan narrative a great many lines) describing her beauty in terms of adornment, house, and blanket, and a third verse with a number of lines enumerating the kinds of food she has brought. The third and concluding scene of the act has five verses describing the man and woman together. Each is a line beginning with "now" and not "then." Mr. Simpson's verses usually begin with both ("now then"). Here the "now" of summation is repeated five times, and the "then" that moves to a succeeding point is suppressed. Time indeed is suspended.

All this can readily be associated with the implicit model for Mr. Simpson's handling of the story, the model of a successful guardian spirit quest. In the first act narrativity began by moving steadily to the abandonment, then circled round three times to the repeated final line of being entirely alone. In this second act narrativity moves steadily, almost ploddingly to the moment of success, and then virtually ceases. Two things are required of a guardian spirit quest: to go alone, to obtain signs of the pity of a power.

In the appended text, again the first two scenes move steadily ahead, and the third presents a portrait as if the two women were to be frozen forever, one reproaching and weeping, one keening, one reproaching and weeping. The portrait etches the apartness of the daughter, come into knowledge of sexuality and blood unattended, only she knowing. It stands implicitly over against expectations of a girl's puberty rite, sponsored, managed, gifts given to make it remembered by others, within a family and community.[33]

A subtler form of subtext and symbolic meaning emerges when a certain characteristic of the narrative action is linked to a tellingly placed suspension of narrativity itself. One such emerges in Cultee's Kathlamet telling of the myth of the Southwest Wind, if one considers that some portions of the ongoing action of a myth are presented with quoted speech on the part of the actors, while some are described without it. A group make their way into the sky to overcome five brothers who are repeatedly destroying their homes. The culminating conflict between the two parties is narrated vigorously, to be sure, but succinctly: this happens, this happens, this happens. The larger part of the text is devoted to the interaction of the party that goes to the sky, much of it incidental to the outcome, much of it displayed through what they say to each other. The speakers, indeed, are small animals, not strong ones. And after the victory, when they return, a good many are left behind in the sky, and their names are recited, one after the other. The two things seem to go together: small animals talking, a litany of such creatures now in the sky as stars, to suggest something besides the principal outcome, the overcoming of all but one of the Southwest Winds. That, I think, is a sense of the domestication of the sky. Small creatures accomplish it, some of them are forever there now. In sum, suspension of action in a litany here is linked with one of the two modes of narrative progression, a mode (quoted speech) whose quality of focusing and dramatizing voices is like pausing for a set piece.[34]

Another myth links set pieces to a subtext and intertext having to do with the natures of women. In Victoria Howard's "Gitskux and His Older

Brother," the latter part begins when Grizzly Woman has killed the older brother's first wife and all the community and taken the younger brother with her. The older brother, alone, comes to a house, enters, and sees what he takes to be a hunter entering the other end with a deer. Later, the same person reenters and lets down her hair: it is a woman. At night he lies down away from her bed but step by step she causes him to be bitten by insects and, as the fifth step, to end beside her. Soon she tells him that he is to be the hunter.

This is done in ten lines of verbal exchange. Unlike every other part of the myth, the lines have no smaller groupings (three, five, three pairs, anything). Their internal shape is not one of parts, not quite one of linear progression, but in words used more as a circle within which places are exchanged: the two, she to him, he to her, the two.[35]

> Now the two stayed.
> She told him,
> > "Now you will be doing the hunting.
> > You will have thought,
> > > 'Perhaps there is some man.'
> > Here I have lived alone,
> > I would be the one hunting."
> "Indeed,"
> he told her.
> Now that is what the two did.

Formally, the story is about the brothers of the title, the younger active and alert to what happens, the older passive and needing instruction. They belong to a matrix of younger and older brothers, one smaller, one larger, drawn from Panther, Fisher, Marten, Mink, and Wildcat, that is widespread in the region, but in character, they stand in contrast. The myth might also be said to be about Grizzly Woman, who initiates most of what happens. She comes to the unnamed older brother (actually, Panther) as a wife. In the event she kills the first wife and puts on her skin, but the wife had foreseen it (this is told out of temporal order, after the event), the brothers test her, and kill her. She returns, kills and eats all the people, and takes the younger brother off to be a slave on whom she will wipe her anus. After the scene quoted above, the second wife is able to tell the older brother what has happened to the younger, and how to rescue him; after a poignant recognition scene, Grizzly Woman is again

killed. The second wife, having cleansed Gitskux (evidently Fisher) five
times, restores his long black hair, making it fall not only to the ground,
but even a little longer than before. Here again there are ten units that
stand apart. The first five verses form an arc, but the sequence does not
stop, it barely pauses, a caesura, as it were, as the combing continues to
its ultimate result.

These two ten-part displays cannot be said to suspend narrativity, time,
entirely. A further point is reached. Yet they hold us within a frame that
is formally apart, an extended formal unity not otherwise found. And they
connect with a subtext brought out in doubling wives, their foreknowledge, and Grizzly Woman's donning the skin of each. Grizzly Woman
wishes to be accepted as a human wife (but fails). Implicit in the contrast
between her behavior and that of the true wives is the question of strength
in women. Grizzly Woman tries to control what she does but cannot; she
kills and degrades. The true wives defend and foresee, and the second
knows what has to be done to kill Grizzly Woman forever (not only burn
her, but mash her bones and blow them away). She does not need a man
to hunt, yet can have the older brother be the hunter; having directed the
rescue of the younger brother, she can restore him and give him black
hair longer than before. That, I submit, is strength, a womanhood so
strong and secure that it not only chooses its partner, but is a freely giving
source of identity in men. In contemporary terms, aggression versus assertion.

This myth is one of four that form a cycle of intertextuality that I can
only indicate briefly. Another myth also ends with Grizzly Woman destroyed for good by having her mashed bones blown away. The tendency
in folklore in such cases has been to pardon native inconsistency. To do so
mistakes the reason such myths exist. Queen Victoria can have died but
once, but Grizzly Woman can die as often as there are motives to think
through what she best enacts. Each of the myths in which she dies for
good indeed complements a myth that has ended with her alive. Each pair
contrasts in the gender of her active opponents and in her motivational
concern. In the pair in which the opposition is by male protagonists, her
motives have to do with being a wife. In its first myth sons revenge a
mother, in the second brothers restore a wife. In the pair in which the
opposition is by female protagonists, her motives are revenge against
women, first one, then all. In its first myth a daughter overcomes a
mother, in the second a mother-in-law. In the first of each pair a child or

children are pursued, and are aided by a bird; in the first of each pair Grizzly Woman ends without kin, destroyed by others and herself. There are other connections as well. Although nothing is recorded to indicate that Victoria Howard thought of these four myths together (she did not tell them together), either she or the women from whom she heard them evidently have thought them through to the point of alignment in terms of common concerns and elements of frame.[36]

A striking suspension of narrativity through inserts occurs in Victoria Howard's "Seal Took Them to the Ocean." As discussed under (i) in relation to Alter, the main narrative has to do with the men who go under the ocean and engage in dangerous contests. Between the contests and return come two scenes, not of action so much as observation by Blue Jay, disclosing Sturgeon. After the return, Blue Jay fatally attempts to imitate Sturgeon, killing his wife, to the dismay of others. The scenes with Sturgeon and Blue Jay interrupt the progress of the main action, and are themselves disjunct. They connect with the opening account of the relation between two brothers, and the remark at the end that he, Seal Hunter, despite heroic success, remains poor with all his people, evidently having violated reciprocity at the outset. The inserted, disjunct sequence shows the principle as more than a relation between persons such as brothers, one of whom has ceased to share. It presents reciprocity in the fundamental terms of life (life-sustaining food) and death, as inherent in the being of the world. In his cleverness (and with advice) Blue Jay has helped his side defeat the people under the ocean in contest after contest with life at stake. Like the chief with regard to the shining of the sun, however, he overreaches. He interprets a providential gift as one more in a series within the control of beings like himself. The emulation destroys.

IV

A. J. Greimas has proposed a model of the elementary structure of signification to which the course of a narrative is held to correspond.[37] It is interesting to see that such a model, accepted as part of narratology, has application to a myth discussed in this essay, not only in terms of semantic units, but also in terms of ethnopoetic form.

The model is that of a "semiotic square." A unit signifies in terms of relations with its contradictory, its contrary, and the contradictory of its contrary. For a concept such as "smart" or "proper" (s_1), the contradictories would be not smart, or not proper ($-s_1$); the contraries, dumb, or improper (s_2); the contradictories, not dumb, not improper ($-s_2$). The course of a narrative can be said to correspond to a movement along the square, through operations or transformations, from a given unit to its contrary or contradictory.

The model can be applied to the appended text. The four states would be the opening consanguineal situation in which the trio (older sister and mother, younger brother and uncle, niece and daughter) live together (s_1); the addition of the affinal "wife" (a man disguised) who comes to the brother (s_2); the girl's discovery of the murder of the uncle by the "wife," now gone ($-s_2$); the daughter's remonstrance and the mother's lament, as their relationship ends ($-s_1$). The movement is from opening moment to its contrary; from contrary to contradictory; and from contradictory to its contrary, which is contradictory of the initial state. The four states can be highlighted as follows:

s_1: consanguineal family ("they lived there")

s_2: augmentation by affine (daughter's warning, mother's reproach)

$-s_2$: loss (uncle murdered, "wife" gone)

$-s_1$: separation (mother : daughter)

These four states intersect the ethnopoetic, or rhetorical, form of the text. The text has three scenes, consisting of three stanzas, three stanzas, five verses, respectively. Each scene begins with specification of a relation between participants and location. The four states of the semiotic square overlap the formal demarcations. Each scene involves two states. In particular, the second and third scenes continue a preceding state (relation), and against that a new one begins.

The initial state (s_1) is expressed in the first verse, an introductory descriptive statement. It is a statement of a kind with which such myths commonly begin: so and so lived there. The second state (s_2) is introduced by the next verse. This state continues into the first part of the next scene. The third state ($-s_2$) is introduced in the second stanza of the second scene, and continues through the third verse of the third scene. The fourth state ($-s_1$) is in the concluding two verses of the third scene.

The intersections of the subsequent states of the semiotic square coincide with markers of narrative time. As said, the first state is a conventionally continuing one. The second state is introduced with the first reference to a specific moment of time (a "definite indefinite" time, "I do not know when it was"), and the third state by the only other (the same expression of "definite indefinite" time). These are the only occurrences of the expression in the narrative. Each is salient against the background of what precedes it. In scene (i) the opening "they lived there" indicates a stable continuing state. The next verse punctuates it with arrival of a woman. In scene (ii) the opening lines about going to bed are not in a narrative tense, but in a future of characteristic activity, "they would," continuing the sense of the preceding stanza of "a long long time . . . like that." The next verse punctuates it with something dropping onto the girl's face.

Finally, the fourth state coincides with a shift from the primary tense of narrative sequence to a tense that is associated with continuing states. The actions of the preceding scenes have been set in the remote past (marked by *ga-*). The third scene (continuing the third state) opens with *na-*, the first use of *na-* in the text, but the other tenses of the first verses, and the first tense of the third verse (all within the third state) are *ga-*. The last tense in the pivotal third verse is *na-*, as are all the tenses of the last two verses (the fourth state).[38]

That the fourth state is contradictory of the initial state is marked by lexical selection and framing on two counts. The myth shows the consequences of acting as does the mother, who insists on observing social norms at the expense of empirical evidence. There are actually two consequences, each enacted in a sequence of the three verses. To recognize this, one must recall that in Chinookan and other languages with three- and five-part patterning, a sequence of five can be organized around its third member as a pivot, completing one three-member series and initiating another.

The first three verses of the scene relate the girl's discovery of blood, then that her uncle is dead, and give her remonstrance to her mother. This series discloses the first consequence of acting like Seal, the death of the man. (It uses the present tense for immediacy.)

The second series of three verses discloses the second consequence, the breaking of the relation between the girl and her mother. The girl remonstrates and weeps, her mother does not answer but formally laments, the girl again remonstrates and weeps.

A choice of verb forms coincides with the distinction among consequences, and, as described, so does the distribution of past tenses (granted a line of anticipation). The third verse (consequence 1) continues the use of the transitive, addressing verb "told." The concluding two verses have the intransitive, broadcast verb "said." And the selection of a marker of simple pastness, *na-*, in the last two verses brings the narrative round again to a continuing state, although one far different from that with which it began.

The two contradictory states thus are integrated within the movement of a single scene. The integration within five verses may have a further appropriateness to the second consequence, if one interprets this third scene against the expectations of the first and second.

On the one hand, in the preceding scenes a verb of saying precedes each turn of talk by the daughter, but not the turns of the mother. Her words come in direct response, nothing intervening. In this third scene, all three turns at talk are enclosed on each side: "The girl told her . . . she wept"; "Seal said . . . she kept saying that"; "The girl wept, she said . . . the girl wept." The separation seems iconic.

On the other hand, the pattern of the preceding scenes is threefold: participants and (a change of) location, verbal exchange, verbal exchange. If the third scene is heard in terms of the same pattern, then the breaking of the relation between mother and daughter is expressed yet again. The first two verses identify participants and a change of location: the girl moves to discover her uncle. The third and fourth verses give two turns at talk, but it is not truly an exchange. The daughter addresses the mother, but the mother speaks broadcast in lament. There is a further turn at talk by the daughter, but then there is no further talk at all. Formal expectations as to a sequence of verses have been fulfilled, to be sure; the scene ends with a fifth. But expectations from the first two scenes of a second verbal exchange are denied. That in itself may suggest an absence of completion, a silence that highlights what has happened.[39]

In sum, both the primary and secondary plots and consequences are given in this final scene: the outcome for the man in its initial arc of three stanzas, the outcome for the relation between mother and daughter in its second.

That the relations proposed by Greimas find overt marking within a culturally specific narrative form suggests the scope of their relevance and its standing as narrative.

V

Intricate, motivated form may be accepted as a sign of literary art. In the story "Seal and Her Younger Brother Lived There" it is an outcome, not only of art, but of change, of a transvaluation of dramatic values. Seal is a woman's inversion of a myth told elsewhere to entirely different purpose.

Along the North Pacific Coast there are a number of recorded myths of a man or men seeking revenge. A father or son has been captured and is near death; a wife has been stolen; a sister has been killed by her husband. All have in common a journey to an enemy village. There the avengers disguise themselves as wives of the chief, or, in one type, a man dresses himself as his sister, his identical twin. They are almost found out. This may happen several times, but the climactic moment is at night within the house, when going up a ladder to bed. A child (not hitherto mentioned) calls out that it is not a woman, but a man; it has a knife, or a penis, beneath its dress. An older person shushes the child, and the avengers succeed. They kill the chief and, if the victim was father or son, rescue him.

In such a story, the child's crying out is a last, perhaps poignant, moment of suspense. For Mrs. Howard it is the focus of an exploration of relations between mother and daughter. Dramatic motivation (suspense) has found motivation in experience of life.

VI

This last speaks to a kind of change not much noticed in regard to Native American myths. For a long time narratives have been considered mostly as properties of groups, narrators as witnesses to tradition. Today one still sees stories identified by the name of a tribe or culture, that is, a group, not a person. The man who skillfully and sensitively preserved the Clackamas narratives of Victoria Howard published them as *Clackamas Chinook Texts* and discussed them as evidence of the Clackamas in general, not of Victoria Howard, of a woman, who had been born into the remnant of a shattered group. In such a context change is taken as occurring from tradition to tradition, group to group.

There will always be much to learn from study of difference and change at such a level. One value of the work of Lévi-Strauss is that he discovers new collocations that give new perspectives.[40] It is what makes possible recognition of individual transformations of the sort found with Victoria Howard. One must read, and reread, seeking to recreate in the mind something of the resources and alternatives a narrator might have had. Each story may bring into relationship details and stories otherwise not particularly noticed.[41] Those who interpret change and artistry must as much as possible have in mind what a narrator might have had in mind. No scholarly resource will suffice, for lists of motifs and tale-types abstract from details and vantage points that may matter in the given case. Each tradition indeed needs its own guide, and where traditions no longer live in the minds of narrators, they must come alive again in the minds of readers. The goal of such comparison, as envisaged here, is not reconstruction (of a past starting point), reduction (to a structure), or reflection (of a culture), but to identify resources and relations so as to interpret something emergent.

Much of the current study of oral narrative focuses on the event of narration itself, on narrators as performers. Focus on occasion brings attention to change as between one performance to another, one performer and another, and within a performance itself.

Such differences might best be called variation, rather than change. There may not be a fixed (memorized) original, or if there is, it may not itself change. Think of narrators in command of resources of both content and form: content, in the sense of story frames, matrices of actors, sequences of incident, image and event, and form in the sense of conventions for the ordering of relations between narrative units (lines, verses, stanzas, scenes). Think of audiences conversant with these things as well. One telling might differ from another simply in explicitness. "But the story [text] doesn't say that it was a feather," I said once to Hiram Smith, a Wasco friend of almost forty years. "Everyone knows it was a feather," was his reply. A pronominal prefix ("it") could be enough.[42]

The mood, interests, and identity of the narrator, of the audience, the relation between the two, affect what and how much is said.[43] The cases to be taken up below are examples, and such variation is familiar in the conception of the oral-formulaic poet as one who draws upon a stock of precoded expressions, adapting length of performance to occasion.[44] Generative adaptation, whether of epic or other genres, is being carefully studied today in many parts of the world.[45] On the native North Pacific Coast, a striking instance of adaptation to occasion is when a story that validates privileges being ritually assumed by an heir is told in outline to a public assembled outside the place of investiture. To share the full story would give away something itself protected as hereditary right, but enough is told to show that the right is genuine.[46]

Tellings to outsiders, especially in English, may be more elaborate, because they make explicit motives and details that a native audience would be expected to know. Sometimes a practiced source may even take on the role of collaborator, carefully interspersing ethnographic and linguistic explanation.[47]

Sequences within a myth and of myths may affect their components. One widely popular story has a trickster-transformer juggle his eyes, throwing them up to fall back in his sockets, only to have them stolen by a passing bird. Having made imitation eyes from a flower, he deceives someone else into thinking his eyes are superior, and trading. In a version told in Klamath by Patsy Ohles, the juggling is a major focus, as Coyote first admires the sound the eyes of Beaver make ("lolololok!") when Beaver juggles, then learns to do it himself. In a sequence told in Santiam Kalapuya by William Hartless, there is no juggling at all. The sun got warm, he became sleepy, he went to sleep, Blue Jay stole his eyes. The loss of eyes is barely described, and the focus of the scene is on the sequel, one of a series of scenes in which Coyote trades body parts.[48]

Creative recombination of myths in sequences is so common that it can be grounds for suspicion of authenticity when sequences from related but different communities are too much alike.[49] Stories vary, then, by incorporation in larger sequences. So also genres other than story, such as songs, may vary when incorporated within one.

If one performance is the one recalled, or best recalled, by someone who later undertakes to tell it, variations of course may lead to versions. And sometimes variation and remaking go hand in hand for the narrator himself. Such seems the case with Charles Cultee's two tellings (1891, 1894) of the "Salmons' myth," discussed above (see n. 24). In each a first part of acceptance by Salmon of insult is followed by a second in which Salmon reasserts authority. In the first telling reassertion goes with abrupt, marked change of poetic form; in the second the key to reassertion is a new ending in unmarked form.[50]

I have emphasized a kind of change that occurs between performances, or perhaps without anticipation of performance at all. Change because of personal felt need to reflect, to interpret experience, with narrative as framework and resource. Change for which the narrator is not so much witness, or performer, as "remaker," interpreting fundamentals, deconstructing and reconstructing both.[51]

So, at least it seems, must have been the case for the late Linton Winishut of Warm Springs, Oregon. Some years ago he told six hours of myth to Virginia Hymes, while others in the household watched television. He said he had had to memorize it as a child and also that he had never told the whole cycle before. If so, then in between childhood and advanced age the cycle had become a vehicle for asserting foreknowledge, for weaving myths together around the figure of a Coyote who constantly predicted correctly what would occur. Another might say both how fine it was that Mr. Winishut was bringing out old words again and that the stories were not well told. What one has, I think, is an assertion of the validity of the tradition itself through the voice of its most salient protagonist. The satisfaction and confidence that gave might, but for chance, have remained a private matter.

So, I think, it was for Victoria Howard, living in Oregon City without other speakers of her language, and for Charles Cultee, living in Bay Center, Washington, with one or two others still knowing some Kathlamet, but neither with a community and occasion for myth, so far as we know. With Victoria Howard we have again and again a fundamental reshaping of narratives known elsewhere from the perspective of male protagonists. Such is the case with "Seal Took Them to the Ocean," in which a myth told elsewhere as male adventure has a crucial woman advisor, an outcome in which adventure is explicitly not rewarded, and a subtext of reciprocity. Such is the case with her handling of the figure of Salmon. Such is the case with the first myth of the pair about Grizzly Woman that focuses on women protagonists. Cultee told Boas a myth (known elsewhere) in which five brothers seek in turn to rescue a sister who has been taken by a bear. The fifth succeeds, killing the bear. In Mrs. Howard's narrative we know nothing of any brothers until a revelation after the fourth has come and been killed, and no fifth comes. The niece-daughter and sister-mother take his place. Again and again Mrs. Howard's narratives think through narratives from the standpoint of the women in them. Again and again these tellings seem to show the effect of growing up in a shattered culture, one in which caretakers are uncertain, unreliable, and in which women must muster what strength they can.

Cultee's Sun's myth uniquely reverses a type of frame known far and wide. In the Southwest, among the Navajo, Apache, Acoma, and others, a woman is magically impregnated by the Sun. Her two children go to seek their father, who tests them severely. They endure, obtain his powers of lightning and the like, and go about the world eliminating dangerous beings. Among the Kwakwala (Kwakiutl) of British Columbia a woman similarly conceives, bearing Mink, who is teased by other children, and seeks his father. Welcomed, he is allowed to carry the sun, but goes too low (Phaeton). Elsewhere in the Northwest, myths of a man put through life-threatening tests by a prospective father-in-law are widespread (for example, the Tsimshian myth of Asdiwal, studied by Lévi-Strauss).

In all of these one can see something of the frame of the Kathlamet myth, except that all have to do with the world before the people have come. The Kathlamet myth does not tell of a world being begun, but being ended. Nothing has to be established, by going or by staying. The protagonist is not tested but welcomed. The destruction from carrying the sun is not what might be expected of a certain character (Mink), but the consequence of the act of a human who might have chosen otherwise. There are other myths of hubris, to be sure, in which characters must learn the limitations of their nature (Coyote seeking to trade body parts [Kalapuya], Coyote or Blue Jay seeking to emulate their hosts). Again, these stories are set before the people have come, when the world is being set right. In the Kathlamet myth the world of people is already right, and an offer is made to make it more than right, but in the end it is destroyed. It is difficult not to see in this unique myth a reflection on the destruction of communities in western Oregon through introduced disease that began in isolated cases in the late eighteenth century, and became widespread in the early nineteenth. Here history is absorbed and interpreted in terms of a fundamental tenet of the way of life, participant maintenance, and reciprocity among the beings of the world, ineluctably conditioned by their respective natures. The theme of hubris, of overreaching one's nature, in stories of a bungling host is generalized to the fate of a people whose leader has only to receive. Perhaps there is also a resonance of accepting things not properly Indian from the new natures who had come, the Whites.[52]

Myths are indeed good to think, it seems, and those who have absorbed them may carry certain of them with them all their lives. Artistry is inseparable, one may think, first, from eliciting absorbed attention that makes the heard myth part of one's imagination, then from offering patterns and details that can give expression to new understandings. Depth of realization, interlocking form and detail, seem most present in just those narratives with depth of transformation, through depth of identification and reflection.

In part such tellers of Native American myth are like users of Greek myth as described by Jameson: "The attitude of the user of myth may be compared to that of a historian who is convinced of the outlines of the history he is studying but feels free to rearrange, reject, and add to the incidents and persons reported by tradition in order to make sense of his subject. The analogy is cogent since, as we have seen, for the Greeks myth was in fact a kind of history. The originality of the Greek artist lay in the sense he made of his material."[53] And in part they are like the medieval authors characterized by C. S. Lewis. The situation is different, in that there can be transforming imagination, and penetrating imagination, and there may be efforts to heighten (characteristics he denies to these medieval authors), but whether engaged in change or not, it is true to say: "It is a realizing imagination . . . their matter and their confidence in it . . . possesses them wholly. Their eyes and ears are steadily fixed upon it, and so—perhaps hardly aware how much they are inventing—they see and hear what the event must have been like. . . . They sometimes profess to be deriving something from their *auctour* at the very moment when they are departing from him . . . like a historian who misrepresents the documents because he feels sure that things must have happened in a certain way."[54] Remakers of myth have no *auctour* before their eyes, but voices and images in their minds, as may someone who has much of the Bible, or Milton, or Shakespeare by heart. Perhaps the fact that it is the hearer of a myth who must supply the images involves a mingling of what was said and what imagined from the outset. To have heard more than one performance, perhaps more than one performer, will have taught that rightness is not a question of always the same words. To have understood that myths have only partly to do with the past, that myths are a dialogue between past, present, and future, will allow them to "realize" (in two senses) what must have happened, from reflection on any of those three vantage points: received tradition, present circumstance, projected need.

Coyote pronounced that swallows would fly upriver in the spring when the salmon are about to come. How do we know that is true? Because we see that it happens. Why does it happen? Because Coyote said it would in the myth.

Circular, to be sure, but such circularity can be creative, a spiral. Caretakers insist on propriety, blinding themselves to danger in their own house. Why does it happen? It must have happened in a myth.

It is inherent in the dialectic of thinking myth, then, for myth to change. It must change, if it is to be coherent with experience. It must give pleasure of shape and detail, if it is to convince. And it must be abstract. Indeed, it is.

In discussing Riffaterre (1c), I mentioned that among the American Indian languages I know best, those that once prevailed along the Columbia River, from its Pacific mouth past the Cascades into the treeless plateau, a term for "myth," *k'ani,* means, "nature." To refer to a myth of the hero Salmon as *I-gunat i-ya-k'ani* is to say "Salmon his-nature." Such a title indicates that the point is to show the consequences of having that nature, of acting as does Salmon in the story in question. An aged Wasco woman of Warm Springs, Annie Smith, once told me that people may hear and read the myths today, but not understand them, not realize what they teach. I take her to have meant that it is not enough to know what a story says. One must know that it shows the consequences of having a certain nature and so acting in a certain way. Simple enough, one might think. But in the tradition, when a trickster such as Coyote acted with greed or lust, people might well laugh, but they would attend as well to the consequence of acting that way.[55]

Myths in effect are thought-experiments.[56] Actors enter into a hypothetical experiment cast in narrative terms. The narrative exhibits the consequences, if a single motive were to have its course, embedded in an actual personality and not crosscut by circumstance. In this respect, the myths can be said to be abstract calculi of motives, providing by verbal means a symbolic "laboratory" for cognitive understanding.

It is possible for a story to be retold, much as it had been heard, without much active involvement. Again and again, however, it appears that those who most knew myths and best told them had experienced them, some of them at least, deeply. In part they were agents of selection, finding in certain stories, rather than others, a fundamental or radical myth of personal meaning.[57] These might not be the myths most widely known, of which almost everyone could give an account, part of public conversation, when salmon came or one passed a place. Understanding of Native American myths as artistry and insight has to be in terms of the concerns, imagination, and resources of individual narrators. That does not imply only a very few. Those who stand at the end of traditions, such as Victoria Howard of Clackamas, and Charles Cultee of Kathlamet, stand out alone against a context of loss, but were there access to their communities a century before, very likely there would have been many such.

VII

Little of what has been said has to do with the oral existence of myths as a cause of change. Some still may hold that oral myths change just because they are oral, without writing, without institutions that preserve texts and records. Others may expect such traditions to be preserved by memorization, almost from time immemorial. Some American Indian people themselves will hold this to be the case, and four impressive volumes of analysis of New World myths find in them a system that preserves, despite all change, an ancient knowledge.[58] Neither view is wrong, but neither is right. Orality ensures neither. One cannot read off a mode of cultural life from this one physical means, just as one cannot ascribe the same mode of life to every group that gathers and hunts. Technological determinism is not accepted when technocrats and Marxists propose it; why then when classicists and media theorists do? The common fact of oral tradition did not make American Indians and West Africans the same in interactive style or other modes of communication. The effect of orality, as of writing, depends on the practices of which it is part. In classical India remarkable analytic feats in grammar and other fields were orally created and orally preserved, through memorized sutras, for centuries.[59] The Nootka of British Columbia say that accounts of the origins of family crests and privileges are true, because transmitted in unbroken succession from the person to whom the originating experience happened.[60] When the Coos of the Oregon coast told myths in winter, those hearing repeated each sentence.[61] Such practices may support considerable stability, as may the meaningfulness of traditions to individuals. Some of the most valuable knowledge now preserved of Native American culture is due to remarkable individuals, who remained in command of a language and narrative tradition for years with no one with whom to share them. At the same time orality may permit divergent versions of events and narratives to continue side by side without prejudice, until the writing of one privileges it and disrupts.[62] In general, orality, like writing, is a means which may be shaped to a variety of ends.

VIII

Myths, then, change in response to personal desire. One may think them through out of existential need. There is satisfaction in this. There is also an element of sheer pleasure in the world and form of the myths, and the situation of telling and listening. If one has the opportunity just to be with people for whom myths and their actors have been part of imaginative life, one learns this. One evening a Wasco friend brought her aunt to a workshop my wife and I were giving on the languages, and afterwards had me read to her aunt a story she knew I had written down from someone else. "That," she said, "is her reward"—to hear the language and the form and to chuckle.

The principal "bearers of tradition," as a phrase once had it—"recreators of tradition" is more accurate—were such often because of pleasure. The last source of narrative in the Coos language of the Oregon coast, Annie Miner Peterson, survivor of many cities, occupations, and husbands, pointed out to her rapporteur, Melville Jacobs, that

> the reason she knew so many more stories than Mr. Drew [source for another linguistic anthropologist two decades before], and could tell them as well as she did, was because she enjoyed going out with the older people when they went root digging, berrying, camping out; she liked to accompany the older people in all their out of door activities. . . . There the people recounted and discussed folktales incessantly when they were drying salmon, camas digging, hunting, or camping out during travelling. Other and somewhat younger people at Yachats Reservation stayed at home more and seemed to have less attentiveness for the stories of the older people, which is why they learned fewer [of them]. (130)

The literature about myths mostly ascribes them to modes of rationalization of a natural world and social order: how a world came to be. Myths do serve ontology, social organization, ethics. A common cause of change is proliferation of a type of story for the sake of social identity. Just as mythographers in classical Greece connected a locality or town through narrative to someone mentioned in the Homeric poems, so the lineages of the Bella Coola, Bella Bella, Kwakiutl, and the like, of the North Pacific Coast, would proliferate legitimating accounts of their origin on a common model.[63] I have stressed that they not only rationalize, but explore, and for individuals as well as groups. Let me say now that there is here an evident element of desire and pleasure as well.

Probably the most familiar cause of myth is to explain something about an animal or the topography. Such are the stories perhaps most often retold for children, and the principal stuff of a long-selling anthology.[64] Myths do often enough end with explanations of why a chipmunk has stripes and bears no tail. Any location may have an account of its name.

To think of explanation only in terms of such motifs, however, is to mistake passing clouds for the sky. Myths may *enact* explanation, without such motifs, as we have seen. And beyond motifs and calculi of motive, there is a general, constitutive openness to being, a cognitive eros of the sort experienced by Tillich.[65]

The world of myth is an open world. No one narrator has knowledge of all the myths, of all that might have happened. That is why Victoria Howard can end a Clackamas myth with "Now I know only that far." It is not that there is more to the myth, it is that there may be more to the world.[66] Nothing in the nature of the world need be in principle without a story. That is why one finds myths that seem hardly myths at all. Butterball Duck's wife sings that her husband is ugly, he sings that her clitoris is short, and that is all. But that gives something of the nature of such ducks. Notes Jacobs: "All the Coos knew this little thing. It is called a myth like any myth of greater length, because it narrates an occurrence of the myth age. When a Coos saw a butterball duck he would quote the lines, sing the song and laugh merrily" (183). Cognitive eros: asking Hiram Smith the name in the language (Wasco) for, say, "otter," one gets not just a name, but where they are seen, how many, and the sliding that otters characteristically do. And so with other coinhabitants of the world. Myths inhabit a world closely observed, and enjoyed in the observing.

Such enjoyment goes with the pervasive presence of a kind of story frame. The people of the myth world gather and come forward one by one. It may be for each to sing its guardian spirit song in winter; to decide who shall be elk when the human beings come; to compete for a chief's daughter. Whatever the reason, each has a moment of activity, perhaps only a song. Conversely, a traveling protagonist may encounter plants, plants and animals as foods, trees, one by one, identify each, pronounce about it.[67] Or encounter places and rivers, and name each one. Scholarly indexes will distribute the stories that do this under different headings, according to principal actor and associated plot. But what unites and defines such framing myths cuts deeper: not a principal actor, but a category of being; not a plot, but a stage.

Repertoires may change to include more of the world. If someone tells an adventure one does not already know for a character one does know, or for a character one did not know had a story, if a pushy field-worker simply asks, "Do you know a story about . . . ?" the response is, "I never heard that one," not that there is no such story.

A living tradition incorporates new elements, as when in the Navajo origin myth, the people, coming in four stages from below the earth, bring with them the horse, or when the late Linton Winishut of Warm Springs, Oregon, elaborating the role of the trickster-transformer Coyote as prophesier of what is to come, has Coyote at one point fly over the Pacific and compares a man who carries the sun to a jet plane. Perhaps every Indian group has a story in which some old person foresaw the coming of the Whites.

A living tradition incorporates new stories. French-Canadians reached Oregon early in the nineteenth century, and at least one who married a Kalapuya woman left a fine set of stories of Petit Jean, told early in this century fluently in Mary's River Kalapuya.[68] Hiram Smith, a Wasco of Warm Springs, Oregon, directed my attention to some fine Coyote stories he hadn't heard before that had been on public television.

A living tradition changes stories so as to keep them. Mr. Smith shared with me stories that he classified as "the kind of Coyote stories Tom Brown tells" (Tom Brown was a quite elderly Warm Springs Sahaptin). No myth world, but the same trickster-transformer, coming along, who bribes his way out of a trap with dollar bills that turn into excrement when the trapper gets home. A subsequent generation has the story, with Coyote bribing an anthropologist with money and a story, the money turning into fur and dirt, the story, when he plays his tape for other professors, turning into droppings.[69]

But such change is not new, due to the impact of Whites, nor has it been incidental.

And how can one explain that reflections which might never find an audience took and kept the form of stories, for Charles Cultee, Victoria Howard, and others, except to say that narrative is a way to think the world one knows, a way that even in inner enactment is satisfying in both content and form.

Altogether, the pleasures of imaginative life and satisfying form. Not a fixed corpus, memorized and recited, though there can be that, but a genre engaging the world. A resource for imagining what must have been and, therefore, what may be, in relation to what is; a way to give experience and speculation a shape that is flexible yet certain—open at point after point to elaboration, curtailment, an even tenor or intensification, full of voices, yet ineluctably the realization overall of a finite rhetoric, one that comes round and again comes round, and can have rather a classical sound.[70] A mingling of forms and meanings that must be abstract, that must change, that must give pleasure.[71]

APPENDIX

SEAL AND HER YOUNGER BROTHER LIVED THERE

They lived there, Seal, her daughter, her younger brother.   [i](A)
I don't know how long, now a woman got to Seal's younger brother.
They lived there.   (B)
    They would go outside in the evening.
The girl would say,   5
    she would tell her mother,
        "Mother! Something is different about my uncle's wife.
        It sounds just like a man when she 'goes out.'"
"Shush! Your uncle's wife!"
A long long time they lived there like that.   10 (C)
    In the evening each would "go out."
Now she would tell her,
        "Mother! Something is different about my uncle's wife.
        When she 'goes out' it sounds just like a man."
"Shush!"   15
Her uncle, his wife, would lie down up above on the bed.   [ii](A)
Pretty soon the other two would lie down close to the fire,
    they would lie down beside each other.
I don't know when at night, something comes on to her face.   (B)
She shook her mother,   20
    she told her:
"Mother! Something comes on to my face."
"Mmmm. Shush. Your uncle, they (two) are 'going.'"
Pretty soon now again, she heard something escaping,   (C)
She told her,   25
    Mother! Something is going t'úq t'úq [dripping].
    I hear something."
"Shush. Your uncle, they are 'going.'"

The girl got up,   [iii](a)
    she fixed the fire,   30
        she lit pitch,
            she looked where the two were:
                Ah! Ah! Blood!
She raised her light to it, so: (b)

her uncle is on his bed,   35
   his neck cut,
      he is dead.
         She screamed.
She told her mother,   (c)
   "I told you,   40
      'Something is dripping.'
   You told me,
      'Shush, they are 'going.'"
   I had told you,
      'Something is different about my uncle's wife.   45
      She would "go out,"
         with a sound just like a man she would urinate'
   You would tell me,
      'Shush!'"
She wept.   50
Seal said,   (d)
   "Younger brother! My younger brother!
   They [house-posts] are valuable standing there.
   My younger brother!"
      She kept saying that.   55
As for that girl, she wept.   (e)
She said:
   "In vain I tried to tell you,
      'Not like a woman,
      With a sound just like a *man* my uncle's wife would urinate.' 60
   You told me,
      'Shush!'
   Oh oh my uncle!
   Oh my uncle!"
      She wept, that girl.   65

NOTES

1. Wallace Stevens, *Transport to Summer* (New York, 1947), pp. 115–48.
2. John Miles Foley, *The Theory of Oral Composition: History and Methodology* (Bloomington, Ind., 1988). The limitations of its extension to Anglo-Saxon poetry are commented upon by Jeff Opland, *Anglo-Saxon Oral Poetry: A Study of the Tradition* (New Haven, 1980), ch. 1. Some of the recent New World work can

be seen in my *"In Vain I Tried to Tell You"*: *Essays in Native American Ethnopoetics* (Philadelphia, 1981); Dennis Tedlock, *The Spoken Word and the Work of Interpretation* (Philadelphia, 1983), and *Recovering the Word,* ed. Brian Swann and Arnold Krupat (Berkeley, 1987).

3. Walter Ong, *Orality and Literacy* (London, 1982).

4. A fact discussed forty-five years ago by the linguist and folklorist Melville Jacobs, *Kalapuya Texts* (Seattle, 1945), pp. 6–7. Cf. Dell Hymes, *Foundations in Sociolinguistics* (Philadelphia, 1974), p. 192, n. 4.

5. Robert Alter, *The Art of Biblical Narrative* (New York, 1981), pp. 184, 17; hereafter cited in text.

6. "Seal and Her Younger Brother Lived There." The text was told in 1930 in the Clackamas Chinook language of the Willamette Valley of Oregon by the last speaker of that language, Victoria Howard, to the anthropologist Melville Jacobs. It is discussed in chs. 8 and 9 of *"In Vain I Tried to Tell You."* (Ch. 9 is revised from an article entitled "Discovering Oral Performance and Measured Verse in American Indian Narrative," *New Literary History* 8 [1977]: 431–57.) I will refer to the text several times, and this presentation and discussion go beyond what has been previously published. The fact that continued reading does not exhaust the text may itself be an indication of a quality that is literary.

7. "Grizzly Bear and Black Bear Ran Away with the Two Girls," in Melville Jacobs, *Clackamas Chinook Texts,* 1 (Bloomington, Ind., 1958).

8. "Panther and Owl," in Franz Boas, *Kathlamet Texts* (Washington, D.C., 1901). But in a Koyukon Athapaskan myth (Alaska), shared with me by Eliza Jones, the beaver asks a young woman who has fallen to the bottom of the river about each of four body parts only to be sure that she is all right.

9. "Sun's Myth," in Boas, pp. 26–33. The scene is evidently inverse to a type in which young men ask their grandmother to whom salmon spears and other fishing gear belong, and when told they are hers, know she lies ("The Otter Brothers Recover Their Father's Heart," in Edward Sapir, *Takelma Texts* [Philadelphia, 1909]).

10. See the discussion of Philip Kachlamat's telling of "Coyote's People Sing," in ch. 3 of *"In Vain I Tried to Tell You."*

11. Not that it is absent. Chinookan speakers make good use of consonantal changes that express augmentative versus diminutive. When Coyote borrows the wrapped-around penis of an old man, he attaches the latter's *i-galxix* (large) to his *i-k'alxix* (small).

12. Philip Kachlamat, a Wishram Chinook speaker, told it to me in the Rainbow Cafe above the Deschutes one evening in the summer of 1956. See *"In Vain I Tried to Tell You,"* pp. 87–91, 203–8.

13. See my "Bungling Host, Benevolent Host: Louis Simpson's 'Deer and

Coyote,'" *American Indian Quarterly* 8 (Summer 1984): 171–98, for "Benevolent Host" as part of the name of a type that has been called simply "Bungling Host."

14. See my "Anthologies and Narrators," in *Recovering the Word,* pp. 68–75.

15. To be sure, I believe another myth is sequel to this, one in which another daughter overcomes the Grizzly Woman who comes to her father, a chief. See "Grizzly Woman Began to Kill Them," in *"In Vain I Tried to Tell You,"* ch. 10.

16. See ch. 4 of *"In Vain I Tried to Tell You."* I have since revised the account of acts 2 and 3.

17. See my "Particle, Pause and Pattern in American Indian Narrative Verse," *American Indian Culture and Research Journal* 4, no. 4 (1980): 7–51. The text was recorded by Dennis Tedlock and published in his *Finding the Center* (New York, 1972; Lincoln, Neb., 1978).

18. In the next stanza, to be sure, he sees a very little bit of flame, takes the flame, builds a fire. But he has seen the flame already; that is why he dries his tears.

19. Michael Riffaterre, *Fictional Truth* (Baltimore, 1990), pp. xiv–xv; hereafter cited in text.

20. See Virginia Hymes, "Warm Springs Sahaptin Narrative Analysis," in Joel Sherzer and Anthony C. Woodbury, *Native American Discourse: Poetics and Rhetoric* (Cambridge, 1986), pp. 62–102, and our book on such patterns in English narrative, being prepared for Mouton.

21. Kenneth Burke, "Psychology and Form," *The Dial* 79 (July 1925): 34–46; reprinted in his *Counter-Statement* (New York, 1931; Berkeley, 1968).

22. Burke, pp. 34–46.

23. See the last section of my "Two Types of Linguistic Relativity," in *Sociolinguistics,* ed. W. Bright (Berlin, 1966).

24. See my "Language, Memory, and Selective Performance: Cultee's 'Salmon Myth' as Twice-told to Boas," *Journal of American Folklore* 98 (1985): 391–434.

25. See detailed comparison in chs. 3 and 6 of *"In Vain I Tried to Tell You."*

26. The sequence is analyzed in my "Anthologies and Narrators." Versions of the last episode are recorded from many narrators, but none say how the tip can still be Coyote's, once he has added the old man's penis to his own. The later recovery of his own tip would seem to require adding the old man's instrument like extra lengths of hose behind a nozzle. Often enough the old man is said to feed his penis constantly with wood chips. Sometimes such a version has Coyote forced to trade back, simply because the voraciousness wears him out. Always, however, a tip inside the girl is simply stuck, not calling for food. Evidently the point of the penis depends on the point of the story.

27. Livingston Farrand and Bettina Kahnweiler, *Traditions of the Quinault Indians* (New York, 1902), pp. 85 ff.

28. The idiomatic phrases "I don't know at what time" and "I don't know when at night" consist of the stem "to think," used as uninflected particle, and a compound adverb, "how / what—with reference to time," plus in one case a postposition for "when" and in the other the noun "night." See below on their use in the appended text with regard to Greimas's semiotic square.

29. I echo the language used by Riffaterre (*Fictional Truth,* pp. 32–33) in analyzing a passage from Trollope's *Barchester Towers.* To be sure, Victoria Howard does not speak in her own voice, as Trollope does in his, but the remonstrance, unique in all known versions of related myths, is hers.

30. Boas, *Kathlamet Texts,* pp. 26–33. Cf. n. 9 and my "Folklore's Nature and the Sun's Myth," *Journal of American Folklore* 88 (1975): 345–69.

31. See my "Bungling Host, Benevolent Host."

32. Cf. ch. 8 of my *"In Vain I Tried to Tell You,"* pp. 286–91.

33. Cf. Leslie Spier, *Wishram Ethnography* (Seattle, 1930), p. 262.

34. Cf. Alter, *The Art of Biblical Narrative:* "As a rule, when a narrative event in the Bible seems important, the writer will render it mainly through dialogue, so the transitions from narration to dialogue provide in themselves some implicit measure of what is deemed essential" (p. 182).

35. See my "Victoria Howard's 'Gitskux and His Older Brother': A Clackamas Chinook Myth," in *Smoothing the Ground,* ed. Brian Swann (Berkeley, 1983), pp. 129–70; cf. pp. 155–56.

36. The myths concerned with revenge against women are (a) "Grizzly and Black Bear Ran Away with the Two Girls," then (b) "Grizzly Woman Killed People." The myths concerned with being a wife are (c) "Grizzly and Black Bear Ran Away with the Two Girls," then (d) "Gitskux and His Older Brother." The order of narration in her work with Jacobs was (c) (notebook 6), (d) (notebook 12), (a) (notebook 14–15), (b) (notebook 15). In other words, first the second of each pair, then the first of each pair. The four texts (abcd) are in Jacobs, *Clackamas Chinook Texts,* 1, 2, as no. 17, pp. 156–66; no. 34, pp. 315–21; no. 14, pp. 130–41; no. 16, pp. 143–56, respectively.

37. A. J. Greimas and Joseph Courtès, "The Cognitive Dimension of Narrative Discourse," *New Literary History* 7 (1976): 433–47; Gerald Prince, *Dictionary of Narratology* (Lincoln, Neb., 1987), pp. 85–86.

38. In strict chronological contrast, *na-* would indicate past of about a day ago, but does not do so here. The tense prefixes within the girl's remonstrance show as much. In the third verse of the final scene, the girl says "I told you" twice with the tense prefix *i-,* indicating action earlier in the same diurnal period. She next says "I had told you" with the prefix *ni-* and the direction marker *t-,* indicating action over a period earlier than that, but (because of the *t-*) nearer rather than farther back. She then confirms the implication of a period of time

by using the future, "You would tell me . . ." Her second remonstrance has only the *i-* of the immediate past.

In sum, the quoted narration of what has happened makes precise reference on either side of "yesterday," the meaning of *na-* if taken as part of a chronological series. "Yesterday" makes no sense in relation to these motivated indications of relative time.

Evidently *na-* has another significance here. Its use in other texts and in elicited forms shows that it does have reference to the past, and here it at least indicates a lessening of the distance indicated by *ga-* (the most remote marker). In narratives *na-* is favored by intransitive verbs of personal state such as "weep" and "think" (a point investigated by Robert E. Moore; see Robert E. Moore, "How Coyote Thinks: Exploration of a Narrative and Linguistic Option in Upper Chinookan." B.A. thesis, 1980, Reed College, Portland, Ore., and "An Optional Form and Its Patterning in Kiksht Narratives: Semantics, Metapragmatics, Poetics," Working Papers for the 17th International Conference on Salish and Neighboring Languages, 9–11 Aug. 1982, Portland State University.) But it is not required by such or restricted to them. The key would appear to be that the shape *na-* is an old marker of location in the language family. There is reason to think that in the set of initial tense-prefixes it may retain a sense of aspect as well as of tense, of "where" as well as "when." Its use here may have a sense simply of location in past time, perhaps with a sense of states that endure as well as occur: she will continue to be up (l. 29), to weep (ll. 50, 56, 65), to say (ll. 51, 55, 57) (but not fix fire, light pitch, look, raise her light, scream).

39. Cf. Alter, *The Art of Biblical Narrative:* "When does the dialogue break off sharply, withholding from us the rejoinder we might have expected from one of the two speakers?" (p. 183).

40. Although in the last volume of his four (n. 58), sometimes taking details out of context and misrepresenting them. See discussion at the end of my "Anthologies and Narrators" and the beginning of my "Language, Memory and Selective Performance."

41. Working with myths told by Philip Kachlamat in the spring of 1933, I thought at first that one, involving an alternation of languages, was unique. Then a Quileute myth came to attention, then a Tsimshian in a new collection, then a Kalapuya. This last reminded me that everything must be used. It was not obtained in the Indian language, and it was obtained by a person scholars put down as a popularizer of limited understanding. But here was unique testimony, not recorded by the anthropologists who had worked with the very same narrator, helping to illuminate a newly recognized semantic field.

42. Cf. *"In Vain I Tried to Tell You,"* pp. 111–15.

43. Among Indian people someone in the audience, perhaps the audience as

a whole, would respond with a certain sound ([*i* . . .] among Sahaptin-speakers in Oregon and Washington). A decline in that sound, or its absence, would let the narrator know the audience to be losing interest, falling asleep. When George Forman, a Wishram living at Yakima, did not recall a story, he would not say he had not heard it, but that he had fallen asleep when it was told.

44. For recent surveys of the work begun by Milman Parry and Albert Lord, see Foley, *The Theory of Oral Composition.*

45. Cf. Stuart H. Blackburn, *Singing of Birth and Death: Texts in Performance* (Philadelphia, 1988); S. H. Blackburn et al., *Oral Epics in India* (Berkeley, 1989); Peter Metcalf, *Where Are You, Spirits? Style and Theme in Berawan Prayer* (Washington, D.C., 1989); M. Mills, *Rhetorics and Politics in Afghan Traditional Storytelling* (Philadelphia , 1991); D. Reynolds, "The Interplay of Genres in Oral Epic Performance: Differentially Marked Discourse in a Northern Egyptian Tradition" (Cambridge, Mass., in press); Joel Sherzer, *Kuna Ways of Speaking* (Austin, Tex., 1983, 1990); and the general discussion in Richard Bauman and C. L. Briggs, "Poetics and Performance as Critical Perspectives on Language and Social Life," *Annual Review of Anthropology* 19 (1990): 59–88.

46. T. F. McIlwraith, *The Bella Coola Indians* (Toronto, 1948).

47. See the discussion of Philip Kachlamat's telling of "Coyote's People Sing," in ch. 3 of *"In Vain I Tried to Tell You."*

48. See "Coyote and Badger," in M. A. R. Barker, *Klamath Texts* (Berkeley, 1963), and my "Anthologies and Narrators." Mr. Hartless, like other Kalapuya narrators, knew also a sequence in which Coyote loses his eyes by throwing them out of a tree in which he is trapped in winter. The sequel is that he finds where people are gambling with them and gets them back. The sunny setting of this scene may serve to contrast it and its sequel (imitation eyes) with the other.

49. Cf. R. Brightman, "Tricksters and Ethnopoetics," *International Journal of American Linguistics* 55 (1989): 179–203.

50. Perhaps remembered between performances, perhaps constructed. Either way, after telling the story in 1891, Cultee continued to think about it, although having no way of knowing he would be asked to tell it again. The case shows that interpretation should not separate narrative content from poetic form, or, as so often the case with Native American narratives, neglect poetic form.

51. *Maker* is not an ideal term, but "author" will not do, for narrators did not think of themselves as authors in the sense of personal originators, and the verb that goes with "myth" in Chinookan is "make."

52. One early term for Whites, because of their extraordinary nature, used the stem for "nature," -*k'ani*. On myth as interpretation of history, cf. *Rethinking History and Myth: Indigenous South American Perspectives on the Past,* ed. Jonathan D. Hill (Urbana, Ill., 1988), and Paul R. Sullivan, *Unfinished Conversations: Mayas and Foreigners between Two Wars* (New York, 1989).

53. Michael H. Jameson, "Mythology of Ancient Greece," in *Mythologies of the Ancient World*, ed. Samuel Noah Kramer (Garden City, N.Y., 1961), p. 234.

54. C. S. Lewis, *The Discarded Image: An Introduction to Medieval and Renaissance Literature* (Cambridge, 1964, 1967), pp. 204–11.

55. Earlier, Whites found Coyote stories disgusting. Enlightened people now find them funny. Neither univocal response does justice to the moral complexity of the tradition and its enactments.

56. Cf. Dell Hymes, "The Methods and Tasks of Anthropological Philology (Illustrated with Clackamas Chinook)," *Romance Philology* 19 (1965): 325–40.

57. On continuation of myth as selection in history, see Hans Blumenberg, *Work on Myth* (Frankfurt am Main, 1979; Cambridge, Mass., 1985).

58. Claude Lévi-Strauss, *Mythologiques*, I–IV (Paris, 1964–71).

59. Cf. F. Staal, "The Independence of Rationality from Literacy," *European Journal of Sociology* 30 (1989): 301–10.

60. Susan Golla, who is engaged in an extended analysis of such accounts, many of them recorded many years ago by Edward Sapir and still unpublished, made this point in a talk at the University of Virginia.

61. Melville Jacobs, *Coos Myth Texts* (Seattle, 1940): "It was expected that child auditors, if not older people, repeat in unison each phrase or sentence verbatim after the raconteur. 'They kept on telling it until the children got it right. They wanted them to have it right. They did not want them to get it mixed up and "lie" when they told it' (Annie Miner Peterson)" (p. 130; hereafter cited in text). When told to adults only, just one auditor repeated each sentence verbatim. This is an aspect of conversational etiquette: the person spoken to usually if not always repeated verbatim what was said to him.

62. I owe this point to Dennis Demert.

63. Thus Franz Boas, *Bella Bella Tales* (New York, 1932), writes that "the desire for privilege and for the authorization of privilege is a source of the exuberant diversification of Kwakiutl mythology" (p. viii). Cf. McIlwraith, *The Bella Coola Indians*.

64. Ella Elizabeth Clark, *Indian Legends of the Pacific Northwest* (Berkeley, 1953).

65. Paul Tillich, *Biblical Religion and the Search for Ultimate Reality* (Chicago, 1955), p. 72.

66. See my "Discovering Oral Performance," in *"In Vain I Tried to Tell You,"* pp. 322–27, 330–31.

67. Not that a narrator would wish to exploit the possibility to the limit. A frame widespread in the Pacific Northwest is one in which in the course of a myth a protagonist questions trees and shrubs one after the other. If the answer is favorable to the questioner, they are rewarded by a pronouncement as to how they will be useful to the human beings who are about to come; if not, not.

Relating a Nehalem Tillamook myth of two Wild Women asking tree after tree how well they looked, Clara Pearson, after thirteen trees, concluded "That is ended. That is enough. It is too tiresome. They asked too many things, grass, dirt, rocks, everything" (Elizabeth Derr Jacobs, *Nehalem Tillamook Tales,* ed. Melville Jacobs [Eugene, Ore., 1959], p. 150; 2d ed. Corvallis, Ore., 1990).

68. By a superb narrator, William Hartless, recorded in 1914 by L. F. Frachtenberg, and edited by Jacobs in *Kalapuya Texts,* pp. 275–85.

69. B. Toelken, Foreword to *Giving Birth to Thunder, Sleeping with His Daughter: Coyote Builds North America,* by Barry H. Lopez (Kansas City, 1977), pp. xi–xii.

70. With apologies to Wallace Stevens, "The Pleasures of Merely Circulating," in *The Man with the Blue Guitar* (New York, 1937, 1952), p. 168.

71. Reflecting on this essay, I realize, that its concerns, and the concerns of those whose narratives it is about, fit naturally with what Kenneth Burke thought and wrote about more than fifty years ago—vocabularies of motive, attitudes toward history, orientations, frames of acceptance (and rejection) caught up in history, actors acting in terms both of a sense of piety (what goes with what) and categories essentially poetic (comedy, plaint, burlesque, tragedy), and that it ought not to be a surprise, having been his student for nearly forty years. (Cf. Kenneth Burke, *Permanence and Change* [New York, 1935; Berkeley, 1984), and *Attitudes Toward History* [New York, 1937; Berkeley, 1984]).

7

LITERARY INVENTION, CRITICAL FASHION, AND THE IMPULSE TO THEORETICAL CHANGE: "OR WHETHER REVOLUTION BE THE SAME"

෴

Murray Krieger

I. DIALOGUE

THE DESIRE TO UNIVERSALIZE OUR EXPERIENCE, to affirm the unity of *being* over the ever-changing variety of *becoming,* is as old as the philosophic urge, an urge we have known since the dawn of humanity as thinking creatures. Trapped within what our own experience permits us to see, we retain the need—as old as Plato's in his war against the Sophists—to try to account for what we must believe is outside those limits, ready to be experienced by everyone. But the philosophic urge in us seems opposed by what Bergson saw as the temporal flow of our experience, which is constantly differentiating itself, except that the universalizing impulse wants to prevent us from seeing that differentness. So we tend to reify the common elements we presume to find, treating them as universals that enable us to freeze the ever-changing flow of experience, and then we congratulate ourselves for our philosophic perspicacity.

But this universalizing is exclusively spatial because the very notion of time and its changes is enemy to the desire of our intellect to contain and give structure to the varieties of historical experience. Indeed, the intrusion of a precise and discriminating historical consciousness has long been

179

a deconstructive act, because in introducing change it gives the lie to our universalizing ambition by relativizing it, that is, by subjecting it to its place within our necessarily partial and contingent perspective. Change thus makes of our universal claims no more than creatures of our historically determined needs; it reduces theoretical grandeur, built on a single, time-defying, all-inclusive structure, to the culture-bound relativism of permanent revolution. In the realm of pure temporality it is as hard to clutch at a constant as it was way back in the realm of paradox ruled by Zeno. For when it comes to our grasping at solid things, the realm of temporality *is* the realm of paradox.

To the extent that our theoretical ambition is undercut by the historical persistence of change, we must see universal claims downgraded from the truths we attribute to nature to the deluding reifications projected by the partisan interests of historically conditioned institutions and their agents. So change replaces theory, institutional sway replaces nature. And the language of theory, for all its ambition, is seen as responsive only to its self-serving assumptions rather than to the external data it pretends disinterestedly to account for. It can be treated, then, as just another expression of an archive preserved by its moment in history; it is not permitted to step outside that archive even long enough to explain either that moment in history or anything else. Where all is historically contained and controlled, there change will reign, an enemy to all universals but itself. Of course, the claim that change is the only universal is a self-denying one in that the dynamics of change should not allow even that single universality, since that would acknowledge a sameness about change. Still, our time-bound condition seems to encourage us to affirm change, in all its ever-changingness, as the only timeless truth we would, though with some embarrassment, allow to stand.

I have been assuming an either / or relationship between theory and change—to admit one is to exclude, even preclude, the other; but one could seek to bridge this disjunction by proposing a theory *of* change, such as the theory of progress or of cyclic repetition. There is a special temptation to absorb history's moments within one narrative form or another. But I would put aside such proposals by pointing out that they *are* simply other theories, disguised versions of spatial thinking constructed out of closed, all-encompassing metaphors.

It is hardly new to observe the scholar's necessary habit—because he has a theory—of converting history's accidents into pattern. Once it has happened, history does appear irreversible. I prefer to treat change more radically, as a temporal particular that represents the errant moment in its momentous potential to disrupt the formation rules that govern all theories, antihistorical theories as well as theories of history.

Words themselves are major perpetrators of our self-deceiving habit of reifying our experience, freezing its temporality into their own ontological space. Their very being militates in favor of theory and against a fluid experience. The substantives we use, with their deceiving implication that one word represents one thing, suggest constants beyond history's changes. Even as we may describe radical changes from one historical moment to another, we retain the generic noun and with it the sense that it is a common, *essentially* unchanging entity that is undergoing minor, though untransforming, alteration. If we ask, "What is it that changes?" the language of the question itself persuades us to a single, constant "it," whether it be "art" or "the aesthetic" or "poetry" or "drama" or "fiction" or whatever, as we allow the nominal subjects to trick us into essentializing them. It may be, as some poststructuralists might argue, that the generic term, representative of a static nominalism of language, has indeed induced us into a false essentialism, so that we have, not the changing single entity (the "it") we think we are talking about, but only a constantly shifting field of differences which we carelessly mislabel as if it were one thing.

Still, the theoretical impulse in us persists and need not be altogether denied. Our discourse requires those very universals that may render that discourse untrustworthy because it blurs the facts of change. Nevertheless we can, in our antinominalistic desperation, point to the fact that culture *does* function and establish its continuity by means of the verbal genres it holds onto in spite of the shiftings of time. Culture takes its generic nouns seriously, even literally; it allows those generic nouns, as its linguistic norm, to shape its development: from the inside, culture uses its myths to function and to produce more culture. These are effects that the historian and the theorist must take account of, regardless of what the demythologizer may persuade us is really going on outside the comforts of those productive, if deceiving, constructs.

But I have now, by way of language, moved these issues into the realm of literary history and literary theory, and in no area is the conflict between continuity and revolution, between the designs of theory and the randomness of invention, more evident. Seen from the ambitions that give rise to it, literary theory exists to create a discursive unity that can accommodate history's variety, to synchronize the diachronic. Making transhistorical claims, literary theory seeks systematically to account for a broad variety of works of many periods and literatures, flattening out the changes—even the apparent revolutions—that may occur among them. Until recently, without self-questioning, literary theory has traditionally assumed that there *is* literature, and thus that there are peculiarly literary works; that consequently there is a legitimate discourse that creates a system to illuminate the performance of each of these works and— by extrapolation—of that body of works lumped together as what we create as our literary canon. Critical discourse and theoretical discourse about criticism were thus legitimized, and the criteria for our judging the relative value of this discourse rested upon those secure assumptions concerning the primacy of those literary works to which such secondary critical discourse or tertiary theoretical discourse was ultimately to be beholden.

But these so-long-secure assumptions have been not only put in question but utterly undermined in recent years. Instead of judging the face-value claims made by rival aesthetic systems to account with consistency for the special kind of writing to which they were responsible, we are to see these claims as contingent upon other than theoretical objectives. There has been a shift in emphasis from questions about the *inside* of theory—What does it account for? What does it leave out? Does it, in the relations among its terms and propositions, argue acceptably?—to questions, apparently from *outside,* that put in doubt the theoretical enterprise itself: What are the pressures leading to the position taken? What is the relation between its principles and its favored literary works? What nontheoretical subtext leads it to the critical judgments it asks us to make? In other words, what are its historical contingencies, however transhistorical it wants its claims to be?

This shift reflects the recent transfer of interest from what we have called *literary* theory to what is today—after the Frankfurt School—called *critical* theory. The earlier secure ambitions of literary theory have been turned problematic by the critical theorist who deconstructs it by exposing its contingencies. But as we gave vent to that deconstructive impulse, which I have here related to our consciousness of temporality, we created a theoretical discourse beyond what we had earlier thought of as theoretical discourse—a metatheoretical discourse, the only discourse that is now allowed to be genuinely theoretical. From this high ground we could view earlier so-called theories as bivouacked within their unchallenged parochial assumptions, assumptions that now could be demonstrated to be historically or linguistically or institutionally contingent; they could no longer be assumed without self-deception, the self-deception of a pretheoretical naïveté. (For example, a movement that thought itself as theoretical as the New Criticism did can now be declared untheoretical in that it failed to undermine itself by acknowledging its own extra-theoretical motives.) So *critical* theory (or metatheory) these days, perhaps in imitation of what the critical philosophy of Hume and Kant did to the metaphysics of the eighteenth century, means to put what we previously thought of as theory out of business by ungrounding it. And what we used to think of as "extraneous" issues, as issues irrelevant to the theoretical project, become those that are central to our concern.

Theory, then, is no longer to be treated as an insular, self-directed enterprise. Of the many kinds of pressures (social, political, literary, or whatever) that help shape what may masquerade as the pristine theoretical claim, rendering it anything but pristine, I would like to concentrate upon the influence of literary fashion in creating critical fashion, upon the role of literary invention in helping to justify critical invention. Literary and critical fashions can be interrelated, and their recent sequence traced, even as we seek to avoid an easy overall narrative for them. Since I earlier ruled out the assimilation of change—and hence of changing fashions—to an all-consuming theory of history structured according to any myth of progress, I must treat them—without hindsight—as a sequence of wayward accidents, each subject only to local forces and not to a rationalized, timeless pattern. In our present theoretical context, it is not impertinent, or an indulgence in idle academic gossip, to concern ourselves with fashion and, consequently, with the politics of criticism and even the imperialism of critical movements, along with their invented theoretical justifications.

Indeed, we can look at the history of recent criticism—especially as it is related to the privileging of one or another kind of literary work—as a succession of would-be empires, movements that have gone through similar stages in their rise and—too soon thereafter—their fall. If we take the word *movement* literally, in thinking of literary and critical movements, we find in it this group commitment to change, to forgo rest for activity itself. This need of a movement to keep moving finds itself in continuing conflict with its desire to establish itself as a dominant, unchanging institution.

Each movement, as a would-be empire, can be seen as deriving its force for change more from the kind of literary culture it wishes to bring into being than from its commitment to advance its internally directed argument toward theoretical truth. It is thus related to literary change as the latter stimulates the rise and fall of literary fashions, with a subservient literary criticism anxious to defend and expand the influence of a particular brand of literary invention. Does critical or theoretical invention follow upon literary invention in its attempt to justify it, does it anticipate literary invention, or is the relationship between the two symbiotic, the interplay of two sides of a single inventiveness? The answer to this question can hardly be determined, and in any case it is probably less important than our need to recognize the contamination of theory by the world of literary fashion.

Some years ago Emerson Marks introduced a phrase, "pragmatic poetics," that I find extraordinarily helpful.[1] Marks used the phrase to describe those poetic theories that derive much of their motivating force from the special kind of poetry they are trying to license. This seems obvious enough: one cannot know Dryden without recognizing that much of his criticism was intended to validate specific poetic styles, that his "Essay of Dramatic Poesy" was written in part to justify the changes he introduced into dramatic styles and forms. Nor can one read Wordsworth's 1800 Preface without seeing the extent to which it is meant to serve as a document in poetic politics, so that it has the pragmatic function in the end less to create a new theory than to make way for a certain kind of poetry, a kind of poetry which Wordsworth is writing and which is not being admitted into the canon, to create—in other words—room in the canon for entries like this that are otherwise likely to be rejected. In order to change the criteria for entry into the canon, one must transform the theory, because each theory authorizes the inclusion of certain works and the exclusion of others.

Early in our own century T. S. Eliot's criticism undertakes a similar task. Eliot's important essay on the Metaphysical poets, his review of the Grierson anthology, sought to persuade readers to take this anthology and these poets seriously, although room had to be made in the canon in order to justify our seeing them as having a place within it. And this was the task of Eliot's essay. So, viewed from the role it seeks to play in the history of literary taste, poetics can indeed be seen as pragmatic. Though the critic's text is apparently addressed to the solution of theoretical problems—to finding adequate and coherent descriptions of the poet's creative act or the reader's poetic experience or the poem itself resulting from the poet's act or stimulating the reader's, together with the function of all these acts in society—though the critic's text may appear to be addressed to these problems—it may actually be meant to create a taste that can sanction transformations in the kinds of poems that are written and read, to prepare poets to write them and audiences to read them. In such critical works we can glimpse the dream of literary empire.

Let me use the fortunes of the American New Criticism as a model of the history of critical empire. As I said, the movement begins by seeking to make room for a kind of poetry that until this moment has not been accepted, to authorize and justify changes that a new school of poetry is seeking to introduce. But first it has to get rid of the kind of poetry that has been the most readily accepted. So it attacks texts of that kind, as Eliot and those who followed him into the New Criticism attacked poems of the Romantics and Victorians and Edwardians and Georgians, viewing all these as a continuous, hardly changing development without a disruptive theoretical moment in it. To counter these, they reintroduced an entire school of poets, in this case the Metaphysicals, who had not been taken seriously as candidates for the canon for a long, long time. One could not take them seriously while holding the canon based on Romantic and Victorian poetic values. And for the New Critics the two kinds of poetry seem mutually exclusive. Their preferences require and are accompanied by a literary theory that justifies them. If I seem to be cynically reductive in this account of the genesis of the New Criticism, it must be remembered that I am talking now as a historian might when he looks at the succession of critical movements rather than as a theoretical scholar might when he surveys a number of rival seekers after aesthetic truth. Still the symbiotic relationship between the revolutionary developments in literature and in literary theory seems hard to deny.

We can note, for example, that one of Eliot's major doctrines is that of impersonality, the need for the poem to avoid reflecting the autobiographical poet, so that when the word "I" is used in the poem, it must be seen as referring to a dramatically conceived character rather than to the poet's person. This is just the doctrine needed to reject the one kind of poetry—the Romantic—in which the poet seems to invest himself autobiographically and immediately, without dramatic distance, in the "I" of the poem. The "I" in Shelley's lyric seems to be Percy Shelley himself and not an invented persona, just as the "I" of "Let us go then, you and I" in *Prufrock* does *not* seem to be the living, breathing T. S. Eliot. Justifying this shift is a theory of Romantic poetry in which the relationship between the "sincere" author and his poem can be utterly unproblematic, so that we can slip easily (too easily for the New Critics) from "the man who suffers" to "the mind which creates" (in Eliot's words). It is this distinction which, Eliot argues, the Modernist poet must use his medium to reestablish. Since, for this theory and the contemporary poetry that accords with it, Donne and Marvell are much more acceptable precursors than anyone who wrote in the nineteenth century (or in the eighteenth, for that matter), what must follow is a rewriting of the whole history of English poetry with a new set of heroes and a new set of villains, and with a new poetic canon emerging out of it. The first step in the creation of the critical empire has been taken—knock down the old gods to set up the new—following the model of political revolution.

This opening stage of empire is forcefully undertaken by the New Critics, as just about all authors from Milton to poets immediately preceding Eliot are newly excluded from the tradition, which, having moved through the Renaissance poets to the Metaphysicals, is seen as having been suddenly disrupted, and, after a gap of centuries, at last having its continuity restored with the coming of the Modernist poets. This radical rewriting of the history of English poetry is formalized in 1939 by Cleanth Brooks, the model New Critic. In *Modern Poetry and the Tradition,* his last chapter, "Notes for a Revised History of English Poetry," is just the revision that Eliot licenses, with everything from the beginning of Milton until the beginning of Eliot somehow a mistake, a tradition gone wrong. But with Eliot we have a refreshing of what should have been the tradition all the while, so that we can now move along with it.

The first movement of the empire, then, is the most radical one. It is youthful, it is vigorous, and it is incautious, if not—from the distance of a future moment—a little silly, but it gets the job done of putting the new empire in place of its predecessor. Only eight years after *Modern Poetry and the Tradition,* Brooks published *The Well Wrought Urn* (1947), and in this book we discover a second phase of empire. Eliot is just in the process of recanting his own attack on Milton, and Brooks is recanting many of the exclusions of his earlier book. *The Well Wrought Urn* is devoted largely to those poets who were excluded before: between the opening with Donne and the closing with Yeats, we find Milton, Pope, Gray, and even Tennyson himself. (I have overlooked Shakespeare and Herrick, poets who had always been acceptable.) Those previously excluded poets have now become candidates for *The Well Wrought Urn*. But we note that Brooks's first chapter is on John Donne and bears the title "The Language of Paradox." It sets forth a model for the striking discovery that Brooks has made: that he should not have excluded these other poets since they really were in the tradition after all, but only because, if one looks closely enough, they can be made out to be just like John Donne in being filled with paradox. The same names are now seen to have produced profoundly changed poems, though poems with the familiar titles and words.

Here is the second stage of empire: the empire relaxes, it learns to include, though always on its own terms. Those that the empire in its early vigor had turned out it now absorbs by way of a totally new reading controlled by the terms established by those privileged writers to whom those being newly admitted can be assimilated. The appearance of catholicity rests on a universal rereading, so that all literature reveals a universal sameness, a sure sign that the movement is about ready to disintegrate.

Catholicity, then, is a disguised form of hegemony: scholars working in every literary period on all sorts of poems are now enabled to find a renewed critical awareness, can write endless "reconsiderations" as the monolithic method accumulates its all-too-consistent interpretations. The ensuing weariness leads to a restlessness that will produce countermovements. We are well into the third stage, with the empire in decline. The pretenders to a successor-empire derive their motivation from the desire to restore to primacy those poems at first rejected or at least neglected and later brought back only under what subsequently appears to be the false colors of an alien standard.

In the case of the dying moments of late New Criticism, it is the need to recover Romanticism—in its unbounded vision and spirit—that stimulates first dissent and then overthrow. The year 1957, with the publication of Frye's *Anatomy of Criticism,* is properly thought of as the turning point. From this time onward there is a continuing desire for newer, revolutionary movements, although a common interest in opposing the New Criticism and recovering Romanticism is at work in them all. In order to recover Romanticism, it then seemed, one had also to recover the author, recovering consciousness as well as vision, so that in the late 1950s and early 1960s the interest in Frye is accompanied and surpassed by an interest in the "critics of consciousness." Frye and those who tried to create a school of Frye rejected the study of individual texts as micro-systems, the New Criticism's self-sufficient contexts. Instead, for them literary works were conceived of as displacements of the universal arche-types themselves, all by-products of the single quest myth of romance that assimilates all works to its universal dream. This dream, the grand collective that is literature, must be treated as the capacious haven that converts all apparently particular works into its categories.

But Frye's prodigious project, despite the efforts of the apostles that it managed momentarily to capture, was challenged almost at once by the critics represented in America by Georges Poulet. J. Hillis Miller reflects his conversion to the so-called Geneva critics from his book on Dickens onward—at least until he is in the early 1970s converted away from Pou-let and to Derrida.[2] Miller and other "critics of consciousness" are inter-ested almost exclusively in just those questions that the New Criticism would have ruled out, namely, the extent to which the work reflects au-thorial consciousness, becomes part of a phenomenological horizon, pro-jects the author's "feel" of his reality as it figures itself to him. There is a rhapsodic union among the author, the world of his work, the characters he creates, and the reader, as all pour into one great bath of consciousness. The critic ought not to distinguish for analysis the reader's experience from the author's consciousness, or either from elements in the literary work, because they all blend into one another. Such blending, such ab-sorption of represented events and characters into a fused consciousness, is characteristic of the appeal of that Romantic imagination which the New Critics had outlawed and which criticism in its wake was seeking to recover.

Shortly afterwards, structuralism, borrowed from Paris, entered the scene as the new movement. It was committed to *difference* as its govern-ing linguistic principle, and thus rejected the emphasis on identity fos-tered by consciousness critics, their bringing together of author, work, and reader into a single undifferentiated consciousness. Structuralism, in its reaction against existentialism, had to reject consciousness itself as a mystifying point of origin. The structuralist is committed to the primacy of language, so that, in his flight from origins, he sees the "I" not as a representation of authorial consciousness but only as the grammatical subject of an utterance that calls for a predicate. Instead of all verbal creation being traced to its origin in the author's *cogito,* as in Poulet, it is—as Roland Barthes would say—language itself that writes texts, so that texts are created by other texts, thanks to a notion of intertextuality that quickly turned structuralism into poststructuralism.

Each of these movements that follow the New Criticism has its own imperialistic ambitions, so that each begins by appropriating works with which it is most comfortable at the expense of others. Indeed part of the reason for the theory to press its claims is that it wants to account for the spirit of works that have been left out of the corpus associated with earlier criticism, especially the New Criticism. We know how exciting Northrop Frye is on Blake, and he should be, since it *was* his interpretation of Blake that expanded into his general critical system. The last portion of his book *Fearful Symmetry* sets up in miniature the categories out of which his *Anatomy of Criticism* will grow. So Blake is the figural subject for Frye, as will be other writers engaged in what he thinks of as the quest romance. While he deals persuasively with such writers, it is more difficult for him when he turns to Milton or to those works of Shakespeare that are less conducive subjects for him. Still, Frye and many of those who follow him put themselves in jeopardy as they move into the imperialistic stage of their enterprise, seeking to extend what works so effectively with certain literary texts to authors and works we would think of as less hospitable and trying to make them work as well. Or we may observe that Poulet seems to be writing over and over again about his ideal subjects, Proust and Mallarmé, even when his nominal subject shifts—even to as apparently alien an author as Balzac. In the transformation Poulet—with imperial confidence—works upon Balzac, all becomes misty as Poulet dissolves Balzac's heavily furnished social reality by absorbing it into an airy vision formed through his primary commitment to other writers.

I do not mean to suggest—as perhaps I have—that it was the desire to supplant and reverse the American New Criticism that got these movements going. Some of the European origins of these movements occurred without any knowledge of who the New Critics were or what they were doing. And there are ample philosophical reasons related to developments in aesthetics, as well as psychology, linguistics, and social theory to explain why these movements came along as they did and when they did. Still, on the American academic scene the adaptation of these movements for domestic use in the classroom can be related to a general and severe reaction against the New Criticism, and, even more, a reaction against its privileged texts or its rereadings of texts to make them privileged, in favor of other texts and other rereadings.

In the United States structuralism moved to poststructuralism so quickly that the structuralist vision itself almost never took hold on its own. Beginning with a widely attended international seminar on "the structuralist controversy" held in the autumn of 1966 at Johns Hopkins, the poststructuralist era had arrived. At that conference a young philosopher named Jacques Derrida, only a year before he was to publish three books which were to institutionalize deconstructionist thinking, delivered his blockbuster essay on "free play," and poststructuralist deconstruction was here before structuralist construction could finish its work. From this point most writers whom people might identify as structuralist were busy demonstrating what made them *post*structuralists as they dissociated themselves from what they saw as the somewhat mechanistic works of theorists like Genette or Todorov or Eco. The previous drift toward diagrammatic method and toward the false security of the social sciences turned another way; and to the name of Derrida the names of Michel Foucault and Jacques Lacan—a considerably older thinker suddenly now brought to center stage—were added. Foucault gave us a new way of thinking history, returning history to the structures of language that shape it in the directions toward which the rhetoric of power presses its forces. Lacan gave us a new Freud by rooting the unconscious in sign functioning.

But it was the Derridean and post-Derridean versions of deconstruction, as adapted to the literature classroom, that made the serious bid for empire, carrying many newly won followers with it. And it is not difficult to find among many of those seeking to implement this thinking the desire to license some writing that the New Criticism would not permit and that the Modernist movement in literature would not sanction. As our Modernist giants seem to call for the New Criticism as a way of getting themselves read and adequately interpreted, so the experimental post-Modern forms we encountered after the Second World War now seemed in the deconstructionists to find a theoretical justification.

We see the easy companionship of modernist literature and the New Criticism as early as the work of T. S. Eliot, their major precursor and announcer both as poet and as critic. In Eliot and in his followers Modernist poetry and the criticism that licensed it walked hand in hand.

Further, the kind of poetry being sponsored in university writing workshops and the rapid growth of the workshop as an agency for writing "official" poetry as well as novels reflected what was being called for in the English departments by the younger New Critics who had taken their place in the academy. But as the literary movement grew tired, rich with its successes, other young scholars became as tired of the so-called academic poets as they were of academic criticism, having had a surfeit of both. They were ready to welcome a kind of criticism which could license a poetry that had freed itself from what were looked upon as our most neoclassical Modernist formulas for closure.

The deconstructionist critics seemed to provide the justification for finding a new, opening voice or—what became more common as the movement grew—for imposing that newly discovered voice on those older works we thought we knew under other guises for so long. In their earlier days what happened, in effect, was that Wallace Stevens as a Modernist model was out, and William Carlos Williams as a post-Modern model was in. Similarly, the Ezra Pound associated with Eliot was out, and the Pound associated with Williams was in. That is to say, they abandoned the Modernist tradition of poetry emblematized as the well wrought urn—whether the golden bird of Byzantium or the Chinese vase of *Burnt Norton* or the jar of Tennessee. This was the tradition that developed from the French Symbolist poets through Yeats and Eliot to the late formalism of Stevens, whose poetry represents in a special way the Modernist poetic because, as the ultimate act of closure, his carefully wrought poems quite self-consciously become their own poetic. Instead, they embraced the radical post-Modern attempt to turn poetry into a much freer, looser, open association of relaxed words, not so much wrought as merely talked, and thus more closely in touch with everyday life and language. So the poetry that is sanctioned moves, as I have said, from the kind of verbal intensity found in Stevens to the casual prosaics found in Williams.

It must be conceded that in the Modernist critical movement there was—for Hillis Miller, for example—another, more Modernist version of Williams, less unfit for the company of Stevens, as later there would be another, post-Modern version of Stevens. Indeed, for Miller both Stevens and Williams are his subjects and made to serve his critical interests, at the several different stages in his theoretical development. These divergent readings of major Modernist and post-Modern voices, like the alternating emphases given to the widely varied work of Pound, help mark

out the succession of literary and theoretical moments for other poets and
for critics.

I can trace this theoretical succession more easily, with Stevens and
Williams used as respective model poets, by using Joseph Riddel as our
exemplary critic. Like Miller, Riddel had early been deeply influenced by
the work of Poulet, writing his book on Stevens out of that attachment.
Shortly after Miller, at the beginning of the 1970s, turned against Poulet
to endorse the newly discovered Derrida, Riddel followed, turning to
Williams and writing his second major book, *The Inverted Bell: Modernism
and the Counterpoetics of William Carlos Williams* (1974), in which the treatment of Williams is introduced by a lengthy and controlling chapter on
Heidegger, surely an unlikely precursor for Williams. Williams is presented as the "decentered poet" who practices "the poetics of failure" in
order to counter the poetics of Modernism. The replacement of the previously idolized Stevens by the previously neglected Williams is the expected first move toward empire. Riddel and others who share his
deconstructionist commitment now license many writers—for example,
a newly conceived Pound—and repress others.

But the second stage follows, that of imperialist expansionism, as they
rediscover (among others) Wallace Stevens himself, who, it now turns
out, is really post-Modernist more than Modernist, a riper subject for the
deconstructionist than he had been for the New Critic or (later) for the
consciousness critic. James Joyce, a Modernist superstar, similarly becomes a welcome post-Modern subject for other poststructuralist critics,
for example, for Riddel's student Margot Norris. Even Ralph Waldo
Emerson finds himself subject to Riddel's transformations. So the canon,
which is enlarged or even exploded at the start of the movement, tends
after awhile to turn out to be not so different after all, even though the
readings within it *are*. By now, in a development of this revolution that
makes it all too like the earlier revolution of the New Critics that it seeks
to undo, just about everything seems to have become grist for the deconstructionist's mill as the movement starts its decline. Examining work
after work in the infinite openness of literature, or of criticism as literature or theory itself as literature, the deconstructionist finds in the very
nature of writing the tendency to turn against itself, to suffer—through
"troping"—the necessary burdens of "erasure" and "double inscription"
(their terms) so that the deconstructionist can do his work on an immense
variety of subjects in the different writing genres throughout the several

historical periods. Through the hegemony of theory, universal sameness conquers once again, and the impatience of readers of criticism that leads to overthrow seems sure to follow. And the newly reborn social-historical critics have been waiting in the wings.

I acknowledge, however, that I have myself been guilty here of turning recent academic experience into a theory, reducing history's sequence of changing moments into the march of sameness, thereby denying each marcher's claim to be different. I have converted the temporal into the spatial structure of *my* narrative forms. For the human mind cannot allow history to unroll without projecting a form upon it: our formal, universalizing impulse would make theorists of us all. The need to proclaim the differentness brought by each agent of revolutionary change is always in conflict with the sameness of the enterprise that proclaims it. This need is also in conflict with the imperialistic desire—and hence the program— to impose this special version of differentness upon others, thus making it their sameness. There is always the temptation to allow the commitment to the phenomenon of change to freeze into the commitment to a single, privileged change in an often self-deceived attempt to universalize it.

The threat to the newness of present change by the compelling uniformity of the past reminds me of Shakespeare's Sonnet 59, the twelfth line of which, as the climax of its three quatrains, expresses succinctly the theme of this paper.

> If there be nothing new, but that which is
> Hath been before, how are our brains beguiled,
> Which, laboring for invention, bear amiss
> The second burden of a former child!
> O, that record could, with a backward look—
> Even of five hundred courses of the sun—
> Show me your image in some antique book,
> Since mind at first in character was done,
> That I might see what the old world could say
> To this composed wonder of your frame:
> Whether we are mended, or where better they,
> Or whether revolution be the same.

"Or whether revolution be the same." It is indeed a most fitting title. The proclamation that something new has occurred, in light of which nothing can ever be the same, that here is a change that transforms history, is always threatened with the grudging concession that it has happened before, with as much ardor, and just this way. The Adamic dream of a new origin, though based on the denial of older "myths of origin," has its inner irony too easily exposed. Even the specially strenuous claims of recent deconstructionism that it has undermined the ground for all previous thinking has been followed by a more skeptical awareness that sees it as a continuing element in history instead of as history's undoer.

The tendency of the self-proclaimed revolutionary to become the imperial expansionist reminds us that literary history and theory can be seen—especially these days—as slipping into the realm of the fashionable. Indeed, my own earlier reduction of theory to the contingencies of its extratheoretical motives has emphasized the dependence of theory on the historical march of changing fashions. It is this march to which I have already denied the rationalization of a progressive shape. Each new fashion, undermining theory as a stabilizing force by privileging only the latest and disruptive change, leads to the idolatry of the new, especially the new-as-revolutionary, as the changer, though by now our skepticism should keep us from thinking it necessarily, or even probably, better than what it seeks to replace.

Probably it was the New Criticism that initiated this obsession with being fashionable some decades back, just as the succession of rapidly moving theories—most of them with short lives—began only with the demise of the New Criticism. Fashion, as an extraneous but significant stimulant for theoretical allegiance, probably entered American literary institutions with the New Criticism by the late 1940s and the 1950s. That is, the New Criticism was the first of the movements to attract followers to itself as *the* fashionable movement, the movement of the moment. By the mid-1950s, large numbers of young people, often with uncritical alacrity, were jumping on the New Critical bandwagon, turning out explications by the dozens, like eggs. I suspect that was the beginning of the major role played by "fashion" in stocking movements in American criticism with followers.

The New Criticism was the last theoretical movement that enjoyed the great good fortune of having no important theoretical competitor on the scene, perhaps because it was the first American critical movement that meant to found itself on an explicit, though often poorly formulated, theory. To be sure, there were early versions of Freudianism and Marxism

that offered themselves as alternatives, but these—in the early forms that
marked their entry into literary criticism—pretty well wiped themselves
out by being rather superficial and often simplistic in their claims and
their readings. They are not to be confused with recent, theoretically
serious uses of Freudianism and Marxism that coexist with poststructuralism and have become important participants in the theoretical debates.
But their earlier versions were hardly competitive. So the New Criticism
had the scene pretty much to itself and exercised a dominion that for years
brought aboard it (or behind it) larger and larger numbers of derivative
scholar-critics. The major arguments then used against the New Criticism
were, almost entirely, arguments against theoretically based criticism itself, usually in the name of historical scholarship or social relevance,
rather than arguments for an alternative theory.

Once past the New Criticism, perhaps we felt instinctively that we had
made a mistake by trusting in one movement so long and so fully without
any competitor. That may be one reason why we have, after the New
Criticism, changed allegiances so often during the recent succession of
movements I have been tracing here. A more likely reason is that once
theory, having been introduced for the first time to an American academic
audience, found itself in the academy, it began to pursue its concerns with
such intensity that, inevitably, a considerable variety of competing theoretical kinds was to replace the relative hegemony of the single theory
that the New Criticism represented. Once, thanks to the New Criticism,
the Pandora's box of critical theory was opened, we became too over-
whelmed by the flood of questionings and self-questionings for a single
set of answers to satisfy very many for very long.

So either we learned not to be so monolithic in our theory and thus
sponsored an increasing variety of competing theories, or our increasing
interest in theory simply prompted more and more varied theoretical proposals to vie for supremacy. Or both, Whichever the case, since the decline of the New Criticism there has been this rapid succession of
competing movements. Only a very few years ago many of us believed
that finally a movement had thrust itself upon us—the first since the New
Criticism—that might claim as general a following and as unquestioned
a dominance, however vocal its antagonists. I am speaking, of course, of
the deconstructionists, represented in the United States most vividly by
the so-called Yale School.

It did seem for awhile that deconstruction might well achieve the kind of broadly based following and lasting control that would permit it a reign that would last a little while, even if not as long as the New Criticism did in our earlier innocence. This succession was made the more ironic since some antagonists presently accuse the Yale deconstructionists of domesticating Jacques Derrida's practice of deconstruction—subjecting it to the Western literary canon and to American pedagogical habits— thereby turning it into a newer, if more reckless, version of the New Criticism. However, those expectations of an extended period of dominance by deconstruction were short-lived, because it has now become clear that it does not sustain anything like the sway that the New Criticism had: having barely arrived, it is already, I think, showing signs of being on its way out, even in the United States, which has held onto it longer than Paris did. Right now the threatening successor is a new social criticism, sometimes referred to as New Historicism, which usually derives from the work of Michel Foucault and is sometimes reinforced by a neo-Marxism. Though Foucault clearly specifies his serious differences from Marxism, his work is seen by many Marxists as being compatible with their interests, even when they are anxious to assert their disagreements with him. These groups have been doing battle with the deconstructionists, treating the latter as lately arrived formalists trapped within textuality and hence cut off from the sources of social power. In its aggressiveness this group appears clearly to be in the ascendancy.

As we would expect from theorists so concerned with the role of power, the new historicists and their methodological allies—whether Foucaultians or neo-Marxists, or feminist versions of these—can be seen as also moving through the earlier stages of empire in accordance with my narrative model. Much of their initial energy was spent seeking to reshape the literary canon by introducing into it works previously excluded. From here they were led to question the grounds for the inclusion of all its members. They reviewed the canon in order to sensitize us anew to the role of dominant discursive formations in the shaping of its individual member-works, so that the latter are to be seen as reflections of the historical dispositions of power. Armed with these political claims, they could dispute the grounds used by our culture to support the selection of the members of the canon since these would require value criteria that were now to be rejected as politically suspect. The canon, erected on hierarchical principles, was seen as privileged by a power structure that excluded all that would challenge its dominance, so that a newly arising power could persuasively argue for introducing works previously repressed by the supporters of the canon: from feminist, minority, and Third World writings before excluded by sexist, racist, and ethnocentric pressures within the dominant culture. Now, these theorists were, presumably, not arguing for such writings to be canonized since they rejected the very notion of canonical value as an elitist deception. It would be a crucial tactical and historical error, they argued, to try to show that these excluded works shared desirable properties formerly seen only in works of the dominant culture, so that they could be admitted to the club only on the old terms. Their argument means to be far more destructive of their predecessors, all now seen as so many minor alternations within a hegemonic discourse serving a political unconscious in need of being confronted and redirected.

An egalitarian principle, on the other hand, would insist that these works be admitted for reasons of justice and the need to compensate for a political repression that previous claims of aesthetic value had served to disguise. Yet these moves have been following an imperial strategy like the one I suggested for the others: they begin by reshaping the list of works to be read and studied, and then, with an expanding ambition, enlarge upon the arguments for this reshaping in order to reread all the texts in the canon, re-creating them to accord with a universal claim that would change the way we approach all texts by revealing the primacy of the political unconscious. Of course, there seem to be reasons to think that the New Historicism represents a movement more revolutionary than previous ones because it would undermine all the distinctions that allowed those others to vie with one another, seeing them all as trivial distinctions, inconsequential varieties within a middle-class series of competitive dances now unmasked by historicist analysis. But we have before seen such radical claims of total deconstruction (of all that preceded) appear from the distance of time as less than utterly disruptive after all. Rather than the undoer of previous theories, then, this one, too, may turn out to be only another competing theory to join the ever-enlarging dialogue.

So the conflicts among divergent critical theories in the United States continue, and we are not likely again to have a generally recognized commanding doctrine for an extended period of time. Too many of our younger would-be theorists, anxious to be in fashion, do not know which way to jump, or for how long. They too often try to be sure that it is onto the latest thing moving. Thus I have been led to take that word *fashion* seriously, however trivial it seems, because the trivial *is* serious in this matter so long as one is trying to record the history of contemporary critical theory in the American academy, in which fashion, and the idea of the new, have become important motivating forces.

Yet our recent concern with whether a particular critical perspective is in "fashion" makes us argue over whether it is "new" or whether it used to be "new" but now is old, whether it has been superseded by a perspective that is "newer," and whether the perspective I am about to pull out of my pocket is "newest" of all. It is amusing—but, I fear, more than that too—to observe the failure of self-consciousness and of historical awareness in our critical theorists or historians of theory as they throw about that adjective *new* in dealing with the "old New Criticism," the "newer criticism," or—as some defenders of the Yale School (or those who would already claim to succeed them) sometimes use the phrase—the "newest criticism." The adjective can be thus thrown about as if the user were not fated to live long enough to watch it fade, with the passage of time, into a joke that history helps to make upon itself. At earlier moments in the history of criticism, other movements of course have thought of themselves as new and even called themselves "new." But it is self-evident that only the failure of a historical perspective could permit the pursuit of being fashionable—the latest thing going—to sanction the absurd appellation "new" that history must render vulnerable almost as soon as it is uttered. Only because what we used to think of as the "New Criticism" is now old is it necessary for its successors to be thought of as "newer" or, most absurdly of all, as "newest."

The use of the qualifier *post* is at least as bizarre, if one views it within the precincts of history. *Post* has had to be invoked mainly because of the historical naïveté that permitted the use of other words, like *new,* which already represent the latest thing. But, once the latest has become only *be*lated, something must come after it in order to give the lie to the most-up-to-dateness of the word now being passed by. The *now* of the new has become *then,* in which case the new must become old. But since the word *new* is not changed, we now have to have something that is—paradoxically—post-new. Thus we have the "post–New Critical" or, more strangely, the current discussions of "post-Modernism" as our rebellious successor to "Modernism." Those literary movements, I have suggested, are accompanied by the fashionable and new doctrine of structuralism, which has been succeeded—as we all know—by the post-fashionable, post-new doctrine of poststructuralism. What sort of conception of time is required to conceive of a post-Modernism—as if Modernism were not newness enough—I find difficult to describe, although it is clear that our commitment to the pursuit of the newest fashion—in literature as in critical theory—has permitted us to use these terms without the embarrassment they ought to bring with them. Yet with the latest "newest" or the last claim of "postness," must history stop now, now that its eschatology has been announced by the superlative beyond which there is to be no further "post," nothing newer? For we must note that the prefix *pre-* is *not* in use, since there is no sign that current movements, for all their commitment to a continuing temporality, want to look beyond their own present to a future they might prepare for. After Matthew Arnold, critics have not—like him—offered to sacrifice themselves for a moment yet to come. We rather have wanted self-consummation, not mere *pre*figurings.

Here we return to the central irony for all fashionable movements at the height of their imperial power: the rejection of the past for the new, newer, newest, and post-newest is accompanied by the desire for change to have a stop with this last—very last—change. So change does indeed seek—each instance—to universalize itself. Even in its most radical undoing of the universal pretensions of theory, change manages to make a claim for its own privileged truth, applicable generally beyond the limited perspective, the time-bound contingencies it would impose on others in bringing itself into being. It is in this form that the theoretical urge persists even in its antagonist, even—that is—in spite of the antitheoretical critique which is a metatheoretical critique that would subvert this urge. And even the critic who as antitheorist would be a metatheorist, the critic who would use the contingencies of change to make the insulated objectives of theory no longer tenable, finds himself playing the theoretical game.

So whether in literature, in the theory that would accompany it, or in theory *as* literature, change is the blessed creature of invention, beyond all theories to predict; but fashion is the seductive betrayer of change, leading it into dogmatic fixity—and hence into theory—in spite of itself. Given the appetite of our theoretical urge, which victimizes would-be antitheorists as well as theorists, how could we not expect fashion, despite its dependence on temporal changes, to seek—however vainly—to bring change to a stop, to want not to be surpassed? Even the speaker in Shakespeare's sonnet, having come down to the defeatist concession, "Or whether revolution be the same," nevertheless concludes—in the spirit of the myth of progress—by affirming in the couplet the superiority of the newest arrival: "O sure I am the wits of former days / To subjects worse have given admiring praise." We can reinforce this conclusion with the stronger claims of other sonnets (Sonnet 106 is perhaps the most brilliant example) that the superiority of the latest arrival makes him an ultimate consummation, a permanent realization, the end to history:

> I see their antique pen would have express'd
> Even such a beauty as you master now.
> So all their praises are but prophecies
> Of this our time, all you prefiguring.

"Permanent revolution" has been converted to a revolution for permanence.

Whether in Shakespeare's sonnet or in theory, where the claim to continuing difference thus ends in a single model for emulation that would produce sameness, a mental construct has been put forward, beyond history's contingencies and secure against further change, with all the risks of that daring, positive act of construction. With each new movement, history is eventually revealed to have a hidden agenda, a suppressed desire for an eschatological finality realized only now. Revolutions are not fought—with all their disruptions of the past or what is now being turned into the past—only to prepare for further revolutions which would turn this privileged present also into the past.

However, as in Shakespeare's sonnet, the word *revolution* may be read another way, promising not disruption but the patterned turning of the earth itself in the circular movement suggestive of universal order. We have spoken of *revolution* only as the noun deriving from the verb *revolt;* but by etymological accident it is also the noun deriving from the related verb *revolve.* Though the act of revolting asks for no more than one turn—one reversal—it may be seen as but a part of a larger revolving that goes beyond by bringing the turns around, and turning yet again—and again. However paradoxically, *revolt* and *revolve* may each equally claim the noun *revolution* as its own—or rather the noun *revolution* may be seen as encompassing both, absorbing the disruption of one into the larger continuity of the other.

So *revolution* may, in spite of itself, be converted into the routine, taming change by taking its *dis*continuity out of it. Where *revolution* in this sense is found to be "the same," there theory can with some dubious confidence begin again; and change—for all the temporal disruption it threatens—can, we hope, be accommodated after all. But even in going this far I speak not as a champion of theory so much as its victim, a willing victim.

II. EPILOGUE

Because I am theory's victim, I must carry these oscillations to one further swing. My treatment of these post–New Critical fashions in theory has emphasized their narrowly political character—that is, it has emphasized the role they seek to play in the politics of criticism in the academy and the rival claims to power within that limited domain. But within those modest, intramural, clubby empires, we have seen imperial ambitions shaped also by a serious and honest concern with the workings of literature, though workings shaped as each competing theory would shape them. Still, these interests, like the pragmatic poetics that they foster, enable us to view these movements not as attempts to answer theoretical questions within their own realm so much as attempts to re-create a history of literature and take control of the interpretation of literary texts.

Recent social and historical theorists, in a rush to replace the deconstructionists with their own new prominence, would be quick to point out that I have too narrowly restricted the extratheoretical motives of these movements to matters of literary preference, to questions about which works were to be valued and what in the works made them worth valuing. In other words, social theorists would charge that I treated the "pragmatic" in the pragmatic poetics that concerned me earlier as exclusively literary, despite the fact that many other pressures related to desire—social-political pressures, economic pressures, psychoanalytic pressures—drive critics to shape their theories as they do and, they would argue, are more crucially causative. We can see literary criticism and theory as the more deluded about the purity of their theoretical quest as we move the subtext of that quest further and further from the "literary" sphere, but critical theory in its social-political dimension is to set us straight. So these days the pragmatic motive is offered the more insistently as it leads us away from the ostensible objective of literary theory. Perhaps I have implicitly acknowledged as much in my free use of political metaphors (words like *hegemony, empire, domain, revolution,* etc.), thereby confirming the ease with which the literary slides into the political and the political into the literary. The role of power in creating acts of repression and exclusion in the social-political metaphoricity of our language has been well established by Foucault, and recent theorists boldly expand his insights and ally them with Marx's in order to bring deconstruction back to the material realms of power from the play of intramural textuality.

Having conceded as much as I have to the pragmatic as it diverts us from theoretical pursuits apparently addressed to problems strewn across theory's path, I still want to suggest the value of examining theoretical problems, and proposed answers to them, in their own right, as if they were independent of the hermeneutics of suspicion. In doing so I have been assuming that these are questions worth discussing in their own right, as if the critical texts, with their theoretical implications, had a speculative objective that made one more satisfactory than another: as if, in other words, the theoretical game is one worth playing. Yet my own earlier concern with the pragmatics of critical theory, and especially of recent critical theory, might well suggest that the hidden agenda or sub-text undercuts the pretensions of theories to mean what they ostensibly mean and to accomplish what they ostensibly accomplish. Does the interest in pragmatics, especially when shown to be insidiously directed by social-political institutions, preclude the theoretical enterprise as one that can be undertaken without self-deception?

This question becomes the more urgent with the increasing dominance of the New Historicism as the latest post–New Critical theoretical fashion.[3] Its own social-political focus leads it to see all theory as a surreptitious rhetoric, pursued out of a desire not to solve problems but to manipulate attitudes. At a colloquium in the School of Criticism and Theory not many years back I recall Stanley Fish (a New Pragmatist more than a New Historicist) exclaiming, "Power is the only game in town," and Edward Said—from the other end of the political spectrum—shouting his assent. As we in the American academy saw in the late 1960s and early 1970s, it may not have been unreasonable for students to make the charge—and for faculty to respond sensitively to it—that the treatment of literature that bestows privilege upon self-consciousness and irony seemed a shrewd and efficacious tactic for ensuring political paralysis by undermining the clear lines of programmatic doctrine upon which political commitment and, ultimately, political action rest. Such a criticism, after all, permits in its canon of works only those whose thematic complexity ensures the evasion of any ideological commitment. Hence the New Critical theorist was seen as the servant of the status quo and of the military-industrial complex that guarantees the status quo. The post-structuralist school of textualist deconstruction today inherits the political charges previously leveled against the New Criticism, thanks to its own entanglements in the web of self-undoing meanings which, it is claimed, cuts textuality off from the world. But, as we have seen, the charge of the social deconstructionist is still broader, claiming that the history of Western theory, up to and including textualist deconstruction, consists of so many staged debates all locked within a common set of exclusionary political assumptions that trivializes their differences.

This attempt at social deconstruction, which claims a rising popularity these days, would bring the enterprise of literary theory to an end altogether by relegating its announced mission to the realm of bad faith. For this rhetoric of power is, of course, using its argument to make its own bid for power, whether political or merely academic. The one difference between it and its predecessors is that its devotion to pragmatics as agent of both deconstruction and its own theory means that its bid for power is more naked than that of its rivals.

The arguments that could be used against such political reduction are the ones we have become familiar with when others have made similar moves in the history of theory. They depend, I fear, on resurrecting the author as a willful "subject," if I may use a term now rejected as obsolete. Granted the hold that our moment in history and history's institutions have upon us, have we no freedom of will to formulate and address a problem, and to construct our discourse in order to cast light upon that problem? Granted that we are often self-deceived in our belief that we think and write as utterly free agents, granted that the subjects we choose to write about are not "natural" subjects for us so much as they are institutionally imposed, is all that we work so hard to make our texts say only a disguise for the attempted manipulation of a reader by the subtext? If an effect of our reverence for literary interpretation should be that master texts would complicate the desire for a life of political action, does this destroy our analyses by turning us into agents of the counterrevolution? Even if it could be demonstrated that one extraneous effect of a given theory was that it restrained the revolutionary impulse, are we justified in arguing that such an effect was actually the reason the theory was being put forth, leading us to reject the theory as having been maliciously conceived as part of a general conspiracy? Or should we examine a theory's claims, even if the hope of doing so disinterestedly is a scholar's naive ideal? To vitiate those claims by impugning their motives, and to impugn their motives by calling a subsidiary effect a primal cause—and, consequently, to impugn our motives as examiners—is to revert to a determinism that has been effectively refuted in the past. In other words, is this recent social theory, beneath its newly sophisticated language, finally distinguishable in the thrust of its argument from the political reductionism we remember from the "vulgar Marxism" in the America of the 1930s?

The easy dismissal of manifest content, the result of the writer's labors at the surface and the interstices of his text, in the interest of the latent content supposedly unearthed by the highly motivated, strongly programmed interpreter, justly arouses the suspicion of other interpreters, although these latter had better also beware of their own motives, whether they search for other latencies or focus upon the so-called text itself. Our propensity to misread texts willfully in order to make them serve our goals, like the writer's similar propensity to write texts that way, need not preclude our possibility of saying something about the text as our ostensible object, or the text's possibility of saying something about *its* ostensible subject. Surely, we are the farther from those possibilities as we deny ourselves the chance to read the manifest text by asserting that only the latent text, together with the power relations to which it points, is "real." The unabashed Platonism that denies manifest appearance for latent essentiality is no less objectionable for assuming a politically fashionable shape. Nor does the adding of a psychoanalytical turn of the screw help much to allay our concern for this rejuvenated simplification of the problem of verbal representation.

But what about the capacity of the text to generate a complex of oppositional meanings? In response to this, the best of the New Historicists, like the best in any movement, are far less doctrinaire about their reductions. Many of them are sensitive to the problematic character of verbal representation, so that they would avoid the naive simplism of the deterministic claim that a text must be treated as a reflection of the subtextual political pressures that create the dominant language of which it is an example. They prefer to respond to the capacity they find in a text not only to resist the hegemonic discourse but also, through its own internal play—free play, perhaps?—to subvert it. I find such a response, in the spirit, say, of Theodor Adorno, persuasive, but is it still what is today called the New Historicism? Such a conception of texts, and especially of literary texts, as internally cultivating their language of critique has been vital outside this group, to theorists whose concern with history and society is enriched and deepened by textual analysis rather than the other way round. I am thinking of those influenced by the rediscovered Bakhtin and his interest in the dialogical function of texts, in their carnivalizing effect, as they move toward the heterogeneity of the novel, the latter seen as both literary antigenre and index to social dispersion. It is this constant press toward textual resistance and opposition that has more recently been extended in the work of Lyotard, a major voice with a significant following. Here, too, there is a ubiquity of political metaphors, though they are generated by the *différends* of the text.

This response to the text's power to sponsor resistance to the dominant discourse argues for a relationship between history and text that treats the text more as an agent and less as a servant—counter to the thrust of much New Historicism. Still bound to history and its language, the text is yet free to affect, indeed to transform, history and its language. Of course, most New Historicists would accuse those who would attribute this power to the text with cultivating aesthetic paralysis, with indulging in a flight from commitment all too similar to that indulged in by those in the tradition of romantic irony from Friedrich Schlegel to the New Critics to Paul de Man. (They might also have to include among these their apparent ally, Adorno.) So we must confront in the text either the reflection of the totalizing discourse of ideology or permanent revolution through the multiplication of discourses of opposition: either words to support action or words to create continual blockage, not so unlike the old doctrine of aesthetic equilibrium. Today we are witnessing a debate between these versions of textual relevance to political power. It would be bracing, if perhaps old-fashioned, to feel that we are free to choose between these latest competing bids to set the fashion.

I have made my way back to my concerns about the pursuit of fashion, the quest for the "new" which, once it becomes old as it shortly must, is followed by the quest for the newer and then the newest. And on and on, fostered by its historical naïveté, it will go. But the stakes become higher when, with an intolerant presumptuousness, the newest bidder for fashion would, like some of the New Historicists, end the game altogether. In effect, they would put theory out of business: they would reject for good the claim of any theoretical discourse to possess an about-ness. Instead, this rejection of theory would wrap critical discourse about itself, narrowing its circles within its own hidden motives as revealed by its subtext, thereby creating its own form of closure from which no gleam can escape to illuminate what claimed to be objects of independent thought. Should we not resist allowing the power of fashion to dictate the end of our earnest habits of continuing our philosophic questing and questioning, whatever the limitations of an operation that has always proceeded *as if* it can indeed shed more light upon the old and new, but still dark, shadows of our doubts? I have respect for the fictional force of the "as if," but I have more respect for the not altogether forlorn hope of light, even of the merest glimmer.

NOTES

This is a revised and considerably enlarged version of a paper delivered in August 1984 at the plenary session of the 16th FILLM Congress in Budapest. The general subject of the Congress was the relationships among literary change, linguistic change, and critical change.

1. Emerson R. Marks, "Pragmatic Poetics: Dryden to Valéry," *Bucknell Review* 10 (1962): 213–23.

2. A good place to spot this shift in the very process of occurring is Miller's "Georges Poulet's 'Criticism of Identification,'" in *The Quest for Imagination: Essays in Twentieth-Century Aesthetic Criticism*, ed. O. B. Hardison, Jr. (Cleveland, 1971), pp. 191–224.

3. I remind the reader that I want to apply this term to a group far broader than those Renaissance and other scholars in sympathy with the so-called *Representations* group. For my purposes here, various theorists, not only Foucaultian, but also Marxist and feminist, are included in my use of this term, despite important differences among them. For they share methodological similarities in attributing a deterministic role to the power relations within a culture that impose themselves upon its texts.

8

MARGINAL MEN AND
CENTERS OF LEARNING:
NEW CRITICAL RHETORIC AND
CRITICAL POLITICS

ঽঙ

R. K. Meiners

> The transformed life, in case there is one, will be accompanied
> by the old state of mind. The world is ending and nobody will
> know it. They will forget all that was yesterday, they will not
> see what today is, they will not fear what comes tomorrow. They
> will forget that the war was lost, forget that it was begun, forget
> that it was conducted. Therefore it will not end.
> —Karl Kraus

I

ONE ALLUDES TO THE WORDS of Kraus's apocalypse with diffidence
because they imply such severe judgment on those who would transform
the language of real suffering, of generations of work and thought, into
the defecations of metaphor in critical debate. But since Kraus's concern
was quintessentially with the deliquescing of rhetoric into opinion and
publicity, the politics of language in historical society, and the way new
voices appropriate the old by denial, transformation, homogenization,
and amnesia, it is worth the risk. And it is worth carrying the risk to that
nearly analogous situation where we must listen carefully to those powerful moments where languages and practices of great force and example
seem to succeed each other. For it is just here that the questions of what
survives from earlier to later, and how the subverted energies of earlier
discourse remain to trouble and to inform later praxis become at the very
least *interesting,* if only because so many interests are involved. It is in
these moments of succession of discourse that one's interests and one's
language are challenged and threatened. It is very well to write and speak
with one's language constantly parenthesized and bracketed, with each

prediction *sous rature;* it is another matter to listen to successive discourses and to avoid succumbing to that political and theoretical otopathy that denies not only the validity of past argument by the introduction of more, and more problematic, factors but insists in the process that the "old state of mind" is not only quite mistaken in the way it failed to understand the terms of its own metaphoricity but, being superseded, need no longer trouble our reflection and practice. Or, if older discourse is still attended to, then only in the terms by which the present interrogates the inadequate past. This essay proceeds on the assumption that historical knowledge requires the interrogation of purer subsequent forms of theory by the questioning of superseded rhetorics.

The classic and therefore most exemplary modern instance is found in that succession represented by Kant's institution of criticism within the antinomies of reflective thought by the juridical queries of transcendental dialectic, the Hegelian canceling and reinstituting of criticism within a dialectical phenomenology, and the Marxist critique of the dialectic by standing it on its materialist feet. There are enough sedimented discourses there to give us all foot and mouth disease forever, and something heavy, like a large lexicon, should be dropped on anyone who believes it easy to separate idealist from materialist practice or suggests that logocentricism as a diagnosis of our present difficulties is likely either to carry us beyond them or to clarify our relations with a past that imagined us as we try, somehow, to imagine a future.

A far less momentous succession of discourses than that marked by the migration of dialectic from Kant to Hegel to Marx may be represented in the history of critical theory and the teaching of literature in American universities during approximately the past forty years. It is less momentous, and yet these are *our* moments, so we should be privileged at the very least in our ability to attend to them. It is the more disabling when the criticism of the recent past is not attended to because of the assurance that it is not worth attending to, because superseded, and when the very terms of its critique are denied not so much by argument as by being fetishized into the production of new theory. This is approximately what happened when New Critical argument confronted an older historical criticism. It will not be my concern to consider *that* confrontation, though it is still worth considering, along with a more speculative and parenthetical question as to what might have happened if a model of historical criticism such as that represented by Erich Auerbach had been sufficiently present in American institutions to furnish a real antagonism to New Criticism rather than the largely eclectic and untheoretical historicism that prevailed more through default than energy.

When one rereads the relevant texts, and thinks through their publication history, the history of critical theory, and the teaching of literature since the mid-1930s, that history certainly seems to be dominated by two phases of critical practice, with their attendant languages and supporting theories. And one must be retrospectively astonished at the relative suddenness with which the marginal language and practice of New Criticism came to seem to dominate the institutions it confronted, and the later accretion of an inferred model of theory around an aggressively antitheoretical rhetoric. For, make no mistake about it, writers like Tate, Blackmur, Ransom, and Winters were marginal and considered themselves so.[1]

But if the sudden triumph of New Critical language and practice was astonishing, and the development, largely by disciples, ephebes, and assorted commenters and concluders, of a "theory" sufficiently convincing to seem to justify the practices even more so, then neither is more surprising than the swiftness of the reversal. We may take the year 1956–57 as a nicely symbolic turning point, justly chosen by Frank Lentricchia as the moment with which to begin his brilliant survey in *After the New Criticism*. That year saw the publication of both Krieger's *The New Apologists for Poetry* and Frye's *Anatomy of Criticism,* and it is worth remarking to what an extent these two books have furnished models for, first, the imputation of certain ideals of theory *to* New Criticism, followed by the decisive rejection *of* those ideals as inadequate, contradictory, and compromised. For certainly the second phase of recent critical history has been marked by a thorough, irritable rejection of New Criticism and a displacement of it by a criticism bearing various competing ideological commitments but having in common a greater theoretical ambitiousness than what it displaced.

Now, it is not my purpose here to decide whether, if New Criticism is "dead," it is so, as Lentricchia says, "in the way that an imposing and repressive father-figure is dead" or even to inquire into the responsibility for the erection of the "father-figure" into such disabling potency that it continues to trouble the dreams of its successors.[2] Other writers, including Krieger himself, Paul de Man, and Gerald Graff, have turned their attention to such inquiry, and the questions of New Critical prestige and New Critical adequacy or inadequacy are not as such my concern though

they are obviously not entirely irrelevant to it. Nor do I wish to trace
briefly the rival models of theory that have emerged in critical history
with and since Frye. Lentricchia has done much of this work with great
care and acuity, and at various levels of competence this has been the
substance of so much recent critical work that there is no need to add to
it here. What I wish to do is rather different; if related to such enterprises,
it is on the one hand a great deal simpler and on the other nearly impossible, or so the testimony of collective experience would seem to demonstrate. I wish to see whether the modes of argument in which New
Criticism challenged its institutionalized opponents, and the rhetoric that
New Criticism subsequently, in its strongest moments, turned back on
its own institutionalized presence, can be seen even now as a challenge to
that nisus toward forms of theory pure enough to reconcile our deepest
skepticisms with the demands of hermeneutic perpetuity. More simply, I
wish to try to pay some attention to this crucial moment where critical
discourses seem to succeed each other, and in so doing try also to keep
from either being enchanted by the lure of older voices, or to proceed as
if they were not worth hearing, being old; and at least to acknowledge
they spoke as they did and not otherwise.

   I have no intention of pursuing the famous red herring of New Critical
"formalism." Attempts to understand what it was and did by following
that path are going to lead to mystification.[3] Furthermore, in spite of the
equally clichéd charges that the New Critics "separated literature from
life" or "isolated the poet / poem from society" or "denied the relationship
of history to criticism," New Criticism was political from the beginning,
as much a cultural as a literary critique. In the American southerners this
usually took the form of a radical agrarian anticapitalism, but it took
other, less overt forms in the moral concerns of Leavis and Winters, or
that peculiarly Empsonian ambiguity that incipiently pastoralized and
attacked the whiggish Miltonic God. I agree with Fredric Jameson when
he says that "for their contemporaries the agrarian anticapitalism of Leavis
or of the early New Criticism was fairly obvious . . . and [it] has only
come to seem essentially formalist from the hindsight of our own historical amnesia,"[4] because I've thought this since I first edged into acquaintance with the New Criticism in the writings of Allen Tate. What *was*
acutely important about the New Criticism and what had everything to
do with what the New Critics said about literature, how they became
institutionalized, and how they continue to test later movements toward

theoretical totality, was the characteristic rhetoric of New Critical involvement. This includes the way the writer of the New Critical essay
takes his relationship to his ostensible subject (including the texts he
questions), the way the critic marks himself out from his opposition and
then absorbs it, and the way in which Rhetoric itself may be seen both in
concert with and opposed to Dialectic.

II

There are any number of reasons that have been or may be given to reject
the New Criticism, to reprehend its inadequacies, to require a more rea-
soned view of interpretation. I will list some of them, making no attempt
at comprehensiveness. (1) The New Criticism was from the beginning
such a hodgepodge of attitudes and practices conducted by so many different writers that no generalizations about "it" are credible; therefore it
is a pointless enterprise to argue against a ghostly hypostasis. (2) New
Criticism represented a hopeless eliding of Romantic-idealist theory with
empiricist practical criticism, self-contradictory from the beginning,
bound to fall when subjected to scrutiny. (3) New Criticism projected an
ideal of formalist understanding isolated from real historical and social
knowledge. (4) New Criticism was *not* ahistorical, but naively historicist,
and therefore projected a reified bourgeois-historical understanding under
such grossly distorted conceptual images as "the dissociation of sensibility." (5) The New Criticism was both provincial and parochial; isolated
from larger traditions of European thought it was inadequate for the un-
dertaking of the task of formulating a hermeneutic applicable to a larger
range of linguistic experience than a very select tradition of lyrical and
quasidramatic texts. (6) New Criticism unconsciously perpetuated the
greatest antinomies of reflective thought, separating knowledge from
value, making from judging, in disastrous ways. (7) New Criticism pursued a dream of literature beyond science and politics and thus, covertly,
a justification of the status quo of liberal ideology; not a critique of the
institutions it was penetrating but a silent complicity with them. (8) It
settled for partial views, and left no basis (unless in some aspects of the
work of Kenneth Burke and Yvor Winters) for dealing with totalizations
of those views, except as a residual rhetoric resisting totalization. (9) The
New Critics pressed their implacably skeptical intelligences toward the
subtle and intimate behavior of words, but they did so without the benefit
of any systematic understanding of linguistics and, indeed, fended off

possible alliances with linguistics as more unwelcome intrusions of "science"; their skepticism and their knowledge of words was thus turned toward the preservation of a mysterious presence, an "experience" or "unity" beyond the reach of mere language. This should have led not only to linguistics, but to a critique of politics and theology: but the New Critics chose to remain in the skeptical scrutiny of languages.

There could be others, but these are enough. With only (3) and (7) am I in substantial disagreement; and I would grant in some circumstances a certain force even to them. Stricture (9) seems to me the fullest and most formidable criticism, and it is the closest to my own present understanding. Now the great formal fact that these criticisms have in common (to borrow a phrase from Blackmur), succinctly illustrated in (8), is that they all assert in various ways that the New Criticism was *partial:* that it ignored, suppressed, or elided *this* or *that.* Thus they all not only must presume to possess some more complete or total understanding, but they also must assume the status of an after-the-fact judgment, and from a position *outside* the body of work they criticize. And both of these procedures are dangerous.

They are dangerous because the subsequent critic inevitably places himself in the position of "demystifying" from the outside, pointing to a discrepancy between New Critical theory and New Critical practice, when precisely by stepping outside they assume a version of the text's relation to critique denied by the most sophisticated New Criticism. It is rather like staring at the Gorgon: stare if you will, but the creature may stare back even from its antique eyes and one had better be shielded. And if the only shield is that of a more sophisticated theory, then any triumph is so burdened by the petrified distance between the purity of theory and the historically troubled language of real poems that it is a triumph of stone and silence. The importance of critique as practiced by the New Critics themselves was that they refused *both* belatedness and detachment, as can be so easily exemplified by such things as the astonishing early readings by Leavis and Tate of *The Waste Land* and *"Ash-Wednesday";* and this refusal of belatedness and detachment extended also to their self-critiques. It made for theoretical messiness, but it also gave their work its characteristic rhetorical procedures in which analogy, as the knowledge that everything always happens at once, became a substitute for and shadow of dialectical separation and precision.

As the genuine importance of New Criticism involves much more than any theoretical positions it asserted or implied, so any merely theoretical argument with such positions is bound to miss the mark. The real importance of New Criticism is intimately tied to the rhetoric of the New Critical essay and the politics of literary argument and institutionalizing it implied. This most emphatically includes their arguments not only with others but with themselves, and so I shall also wish to observe the rhetoric that shapes the self-critique of some later essays by Tate and Blackmur, the two critics upon whom I will focus for reasons that will become clear. Now the most observable feature of New Critical rhetoric— practiced in widely varying ways by various writers—is its pervasive sense of irony: the way in which it both identified with and separated itself from the object of its critique, whether admired or reprehended, and the way in which it insisted on the space between its discourse and that of any potentially rival position. This is the real significance of all those familiar terms—*paradox, ambiguity, pseudo-reference, morality, irrelevance,* and *tension* are among the most famous. They all simultaneously renounce any claim to totality yet attempt to suggest some "full knowledge" or "unity of experience," or "preconscious whole" somehow mysteriously latent in a text as well as in "poetry" as a whole.

As I have said, any subsequent questioner of this critical mystification and/or bad faith is perhaps in more complicated circumstances than is generally understood, and I include myself in these circumstances. It seems a relatively easy matter, twenty years after I first attacked Tate in letter and in print for his philosophical unsophistication and theoretical poverty, to reiterate and broaden that attack from the advantage of later knowledge. So now, inevitably, I want to know why the skepticism of the New Critics toward the behavior of words in poems *and* societies did not reach to criticism of the ontotheological metaphors of their own discourse and the impacted and fractious assumptions in the baffling ease by which they seemed to relate their "criticism" to "poetry" (joined, at least, by the mysterious hypostasis of the "author" who had written, often enough, both the poetry and the criticism) and to oppose both poetry and criticism to "science" or "sociology" and other suspected modes of writing and thinking. I can question this ease, as I can despise the easy assumption that mortal and theoretic death is a good enough occasion for a poem and the language of defeated persons a good enough medium; but it will be clear that, insofar as I fail to join such estimable writers as Geoffrey Hartman and Edward Said in equalizing poetic, critical, and philosophical text in the mediations of textuality, I still bear the burden of the dilemma raised by New Critical critique. Even so burdened, I now wish to know why the New Critics did not question more the filiations of authority that entailed their own rhetorics, why they did not overtly challenge the issue of whether the "autonomy of the poem" was not as subverted by the pervasive and subtle hegemony of the vastly ignorant State as any other claim—social, aesthetic, religious, scientific—to autonomy.

But now, in the righteousness and power of critique I must, as those subversive poems by Allen Tate suggest a critic should, "think a little of the past" more carefully and the ease with which I seem to triumph over it, and the way that ease is powerfully legitimated by the language of valorization and reification learned as methods to discriminate present difficulties from where I found myself first entering into the margins of criticism.

For in spite of a quarter-century's worth of American understanding learning new and subversive ways of questioning its languages, there are still very few assessments of the inadequacies of New Criticism quite so cutting as some passages written by New Critics themselves. And the very reason they are so "cutting" is that they are criticisms written by poets with that cutting analogical irony in which American Modernists made themselves specialists, which depended more on rhetorical images of dialectic than upon dialectic itself. They were, in Blackmur's great phrase, masters of "irregular metaphysics," and it was not that they despised politics or theory so much as they queried the relation of literature, including literary criticism, to all forms of Authority, whether it came calling itself Politics or Philosophy. Some examples are needed, and I will draw them from the late work of the two critics who remain for me at the real cutting edge of the American New Criticism, Allen Tate and R. P. Blackmur. Turning again to Tate, there is a certain embarrassment that he continues to have things to teach me long after I thought I had ceased to have any real reason other than mere affection to read him. I want to call attention here to that peculiarly exemplary combination of lectures he gave in 1950–51, published as "To Whom Is the Poet Responsible?" and "Is Literary Criticism Possible?" The latter, with almost grotesque irony, was delivered at a Harvard Conference on the Philosophical Bases of Literary Criticism.[5]

The first thing to note in Tate's lectures is the valorizing of "poetry" as a language not only "above" politics but as a challenge *to* politics, on the covert assumption that politics is the language in which the State expresses authority and that the only hegemony the poet may acknowledge is the "full" authority of the "full language" of "the human condition." This is impossible; I used to insist to Tate that "the full language of the human condition" was something a person might dream about but could never experience short of unalienated nature or variously millenary or proletarian apocalypses. Since the major purpose of this exercise is to question the comforts of periodizing and the ease with which later language seems to displace earlier, I need hardly suggest the ironies my later views "find" sedimented in my earlier ones.

The second thing about the Tate lectures worth observing is the profound skepticism with which he allies "criticism" with "the humanities" in the theory and politics of university alliances. I do not suggest that Tate anticipates the movement of criticism to a place in the "human sciences" in the past two decades. Tate's only term for "human sciences" is that peculiarly dated phrase "social science," and he is as caustically dismissive of *its* claims as he ever was. But he is hardly less contemptuous of the "humanities"; if he allies criticism with humanistic study it is only by virtue of the humanities' historical claims to some proprietary interest to the then moribund subject of rhetoric. For it is plain that Tate finally believes criticism's true province is rhetoric, and I am retrospectively surprised that Tate, who understood the traditional claims of rhetoric as well as anyone could have, was still so chary of any claim of politics on criticism, since rhetoric is from its beginning and in its very nature political. That is, in part, explained by his refusal to subvert the power of the poem's language by yielding it up to the language of critical or political narrative. Long ago I accused Tate of mystification on this issue, but it may be more like the truth to say that he felt the poetic moment offered the only possible bulwark against the pervasive irony of his own critical prose, which he took to be a representative prose. There is no real place in Tate or even in Blackmur where the critical moment and the poetic moment hear their mutual languages, and that is the great absence at the center of New Criticism, continually jumped by analogy. But that very absence is responsible, for instance, for that extraordinary draconian image in "Two Whom Is the Poet Responsible?" where Tate imagines adjoining cells for Ezra Pound and Archibald Macleish in the politics of a state that claims hegemony in *all* languages. That image is something like Tate's corrosive farewell to the consuming theme of the autonomy of the

poem; which doesn't mean that he abandoned his views of the high rhetoric of the human city extending to Communion; which Blackmur once
paraphrased as "Diplomacy on the high scale: how we learn to live with
the sons of bitches."[6]

What is perhaps above all worth noticing is the remarkably *discontinuous*
nature of the critical rhetoric in these essay-lectures. All New Critical
essays develop a discontinuous rhetoric. The closer they get to their subject, the further the author claims his "knowledge" is from comprehend-
ing it. Tate suspects theoretical ambition, and he places great gaps
between it and anything he—a mere essayist—might assay. But there is
here hardly *less* discontinuity between Tate's work and, say, Northrop
Frye's later version of criticism, than there is between what Tate is saying
of the finally marginal and uncertain character of criticism and the criticism Tate himself had been writing for thirty years. "Skeptical" is not a
strong enough word for Tate's late view of the critical situation. He is
deeply suspicious of any claim to authority in language, the critic's hardly
less than the politician's.

If Ransom had been less dandified and less American he might, of the
New Critics, have been in a position to insist that these very skepticisms
were within the precincts of critique, to bring something like a European
respect for ideas and theory into the New Criticism without sacrificing
the acuity of its ironic skepticisms (certainly René Wellek, whatever his
other virtues, had nothing to offer along that line). As it was, we can
learn from the best of later New Criticism what happened when it finally
began to cast its eye on the way in which it had become part of the
institution and brought its own earlier procedures into the center of its
late critique, and implied an equally severe critique of those second-order
institutionalizers who had commodified those procedures into "method."

Consider the late essay called simply "Modern Poetry."[7] It is as much a
retrospective as Tate ever wrote, glancing back from 1955 at the century's
poetry and its accompanying criticism. "I am not repudiating the immense, and immensely resourceful, critical activity that began in England
with Hulme, Eliot, Richards and Read thirty to forty years ago, and, in
the United States at about the same time, with the Crocean aesthetics of
the late Joel Spingarn, and with the *Prefaces* of Henry James," Tate writes.
He goes on to mention the essays of Ezra Pound and Irving Babbitt, and
a "second wave of this Anglo-American criticism (I must ignore its French
affiliations) brought forward in America by men as different as Wilson,

Ransom, and Blackmur." His purpose was not to repudiate that criticism but to identify its mode and that of the poetry it accompanied. That mode was "the aesthetic-historical mode," which was not only concerned with "the language of the literary work at its particular moment in time" but is peculiarly marked by the alienation of the "contemplative man" and by the isolation of the literary community. The essay closes with Tate reckoning that he is writing at the end of a "period style" in poetry. He assumes as well that he was writing at the end of a "period style" in criticism. If "aesthetic-historical" is vocabulary too loaded to be used without sinking, we may substitute for it that "bourgeois humanist" who keeps slipping precariously in and out of Blackmur's "Anni Mirabiles" lecture.[8] And both Tate's phrase and Blackmur's phrase, borrowed from the central vocabulary of the tradition they feel they are, self-consciously, ending, have at least the virtue of being used with the utmost self-criticism, with nearly the same combination of irony and historical seriousness as that hunchback in the machine who opens and haunts Walter Benjamin's "Theses on the Philosophy of History."[9]

Thinking here of Tate and Blackmur together, one thinks not only of Blackmur's fine, skeptical late essay on Tate, but of that sort of political and social acuteness rising fully to consciousness in the late writing of Blackmur that was actively present in Tate's earlier criticism and latent in the later writing. What Jameson calls "the political unconscious" is never far from formal articulation in Tate (though a bourgeois unconscious reeling under reification from Jameson's point of view—this last phrase, "point of view," a metaphor so historically crucial it deserves even more than Jameson's brilliant discussion of it).[10] Yet another denunciation of the "liberal, utopian, 'totalitarian' mind" was not what one would have wished from Tate in 1955, but some greater scrutiny of his political and critical scruples at totalitarianism and totalizing. That would have been invaluable; but it also would have been out of his nature. It would perhaps have led him to write the kind of sustained and connected argument similar in kind if not in sentiment to the sort Jameson has so finely produced in book after book. Tate used to wave aside his failure to produce a "real book" as the result of a "poor" or "unfinished" education. But it was more than that, unless "education" is meant in something very like Henry Adams's sense. It was analogous to Eliot's refusal from the beginning to be formally "philosophical" in spite of his training: it was to *insist* on marginality, on alienation as a condition for maintaining the only relation to *civis populi* the "man of letters" (another crucially duplicitous metaphor) *could* with honor maintain in late capitalist civilization.

Tate looked at the activities of "criticism" as practiced by his contemporaries and a generation taught by them and what he chiefly saw was a situation in which "a modern poem becomes history for the fewer before the few, a handful of unprofessional readers, can read it." In this condition, "our critics . . . have been perfecting an apparatus for 'explicating' poems (not a bad thing to do), innocent of the permanently larger ends of criticism." These "permanently larger ends of criticism" include the querying of "explication," the "autonomy of the poem," the writing of endless articles based upon the "explication" of "autonomy," and even the establishment of journals devoted to such arcane procedures. But they also include the querying of subsequent professional strategies where any new text, once noticed, is turned into a textual commodity before any feeling of what it meant to speak or write *those* words in *that* situation might say of the only life in body or mind we have. And the "permanently larger ends of criticism" include also this: "In writing criticism they [the "critics of our time"] forget that they occupy 'posts of observation,' that they themselves are 'trapped spectators'. . . . If what the novelist knows—or the Jamesian novelist, at any rate—is limited to what his characters see, hear, do, and think, why is the critic not similarly confined to place and moment? The answer is that he *is*. But the critic does not see himself, *his* point of view, as a variable in the historical situation that he undertakes to explain: as one motion of the history that he is writing."[11]

It would be less than honesty or charity demands for me to very much insist upon denying the privilege of the last dialectical moment to another. My references and allusions to Fredric Jameson should make it clear I find him an invaluable critic. It would be well, however, even when arguing a view which claims theoretical totality, which logically demands in *The Political Unconscious* to be taken as the resolution of competing antagonisms—a founding discourse, in Foucault's phrase—to bring critique against the very privilege and finality from hypothetical other positions and superseded languages. And so I would say that even a Marxism so subtly persuasive as Jameson's has something to learn, perhaps not by consenting again to becoming a bourgeois "trapped spectator," but at least in some residual suspicion or skepticism, which we may still learn from Tate, at the ease with which our critical discourse may easily turn into a kind of intellectual and emotional imperialism that is the darker side of the political and cultural critique we turn toward bourgeois humanism with all its older and newer criticisms, with the critic cast in the role of a trapped spectator of a vanishing vision.

III

If Thomas Mann was the great modern virtuoso of that bourgeois humanism, and Auerbach and Benjamin its great European critics, the American virtuoso of the literature, intellect, sensibility, and critical politics of bourgeois humanism is R. P. Blackmur. If any of the New Critical critiques of New Criticism still has the possibility of provoking attention to issues no less pertinent after thirty years of increasingly sophisticated theoretical argument, it surely must be Blackmur's—and partly because he has probably been the least read of the New Critics. He is simply ignored, time after time, in contexts where it would seem essential to look at his example. For if Blackmur is only read carefully, it will be apparent that among the many other matters with which he concerns himself, no one ever pointed out the various missing dates and derelictions of the New Criticism with greater power and tact. The 1946 essay "A Burden for Critics" is one of the crucial texts, though there are others to which I will come later. It is hard to know what, in this remarkable essay, to quote, but here is one moment in the essay where Blackmur anticipates the themes that will preoccupy him in the 1950s:

> Almost the whole job of culture, as it has formerly been understood, has been dumped into the hands of the writer. Possibly a new form of culture, appropriate to a massive urban society, is emerging: at any rate there are writers who write with a new ignorance and a new collective illiteracy. . . . Those who seem to be the chief writers of our time have found their subjects in attempting to dramatize at once both the culture and the turbulence it was meant to control, and in doing so they have had practically to create—as it happens, to re-create—the terms, the very symbolic substance, of the culture as they went along.
>
> I do not mean that this has happened by arrogation on the part of the writers; I mean they have been left alone with this subject as part of the actual experience of life in our time. . . . It is getting on toward a century since Matthew Arnold suggested that poetry could perhaps take over the expressive functions of religion.[12]

Blackmur here simultaneously *represents* that "isolation of the literary community" adduced by Tate, and *places* its history by invoking the precedent of that sober bourgeois humanist Matthew Arnold. But I take it that the question is in dispute whether Blackmur is a nostalgist or merely mistaken when he goes on to respond to the Arnoldian suggestion by saying: "All poetry can do is to dramatize, to express, what has actually happened to religion. This it has done. It has not replaced or in any way taken over the functions of religion; but it has been compelled to replace the operative force of religion as a resource with the discovery, or creation, of religion as an aesthetic experience" (BC 202). Now my own belief is that Blackmur is mistaken. He makes no provision for poetry to judge the criticisms that politics and critique presume to make upon it, silently acquiescing in that great tradition running from Kant to Croce to Frye which holds that in poetry there is neither moment nor warrant for judgment. It is no wonder that Jameson, in this at least representative of the most vital and powerful contemporary theory, has focused attention on narrative and other spacious forms including dialectic, resigning the New Critic's preoccupation with specifically "poetic" dilemmas to a discredited critical tradition. It is easy to sympathize. If "all poetry can do" is to "dramatize, to express," then the great temptation is to say to hell with it, it is a self-indulgence difficult to afford any longer. (I speak as one with difficulty and at risk calling himself a poet.) Blackmur is of little use here, and no more is Tate, or for that matter Jameson or Said.

These points, while real, must be taken up on other occasions. For now, here is Blackmur moving in on the difficulties of his tradition and its contemporary crisis: "Why do we treat poetry, and gain by doing so, after much the same fashion as Augustine treated the scriptures in the fifth century? Who do we make of our criticism an essay in the understanding of words and bend upon that essay exclusively every tool of insight and analysis we possess? Why do we have to re-create so much of the poem in the simple reading which is only preface to total performance? Do we, like Augustine, live in an interregnum, after a certainty, anticipating a synthesis? If so, unlike Augustine, we lack a special revelation: we take what we can find" (BC 202).

His response to his own rhetorical question is something very close to a flat "yes" and it is interregnum politics that forces Blackmur's awareness of criticism as a "technique of trouble," to use another of his great phrases, and his even more pointed critique of critical *practice* late in the reign of the bourgeois humanist:

> If we look at the dominant development in criticism in English during the last thirty years—all that Mr. Ransom means by the New Criticism—with its fineness of analysis, its expertness of elucidation, and its ramifying spe-

cialization of detail—we must see how natural, and at bottom how facile, a thing it has been. It has been the critics' way of being swept along, buoyed more by the rush than by the body of things. It is a criticism, that is, which has dealt almost exclusively with the executive technique of poetry (and only with a part of that) or with the general verbal techniques of language . . . it was a criticism created to cope with and develop the kind of poetry illustrated by Eliot's *Waste Land* and Yeats's *Tower*. . . . Eminently suited for the *initial* stages of the criticism of this poetry, it has never been suited to the later stages of criticism; neither Eliot nor Yeats has been compared or judged because there has been no criticism able to take those burdens. (BC 206–7)

This is not unlike Tate's own critique of the New Criticism, but it is simultaneously more complete and less skeptical than Tate's. Blackmur is more willing than Tate to go on at this late stage and say what criticism *should* be doing, what it could hope yet to do: "I suppose what I want criticism to do can as well as not be described as the development of aesthetic judgment—the judgment of the rational imagination—to conform with the vast increase of material which seems in our time capable of only aesthetic experience. This is not to define a revelation or create a society. It is to define and explore the representations in art of what is actually going on in existing society" (BC 207–8).

There is something extraordinary beginning to happen here in Blackmur's rhetoric. The New Critics never wrote in the apolitical and unworldly vacuum their caricaturists depicted (about their epigones I have nothing similar to say), but Blackmur's writing is more and more full of what Edward Said calls "worldliness." And yet it is still quite recognizably permeated with the metaphorical and analogical spacings and hesitations. It has the authentic New Critical fear of language increasingly co-opted by the newly educated proletariat, and yet it is turning not only back on itself but on the agencies of co-option. It is still a New Critical rhetoric, aware of discontinuities and troubles, aware that rhetoric was traditionally a continuous contract in the politics of speech, writing, and hearing, yet doubting the finding within its resources ways to reach "what is actually going on in existing society." It is not only a self-critical rhetoric but a rhetoric written out of a fuller social and historical critical consciousness than that achieved by any other New Critic. Blackmur died before taking his own criticism far enough into what was "actually going on in existing society" to turn back convincingly on its own discontinuities. But in the next decade Blackmur was to go so far in that direction that one is entitled to ask whether any other American critic has gone so far.

His most sustained performance is found in "Anni Mirabiles 1921–

1925: Reason in the Madness of Letters." But the very fact that these 1956 lectures are in large measure retrospective makes them not quite so interesting for my purpose as some other things, though they are indispensable. What makes them particularly important is that everywhere the critic's retrospective judgment is solidly based on post–World War Two cultural and political reality, and everywhere it is a judgment suffused with the feeling of what life in a late capitalist society has become. But the essays that declare the ground on which "criticism" will henceforth have to confront its theoretical and political obligation are "Towards a Modus Vivendi" and the marvelous concatenation in Part II of *A Primer of Ignorance* collectively titled "Pathologies of Culture." They hardly seem to be "critical essays" at all when judged either by the standards of 1930s American left criticism or by the "tory anarchism" of his own tradition. Yet while there is no literary text in view, there is a hypothetical tradition of literary texts mediated by social history, and there is the current social reality in which texts must be studied if they are to be studied at all. Thus "Towards a Modus Vivendi" and the other essays are hardly what one could call political, sociological, or semiotic critique either. Not even the obvious precedent of *Culture and Anarchy* and other Victorian cultural argument are real analogies. This late Blackmur work might be sui generis, were it not for the precedent of Henry Adams and the odd mode of historical and cultural analysis in which he specialized.

Adams as a shadowed predecessor, an archetypal modernist bourgeois meditating the close of his tradition, has hardly received the attention he deserves. It must serve to say here only that Blackmur's diagnosis of what happens when "education" both permeates and fails a society, as well as providing the chief means and major images of hegemony in the relation of dominant institutions to aspiring ones can hardly be given its peculiarly American, insular, and Protestant tonality without invoking the precedent of Adams. One thinks of the history of successive crises, and remembers Arnold, who is certainly in Blackmur's mind. But it is Adams far more than Arnold who presides over Blackmur's vision of the thinness of Anglo-American criticism and its gestures toward European sagacity and Oriental energy. Adams and Arnold: a peculiarly potent and disabling combination with which to confront the aspirations of and failures in institutionalized literary education permeated by "the derangement of the senses" in the literature it presumes to "teach" and the growth of techniques to "manage" that derangement.

This much more must be said about Blackmur's obsession with Adams: both are deeply political critics obsessed by art. For both, art is pervaded by political life yet possessed of a different modality: the ideas of imagination and the ideas of law met in the archetectonic of forms, but they were contemplated separately only in impoverishment. That is why Adams had to resist both Darwin and Marx, to whom he was deeply attracted, and Blackmur could never have written anything like Coleridge's *Statesman's Manual*. That is why Blackmur, later in the subversion of language by the pretensions of poetry, would choose Montaigne rather than Adams's choice of Aquinas as a model of reconciliation. *"Epecho,* I will not move" is the verbal skeptic's response to theoretical totalization; and literature, for Blackmur, was the only possible synthesis of conflicting cultural energies rather than the architecture that for Adams reconciled his own versions of numen and moha. I apologize for this shorthand which I hope will call to mind the relevant anxieties and texts. My summary is analogy operating on analogy to say that both Blackmur and Adams were supreme masters of the analogical rhetoric that shaped the beginning and the ending of the New Criticism, that preferred the logic of the double plot and within that the logic of the subplot rather than the major plot. Unwilling to choose between metaphysics and epistemology, the criticism of Adams, Blackmur, and the New Critics refused to settle for sociology and economics as modes of study adequate to the social order in which they lived because they felt at the bottom of their humanist bones, as Coleridge had inadequately taught them, a phenomenon could never be the explanation of phenomena.

A phenomenon cannot *explain* phenomena, but a phenomenon may *illuminate* phenomena, as well as the ordering that links a given sequence of phenomena; and also the larger ordering that makes the concept of "phenomenon" possible. This is the enabling belief of Imagism, and it lights up the vast emptiness in the slovenly American wilderness never penetrated by Intellect. And, carried to its most acute, which is to say technical and rational, degree, it is Analogy in Blackmur's sense: the relation of attributes rather than substances, the reminder "that there is always something *else* going on" (IM 41). It is such a sense of analogy that informs the rhetoric of Henry Adams, of high New Criticism, and particularly of Blackmur and Tate. I will use the phrase "analogical rhetoric" again, for it is something of a barbarous coinage. It is at the essential center of that in New Criticism which seems to me most characteristic and still valuable in that criticism despite all of its shortcomings and our altered condition. I mean by "analogical rhetoric" a rhetoric which constantly *deals* in analogy and in which the relation between the terms of the analogy is usually ironic, with an irony that is not merely "literary" but political as well, in that the polity of the relationship is continually questioned even as it is advanced. But I mean also a rhetoric which is itself "analogical to" other modes of discourse. It is a rhetoric that *uses* argument, that *uses* dialectic, not in the sense of raw material for production but in the sense of giving successive images of where the vexed places in argument have occurred. And that is why New Critical rhetoric was essentially both marginal and political throughout.

In "Towards a Modus Vivendi" and the other cultural essays Blackmur contemplates with a mixture of sympathy, identification, despair, and something approaching apocalyptic vision—all qualities of that "obliquely cautious" rhetoric which Henry Adams patented[13]—the rise of what he chose to call "the new intellectual proletariat." "Proletariat" used outside (and often inside) Marxist argument is hardly less troubled a word than "bourgeois," and Blackmur was certainly no Marxist. But let us say that "the new intellectual proletariat" is that class of newly educated persons whose abilities to use the analogies have not only been placed in jeopardy by what Blackmur called "the new illiteracy," who mistake the language of publicity including public politics for the language of power, but that class of persons cast off from the practice of power by the language they have learned in the Institutions of Learning and any conceivable use to which existing society might put those institutions:

Call it what you like, the double apparition of mass society and universal education is producing a larger and larger class of intellectually trained men and women the world over who cannot make a living in terms of their training and who cannot, because of their training, make a living otherwise with any satisfaction. The American distrust of the intellect, and the painful shrinkage of the confidence of the intellect in itself turns out to be a natural phenomenon of mass society and universal education. Even in Egypt, the Lebanon and Turkey the intellectual has no collectable claims on society. I think the cause is in the dilution of literacy, and the intrusion of the new illiteracy into higher education. . . . It struck me as much in Cairo or Ankara as in Bologna or Munich or Princeton or Harvard that our distrust of the intellectual, as he becomes a massive phenomenon, is a result of the inadequacy of his preparation and the following failure of the independence of his mind. We think we can make the intellectual with the tools of the new illiteracy. All we do is uproot an increasing number of individuals from any vital relation either to society or to themselves. (MV 8)

It would be good to have Blackmur still writing, capable of observing the elevation of "literacy" to a code word of "the new illiteracy." But there is plenty here to mark the bourgeois humanist at the end of his tether, not least being the reluctance with which he surrenders his marginality and "independence of mind." Along with that, there is the air of prophecy, redolent of Henry Adams, full of reminders of what "is going on in existing society." It is left to the belated reader to confirm with chagrin that the prophecy was substantially accurate:

The existing surplus of talent in the academic proletariat in Western Europe is only an advance form of the surplus which will appear in 1970, at latest, in America and earlier if there is a major depression. This seems inescapable, not only in humane studies, but also in the social and physical sciences. . . . The graduate schools will neither be able to shrink their number of students nor to richen and generalize their standards of study. Or at least they will not be able to do so without the shock of new will on old purpose; and any such shock will have initially to come from outside the universities and aside from the state. It seems unlikely any such shocking force will appear. (MV 25)

Who can say this proved *substantially* wrong, arguable though it is in detail and interpretation? Even in the face of a Reagan and his smile and his psychopomps the last sentence hardly seems too skeptical. Presumably a revolution is needed, but even if we narrow our focus so sharply as to speak only of the Institution of Criticism in the American University, the question remains as Blackmur raised it: Has there been any transformation in the relation of the literary intellectual—the critic—to the hegemonic powers in the culture in this time? The answer is that there has not. And if we do not cease wiping our collective memories free from the real language of historic argument, if every generation must begin anew brandishing its tame military-political metaphors of "strategy" and "revolution," it is unlikely that any *substantial* change will ever occur.

The question that Blackmur is implicitly considering throughout "Towards a Modus Vivendi" and the other late essays is: What is the future of "criticism" under these conditions? It is clear that Blackmur's late answer to such a question is along the lines of: to whatever the theory may be addressed, and no matter the names in which it is dressed, it cannot

but be political. In the preface to his anthology, *First World War Poetry,* Jon
Silkin put it this way: "We shall never not be political again, and the best
way to be this, among other things, is to think *and* feel; and if this
cooperative impulsion is permeated with values we can decently share, we
stand a chance, as a species, of surviving." [14] Blackmur would have shared
the opinion, and gone on to elaborate in his own peculiar way:

> It was a strange dream of the early nineteenth century that by the industrial
> revolution, we obviated politics and had escaped history. History jerks us
> every second. It always has, but it did not matter until there were too many
> of us. We cannot any of us be Swiss except the Swiss: whom we have thrown
> off as a sport, the one possible collection of people impervious to history [not
> even the Swiss in 1982]. But the Swiss have no Djinns in their privies; their
> faces never wince.
>
> The Egyptians, and all the Arab World, wince at the suddenness with
> which they have been thrust into a late stage of Western history, and they
> are perhaps more precarious in that history than we feel we ourselves are.
> (MV 20)

We are all even more precarious, and perhaps we wince rather differently than we might have when R. P. Blackmur was writing these words
in 1954 in that interregnum between the New Criticism and the Newer
Criticism. In 1957 Northrop Frye was to publish his *Anatomy,* that Ca-
nadian Marshall Plan of Criticism so appropriate to Eisenhowerian democracy. Blackmur could hardly have anticipated subsequent changes
when he wrote the conclusion to his dark meditation on the possibilities
of a future for criticism in "existing society":

> At this point, with all the exaggerations and ejaculations in the above para-
> graphs cut down to size, it begins to emerge that literacy (the aim of educa-
> tion) is itself an energy comparable in intensity, delicacy, and mass to the
> energies we locate in the natural sciences. What is more important, imperfect
> literacy, degraded literacy, or what has been called the new illiteracy, though
> it has lost its capacity to control other energies, has not only not lost but has
> gained in uncontrollable and unpredictable energy of its own: much like the
> physical energies themselves when, once released, they are let alone. What is
> needed, from Cairo and Ankara to Paris and New York, is an energy of mind
> equal to both the new physical energies and their natural concomitant the
> new illiteracy. Institutional education alone, like institutional religion in the
> Christian past, is not enough: though these may persuade what is necessary
> into being: the multiplication and heightening of individual intelligence.
> Some people call the mode of this intelligence in action criticism. It had
> better be called the charity of compassionate understanding. Its aim is no less

than a modus vivendi for those who must live together; no more, in the end, than true empire: *della vera città almen la torre.* (MV 30–31)

This was written at the twilight of New Criticism, and if one armed only with the clichés and generalizations about the New Criticism and otherwise ignorant of what work was really done were to read this, such a one might be very hard pressed to say how this resembles the writing of a New Critic. Yet there is one clue: the politics of criticism, the establishment of a modus vivendi that longs for a politics of "true empire" depend, if not absolutely then initially, on the "multiplication and heightening of individual intelligence." This is a politics that begins with the individual: with the isolated and imperial bourgeois intelligence. If this is something like the last representation of New Critical intelligence, then it is a representation of that intelligence as separate, as marginal, as speaking from the midst of failure if not itself failed. To similar issues as to the secrets of criticism, T. S. Eliot opined that the only "secret" is to be "very intelligent." That is, to be sure, a secret; but at this stage one is entitled to wonder whether it is a sufficient secret. This is something like the final declaration of failure of the New Criticism; but if it is that, there is yet something very fine in its self-criticism.

What was needed was a more direct political understanding of the way criticism appropriated the languages of poetry and other literary discourse; but beyond that an understanding of the way that poetry, as "literature" generally, appropriated and triumphed over, in its own imperialism, the rejected languages and marginal voices of the culture (including critical discourse), and used those to subvert the dominant languages. And above all, it needed a more constantly critical and political knowledge of how critics, once they allow their marginal intelligences to become co-opted by the central concerns of institutions, run the continual risk of becoming what Gramsci called "experts in legitimation."

Blackmur never quite found the way to such an understanding, and it is questionable whether any writer—critic, novelist, poet—*can* except in one of those "academic paper solutions" Allen Tate once reprehended in his younger critic.[15] Yet there are ways to sharpen the awareness of the implications—moral, political, historical, literary—of the issues involved, even if one never escapes a certain belatedness in the very terms of understanding, or even a version of that "secondary" position for criticism that Edward Said abhors in his brilliant essay "The World, the Text, and the Critic."

For there are two chief modern manifestations of the ironic mode of "critical secondariness": one is the great mode, more at home in Europe than in America where ideas have always fallen on thin soil, of dialectical critique. This is the continuous and frontal engagement with Power, and yet, since it *is* power—theological, economic, political—that is being confronted, there is a necessary rethinking and respeaking, a secondary quality, in this mode of critique. That other Power may come from the engagement does not change this. The second mode of critical secondariness is what I have called the analogical rhetoric, the disconnected-yet-engaged rhetoric of the American New Critical essay. Every book Allen Tate ever published looks half-enviously in the direction of theoretical consistency, dialectical continuity, and extended argument, and decisively pushes them aside. And yet it would be a very great mistake to think the two great ironical modes utterly separate, that nothing may be learned by the one from the other. To do so is to continue to think that every generation must entirely make its own revolution, and pretty well to resign ourselves to revolving forever.

NOTES

The epigraph is from Karl Kraus, *Die Letzten Tage der Menschheit* (Munich, 1957), p. 659; my translation.

1. See, e.g., Yvor Winters's account in the first section of "Problems for the Modern Critic of Literature" in his *The Function of Criticism* (Denver, 1957).

2. Frank Lentricchia, *After the New Criticism* (Chicago and London, 1980), p. xiii.

3. It isn't that those who impute "formalism" to New Criticism do so quite groundlessly; after all, Cleanth Brooks at one point claimed that his "credo" was that of a Formalist Critic. But whatever writers may be included under the shaky rubric of "New Criticism," their homespun American formalism, even when buttressed by Ransom's idiosyncratic Kantianism, was such a mixed bag that to begin a discussion here is to beg more questions than it's worth.

4. Fredric Jameson, "From Criticism to History," *New Literary History* 12 (1981): 374. In work related to this essay I suggest a sort of development through what I see as the best work of the New Critics—much of Leavis, some of Winters, as well as those texts with which I am chiefly concerned here—certain later essays of Tate and Blackmur—to the current writing of Fredric Jameson and Edward Said. The idea and practice of rhetoric is crucial to this development.

5. In Allen Tate, *Essays of Four Decades* (Chicago, 1968), pp. 17–44. Since

later in this essay I allude to my own earlier criticism of Tate, I should perhaps say here that some thirty years ago I wrote a Ph.D. dissertation on Tate that evolved into the first extensive critical book on his work, *The Last Alternatives: A Study of the Works of Allen Tate* (Denver, 1963). The present essay is part of a larger study in the historical-political context of the relations of contemporary theory and contemporary poetry. In the larger work some use is made of private correspondence between Tate and myself, and that fact may partly account for a certain personal tone which may yet color some references to Tate in this essay.

6. R. P. Blackmur, "San Giovanni in Venere: Allen Tate as Man of Letters," in *A Primer of Ignorance*, ed. Joseph Frank (New York, 1967), p. 176.

7. Allen Tate, "Modern Poetry," in *Essays of Four Decades*, pp. 211–21.

8. R. P. Blackmur, "Anni Mirabiles 1921–1925: Reason in the Madness of Letters," in *A Primer of Ignorance*, pp. 3–80.

9. Walter Benjamin, *Illuminations*, tr. Harry Zohn (London, 1973), pp. 255–66.

10. Fredric Jameson, *The Political Unconscious: Narrative as a Socially Symbolic Act* (Ithaca, 1981), pp. 160, 219–21.

11. Allen Tate, "Modern Poetry," p. 213.

12. R. P. Blackmur, "A Burden for Critics," in *The Lion and the Honeycomb* (New York, 1955), p. 201; hereafter noted in text as BC. Blackmur's "Towards a Modus Vivendi," also in *The Lion and the Honeycomb*, is noted as MV; the one reference to "Irregular Metaphysics," in *A Primer of Ignorance*, has been noted as IM.

13. "Adams, in his several substantial volumes, was the patentee of one of the most obliquely cautious of modern styles" (Geoffrey Hill, *The Lord of Limit* [London, 1984], p. 84). This difficult, oblique, and deeply moral essay will repay any amount of attention.

14. Jon Silkin, "Introduction," in *The Penguin Book of First World War Poetry*, ed. Jon Silkin (Harmondsworth, 1979), pp. 11–12.

15. An allusion to a phrase in a letter from Allen Tate to the present writer; Tate was questioning the canons of theoretical comprehensiveness and consistency that seemed important to his critic.

9

URBAN SIGNS AND
URBAN LITERATURE:
LITERARY FORM AND
HISTORICAL PROCESS

ò

Richard Lehan

WE NOW HAVE A NUMBER OF IMPORTANT BOOKS that connect the evolution of the city with historical events: Lewis Mumford's *The City in History* and his *Culture of the Cities*, Leonardo Benevolo's *The History of the City*, and Wolf Schneider's *Babylon Is Everywhere: The City as Man's Fate* are perhaps the best of those which come to mind.[1] We also have a number of books that connect the city and the literary text: Max Byrd's *London Transformed: Images of the City in the Eighteenth Century*, F. S. Schwarzbach's *Dickens and the City*, Alexander Welsh's *The City of Dickens*, Donald Fanger's *Dostoevsky and Romantic Realism*, and Burton Pike's *The Image of the City in Modern Literature*, just to name a few.[2]

This paper attempts to bring all of these divergent matters together in a way that not only relates urban texts to literary texts but also suggests that these texts are as much influenced by historical change as is the city itself. My assumption is that the literary text codifies ideas and attitudes about the city and that as the city itself changes under historical influence, so do these codes, exhausting traditional modes as they call for new meaning, often by parodying the emptiness of the older forms.

For purposes of this paper, I have divided the evolution of the modern city into three phases: the commercial, the industrial, and the world city—traditional categories, except for perhaps the third, which Daniel Bell refers to as the postindustrial city and David M. Gordon as the corporate city.[3] In what follows I shall argue that we have already gone beyond those terms just as emphatically as postmodern literature has gone beyond the modern.

I

One can argue that the modern commercial city came into being at 2:00 A.M. on Sunday, September 2, 1666, when a fire started in London's Pudding Lane and burned for five days. By the end of it the London of Chaucer and Shakespeare was no more. Christopher Wren designed a new London while the fire was still raging, a plan that would have made the Royal Exchange the center of the city with magnificent boulevards radiating away from it. While Charles II liked the plan, he found it impossible to implement because the real estate rights were prohibitive. Although Wren's plan failed, it tells us a great deal about a shift in ideology: the old idea of the spiritual city, founded as a sacred burial place with the sanctuary in the center, had given way to the commercial city organized around the East India House, the Bank of England, the Royal Stock Exchange, and other trading firms and counting houses. It was this new commercial London that gave rise to a new breed of men who became wealthy from trade and other investments, men who made money by handling money, men like Thomas Gresham, the founder of the Royal Exchange, and the banker Josiah Child, as well as others like James Bateman, John Fryer, Peter Delme, Thomas Harley, Hugh Awdeley, Nicholas Barbon, Theodore Hannsen, Jacob Jacobson, and Peter Fabrot.

In *The Complete English Tradesman* (1726), Daniel Defoe said of this new class, "Our merchants are princes, greater and richer, and more powerful than some sovereign princes," and he contrasted the "immense wealth" of this new commercial class with the declining fortunes of the landed aristocracy.[4] It was this new class that in great part was responsible for the magnificent new townhouses that dominated such squares as Leicester, Bloomsbury, Soho, Red Lion, and St. James, built by such families as the Befords, Harleys, Portlands, Portmans, and Grosvenors. These houses were to the city what the estate was to the country. This was also the London of the new coffeehouses which, among other matters, served as clearinghouses for commercial business, as Lloyds was a clearinghouse for mercantile insurance. Each coffeehouse encouraged a different clientele, but those that served the new commercial investor also supplied commercial information (regarding the arrival and departure of ships, stock listings, and so forth) and thus were in effect the first newspapers. More formal newspapers came into being soon after and were the voice of the city. This was the London that by 1700 had a population of 575,000; by 1750, 675,000; and by 1800, 900,000, or over 10 percent of the combined population of England and Wales. Soon after the turn of the century, London became the first city in the Western world to have a population of over one million.

The literary mind that best understood how this city worked was Daniel Defoe's. A novel like *Robinson Crusoe* recapitulates the historical process: we move in the novel from isolation to community, from individual authority to government by consent, and from a wilderness to a primitive agrarian realm, to the beginnings of a commercial order. We move, that is, beyond the dictates of survival to a form of feudalism (where goods in a hierarchical society are produced for use and not for sale), and then to the beginnings of commercialism. A spiritual agency demands that Crusoe be aware of signs from above—and the storm, earthquake, and his own illness take on special religious significance for him. But equally important, Crusoe becomes an expert observer of the physical world and develops a finely trained empirical eye. By observing how nature works, he learns when he can best plant his corn and when it is safest to risk the tides in order to fish and travel the ocean. Such an understanding of nature allows a certain amount of control over it, from which he eventually moves to a control over the animals and later the humans who come to the island. Although Crusoe will leave the island briefly for a return to England, he returns to the island to divide up the land, allowing some to be taken as community property, but reserving to "my self the Property of the whole," with the right to sell it.[5] Robinson Crusoe is the father of us all—the first of the modern men. And while this novel seems to have little or no connection to the city, it is, I believe, one of our most important urban novels because it explains the cultural and historical process by which the commercial (that is, the modern) city came into being.

If *Robinson Crusoe* anticipates the coming of London, the work that analyzes that London in detail is Defoe's *A Tour Through the Whole Island of Great Britain* in which he gives one whole section of this book to a description of London itself. This is the famous "Letter V," which appears in a two-volume collection of thirteen "letters" describing Great Britain. For Defoe, this discussion of London comes in the center of his book, because London itself is the center of this world, everything emanating from and controlled by its institutions. Defoe's emphasis is upon commercial London as a marketplace and a trade center for the world. He estimates the size of London as seven and a half miles east to west, and five and three-quarter miles north to south, or slightly over forty-three square miles. Within this area he computes there to be 5,099 streets, lanes, and squares, encompassing 95,968 houses. And he estimates the population at 651,580. He describes at some length London moving beyond itself, incorporating the surrounding villages of Deptford, Islington, Miles End, Newington-butts, and Southwark, which in turn had incorporated Newington, Lambeth, and Borough. Defoe argues that the power had been transferred from the Court to the City, from a feudal to an urban realm. The Court now envied the City's wealth, the City had outlived the attacks upon it by the Court, and the Court had to recognize that the City was "necessary" to its very being—both as a source of money and a source of defense. Defoe also saw in his *Tour* that a large urban population made a division of labor necessary, turning the population into wage earners. The ability to earn good wages in turn advanced the commercial base of the society. More than any other document, Defoe's *Tour* showed how London had transformed not only its immediate environs but all of Great Britain, moving the population away from the land and away from the remains of a feudal society toward a commercial society that turned on money. Defoe was the first to see what has now become an axiom: in a premarket society, money follows power; in a market society, power follows money.

But the prosperity that Defoe depicts in the city was not equally shared by those who stayed on the land. Some of the landed families—such as the dukes of Leeds, Devonshire, Marlborough, and the earls of Pembroke, Bradford, and Portland—maintained their wealth by investing in the new commerce or, like the Russells, in the new joint-stock companies. Others maintained their positions by marrying into the new money as did the duke of Bedford when he married his grandson to the granddaughter of Sir John Spencer, a London merchant, or Lord Acton of Shropshire, who married the daughter of a goldsmith from Leadenhall Street. But despite these examples, a kind of class revolution was taking place with the center of wealth shifting away from the landed class and toward a new, urban commercial class that was a monied rather than a landed aristocracy. Only

200 of today's peerage were created before 1800. By 1802 only 17 of James I's creations survived in the male line.

The import of this is that many country estates were taken over by such families of new wealth as the Clives, the Pitts, and the Grosvenors; and a number of old estates went into decline as the source of wealth shifted from the land to the city. This situation became even worse under the influence of the enclosure movement that, between 1760 and 1845, affected an area of more than five million acres of common fields and forced the last of the tenant and yeoman farmers off the land and into a surplus of farm labor, sending many to the cities. The enclosure movement brought new land under tillage and increased the needed food supply, but it was also a land grab influenced by commercial speculation and protected by a new legal and political system.

Almost every novel written near the last half of the eighteenth century touches on at least one of these matters. Richardson's *Clarissa* (1747–48) is most revealing, since the Harlowes are members of the new commercial class intent on marrying Clarissa into another propertied family so that they can increase their holdings and better make claim to the aristocracy. Almost all of the narrative events in this novel are set in the context of the estate as opposed to the city—as is Fielding's *Tom Jones* and Goldsmith's *The Vicar of Wakefield*—novels that involve women who are kidnapped or flee from the estate and are brought into the city where their experiences are unhappy ones. With some indulgence one can even think of *Tom Jones* as a *Clarissa* if only the novel could have been told from Sophia's point of view, or of *Tom Jones* and *Clarissa* as a *Vicar of Wakefield* if only Squire Western or Mr. Harlowe could have been capable of expressing the sense of the lost daughter as well as Reverend Primrose.

Such speculation points to the curious fact that so many of these novels treat the same kind of narrative situation within the framework of the estate as it is transformed by the city. In *Tom Jones,* Paradise Hall remains unchanged and, along with Squire Allworthy, is the moral frame of reference to which the novel constantly returns—just as the estate and the Mr. Knightley figure prevail in the later novels of Jane Austen. But in *Clarissa* something different is happening, and the story is finally played out in proto-Gothic terms.

We have a great many books dealing with the rise of the Gothic novel in this period, but no one to my knowledge has seen the possible connection between the rise of the new city, the decline of the landed estate, and the rise of the Gothic. This seems strange to me because so many of these novels—Walpole's *The Castle of Otronto* (1764), Radcliffe's *The Mysteries of Udolpho* (1794), and Godwin's *Caleb Williams* (1794) come to mind—treat the passing of the estate and locate the origins of so much evil in the city.

The narrative patterns in these and other Gothic novels are very similar. The story is set in the past—in a feudal castle or a landed estate that has been touched by the hand of death and is caught in the process of decay. The connection between the past and the present has been disrupted by a fraudulent claim upon the state, or the estate has come by new owners—often rich merchants or members of the new city's commercial class, or the estate has been intruded upon by the new city types such as the libertine whose hardened heart and jaded virtues are the by-product of his city ways. The end result is that the world of the old father has been disrupted by the ways of the new, and a kind of curse has been put on the land, which disrupts the natural processes in a mysterious, sometimes in a supernatural way.

The symbiosis between the city and countryside was breaking down. When the historical signs of this breakdown were translated into literary codes, what we got was the Gothic novel. And if the relationship between the city and the countryside was unsettled, what was going on beneath the surface of the city was equally unsettled and unsettling. The city was subverting itself from within. In a commercial system, everything comes back to what is for sale; in the case of Moll Flanders and Roxana, this becomes their bodies. Those who cannot fit into the commercial system become homeless, like Colonel Jack and Moll Flanders, and often take to crime or piracy, as in the case of Captain Singleton. The city tries to impose a grid upon nature, to harness its energies and turn a profit; but beneath the grid is an underground, a city within a city, one undermining the other. London as a system is quick to discard what it cannot use. As a result, we get a sense of human detritus as an unfortunate by-product of the city. Such outcasts usually end in the New World: in the American colonies, as is the case with Moll Flanders and Colonel Jack; or in Africa, Brazil, and the South Seas, as with Captain Singleton; or on the Continent, as with Roxana. Thus Defoe's London leads to the world, usually the underdeveloped world, from which it brings in raw material, precious metals, and slave labor for its colonies, and to which it exports its commercial goods and social outcasts.

This paradigm will be repeated over and over, with changes of empha-

sis only, even as the urban structure is transformed from a commercial to
an industrial, to the world city. What we begin to see is that a by-product
of the city is waste—or more specifically junk. Krook's junk shop in
Dickens's *Bleak House* and Boffins's Bower and Mr. Venus's taxidermy shop
in *Our Mutual Friend* testify to how junk is the end product of a commercial society. The city can only function if things wear out and are used
up—and this is true for humans as well, as Little Nell, Jo the street-
sweep, and Little Dorrit all testify. If Dickens tends to concentrate upon
the dereliction of children, orphans, and helpless women, it is because his
appeal is to the heart—that is, to sentiment or the power to do good in
the face of evil. Evil in Dickens's world is always substantial and lurks
beneath the surface of the city. It is often inseparable from the men who
embody the institutions of the commercial city—men like Tulkinghorn
or Jaggers, the lawyers who control those around them by controlling
information, men who know how institutions work or men who have
fathomed secrets that lie buried in the heart.

In *The Journal of the Plague Year,* Defoe brought a commercial observer
into the infected city to read and to interpret the urban signs—the famous H. F. whose final conclusion is that the plague comes from natural
and not divine sources and is thus not an indictment of the commercial
process. As we move from Pepys to Addison's spectator, the text uses an
observer of the city who becomes more distant in the way he observes. In
Wuthering Heights, in the character of Lockwood, Brontë will bring this
spectator into the Gothic countryside where he will misread the signs of
the changing landscape. In his book on Baudelaire, Walter Benjamin discusses this literary figure in detail, refers to him as the flaneur, and sees
him as the new reader of urban signs. "To him the shiny, enamelled signs
of business are at least as good a wall ornament as an oil painting is to a
bourgeois in his salon. The walls are the desk against which he presses his
notebooks; news-stands are his libraries and the terraces of cafes are the
balconies from which he looks down on his household after his work is
done."[6]

In Dickens, this figure becomes the detective who from Nadgitt in
Martin Chuzzlewit to Inspector Bucket in *Bleak House* cuts through the
anonymity of the city, unlocks the secrets that hold many of the characters
in bondage, and helps the summer sun to burn away the winter fog. And
as in the case of Esther Summerson in *Bleak House,* the mystery often
unfolds at the grave, as when Inspector Bucket traces Esther's mother to

the grave of Nemo and unlocks her from the past by revealing her parent-
age. The first cities—Ur and Uruk—were founded as a place where wan-
dering tribes could return to worship the dead, and the idea of the city
has never been separated from the reality of death. But by the time we
get to Dickens, as both F. S. Schwarzbach and Alexander Welsh have
shown, the fate of the living is inseparable from the fate of the dead. As
Schwarzbach points out, both *Oliver Twist* and *Nicholas Nickleby* end in the
graveyard of Agnes and Smike, and "the dead are what link the living to
a vision of their childhood memories which prefigure the joys of paradise,"[7] joys that Alexander Welsh finds ministered to by Dickens's feminine angels. Dickens's city seems to mediate between the living and the
dead. In its worst embodiment it is brokered by the money-counters like
Ralph Nickleby and Quilp in *The Old Curiosity Shop,* John Chester in
Barnaby Rudge, and Jonas Chuzzlewit, or its functionaries like Bumble in
Oliver Twist and Pecksniff in *Martin Chuzzlewit.* In its redemptive possibilities, it is represented by Pickwick, Mr. Brownlow, the Cherryble
brothers, Esther Summerson, Sydney Carton, Pip and Lizzie Hexam—
many of whom must pass through a near terminal illness before they can
function effectively in the city of the living. The city also seems to mediate between nature and civilization. Over and over, Dickens describes
the city extending to a kind of middle ground between the city and the
countryside—a strange, eerie, primitive realm, often a world of marshes,
of water and mud with often a house sinking into the mud, or a sluice
gate, or a mill. Where water and land meet, where the country and the
city intersect, or where the present and past verge, we have narrative flash
points in Dickens's fiction. This becomes a kind of modern hell that many
of Dickens's characters enter before they enter the city itself. Out of this
world comes a primitive evil, slink various human outcasts who are almost mutant forms of humanity. In *Oliver Twist,* Bill Sikes emerges from
and goes to his death in such a region, as does Quilp in *The Old Curiosity
Shop,* and Bradley Headstone in *Our Mutual Friend.* In *Great Expectations,*
Orlick slithers from such a realm with a primitive evil clinging to him.
Such a realm is always on the verge of reclaiming the city, a realm into
which the city is seemingly about to sink. The image—and it is an obsessive one with Dickens—seems to suggest the tenuousness of the city.
Defoe was confident that modern man could impose his will upon nature,
create structures of authority like the city that would minister to the
wealth that it created. Dickens seems less confident of this prospect,

showing us that what is outside the city—first in what it inhumanely discards, and second in what is subterranean in its nature—has the capacity to reclaim the prideful city and its monuments to self.

The most graphic illustration of this pattern is in Hugo's *Les misérables,* where we have a dramatic contrast between Jean Valjean, the urban outcast, and Javert, the police inspector, who embodies social authority. In the original city, the fort stood to protect the inhabitants from threats from without. In the Victorian city, the fort has given way to the prison, protecting the inhabitants from what is within the city. Javert interestingly was born in prison and is using his life to repudiate all that falls outside of urban order and control. This explains his hatred for Jean Valjean, who has been sent to prison for stealing a loaf of bread and whose sympathies are with the poor and the outcast. The famous descent into the Paris sewers is a descent into an urban hell, using the typologies of Dante, a descent that is into the land of the dead, even to the extent that Valjean crosses a River Styx and is released from this hell by a gatekeeper of the dead, Thénardier. As with Dickens, Hugo's characters seem to have to pass through the land of the dead before they can be redeemed in the new commercial city—a theme that will become pervasive in modern literature as one can illustrate from such works as Pound's *Cantos,* Joyce's *Ulysses* (especially the Hades and Circe episodes), and Eliot's *The Waste Land* with its journey to the cemetery at the Chapel Perilous. Other texts like Balzac's *Père Goriot,* in which Rastignac commits himself to the city from the graves of Père Lachaise, and *The Great Gatsby* and *Sister Carrie,* only multiply examples. Those who have passed through the city and into death seem to know the mysteries that unlock the city's doors and to make the passage through it possible. They tell us how fragile we are, how illusory the city's monuments, and how distorting the commercial process can be. The nineteenth-century novel often begins with the young man leaving the provinces to seek a higher and essential self in the city and closes with such a young man trying to be reunited with the family that he left behind. Such is the story of *Great Expectations, The Red and the Black,* and *Lost Illusions.* The more the city seemed to move beyond the human scale, the more technology changed the dimensions in the way man functioned, the more the literary imagination took solace in remnant forms of humanity—the city of the dead and the family that was left behind.

Not only was the city becoming an illusion, but the processes that took place in the city were equally illusory. Defoe believed that commercial value came into being through work; Dickens showed how it came into being through manipulation and speculation. Money began to make money. By the time we get to a novel like Gogol's *Dead Souls,* there is no connection between value and the commercial process. Chichikov goes into the countryside to buy up dead souls (that is, the titles on dead peasants) which he then mortgages at the bank, turning the city of the dead into a commodity. The commercial system promoted schemes that exploited the system itself rather than encouraged useful production. In Gogol's "The Overcoat" and "The Nose," he shows how this process, carried to extremes, anticipates the world of Kafka. As the city becomes less friendly and more hostile, the inhabitants become more alienated, the landscape more grotesque, and the process itself more absurd. H. G. Wells carried this idea even further in *Tono-Bungay* where the patent medicine that makes Uncle Ponderevo wealthy is only slightly injurious to the health of those who use it and where schemes, like the search for quap, move the commercial process into a stage of imperialism (the invasion of the wilderness, the killing of the natives, and the exploitation of natural resources). Conrad would take the imperial city as his subject and show how the demands at the extremities can eat away the heart of the imperial city, leaving even greater waste—the waste of natural resources, of human dignity, and of the urban system itself. T. S. Eliot's *The Waste Land* finds its being right here, in the contrast between the commercial city and the mythic imagination with its cyclical sense of history that allows memory to voice from the city of the dead warnings to the city of the living, as Eliot's Tiresias comes from the underworld to foretell it all in the commercial center of London.

II

If we see the beginnings of the commercial city in the works of Defoe, we see its endings in the works of Dickens, who carries us into the industrial city in a novel like *Hard Times* with its depiction of Coketown. Dickens had anticipated the industrial city in novels like *Dombey and Son* when he described the railroad transforming the urban landscape. Perhaps the most important element in the rise of the industrial city was the invention of the steam engine in 1769 which freed the factory from rural waterpower and moved it into the city, bringing the workers with it, and creating the terrible slums that took hold in all the major industrial cities of the Western world. Burgess and Park of the University of Chicago best described the way the industrial city evolved, passing through a series of concentric circles. "The first ring from the central business district is a zone of transition, of warehouses and the residences of the poor. Then comes a ring of the more solid working class; then the white-collar professions, with the richest pushing outward to escape the intrusion of the other groups as the city grows."[8]

The most complete depiction of the industrial city is not in the sentimental novels of Dickens but in the naturalistic novels of Zola—novels like *L'Assomoir* and *Nana,* which take us to the proletarian depths of the city and to its comfortable heights, the salons corrupted by the money that comes from this social imbalance, from the surplus profit and exploitation of the workers, to put it into the Marxist terms that serve as a subtext for these novels. Zola's world is one of limits; if one is to have great wealth, then there must be poverty. Zola describes the political shifts of the peasants in the countryside as they jockey for profit in the Second Empire. But the physical center of his Rougon-Macquart novels is Paris. While *Germinal* and *La Débâcle* are not city novels, they show how the city controls what goes on in the coal mines of the north or in the intrigue that leads to war. No one can escape the reach of Paris as Zola dramatically shows in *L'Argent.* The biological processes of life and death have been transformed in the modern world, moved from the realm of nature to the realm of the city. In *Le Ventre de Paris* (1873) and *Au bonheur des dames* (1883), he describes two kinds of marketplaces: the Halles Centrales, which supplies food, and the modern department store, which supplies material goods—which show the new industrial city organizing the means to satisfy biological needs. The industrial city was a power structure that organized the way goods came into being, were distributed, and finally consumed. When raw materials or markets became scarce, the city reached beyond itself and created empires in England, France, Belgium, and Germany—a process that would eventually play itself out in two global wars in 1914 and 1939. As Jacques Ellul has shown, as these societies became more technologically sufficient, they also found the means of controlling the masses, the information that reached the masses, and the liberties that were allowed them.[9] The industrial city takes us to the doorsteps of the totalitarian city. Nathanael West showed in *The Day of the Locust* (1939) how an unsatisfied, restless, disorganized mass could easily explode into anarchic protest at the same time that it harbored the potential to be reorganized by a super ruler as was happening in Hitler's Germany.

The city crowd became the subject of new concern. Books like Gustave LeBon's *The Crowd* (1896) had great influence. As LeBon would show, civilization, which had always been directed by a small aristocracy, suddenly had to come to terms with crowds that had the potential to effect the "final dissolution" of modern civilization. George Orwell in *1984* (1949), Jack London in *The Iron Heel* (1908), H. G. Wells in *When the Sleeper Wakes* (1899), E. M. Forster in "When the Machine Stops," all saw that a mass was only one step away from a master, and that the needs of a technological society, with its emphasis upon efficiency and control, played into the hands of totalitarian movements, as Zamyantan had shown in *We* (1924).

In his book on Baudelaire, Walter Benjamin describes Baudelaire's fascination with the crowd, because the crowd embodied an energy that released the imagination. There is a mystery in the crowd, a sense of new possibilities, of new experience—a new lover, as Baudelaire suggests in "To a Passer-by": "Somewhere, far off! too late! *never,* perchance! . . . We might have loved, and you knew this might be!" (45). Benjamin's suggestion explains the sense of discontent the city inculcates because it offers so many possibilities that one feels something is being missed even in the act of experiencing; the city thus becomes inseparable from feelings of restlessness, dissatisfaction, and aimless desire. As West showed in *The Day of the Locust,* such potential can be frightening, at which point it overwhelms our sense of identity, our desire for stability, and when not controlled can lead to frenzy or to the kind of neurasthenia that Eliot describes in *The Waste Land.* When the sense of experience latent in the crowd becomes threatening, when we have no real physical object for our fear, it can lead to the kind of paranoia that Pynchon describes in *The Crying of Lot 49.* The crowd can embody the city and ways of responding to the city, which is why the artist, from Poe to Baudelaire, often escaped into the crowd. As Benjamin has told us, "To Poe the flaneur was, above all, someone who does not feel comfortable in his own company. . . . 'He is the man of the crowd'" (48). Baudelaire is the man in the crowd. He hated Brussels because there were no shop windows. "Baudelaire loved solitude, but he wanted it in a crowd" (50).

It is Baudelaire who takes us into the ways Modernism (the literary movement) rejected the industrial city by establishing an elaborate aestheticism that never let it shine through. Joyce does exactly this in *A Portrait of the Artist as a Young Man* when Stephen Dedalus creates an aesthetic or artistic equivalent for all that he sees in Dublin: "His morning walk across the city had begun; and he foreknew that as he passed the sloblands of Fairview he would think of the cloistral silver-veined prose of Newman; that as he walked along the North Strand Road, glancing idly at the windows of the provision shops, he would recall the dark humour of Guido Cavalcanti . . . ; that as he went by Baird's stone cutting works in Talbot Place the spirit of Ibsen would blow through him like a keen wind." [10] At some point in his career, Joyce also learned that he could transform literary naturalism and the city that emerged from it by superimposing a symbolic or mythic plane of reference upon it, thus establishing a contrast between the diminished city of the modern and the heroic city of the past, a contrast that reinforced his Viconian belief in the cyclical decline of modern man. And what Joyce did in *Ulysses,* Eliot would also do in *The Waste Land.*

III

When such ways of observing the city were challenged, we moved from the modern to the postmodern. In *Mythologies* (1957), Roland Barthes tells us that he distrusts myth for, unlike language, myth does not generate its own meaning; history supplies the meaning that is embedded in myth. The message of myth is taken as natural and true rather than as signs and mental processes by which man endows his world with meaning. In *The Empire of Signs* (1983), Barthes applies this idea to a reading of a modern city. Tokyo, he tells us, has no center out of which the rest of the city radiates, as with cities of medieval origin in the Western world. Like Jacques Derrida, Barthes sees everything as writing, including the city on which there are written planes of inscription. As in the literary text, the city becomes a galaxy of signifiers, not a structure of signifieds: "The codes it mobilizes extend as far as the eye can reach, they are indeterminable." [11]

If the city of Defoe suggests the grid, and the city of Hugo the underground, the postmodern city suggests the labyrinth where experience is cut off from memory and memory from signification in a landscape of paranoia that defies repetition and fixity. In a recent essay, Fredric Jameson has tried to develop this idea with a detailed description of the Bonaventure Hotel in downtown Los Angeles, a hotel that fills space without ordering it. Jameson sees an equivalence between this hotel and multinational capitalism, which no longer has a center.[12] American money is invested in Europe and Japan, European and Japanese money is invested in America, and the multinational corporations that control this money invest it throughout the world. In Defoe's commercial city, Englishmen invested English money in English commercial adventures that may have sent ships around the world, but always in the name of England. In Zola's industrial city, Paris becomes the center of the Second Empire, just as London is the center of the British empire for Conrad, the center often weakened by its outreach to the extremities, but the center as something knowable and defined.

In postmodernism, the commercial and the industrial city have given way to the world city, and once again the way the city encodes its messages has been transformed. The literary embodiment of this new city is a work like Pynchon's *The Crying of Lot 49* (1966), the story of Oedipa Maas, the woman trying to come to terms with the world of the father in the maze. In trying to resolve the legacy of Pierce Inverarity, she journeys through Barthes's city without a center, which in Pynchon's novel is Los Angeles, renamed San Narciso since it gives back, like an echo, what is brought to it. All the themes that we saw in Defoe, Dickens, and Zola— the waste, miscommunication, secrets that hold the city together, the dead that beckon from their graves—all seem to leave signs that point toward a secret organization named the Trystero. But like an echo, Oedipa is not sure that the Trystero really exists or is just the rebound of the paranoid suspicions that she has brought to the city. She believes the Trystero had its origins in the seventeenth century—that is, with the rise of Puritanism and the commercial city—and that it moved across Europe, and then an ocean, and then a continent before it arrived in Los Angeles. The Trystero lives off the waste the system leaves behind, lives off entropy—mechanical, communicative, and human entropy—turning commodities into physical waste, communication into noise and then silence, and human resources into death. Such seems the legacy of the city, of Pierce Inverarity's order and control. But like Barthes's reading of the text, Oedipa's reading of the city finds only plural meanings; the networks are many and interact, without any of them being able to surpass the rest. What she ends up with is all signifiers and no signified.[13] Pynchon's *Lot 49* is only one of a number of postmodern novels that have ideologically redefined the city; Gaddis's *The Recognitions* (1955), DeLillo's *White Noise*

(1985), and Pynchon's own *Gravity's Rainbow* (1973) are others that come to mind; and more examples are available in science fiction, especially novels like Samuel Delaney's *The Einstein Intersection* (1967).

As the function of the city changes, its very nature changes, and those changes alter our ideologies that are encoded in cultural signs, including our literary texts. Walter Benjamin has told us as much: "Every epoch not only dreams the next, but while dreaming impels it toward wakefulness. It hears its end within itself, and reveals it . . . by ruse. With the upheaval of the market economy, we begin to recognize the monuments of the bourgeoisie as ruins even before they have crumbled" (176).

The commercial, industrial, and world cities cannot be divorced from the systemic processes that brought them into being—and neither can they be divorced from the ideological processes that they in turn bring into being. For as Roland Barthes has told us, such processes are the means by which man endows his world with meaning. If such is the case, then the consequences for literary criticism are greater than we seem to be aware, because it means that the better we read the city, the better we are reading the literary text.

NOTES

1. Lewis Mumford, *The City in History: Its Origins, Its Transformations, and Its Prospects* (New York, 1961) and idem, *Culture of the Cities* (New York, 1938); Leonardo Benevolo, *The History of the City,* tr. Geoffrey Culverwell (Cambridge, Mass., 1980); Wolf Schneider, *Babylon Is Everywhere: The City as Man's Fate,* tr. Ingeborg Sammet and John Oldenburg (New York, 1963). The recent book by Mark Girourd, *Cities and People: A Social and Architectural History* (New Haven, 1985), could be added to this list. Also relevant to my discussion in this essay are Max Weber, *The City* (New York, 1958); Karl Polanyi, *The Great Transformation* (New York, 1944); Fernand Braudel, *Civilization and Capitalism,* 3 vols. (London, 1981–84); Manfred Tafuri, *Architecture and Utopia: Design and Capitalistic Development,* tr. Barbara Luigia La Penta (Cambridge, Mass., 1976); Richard Sennett, *The Uses of Disorder: Personal Identity and City Life* (New York, 1970); Kevin Lynch, *A Theory of the Good City* (Cambridge, Mass., 1981); and Jane Jacobs, *Death and Life of Great Cities* (New York, 1961).

2. Max Byrd, *London Transformed: Images of the City in the Eighteenth Century* (New Haven, 1978); Alexander Welsh, *The City of Dickens* (New York, 1971); F. S. Schwarzbach, *Dickens and the City* (London, 1979); Donald Fanger, *Dostoevsky and Romantic Realism: A Study of Dostoevsky in Relation to Balzac, Dickens, and Gogol* (Chicago, 1967); Burton Pike, *The Image of the City in Modern Literature* (Princeton, 1981).

3. Daniel Bell, *The Coming of the Post-Industrial Society: A Venture in Social Forecasting* (New York, 1973). David M. Gordon, "Capitalist Development and the History of American Cities," in *Marxism and the Metropolis,* ed. William K. Tabb and Larry Sawers (New York, 1978), pp. 25–63, esp. pp. 53–55.

4. Daniel Defoe, *The Complete English Tradesman* (London, 1745).

5. Daniel Defoe, *Robinson Crusoe,* ed. Michael Shinagel (New York, 1975), p. 237.

6. Walter Benjamin, *Charles Baudelaire: A Lyric Poet in the Era of High Capitalism,* tr. Harry Zohn (London, 1973), p. 37; hereafter cited in text.

7. Schwarzbach, p. 61.

8. As summarized by Tabb and Sawers in *Marxism and the Metropolis,* p. 10. For a more direct understanding of Park's views, see Robert Ezra Park, *Human Communities: The City and Human Ecology* (Glencoe, Ill., 1952), esp. pp. 13–51 and 118–41.

9. Jacques Ellul, *The Technological Society,* tr. John Wilkinson (New York, 1964).

10. James Joyce, *A Portrait of the Artist as a Young Man* (New York, 1944), p. 204.

11. Roland Barthes, S / Z, tr. Richard Miller (New York, 1974), pp. 5–6.

12. Fredric Jameson. "Postmodernism, or the Cultural Logic of Late Capitalism," *New Left Review* 146 (1984): 53–92.

13. The vertigo that Barthes and Oedipa Maas experience, of course, takes on special meaning in the era after Nietzsche, Heidegger, and William James and American pragmatism where an ideal or essential reality is challenged and cut off by the "bracketing" of consciousness or by defining all metaphysical-epistemological problems as semantic and linguistic matters. But Pynchon is not working with figural or other linguistic theories of dispersal in *Lot 49.* The more immediate influence here is a book like Norbert Wiener's *The Human Use of Human Beings* (Boston, 1950), which deals with information theory. Within every system of organization, Wiener tells us, is a process of disorganization (of entropy). As my essay has tried to show, Defoe, Dickens, Zola, and Joyce, in their different ways, saw the way the city, as a social system, disrupted itself from within. This was not a purely linguistic matter for any of these writers—not even Joyce. And it is not a purely linguistic matter for Pynchon, who embodies such disruption in the historical process he identifies with the Trystero. This is why in such readings I think it important to see such disruptions on a historical-cultural-ideological level—and not simply and inclusively in terms of a theory of nonreferential language (for which there is no known proof and which privileges this argument in a way that its proponents attack other arguments for being privileged).

10

RECYCLING: RACE, GENDER AND
THE PRACTICE OF THEORY

Deborah E. McDowell

The old patterns, no matter how cleverly rearranged to imitate
progress, still condemn us to cosmetically altered repetitions of
the same old exchanges.   —Audre Lorde

History, I contend, is the present—we, with every breath we
take, every move we move, *are* History—and what goes around,
comes around.   —James Baldwin

To exist historically is to perceive the events one lives through
as part of a story later to be told.   —Arthur Danto

This was not a story to pass on.   —Toni Morrison

TO SPEAK OF "HISTORICAL KNOWLEDGE" is to stage or enter a
vigorous debate between those who see "history" and "knowledge" as ontological givens and those who don't. I identify with those who don't,
with those who recognize that, despite its basis in a verifiable then and
thereness, often complete with concrete facts and recognizable person-
ages, history is a fantastical and slippery concept, a making, a construction.[1] I side with those who see history, to invoke the current lingua
franca, as a "contested terrain," although it often functions to repress and
contain the conflicts and power asymmetries that define the sociopolitical
field.

That contemporary students of culture and its institutions have by and
large willingly adjusted their assumptions and altered their practices to
fit these axioms, is a salutary development. But I share Renato Rosaldo's
fear that in our zeal to establish historical contingency, to show that *everything* is constructed, human beings tend to "lose their specific gravity,
their weight, and their density, and begin to float." We would do well to
heed Rosaldo's warning against the dangers of declaring historical knowledge constructed and simply ending the discussion there, for we must

"show in historical perspective," however difficult that is, "how it was constructed, by whom, and with what consequences."[2]

Here, I want to take some liberties with time and construe the present moment as the future's past in order to determine what "historical knowledge" of "literary theory" we are constructing at this moment and with what consequences to what specific bodies. In other words, how are we telling the history or story of recent theoretical developments? Who are the principals in that story? What are the strategies of its emplotment? How does it reconstitute timeworn structures and strategies of dominance? Recode familiar hierarchical relations?

As with most everyone else today, at least nominally, I am keenly interested in how race and gender figure into the objects of our critical inquiry, and in this matter of criticism's history, I am specifically and especially interested in where *black American women* and their discourses enter into the record (or not). I agree with Hortense Spillers that "in a very real sense, black American women are invisible to various public discourse, and the state of invisibility for them has its precedent in an analogy on any patriarchal symbolic mode that we might wish to name."[3] But what interests me here is their "visible" invisibility within Anglo-American feminism and Afro-American literary criticism. The laudable project to restore black American women to sight is often rent asunder or, at best, stalled by the far more powerful imperatives of historical legacy and contemporary social design. As Evan Watkins notes, "How we tell ourselves the history of recent theoretical developments . . . takes place in [that] shady zone between the boundaries of intellectual work and social situation, and attempts to resolve its tensions,"[4] but, as I hope to show, those tensions are not so easily resolved.

What follows is not a singular narrative, but rather, a few miscellaneous examples—call them "case studies"—about black feminist thinking that are rapidly assuming a structural relevance and significance that can no longer be ignored. One could raise at least two serious objections here. The first is that a focus on what has been written *about* black feminist thinking eclipses a more constructive, perhaps a more empowering focus on what has been written *by* black feminists.

In her review of Patricia Hill Collins's *Black Feminist Thought,* for example, Farah Griffin commended Collins for moving black feminism "to a new level" by spending "little time castigating white feminists or black men for their failures in regard to black women." She praises Collins for focusing instead "on an exploration and analysis of thought produced by black women themselves. In so doing, she reinforces their status as subjects and agents of history."[5] While I would dispute Griffin's perception that the work of black feminists has been, to this point, determinedly other-directed, I regard her implied call for a necessary shift of focus and address *within* the work of black feminism absolutely essential. But such a shift is, alone, insufficient, for it ignores the often unequally positioned sites of knowledge production and their influence on how and if the work of black feminists is read, on how and if it is read in a way that restructures, not simply annexes, knowledge in ceaseless reflex acts.

One could raise a second objection, and that is that my focus is too strictly and narrowly academicist, and curiously so, if we consider that although its main address is now the UNIVERSITY, black feminist thinking does not stake its origins or find its shelter there, and even when academia is its central site, it strives to extend its borders beyond.[6] While the focus is narrow, its implications and imperatives for the organization and construction of historical knowledge are much broader. The hierarchies and orders of value this construction encodes help to resituate African-American women and other "women of color" in a narrative that underwrites a familiar sociocultural contract, the terms of which are often silent, the print of which is often fine.

As we know, in the emplotment or narrativization of history, much depends on familiar vocabularies of reference, on the circulation of names, of proper names, and some names are more proper than others.[7] I want to talk briefly about the circulation of one name—Sojourner Truth—and the knowledge that name helps to construct about black feminist thinking within the general parameters of feminist discourse.[8]

UNCOVERING TRUTH, OR COLORING "FEMINIST THEORY"
In the opening chapter of her study *Am I That Name? Feminism and the Category of "Women" in History,* Denise Riley begins with a reference to Sojourner Truth and her famous and much-quoted question—"Ain't I a Woman?"—posed before the 1851 Women's Rights Convention in Akron, Ohio. Riley supposes that, in the current historical moment, Sojourner "might well—except for the catastrophic loss of grace in wording—issue another plea: 'Ain't I a Fluctuating Identity?'" The temptation here is simply to find the humor in Riley's rewriting and move on, except that to do so is to miss the sociocultural assumptions that constellate

around it, assumptions that escape the boundaries of Truth's time to project themselves boldly in our own.

Riley's move to appropriate Sojourner Truth introduces a subtle racial
marker that distinguishes between Truth's original words and Riley's
modernization that displaces them. That modernization allegorizes a
common, if sometimes muted, assumption about black women and their
language found in much contemporary literary-critical discussion. That
assumption is that black women, and I should add, women of color more
generally, need a new language, a language in the service of a theory,
preferably a poststructuralist theory, signaled in this context by the term
fluctuating identity.[9]

To trace the move from Sojourner Truth's "Ain't I a Woman?" to Riley's
"Ain't I a Fluctuating Identity?" is to plot, in effect, two crucial stages in
a historical narrative of academic feminism's coming of age. Following
this evolutionary logic, academic feminist discourse can be said to have
"grown out of," or to have outgrown, an attachment to what Riley terms
that "blatant[ly] disgrace[ful]" and "transparently suspicious" category—
"Woman." That category happens to be personified by Sojourner's rhetorical and declarative question. Riley concedes that Sojourner represents one
move in a necessary "double move" of feminist theory which recognizes
that "both a concentration on and a refusal of the identity of 'woman' are
essential to feminism."[10]

Constance Penley makes essentially the same point in *The Future of an
Illusion.* Whereas in Riley's study Sojourner marks the point of departure,
in Penley's she marks the point of closure. In the last two pages of the
final chapter, she walks on to take a bow with Jacques Lacan. His "noto-
rious bravura"—"the woman does not exist"—is counterposed to Sojourner Truth's "Ain't I a Woman?" Echoing Riley, Penley explains this
counterposition as "two ideas or strategies . . . vitally important to feminism," though they might appear completely at odds. Penley classifies
the one strategy—represented by Lacan, Althusser, and Derrida—as
"epistemological" and "metaphysical"; the other, represented by Sojourner
Truth as "political." That Truth's declarative question—"Ain't I a
Woman?"—might be read as "political" *and* "epistemological" simultaneously seems not to have occurred to Penley, partly because she manip-
ulates both these categories—consciously or not, to conform to an already
polarized and preconceived understanding.[11]

Is it purely accidental that, in these two essays, Sojourner Truth comes to represent the politics but not the poetics that feminism needs? Is hers a purely neutral exemplarity? Agreeing with Gayatri Spivack that "it is at those borders of discourse where metaphor and example seem arbitrarily *chosen* that ideology breaks through," [12] I would argue that Sojourner is far from an arbitrary example. Possible intentions, notwithstanding, Sojourner Truth is useful in this context both to a singular idea of academic feminism, in general, and, in particular, to recent controversies within that discourse over the often uneasy relations between epistemology and politics. Black women figure prominently in both the general and particular dimensions; in the former, by their absence; in the latter, by their complicated presence.

The belief that feminism and whiteness form a homogeneous unity has long persisted, along with the equally persistent directive to feminist theorists to "account" in their discourses for the experiences of women of color. The unexamined assumption that white feminist discourse bears a special responsibility to women of color helps to maintain the perception that feminism equates with whiteness and relates maternalistically to women of color.

Such assumptions are implied in the recently published *Feminist Theory in Practice and Process*. In "Naming the Politics of Theory," one section of the introduction, the editors challenge "feminist theory . . . to recognize the myriad forms of black women's race, gender, and class politics and to envision theories that encompass these lived realities and concrete practices." [13] Elizabeth Spelman's observation is useful here: "It is not white middle class women who are different from other women, but all other women who are different from them." [14]

That difference has become magnified and has assumed an even greater urgency since academic feminism, like all discursive communities on the contemporary scene, has accepted the constructive challenge to take its processes into self-conscious account; that is, since it has accepted the challenge to "theorize" about the work it does and the claims it makes. The strain to fulfill both requirements—to "theorize," on the one hand, and to recognize material "differences," on the other, has created a tension within academic feminist discourse (read *white*). That tension is often formulated as a contrast, if not a contest, between "theory" and "practice-politics" respectively.

I must rush to add that race (here, read *black*) and gender (here, read *female*) are not the only stigmatized markers on the practice-politics side of the border between theory and practice, for they trade places in a fluid system of interchangeability with differences of nationality, sexuality, and class.[15] The now quiescent French-American feminist theory debate— illustrated most controversially in Toril Moi's *Sexual / Textual Politics*— provides one example of what I mean. Moi clumps Anglo-American, black, and lesbian women on the practice-politics-criticism side of the border; French women, on the theory side. After blasting the claims of Anglo-American feminist criticism, Moi then turns to answer those who well "might wonder why [she has] said nothing about black or lesbian (or black lesbian) feminist criticism in America. . . . The answer is simple: this book purports to deal with the theoretical aspects of feminist criticism. So far, lesbian and / or black feminist criticism have presented exactly the same *methodological* and *theoretical* problems as the rest of Anglo-American feminist criticism" (emphasis in text). Moi adds, "This is not to say that black and lesbian criticism have no . . . importance," but that importance is not to be "found at the level of *theory* . . . but the level of *politics*."[16]

In the context of these critical developments, the use of "Sojourner Truth" projects myriad meanings needed to perform the work of distinction and differentiation in the culture of academe. To begin with, as a metonym for "black woman," the name can be read as a mark of racial difference and distinction within "feminist theory," which points up its internal conflicts and ambivalence over the relative merits and value of "political" discourse. That racial difference is frequently hidden in itineraries represented as "purely" (and thus neutrally?) epistemological, is evident in the following summary by Jane Flax: "Feminist theorists have tried to maintain two different epistemological positions. The first is that the mind, the self, and knowledge are socially constituted, and what we can know depends on our social practices and contexts. The second is that feminist theorists can uncover truths about the whole as it 'really is.' Those who support the second position reject many post-modern ideas and must depend upon certain assumptions about truth and the knowing subject."[17]

The assumptions about Truth examined so far—both explicit and implied—cast her categorically in that second position, despite the fact that the short text of the "Ain't I a Woman?" speech is a compressed but powerful analysis and critique of the social practices within the context of slavery that depend on biases of class and race to construct an idea of universal or True Womanhood. She challenged that dominant knowledge, offering and authorizing her experiences under slavery as proof of its underlying illogicality.

The "truth" that Truth knows, then, is not reducible to a mere statement turned slogan that acts as theory's Other, or theory's shadow side. The politics contained within *that* epistemology, within that way of knowing Truth, must be interrogated and the foundations on which it rests laid bare. When we remember the full content and context of Sojourner Truth's speech, as well as its degrading aftermath, those foundations are sharply exposed.

After Truth delivered the speech, which turns on references to her body and its exploitation during slavery as a reproductive machine, one Dr. T. W. Strain alleged that she was a man. To prove that she wasn't, Truth bared her breasts.[18] The scene concludes with Truth's fixity in the body and, thus, effectively, in her distance from the "proper" white feminists enlisted to "verify" her sex. Her recuperation in these modern contexts forges a symbolic connection with that prior history, a conjunctive relationship to that past. It is precisely this earlier scene of verification that is being symbolically reenacted today. The demand in this present context is not to bare the breasts to verify womanhood but to bare the evidence that would verify knowledge that "black womanhood" is a discursive formation fluctuating in time.

But the selection of Sojourner Truth as metonym raises still other problems that connect to the relation between the symbolic and the social, the relation between the present and the past. The fact that Sojourner Truth was illiterate and that the words by which we know her were transcribed by stenographic reporters or admiring white friends has only begun to be interrogated with any complexity. Recent work by Nell Irvin Painter has begun to engage the nexus of paradoxes, ironies, and contradictions of these transcriptions and to inquire into why, until recently, Sojourner Truth, a "naive rather than an educated persona, seems to have better facilitated black women's entry into American memory" than any of her educated black female contemporaries. Painter's point is obviously not that only lettered or tutored black women should have facilitated that memory but that Sojourner Truth as figure keeps alive the "disparities of power and distinctions between European and Euro-Americans and natives, domestic and foreign."[19]

As a sign to a rematerializing critical discourse of its sins of omission around race, the utterance of Sojourner Truth or any other metonym for black woman seems to perform for some an absolution of critical guilt; but the utterance is all. "Sojourner"—or any other metonym for black woman—is one of which no more need be said. Truth's experiences beyond popularized clichés are not fully addressed. She is useful simply as a name to drop in an era with at least nominal pretensions to interrogating race and the difference it makes in critical discussion.

But the repetition of Sojourner's name makes no *real* difference. In dominant discourses it is a symbolic gesture masking the face of power and its operations in the present academic context. As a figure summoned from the seemingly safe and comfortable distance of a historical past, Sojourner Truth is removed from the present social context and can thus act symbolically to absorb, defuse, and deflect its conflicts. However, "Sojourner Truth" stirs up far more controversy than it settles, preventing any easy resolution of feminism's conflicts. The name contains locked within it the timeless and unchanging knowledge (the very definition of "truth") of race and gender embedded in Western philosophy that now find their way, like the return of the repressed, into the organization of knowledge in contemporary academe.

The repeated invocation of "Ain't I a Woman?"—detached from historical context—neither captures its immediacy for Truth's time nor reactivates it for our own. Correspondingly, the repeated invocation of "Sojourner Truth" functions not to document a moment in a developing discourse but to freeze that moment in time. Such a chronopolitics operates not so much as history but as an interruption of history, at least as black women might figure in it, a phenomenon not unlike Hegel's description of Africa as outside the "real theatre of History," of "no historical part of the World." "It has no movement or development to exhibit. . . . What we properly understand by Africa, is the Unhistorical, Undeveloped Spirit, still involved in the conditions of mere nature, and which has to be presented . . . on the threshold of the World's history."[20]

The proposition that Black feminist discourse is poised on the threshold of "Theory's" history has predictable consequences. Not least, this view helps to reconstitute the structures and strategies of dominance, even in work that strives zealously in an opposite and oppositional direction.

GENDERING AFRICAN-AMERICAN THEORY

We can observe such strategies of dominance in *Gender and Theory,* a recent anthology edited by Linda Kauffman. Kauffman tries studiously to prevent a reproduction of the simplistic divisions and antagonisms between black and white, male and female, "theory" and "politics." She explains in her introduction that while the title—*Gender and Theory*—posits a couple . . . the essays are arranged to permit men to respond to the essays by women and vice versa. That "structure is designed . . . to draw attention to such dichotomies in order to displace them by dissymmetry and dissonance."[21] Despite that goal, these very oppositions are evident nonetheless.

In fact, we could argue that if theory is often to "practice-politics" what Europe is to America, what white is to black, what straight is to gay, in Kauffman's anthology, theory is to practice what black male is to black female. This reductive accounting has entered the contemporary critical record and has constructed black women as categorically resistant to theory. To be sure, some black women have indeed helped to foster this perception and to encourage the metonymic strategy of choosing the name of any black woman to summarize the critical position of all.[22]

"Race" in Kauffman's anthology is constructed once again as synonymous with "blackness." Barbara Christian's "The Race for Theory" and Michael Awkward's response, "Appropriative Gestures: Theory and Afro-American Literary Criticism," are placed at the very end of the volume and thus apart from the preceding pairs of essays, none of which interrogates the racial inflections of "gender and theory." The racial opposition coordinates with a gendered opposition between male and female and a gendered opposition between theory and practice.

The question Kauffman poses in her introduction—"In what ways are Afro-American theory and Afro-American feminism complementary, and what ways are they antagonistic?"—gets answered in the two concluding essays: "Afro-American theory" is gendered male and Afro-American feminism is gendered female, and they function effectively as structural polarities. Such a seemingly innocent structure has already quickly decided its conclusion: Michael Awkward's response to Barbara Christian calls for a "theory" to her "practice."

One of the strengths of Awkward's response to Christian lies in its implicit recognition that poststructuralist theory cannot be homogenized, nor can it stand synecdochically for all theory. Although it is clear that he thinks Christian has missed the theoretical mark, he asserts that Barbara Smith's "Toward a Black Feminist Criticism" was "essentially a theoretical statement" "if not [a] post-structuralist discussion of critical practice and textual production." Smith's essay, he goes on to say, "theorizes despite its lack of a clearly informed awareness of deconstruction, reader-response theory, [and] semiotics."

Here, Awkward's vocabulary—"if not" and "lack of"—essentially negates whatever value he initially assigns to Smith's essay, which is structured as the negative of the positive—poststructuralism, the sole frame of reference. In an uncritical assertion of the synonymity between black women writers and "black women" as critics, Awkward offers a cautionary note: "If this field [black women's literature] is to continue to make inroads into the canon, if it is to gain the respect it doubtlessly deserves as an ideologically rich literary tradition, within an increasingly theoretical academy, it will require that its critics continue to move beyond description and master the discourse of contemporary theory."[23] If, as Awkward suggests, "black women's literature still does not assume the prominent place in courses and criticism" that it merits, I would ask whether that marginality can be explained exclusively by the lack of theorizing on the part of black women or rather whether that marginalization is often structured into the very theories that Awkward wants black women to master. Again, my point should not be read as a simplistic rejection of theory, as it is narrowly associated with poststructuralist projects, but as a call for a more searching examination of the processes and procedures of marginalizing any historically subjugated knowledge.

Awkward's essay does more than close Kauffman's volume; it performs a kind of closure, or functions as a kind of "final word," which extends far beyond the boundaries of the collection, *Gender and Theory*. He leaves intact the clichéd and unstudied distinctions between "theory" and "practice," represented by Paul de Man and Barbara Christian, respectively. It is paradoxical and ironic that an essay that privileges poststructuralist theory and extols de Man, relies on an uncritical construction of theory as an autonomous entity with semantic stability and immanent properties that separate it from practice. It is all the more ironic that such a dichotomy should dominate in an essay that valorizes a body of theory that emerged to blur such inherited and unmediated oppositions. But such dichotomies mark a difference and issue a set of limits—social limits—with implications that extend beyond the academic realm. In identifying with Paul de Man, Awkward consolidates his own critical authority against Barbara Christian's, making theory a province shared between men.

NOTES TOWARD A COUNTERHISTORY

Where might we go from here? I would start with the forthright assertion that the challenge of any discourse identifying itself as black feminist is not necessarily or most immediately to vindicate itself as theory but to resist the theory-practice dichotomy as at once too broad and too simple to capture the range and diversity of contemporary critical projects, including the range and diversity in the contributions of black women to that discourse. A far more valuable and necessary project would proceed from the commonplace assumption that no consideration of *any* intellectual project is complete without an understanding of the process of that project's formation. And thus any responsible accounting of the work of black women in literary studies would have to provide a history of its emergence and to consider that emergence first on its own terms.

Of course, part of the historical accounting of recent critical production is well underway, but unfortunately it leaves questions of the relations between race and critical discourse largely unexplored. A counterhistory, a more urgent history, would bring theory and practice into a productive tension that would force a reevaluation of each side. But that history could not be written without considering the determining, should I say the overdetermining, influences of institutional life out of which all critical utterances emerge.

It follows, then, that we would have to submit to careful scrutiny the past two decades, which witnessed the uncanny convergence and confluence of significant historical moments, all contributing to the present shape and contours of literary studies. These are: the emergence of a second renaissance of black women writing to public acclaim; a demographic shift that brought the first generation of black intellectuals into the halls of predominantly white, male, and elitist institutions; the institutionalization and decline of Afro-American studies and Women's Studies; and the rising command in the United States academy of poststructuralism, regarded as a synonym for theory.

Our historical narrative would have to dramatize the process by which deconstruction came to stand synecdochically for poststructuralist theory, its dominion extending from the pages of arcane journals of critical theory to the pages of such privileged arbiters of culture as the *New York Times Magazine* and *New York Review of Books,* to the less illustrious pages of *Time* and *Newsweek.*[24] The analysis would have to explore how deconstruction became associated as much with an ideological position as a revitalizing and energetic intellectual project at roughly the same time that a few black women, following Barbara Smith's challenge, began to articulate a position identified as black feminist criticism. Smith focused on recuperating the writings of black women for critical examination and establishing reading strategies attentive to the intersections of gender, race, and class in their work.[25]

If we were to isolate the salient terms of black feminist criticism and poststructuralist theory for this historical narrative, they might run as follows:

1) While black feminist criticism was asserting the significance of black women's experience, poststructuralism was dismantling the authority of experience.

2) While black feminist criticism was calling for nonhostile interpretations of black women's writings, poststructuralism was calling interpretation into question.

3) While black feminist criticism required that these interpretations be grounded in historical context, deconstruction denied history any authoritative value and truth claims, and read context as just another text.

4) While the black woman as author was central to the efforts of black feminist writers to construct a canon of new as well as unknown black women writers, poststructuralism had already rendered such efforts naive by asking, post-Foucault, "What Is an Author?" (1969) and trumpeting post–Roland Barthes, "The Death of the Author" (1968).

5) While black feminist critics and Afro-Americanists more generally were involved in recuperating a canon of writers, a critical vocabulary emerged that subordinated texts and traditions to textuality.

But the salient terms of these admittedly tendentious synopses would also have to reveal some useful correspondences. Both black feminist criticism and deconstruction see the regulation and exclusion of the marginal as essential to maintaining hegemonic structures. Both describe the structural and hierarchical relations between the margins and the center. Our narrative might then pause to ponder how these two reading strategies came to be perceived as antithetical. How their specific *units* of critical interest came to be polarized and assigned an order of intellectual value that drew on a racist and sexist schema with heavy implications and investments in the sociopolitical arrangements of our time.

CHOOSING SIDES

What viable position can be taken in this context? We might begin to assert a provisional conclusion: When the writings of black women and other critics of color are excluded from the category of theory, it must be partly because theory has been reduced to a very particular practice. Since that reduction has been widely accepted, a great many ways of talking about literature have been excluded and a variety of discursive moves and strategies disqualified, in Terry Eagleton's words, as "invalid, illicit, non-critical." [26]

The value of Eagleton's discussion of literary theory lies mainly in its understanding of how critical discourse is institutionalized. In that process, the power arrogated to some to police language, to determine that "certain statements must be excluded because they do not conform to what is acceptably sayable" cannot be denied. [27] The critical language of black women is represented, with few exceptions, as outside the bounds of the acceptably sayable and is heard primarily as an illicit and noncritical variety of critical discourse defined in opposition to theory. Its definition and identity continue to be constructed in contemporary critical discourses, all of which must be recognized, distinguished, and divided from each other in the academy's hierarchical system of classifying and organizing knowledge. To be sure, the discourses that exist at any given historical juncture compete with each other for dominance and meaning, compete with each other for status as knowledge, but we must be constantly on guard for what Biodun Jeyifo is right to term a *misrecognition* of theory, although this misrecognition has "achieved the status of that naturalization and transparency to which all ideologies aspire and which only the most hegemonic achieve." [28]

Given this *misrecognition* of theory and the privileged status it enjoys, even in moments of embattlement, it is readily understandable why some black feminists and other women of color in the academy would argue for the rightful *recognition* of their work as theory. While I would not presume to speak for or issue directives to "women of color," which would, in any case, assume a false and coherent totality, I openly share my growing skepticism, about the tactical advantages of this position.

I am far more interested, for the moment, in joining the growing number of critics—many of them Third World—who have begun to ask the difficult questions about the material conditions of institutional life and to view theory, in its narrow *usages* (rather than in any intrinsic properties

to be assigned to it), as an ideological category associated with the politically dominant. It is important that such a statement *not* be read as a
resistance to "theory," but one that inquires into why that category is so
reductively defined, and especially why its common definitions exclude so
many marginalized groups within the academy. Such is Barbara Christian's point in "The Race for Theory," although in their rush to contain
her inquiry, critics missed those aspects of value in her critique.

The question that Christian raises about the reassertions of racially
coded territorial assumptions and imperatives implied in the distinction
between theory and practice are echoed in the writings of a growing number of students of minority and postcolonial discourses. For example, Rey
Chow addresses the problem of "the asymmetrical structure between the
'West' as dominating subject and the 'nonWest' or 'Third World' as the
oppressed 'other.'" She argues that "contrary to the absolute difference
that is often claimed *for* the 'Third World' . . . the work of a twentieth-
century Chinese intellectual foretells much that is happening in the contemporary 'Western' theoretical scene." [29] Chow's observations go far
beyond and far deeper than a plea for a liberal pluralist position here,
beyond a plea for "equal time." Neither she, nor the growing number of
Third World intellectuals who have begun to interrogate the uses to
which theory has been put for the past twenty years, is so naive as to
suggest that the power of theory's gravitational field can be so simply and
reactively resisted. Most of us know that the debate over the uses and
abuses of theory, formulated as such, followed by a growing demand to
choose sides, is sterile and boring. But more importantly, it diverts us
from the more difficult pursuit of understanding how theory has been
made into an exclusively Western phenomenon inextricably attached to
the view that it does not and cannot exist outside a Western orbit.

That view is especially apparent in what Edward Said refers to as a
"maddening new critical shorthand" that "makes us no less susceptible to
the dangers of received authority from canonical works and authors than
we ever were. We make lackluster references to Nietzsche, Freud, Lacan
as if the name alone carried enough value to override any objection or to
settle any quarrel." [30] Said's list of names requires others who are said to
embody the most popular terms of critical opprobrium. I am concerned
to note that often these are the names of black American women. Their
assignment to the political, the empirical, the historical camps helps to
construct an identity, a subjectivity for black feminist thinking among

the general critical discourses of our time. That identity has so far been anything but fluctuating. It has been solidly fixed to a reference schemata and a racial stigmata that we have seen before.

NOTES

This is a slightly altered version of a talk presented at the Commonwealth Center for Literary and Cultural Change, University of Virginia, as a part of a general symposium, "Is Knowledge Gendered?" and a specific panel on "Race and Gender in the Teaching of Historical Knowledge." I thank Susan Fraiman and Rick Livingston for helpful comments and suggestions.

My epigraphs are drawn from Audre Lorde, "Age, Race, Class & Sex," in *Sister Outsider: Essays and Speeches by Audre Lorde* (Trumansburg, N.Y., 1984); James Baldwin, *The Evidence of Things Not Seen* (New York, 1985); Arthur C. Danto, *Narration and Knowledge* (New York, 1985); and Toni Morrison, *Beloved* (New York, 1987).

1. While certainly not peculiar to this, this philosophy of history has long been prevalent in the writings of African-Americans, especially in the historical, or documentary, fiction produced so insistently for the past twenty years. Random examples would include John A. Williams's two metahistorical novels *The Man Who Cried I Am* and *Captain Blackman* (1972), in both of which history is a suspicious text constructed by paramilitary conspiratorial agents. Other examples include Ishmael Reed's *Flight to Canada* (1976) and Sherley Anne Williams's *Dessa Rose,* derived from her short story "Meditations on History." For a discussion of history and documentation in African-American fiction see Barbara Foley's "The Afro-American Documentary Novel" in her *Telling the Truth: The Theory and Practice of Documentary Fiction* (Ithaca, 1986). The charge that history is a construction of the imagination has been articulated in such "nonfiction" as Hayden White's *Tropics of Discourse, The Content of the Form: Narrative Discourse and Historical Representation* (Baltimore, 1987) and *Metahistory* (Baltimore, 1973).

2. Renato Rosaldo, "Others of Invention: Ethnicity and its Discontents," *Voice Literary Supplement,* Feb. 1990, p. 27.

3. Hortense Spillers, "Interstices: A Small Drama of Words," in *Pleasure and Danger: Exploring Female Sexuality,* ed. Carole Vance (New York, 1984), p. 74.

4. Evan Watkins, "The Self-Evaluations of Critical Theory," *Boundary 2,* 12–13 (1984): 359–78.

5. Farah Griffin, *Women's Review of Books* 8 (Feb. 1991): 14.

6. As efforts to fix origins are vain and subject to the desires and needs of those in a given historical moment, I propose no definitive boundaries here, but the speeches of Sojourner Truth and Maria Stewart would have to figure promi-

nently in any narrative of the origins of black feminist thinking. For a discussion of the wider reaches of black feminist thinking, see Patricia Hill Collins's discussion of the implied audiences in her recent book *Black Feminist Thought*. "I explicitly wrote for a broader readership than a strictly faculty or graduate student audience" and avoided "academic jargon" so as to make the "ideas in my book accessible to a wider community" ("The State of the Art," *Women's Review of Books* 8 [Feb. 1991]: 23). See also Bell Hooks, who described her book *Ain't I a Woman?* (Boston, 1981) as written primarily with an audience in mind of black women who worked at the phone company. She accepted their challenge to "write a book that would make our lives better, one that would make other people understand the hardships of being black and female. It was different to be writing in a context where my ideas were not seen as separate from real people and real lives" ("*Ain't I a Woman?* Looking Back," in *Talking Back: Thinking Feminist, Thinking Black* [Boston, 1989], p. 152).

7. For a discussion of the use of charismatic names to legitimate critical arguments, see Martin Jay, "Name Dropping or Dropping Names? Modes of Legitimation in the Humanities," in *Theory between the Disciplines,* ed. M. Kreiswirth and M. Cheetham.

8. For a discussion of Sojourner Truth as "standard exhibit in modern liberal historiography," see Phyllis Marynick Palmer's "White Women / Black Women: The Dualism of Female Identity and Experience in the United States," *Feminist Studies* 9 (1983): 151–69.

9. Rather than attempt to provide an extensive inventory here, let me call attention to certain benchmark statements from women of color about the injunction to theorize. In her controversial essay "The Race for Theory," Barbara Christian discusses the pressures she feels to "produce a black feminist literary theory as if [she] were a mechanical man" in *Gender and Theory,* ed. Linda Kauffman [London and New York, 1989], p. 227). Gloria Anzaldua notes that "what passes for theory these days is forbidden territory" for women of color, which makes it "*vital* that we occupy theorizing space," even as we understand that "what is considered theory in the dominant academic community is not necessarily what counts as theory for women of color" (Introduction, *Making Face, Making Soul / Haciendo Caras: Creative and Critical Perspectives by Women of Color* [San Francisco, 1990], p. xxv).

10. Denise Riley, *"Am I That Name?" Feminism and the Category of "Women" in History* (Minneapolis, 1988), p. 1. By her admission, Riley's is a concession to pragmatism. She maintains that "it is compatible to suggest that 'women' don't exist—while maintaining a politics of 'as if they existed'—since the world behaves as if they unambiguously did" (p. 112).

11. Constance Penley, *The Future of an Illusion: Film, Feminism, and Psychoanalysis* (Minneapolis, 1989), p. 179.

12. Gayatri Spivack, "The Politics of Interpretation," in W. J. T. Mitchell, *The Politics of Interpretation* (Chicago, 1982), p. 346.

13. *Feminist Theory in Practice and Process,* ed. Micheline R. Malson et al. (Chicago, 1989), p. 7.

14. Elizabeth Spelman, *Inessential Woman: Problems of Exclusion in Feminist Thought* (Boston, 1988), p. 162.

15. In a perceptive and persuasive essay Judith Roof argues that "while the materialist commitment to gender and the economic" are defined as "'analysis,' a racial or lesbian commitment is defined differently, as anachronistically political—'liberationist'—as activism instead of analysis." She asks, "Why for this moment are gender and class cerebral and race and sexual orientation experiential?" ("All Analogies Are Faulty: The Fear of Intimacy in Feminist Criticism," in *A Lure of Knowledge: Lesbian Sexuality and Theory,* forthcoming).

16. Toril Moi, *Sexual / Textual Politics* (London and New York, 1985).

17. Jane Flax, *Thinking Fragments: Psychoanalysis, Feminism, and Post Modernism in the Contemporary West* (Berkeley, 1990), p. 140.

18. For a brilliant discussion of this scene and of the materiality in which black women were embedded more generally, see Haryette Mullen, "'Indelicate Subjects': African-American Women's Subjectivity," *Subversions,* Winter 1991, pp. 1–7. See also Valerie Smith's "Black Feminist Theory and the Representation of the 'Other,'" in *Changing Our Own Words: Essays on Criticism, Theory, and Writing by Black Women,* ed. Cheryl Wall (New Brunswick, N.J., 1989), pp. 38–57. There, Smith discusses tendencies prevalent in the discourses of Anglo-American feminist and male Afro-Americanists to invoke the experiences of black women who become fetishized Others. She also links this association of black women as embodied Others to "classic Western philosophy as well as to nineteenth-century cultural ideas and ideals of womanhood. Such ideas of womanhood excluded slave women who were pinned in the body and therefore associated with animal passions and slave labor" (p. 45).

19. Nell Irvin Painter, "Sojourner Truth in Life and Memory: Writing the Biography of an American Exotic," *Gender and History* 2 (1990): 3–16. Painter traces the evolution of Sojourner Truth as historical legend and how the dominant representations of her, in both her time and ours, reflect various power asymmetries and hierarchies.

20. Georg W. F. Hegel, "Geographical Basis of History," in *The Philosophy of History,* trans. J. Sibree (New York, 1991), p. 99.

21. *Gender and Theory,* ed. Linda Kauffman (New York, 1989), p. 2.

22. Such a perception derives in large part from the wasteful battle waged on the pages of *New Literary History* 18 (1987). See Joyce Ann Joyce, "The Black Canon: Reconstructing Black American Literary Criticism"; Henry Louis Gates, Jr., "'What's Love Got to Do with It?': Critical Theory, Integrity, and the Black

Idiom"; Houston A. Baker, Jr., "In Dubious Battle"; and Joyce Ann Joyce, "'Who the Cap Fit': Unconsciousness and Unconscionableness in the Criticism of Houston A. Baker, Jr., and Henry Louis Gates, Jr." Christian's "The Race for Theory" added significantly to that perception.

23. Michael Awkward, "Appropriative Gestures: Theory and Afro-American Literary Criticism," in Kauffman, *Gender and Theory,* p. 243.

24. Jonathan Arac, Wlad Godzich and Wallace Martin described the spread of deconstruction in their preface to *The Yale Critics* (Minneapolis, 987). In his estimation, "critics doing the new work most respected by a professionally authoritative screening group have drawn heavily from the Yale critics. In thirty-five essays that recently reached the Editorial Committee of *PMLA*, the American critics most cited were Miller . . . de Man, Bloom, Hartman and Derrida." Yet another and related sign of their powerful sway, Martin observed, was deconstruction's spread "from elite private institutions to public institutions," embracing "much more of the United States" and enrolling much "broader student bodies."

25. Barbara Smith, "Towards a Black Feminist Criticism."

26. Terry Eagleton, *Literary Theory: An Introduction* (Minneapolis, 1983), p. 203.

27. Ibid.

28. Biodun Jeyifo, "Literary Theory and Theories of Decolonization." Unpublished manuscript. Also see his "On Eurocentric Critical Theory: Some Paradigms from the Texts and Sub-Texts of Post-Colonial Writing," in Helen Tiffin and Stephen Slemon, eds., *After Europe: Critical Theory: Post-Colonial Writing* (Sydney, 1989).

29. Rey Chow, "'It's You, and Not Me': Domination and 'Othering' in Theorizing the 'Third World,'" in *Coming to Terms: Feminism, Theory, Politics,* ed. Elizabeth Week (New York, 1989), p. 161.

30. Edward Said, *The World, the Text, and the Critic* (New York, 1983).

11

"SEISMIC ORGASM":

SEXUAL INTERCOURSE,

GENDER NARRATIVES,

AND LYRIC IDEOLOGY

IN MINA LOY

૨ઢ

Rachel Blau DuPlessis

The only point at which the interests of the sexes merge—is the
sexual embrace.

—Mina Loy

MY FIRST CONCERN IS "INTERDISCURSIVITY": some tentative beginning on "the historical study of the orders of language."[1] This is an
attempt to read poetry in ways that incorporate thematic, technical, and
rhetorical matters into specific social situations and debates. My second
concern is with a historically framed problem of representation. It is generally accepted, and visibly true, that the representation of sexually explicit and sexually frank materials is a characteristic of at least certain
modernist texts, and that the "sexual embrace" becomes problem, symptom, solution, cure-all, from Joyce's apotheosis of Molly Bloom and
Stein's "Lifting Belly" to Eliot's "Lune de Miel" and moments in *The Waste
Land* set in the "supine" aftermath of sexual intercourse. These representations and others focus directly on sexual activity; we can read that "embrace" as a site wherein various agents and cultural processes are defined.
The modernist frankness of Mina Loy evokes these issues, since this un-
derknown writer produced a work whose depiction of sexuality, if not
unique, is a provocation to the study of the social codes of the lyric and
some historical meanings of the representation of sex.[2]

Mina Loy's thirty-four-section "Love Songs to Joannes" (1915–17), is a

poem at a cultural pressure point of female subjectivity and sexual relations.[3] In "Love Songs," Loy traces the course of a love affair, involving
open sexual desire, through her pursuit of an apparently flagging partner,
the complex of satisfactions and dissatisfactions centering on a split between sexual urge and suspicious analysis, and finally a consideration of
sexuality and reproduction; these concerns intersect with feminist issues
in Loy's short "Feminist Manifesto," a declarative prose work from the
same era.[4]

The last proposition of the "Feminist Manifesto" reads: "The realisation
in defiance of superstition that there is *nothing impure in sex*—except in
the mental attitude to it—will constitute an incalculable wider social
regeneration than it is possible for our generation to imagine." Loy's forthright critique of a "mental attitude" deemed "superstition," not to speak
of her forthright willingness to discuss sex (sexuality, gender, sexual intercourse are all mingled in the term), are clear ruptures with dominant
ideology.[5] This sexual radical position appears in the "Feminist Manifesto," which redefines feminism in the same ways as Dora Marsden's edi-
torials in the 1913 *New Freewoman*. It is plausible that Loy knew Marsden's
work and the radicalism of the journal, but even if she did not, her claims
have much in common with the specific feminism of Marsden's anarchist
"Überfrau."[6]

In her "Feminist Manifesto" Loy is unsubordinate, sexually blunt, ea-
ger to transcend and eradicate (by the power of individual agency and
will) any prior world history of female servility—what Marsden would
call Bondwomen in opposition to the modern Freewoman behavior, and
what earlier feminists Gilman and Schreiner called Parasitism and Prostitution, as did Loy.[7] Loy situates herself at a nexus of historical change,
indeed, as do the writers of all manifestos, at an apocalypse of immediate
and total change. Yet the absolutism of her rejection of prior female strategies and her repeated tropes of destruction might be termed "suspect
places," in the words of her poem (sec. 1), a woman both protesting, and
protesting too much. In Loy's view, the feminist movement is "*Inadequate*"
because it depends on political reforms calling for "equality" (among
them, female suffrage, equal education, and professional opportunity).
More particularly, women should deny any conventional restrictions based
on banal complementarity: "Leave off looking to men to find out what
you are *not*—seek within yourselves to find out what you *are*" (*LLB* 269).[8]

Loy has a liberatory view of sexuality. The manifesto calls for free love

brought about by "intelligent curiosity & courage" in acknowledging sexual desire, for a critique of "the impurity of sex," for the surgical destruction of virginity at puberty so it could not be a bargaining chip, for "the
right to maternity" for all women, married or not, and for principled
resistance to the "comfortable protection" of marriage. These opinions are
in direct dialogue with both general ideology and with a specific kind of
Victorian and modern reforming feminism called the Social Purity movement, which combines claims for the moral superiority of women and a
denial of female sexuality. Social Purity was hegemonic in the suffrage
movement (1908–14), but not unchallenged. Libertarians and utopian
socialists, as well as feminist sex radicals, rejected the "purity" argument;
these would find chosen sexual unions a moral and ethical kind of sexual
behavior, and would urge the end of sexual repressions. Most dramatic
was the claim that women had a right to and capacity for sexual pleasure,
that women's sexual drive was equal to men's.[9] In contrast, Social Purity
feminists made urgent allegories of gender division in sexual matters: men
were lustful, women were spiritual; men needed their sexual (and the
synonyms were *bestial, animal*) instincts curbed by women as asexual
guardians of an evolutionary superiority, glossed as a minimal need for
the "sexual embrace."[10]

Feminists were found among both sex radicals and Social Purity reformers. As Dubois and Gordon summarize this issue, feminists have long
explored two conflicting traditions about sex. One emphasized its dangers
and its victimizing potential (frequent pregnancy, venereal disease, exploitation). Social Purity feminists sought protection by enforcing those
controls over men that women (in the double standard) had internalized,
by insisting on chivalric honor in men and consensual sex, and by cam-
paigning against vice (prostitution), which often was a campaign for the
"containment of female sexuality within heterosexual marriage" no matter
how oppressive. In contrast, sexual radical feminists were committed to
pleasure, encouraged female autonomy and sexual expression, but did not
see, or thought they had transcended, power relations, and the "male
construction of the sexual experience available to most women."[11]

"Love" as Loy tersely reports in the one-line final section (34) is indeed
"the preeminent littérateur," and Loy might be said to draw on these two
historically available traditions of depiction—pleasure and danger. Loy's
story is more clearly filled with sex-radical evocations of pleasures. "Love
Songs" is not a narrative poem in the normal discursive sense of that

word, but it does "make a progression of realisations." [12] The poem traces a double kind of abandonment: the surrender of inhibition in the sexual sense and then the abandonment in the sense Laurence Lipking foregrounds, the end of love, the desertion of the woman. [13] These two abandonments are not related causally, which avoids a familiar convention of romance, where surrender in love leads to social obloquy. The depiction of reckless and passionate female lust occurs alongside a rather more servile desire to be loved at any cost with concomitant narratives of thralldom and recovery, obsession, rupture, and painful isolation. And while the "Feminist Manifesto" declares, "Women must destroy in themselves the desire to be loved," it continues in a pensive fragment, "The feeling that it is a personal insult when a man transfers his attentions from her to another woman." [14] Along with "the desire to be loved," presumably this insulted feeling must be extirpated too, for the modernity of Loy lies in her defiant desentimentalism, as if feelings—especially those associated with the ideology of femininity—were downright toxic, part of the "rubbish heap of tradition" [LLB 269]. Thus she argues that "love" (accompanied by "honour, grief, sentimentality, pride, & consequently jealousy" [LLB 271]) should be "detached from" sex. Yet the poem seems subject to just such an array of retrograde emotions. Hence the poem stands in a duplicitous, contradictory, and thoroughly problematic relation to the manifesto, sometimes continuing it by other means, sometimes depicting the internal debates in consciousness which accompanied the attempt of this singular woman to purge herself of all her "pet illusions" and the "lies of centuries," as she tried singlehandedly to control feminine ideology.

The poet enters into her consideration of the "wild oats / Sown [sewn?] in mucous-membrane" with the clear admonition "These are suspect places" (sec. 1). [15] She assumes various postures for this investigation, various subjectivities, various "I's." Among them is a "wise virgin" pose, holding an investigatory (Diogenesian, not Dionysian) lantern aloft so it will not be blown out by "the bellows / Of experience." The lantern show (slide show—the sections of the poem offer individual moments of a narrative montage) takes her own cool, analytic "eye" as the source of light, but that analytic "lantern" tries to control a response to inflammatory orgasmic imagery: "An eye in a Bengal light / Eternity in a skyrocket" (sec. 1). [16] Negotiating sexual and analytic passions, the poem's challenge, is often solved by impacted and intellectualized languages of wit graphically describing sexual moments and apparatuses. The gaze of power (nar-

rator's eye as illuminating lens) rests on the man and even—in the first
view we have of him—on his genitalia as a metaphor for him: "The skin-
sack / In which a wanton duality / Packed / All the completions / Of my
infructuous impulses / Something the shape of a man" (sec. 2).[17]

In "Supposed Persons," using terms from alternative feminist perspectives, Carolyn Burke contrasts the lyric poetry of self (consistently confes-
sional, homogeneous, integrated, seeking wholeness) with the poetry of
the subject (a persona, fictive, unstable, taking up positions in language).
She then argues that Loy is a paradigmatic case of female modernism, by
virtue of her use of both, where near-biographical "revelation" itself becomes one among several "supposed persons."[18] This is clearly visible in
this poem, in which Loy seems to call up both an ego-confessing-sincerely
and a fictive-evasive-ironic subject and play between them. At least two
discourses go along with these subjectivities. Moments of hope and loss
often come in (for want of a better term) lyric simplicity ("the moon is
cold") while moments of intellectual dissection are couched in a lapidary
texture and an arcane vocabulary. However, the urge to "sincerity," being
just one of the possible positions of this subjectivity at work, irremediably
ironizes even open confession.

The poem's temporal organization is curious. Despite the fact that the
course of failure of romance appears already to have happened, the poem
is almost uniformly conducted in the present tense and addressed to the
lover as "you," as if the action were happening. The notational quality of
the sections is thereby increased: the poem is as if telegraphed to "you" to
call "your" attention to the intricacy of the narrator's desire for "you." The
reader, as textual substitute for the man addressed, is in a peculiarly intimate, but complex, position. First, it is as if reading were the eroticized
overhearing of a confession. Second, the "I-you" pronouns instead of
"he-she" seem to resist the binary gender ideology of the polarized
sexes. Because of the "I-you" pronominals, their similarity and contiguity
are valued, and both partners seem to have both desire and suspicion
(suspicion of their relationship, and of each other; suspicion as well
about what sexuality means). This may be a kind of equal—though non-
idealized—intersubjectivity that is an attempt to depict a nonhierarchical
arrangement of the sexes.[19] "Voices break on the confines of passion /
Desire   Suspicion   Man   Woman / Solve in the humid carnage" (sec.
12). This set of metonymies suggests at once that both man and woman

have desire and suspicion, and, following the lines of Social Purity binaries, "desire" goes with "man" and "suspicion" with "woman." Yet also the sexually radical "desire / woman" can frame and surround the "suspicion / man." Even the unstable language of extreme fragmentation offers evidence of the positional debates within feminism. In addition there is a sense of an equation to be solved. Solved, perhaps, in that "humid carnage" that overrides gender division, as the epigram I chose from Loy claims (*LLB* 269).

And third, given the "I-you" pronominals, the writer with her speculative "gaze" casts the specular reader's eye as the object of her scrutiny and tries by this reversal to evade the almost inevitable position of prurient or condescending reader scrutiny that any female "confession" has conventionally evoked. The high intellectual language supports this evasion of the gaze of the reader on a beautiful, distressed woman in love. For the early narrative of the poem, its main unit, shows the "Loy" figure enthralled and pursing the lover, traveling to him, even stalking him through city streets at night, at once exhilarated by her passion and debased by it (secs. 5–8). In one of these sections, the female figure is a marionette of passion who "know[s] the Wire-Puller intimately" (sec. 6).

Then with "laughing honey / And spermatozoa / At the core of Nothing / In the milk of the Moon" (sec. 9), and continuing for six sections, Loy composes precisely on or alludes to (hetero)sexual intercourse with a striking frankness of diction, and in a great variety of registers, including terror, danger, pleasure, resistance, lust, controlling wit.[20] These are not, it appears from their tonal differences, narratives of one erotic encounter, but rather six separate, distinct, and precisely noted representations of activities and attitudes that go with sex. She offers special attention to the similarities between the partners at the moment of pleasure when (according to Loy in the manifesto) male-female distinctions dissolve: "seismic orgasm" (sec. 29). For instance, the obliteration of gender distinctions seems especially keen in "humid carnage // Flesh from flesh / Draws the inseparable delight / Kissing at gasps   to catch it," and then to "welded together" and "knocking sparks off each other" (secs. 12, 13, 14).[21] But even Loy's most distinctive phrases—"humid carnage" or "seismic orgasm"—combine pleasurable words and dangerous words. "Carnage" reaches etymologically for "flesh" and connotatively for "carnal," with its historical pun, "dying," but denotatively for "mass slaughter."

Charming and alarming is this haiku, allusively complete in just three lines.

> Shuttle-cock and battle-door
> A little pink love
> And feathers are strewn
>
> (sec. 10)

The shuttlecock of badminton bears irresistible double overtones, and the battledore, a flat wooden paddle (and the old word for badminton itself), is provocatively respelled "battle-door," to suggest the door that it is the object of some seriocomic battle to enter. This first line emphasizes the extreme difference between the sexes. "Pink love" smacks of an ironized eros of knowing possession, rather than unconsummated yearning. So this second line, with its hovering metonyms and spondees, suggests fusion between the opposing players. The "feathers" signal a comic devastation of the "birdie," or cock, a triumph perhaps of the woman, or perhaps mutual "humid carnage" (sec. 12). Once Cupid had wings; now he is a plucked bird.

At the end of the poem, Loy offers herself as a crucified "busy-body" (sec. 31; hyphen from *Others* publication), one of the least charming stereotypes of woman, and a phrase that might bitterly reflect on the poem as a punished instance of kiss-and-tell. Yet "busy-body" also suggests one whose body, literally busy with sexual expression, wrongly assumed that their panorama of sexual embraces would alter "the intimacies / Of your insolent isolation" (sec. 31). Yet this sexual "busy-body" discovers that, despite the claims of the manifesto, even at the moment of—the very point of—the sexual embrace, the interests of this couple drastically diverge, the male to seek solace in egotism and superior separateness. The "Feminist Manifesto" asserts the erasure of polarized sexual differences in the sexual embrace; in contrast, the poem finds that gender saturates everything, and that sexuality is not a privileged site.[22]

Mina Loy's "Love Songs," as is clear, contains a unique concentration on the representation of sexual intercourse, and many imaginatively graphic descriptions of sexual physiognomy. Of thirty-four sections, fourteen (comprising about 40 percent of the poem) are arguably centered on different occasions or acts of sexual intercourse, or may be said prominently to mention sex. And this representation is drastically a-conventional, a challenge certainly to prudes, and, more interestingly, to the hegemonic romance narratives of the lyric genre, but equally well a challenge to another kind of modernist libertarian thinking. For there are aspects of this urgency—the turn to reproductive sexuality at the end—that are, in a modernist context, radically conservative.

The next main portion of the poem (secs. 16–25) narrates the apparent aftermath of romance, with the tentative steps toward recovery, and back-slidings into misery, pleasure in isolated identity, bitterness about betrayal.[23] The "severing" might be of man from woman, with the "heinous acerbity / Of your streetcorner smile" (secs. 18, 24). But it might be self-induced, a bitter self-imposed punishment of exile from him when her emotions (pride, jealousy, sentimentality, and so on) could not be detached from her sexual experience, and she violated the terms of her own brave "Feminist Manifesto."

A key section on the recovery is a private "green" poem of pleasure in isolation and revival—like a Marvellian pastoral.

> Green things grow
> Salads
> For the cerebral
> Forager's revival
> Upon bossed bellies
> Of mountains
> Rolling in the sun
> And flowered flummery
> Breaks
> To my silly shoes
>
> In ways without you
> I go
> Gracelessly
> As things go

(sec. 22)

In her thinking about her long poem, Loy spoke of "Love Songs" as "THE best since Sappho."[24] More than just a chipper touch of self-praise, this phrase seems to indicate both Loy's concern to situate the poem in a tradition of female lyricists, and as well to hint at a playful yet decided set of allusions to Sappho's images. These encodings occur especially, but not exclusively, in this part of the poem, which speaks of her tentative recovery from or rejection of thralldom and romance. Unlike a "sapphic" (that is, lesbian or bisexual) use of Sappho as one might see in H. D., Loy uses the Sappho of unwilling yet persistent feelings of sexual desire: "Desire shakes me . . . it is a creeping thing and bittersweet / I can do nothing to resist."[25] So Loy claims Sappho as the necessary precursor in the frank and free treatment of sexual matters.

In the poem, Loy calls upon certain isolated images of Sappho that have a particular aura in our poetic tradition precisely because they exist a-contextually, in randomly preserved fragments. There is Sappho's sweet apple, unpicked at the top of a tree, and her "cool water rustles through apple shoots," and Loy's comparably watery "apple stealing under the sea" (sec. 16). Sappho had her "feet / in many colored thongs"; Loy notes "my silly shoes" (sec. 22), which break flowers when they walk as do the feet of Sappho's Cretan women. Sappho had a vastly suggestive "dripping towel"; Loy notes (sec. 28) how "a white towel" wipes away the sweat and yellow-white liquids of love-making. Sappho set forth "shoots of parsley"; Loy notes how "green things grow / Salads" for her renewal (sec. 22). Loy even proposed a tricky revision of a famous Homeric line, as did Sappho; in Loy's blunt terms: "The little rosy / Tongue of Dawn," part of the pink palette of the poem, wakes the lovers (sec. 25).[26] One section in the final part of the poem is explicitly Sappho-like in its suggestion of loss; it is the only section which names the man: "The moon is cold / Joannes / Where the Mediterranean—" (sec. 32, cited in full); this brooks comparison with Sappho's "The moon / the Pleiades . . ." fragment and may respond to, or parallel, Pound's deliberate recreation of the fragment: "spring / Too long / Gongola."[27]

A summary set of lines moves away from the sensuous alba of romance tradition, and divides into two categories those who thereupon wake up. The section names "some of us" still "melted" "Into abysmal pigeon-holes / Passion has bored / In warmth." This produces an unsavory combination of the swindled "pigeon," and the slotted, compartmentalized place they nest, not to speak of the duplicity of the word "bored" (sec. 25). These would be, generally, adherents of a feminine ideology of romance. These are distinguished from a more distinctive elite ("Some few of us") who "Grow to the level of cool plains / Cutting our foothold / With steel eyes" (sec. 25). This steely analytic elite has awakened in another sense and will be able to scrutinize the situation of love and sex, examining nature with the care of dispassionate science, not sensual passion, misplaced morality, or curdling personal sentiments of loss. This intellectual move in which "the cerebral forager" takes herself as a one-woman petri dish for the cultivation of sexuality, and then produces herself as the scientist scrutinizing the growths, trumps the sexual radical evocations of intercourse, and the more conventional narratives of passion and loss, thralldom and aftermath, that the bulk of the poem has so far presented.

Nature is thereupon called "that irate pornographist." [28] "Irate" means angry, excited, incensed; "pornographist" makes of nature an angry or emotional producer of texts depicting sexual intercourse. Given Loy's poem, this would put her in precise alliance with nature; she too is an incensed writer who has certainly "shed . . . petty pruderies" in her depiction of sexual intercourse. Yet in what senses would this almost willfully antinatural poet take sides with nature?

Loy first argues, with naturalist panache, that we are some kind of means for nature; nature is a presenter of materials for our sexual arousal, and we are just those human materials upon which nature has to act, containers for natural forces; and that individual niceties, specific feelings, certain kinds of resistance are counterproductive, causing only suffering to the small speck somehow standing up in the face of these forces. Nature "knows us with" "blind eyes"—implacable, amoral (sec. 30). Women and men are, in a kind of Hardyesque fatedness—controlled like cosmic puppets by the force and overwhelming character of "nature"—sexual drives. These "naturalist" feelings about sexuality (that the hard-won individualism of the New Woman stands in the way of and is swept away in the face of cosmic natural drives) seem to be at issue when Loy bitterly calls for a new breed of "sons and daughters" who might have "some way of braying brassily / For caressive calling" and be "seduce[d]" "To the one / As simple satisfaction / For the other" (sec. 29).

> Let them clash together
> From their incognitoes[29]
> In seismic orgasm
> For far further
> Differentiation[30]
> Rather than watch
> Own-self distortion
> Wince in the alien ego
> (sec. 29)

The sexual life of these active and "caressive" paragons will be simple, compared to her "own-self distortion"—perhaps the fact she could not live her own stated ideals, perhaps the way she found herself in the "alien" romance plot. Thus again the assertion that at least in sexual intercourse gender difference disappears is tested and denied by the poem. We need, she argues, some kind of biological evolution for the duplicities and disappointments of gender difference and sexual embraces as we experience them to be transformed.

As she sometimes represents sexual intercourse in the poem, the loss of individual gender binaries was an advantage and a pleasure, the creation of some site beyond gender, just "Me you—you—me" (sec. 13). But there is danger: a lust for orgasm necessarily overrides a sense of ego or boundaries. So the "Nirvana" is terrible / terrifying and terrific / exhilarating, as they "tumble together / Depersonalized / Identical / Into the terrific Nirvana / Me you—you—me" (sec. 13). To be "depersonalized" is a fearsome thing: Loy seems to say that a woman could fear that dissolution of identity. These metaphors of chaos or annihilation in sexual bliss show the dangerous loss of identity, perhaps reversion to a "femininity" of dissolution and passivity, defined by stereotypical gender ideas that Loy has staked herself upon resisting. The pleasures of merging boundaries, the dangers of merging boundaries, are in unresolvable circulation in this poem.

But Loy has another feminist project: the construction of a new female gender identity—where "mistress and mother" are not distinct (*LLB* 269, 270). For Loy, autonomous sexuality and her "freewoman" brand of autonomous feminism involved a radical claim to maternity. The argument toward the end of the poem "Evolution   fall foul of / Sexual equality / Prettily miscalculate / Similitude" strongly suggests that "sexual equality" feminism and "species meliorism" / "human biology" are at odds—a position that seems a slap at the evolutionary claims of Social Purity feminism (sec. 29). The phrase suggests that mainstream feminism is going to be tripped up by natural forces, but that her kind of maternalist feminism, proudly set forth in the "Feminist Manifesto," will not.[31] The genders are not "equal"; a woman must act as if independent of the sex-gender system, contemporary gender institutions, and feminine ideology, and she is bolstered in this by "Nature." The "complete woman" is endowed by "Nature . . . with a faculty for expressing herself through *all* her functions": to claim that her feminism is in tune with nature, and is expressive of its fundamental evolutionary tendencies, certainly becomes an answer to biological explanations of female subordination and gender asymmetry. And yet, at the same time, the linking of sexual activity with reproduction was a conservative position, when the whole history of modern struggles for the acceptance of sexual practices (whether contraception, abortion, homosexual expression, masturbation) has been to valorize non-reproductive "sexual embraces," what Richard Brown wittily dubs "copulation without population." [32]

So there are two intertwined narratives at the end of the poem. One is the intellectual analysis of the amorous failure of these highly developed intellectuals, whose precepts and experiences don't match.

> The prig of passion
> To your professorial paucity
>
> Protoplasm was raving mad
> Evolving us
> (sec. 33, the penultimate)

They are ill-suited to the needs of protoplasm to continue itself, to continue the race. One would not want to produce "foetal buffoons" in whom the bad patterns of the generative parents get mimicked or copied *in utero;* the superior candidates for "vital creation" should produce evolutionary superior children (sec. 30). But these partners are characterized as too far from the origins of life—he by "paucity" (smallness, dearth)—a kind of finicky or impotent withdrawal, and she as a "prig of passion." But since she is assuredly no prude ("prig"), one looks to other meanings; she could be arrogant or smug, a plausible reading of the way the poem tests and tempers her (self-assured) "Feminist Manifesto." Or, interestingly, a reading of "prig" in British slang, a pickpocket, petty thief, or pilferer. She was trying to pilfer a little passion, and more.

Because the second narrative that structures the end, is—to baldly summarize—her extreme rage and grief that she does not have his child, that she did not get pregnant, or that pregnancy was not allowed to happen, barred from happening by contraceptive practices, or even, perhaps, aborted. [33] As she says: "The procreative truth of Me / Petered out / In pestilent / Tear drops / Little lusts and lucidities" (sec. 24). Loy proposes a kind of mourning for the washing away of their sperm and cyprine mixture, [34] a "plastic" substance that was not allowed to become anything:

> The hands of races

Drop off from
Immodifiable plastic

The contents
Of our ephemeral conjunction
In aloofness from Much
Flowed to approachment of———
NOTHING
There was a man and a woman
In the way

(sec. 27)

The next section with its white towel, and images of blank whiteness,
characterizes his abilities at erasure. "I am burnt quite white / In the
climacteric / Withdrawal of your sun" (sec. 28). Not only is it about
thralldom, although plausibly about her wounding by the loss of his illuminating central presence, this section also seems specifically about
withdrawal, combining the words *climax*—a pun on an uncertain tactic
of birth control, and on *climacteric*, or "critical change of life." [35] The "crucifixion" section (one of the final ones) seems to criticize her self as a
"busybody / Longing to interfere so / With the intimacies / Of your insolent isolation." This is not just a criticism of him for narcissism or uncar-
ingness (those familiar tropes of the end of romance), this is specifically
her "crucifixion" as the bearer of a new and controversial idea (she is the
"Caryatid   of an idea"): that women should freely bear the children
of their lovers, and that superior women will bear superior children in a
eugenicist sense. The final sense of loss is not between them, only or
exclusively, but between her, and the missing child.

For in the "Feminist Manifesto," Loy also produced a eugenicist codi-
cil to her maternalist hopes: "Every woman of superior intelligence
should realize her race-responsibility, in producing children in adequate
proportion to the unfit or degenerate members of her sex" (*LLB* 270). It is
specifically ironic to construe ordinary, run-of-the-mill, conformist
women as "degenerate." Given the number of women "unfit" in Loy's
feminist terms, her call for feminist maternity was a rather breathlessly
elitist bio-political principle for meliorism. There is a hidden claim that
superior women, through redefined sexuality and maternity, will lead
the race to a "social regeneration." As she had said, in lines I only half-
glossed earlier, "Where two or three are welded together / They shall

become god" (sec. 13): this is not only about the new fusions in orgasm but about a new holy family—man, woman, and fetus or baby as an ideal one might worship. Perhaps the future paragons of "caressive calling"— more modern sex radicals than she—might be able to have sex without thinking that their combined discharges and ejaculations are "human insufficiencies / Begging dorsal vertebrae" (sec. 29). But Loy exists in an angry mourning for the lack or loss of a child from sex, a rejoining, for radical reasons, of sexual intercourse and reproduction, which is the most traditional justification for the sexual embrace. But this justification occurs so that Loy can claim a radical identity of autonomous, self-chosen maternity. It may also occur so that she can avoid the cliché of contrasting definitions of sexuality in which male and female urges are balanced in apparently "eternal" opposition. To this way of proceeding, Loy announced her fundamental suspicion. The addition of maternity to the sex-gender mix allows Loy to attempt to define female sexuality autonomously.[36]

This brief account identifies one main issue: Loy's representation of sexuality, and not only or simply sexuality in a discrete Georgian blur or fuzz[37]—certainly one convention of depiction—but sexuality as a complex of events and meanings, as a site of struggle among various historically situated discourses of depiction. No human act is natural in an unmediated way and even the most apparently basic and primal (the sexual act) has been constructed with codes of meaning, and, if represented, is doubly invested with codes involving what is seen, what is cut, what is commented on, what is meant. As Michel Foucault remarks: "It is no longer a question simply of saying what was done—the sexual act—and how it was done; but of reconstructing, in and around the act, the thoughts that recapitulated it, the obsessions that accompanied it, the images, desires, modulations, and quality of the pleasure that animated it."[38]

It is a cultural commonplace to identify poetry with "love poetry": certain conventionalized narratives of yearning and urging, distance, loss, seduction by arguments about time, beauty, and loss. Accompanying this commonplace, poetry is often coterminous with "beauty" and with the eulogy of beauty. These ideas belong to a notional cluster that bares some, although not all, root ideologies of the genre. Poetry "is" love poetry; love poetry writes from a romance plot; the central romance plot is "about" a courted woman, and depends, as Margaret Homans argues, "on an implicit plot of masculine heterosexual desire" with specularity, hierarchy, and distance maintained in and through the rhetoric.[39] But when these root ideologies operate in a historical conjuncture—modern times—in which sexualities and gender are problematized, a nonromantic lyric can be a result.

In addition, relatively well enforced female silence is proper to the representation of women in conventional lyric poetry. It is extremely rare, in the canonical "golden treasuries" of verse, that the nymph replies critically to the courting shepherd. Generally we read the articulated love of the male poet-speaker for a female figure, silent in the text by the very terms of "lyric," even if not by terms of the cultural proprietorship of voice, the "allowability" of female speakers and speech.[40]

This question of voice is intermingled with issues about the framing of an iconic figure by "the gaze."[41] For women are a central object for poetry to scrutinize. Beautiful women are a "beauty" of beautiful poetry; the "beauty" of poetry as a genre (as an ideology—a set of deeply naturalized values) is supported and mutually reinforcing in its relation to figures of "Woman" and motifs that surround her. Love, beauty, nature, masks, lies, the fictive and "makeup," beauty raked by time, mediating vision or muse, the pastoral, the carpe diem motif, witchy and tempting female figures, the satire on the functions and aging of a female body, the "most poetical subject" being "the death of a beautiful woman" (or, in a Williams's update of an obsessive power, "the rape of a Beautiful Thing"), or the poignant voice of the female loser—the history of lyric poetry, seen through a goodly proportion of its canonical texts, makes a site through which familiar gender narratives of romance and sexuality can course.[42] I am indicating the discursive construct of the love lyric somewhat globally and unhistorically to suggest simply that when any critical sentiment existed in a (male- or female-authored) voice, the lyric would be, by genre, resistant to it. This means that when women writers take voice, or when male writers become even to the slightest degree suspicious of or discontented with gender identity or sexualities (as Pound does in "Mauberley"), the romantic lyric is no longer plausible and one must invent something like a critical, satiric, or analytic lyric precisely because the writer has ruptured long agreements upon which the romantic lyric rests.

In her own way Virginia Woolf noticed this change when, in the first chapter of *A Room of One's Own,* she indicated that two romantic-poetic melodies—one by Tennyson and one by Christina Rossetti—are no longer current; she says since the First World War.[43] The general gender narratives of the lyric as genre, and the gender issues raised by specific poems, especially when they are reset in their discursive contexts, into specific social situations and debates, make of modern poetry a whole new field for feminist criticism to enter. "The adoption of personae in modernist lyric is, as has often enough been remarked, symptomatic of twentieth-century anxieties about self-identity"; but it has hardly been remarked at all by most considerations of modernism that these "anxieties" and these "identities" are set askew and in new circulation precisely by the intervention of multiple strands of feminist debate.[44] I can do no more than suggest the plausibility of rereading every critical lyric, and then every encyclopedic poem of the modernist canon in an engagement with feminist cultural studies.

Loy, a self-styled feminist writer, in or alluding to the lyric of romance ("the best since Sappho"), and situated at a historical cusp of sexual issues—free love, maternalism—also faces these lyric assumptions at their extreme. Loy's crisp, wickedly learned "intellectual" poetry, the complex "ugliness," the satiric, clinical languages of "Love Songs" demystify the gender ideologies of beauty and of love. In a staggering prose poem called "Ladies in an Aviary" (unfortunately undated in the Conover collection), Loy pointedly criticizes the bird-women, dressed like brides, in their cage, offered sugar, "the sugar of fictitious values" by a "great strong man" who visits, mouthing such familiar statements as "Here is love. . . . 'tis a woman's whole existence," which take a bead on the romance tradition in poetry.[45]

For Loy the "cerebral forager"—with her thick etymology, fragmented colloquialisms, esoteric discourses, scientific languages, polysyllabic tongue twisters—is a writer of "logopoeia"—a poetry of ideas and word-play; intellectual analysis made in poetry; dissenting, and resistant thought and argument. A reader of "logopoeia" cannot respond with pure pleasure at the monodimensional; one is constantly being hit with counterjabs of new registers, bitter undercuts. It is a highly dialogic mode, and recalls to us how socially constructed our responses are: "It takes count in a special way of habits of usage, or the context we *expect* to find with the word, its usual concomitants, of its known acceptances."[46] Hence it can be critical of the common pleasures and beauties of poetry-as-usual. In this category of the usual, I put the gender narratives of lyric poetry: beauty, the gaze on female objects, the play with female silence.

But "logopoeia" also demands that one understand various "logoi"—the
social debates from which the poems drew, and with whose positions they
played.

In her reconstruction of the cultural context in which Loy wrote that
led her, as well as Moore and Stein, to collage strategies of splicing,
Carolyn Burke incisively notes that Ezra Pound invented the term *logopoeia*
in an essay of 1918, precisely to describe the early poetry of Mina Loy and
Marianne Moore.[47] Burke discusses Pound's appreciation of their strategy
of the "dance of the intelligence among words and ideas" and his inability
to perceive that their work had anything to do with (female) gender,
despite his aggressively "phallic" claims of the impact of (male, or nor-
mative) gender on his own writing during the same period.[48] Instead,
Pound ascribes the "arid clarity" of these "girls" to their Americanness.
"Logopoeia" situates itself as, perhaps, a new genre (not a new mode) in
the feminist history of the lyric; it is at least traceable to the resistances
of women poets to conventional gender narratives of lyric poetry, especially the ideology of beauty, and certain narratives of romance.

Central to the lyric is the carpe diem invitation, itself loosely dependent upon the pink (or red) and white beauty of the woman. To this, Loy
makes ironic counteroffers. First, of many "whites": never the assumed
beauty of female Caucasian skin but a male body lengthened like a plant
stretching for inadequate sunlight, or the colorlessness of a man's withdrawal.[49]

> White   where there is nothing to see
> But a white towel
> Wipes the cymophanous sweat
> —Mist rise of living—
> From your
> Etiolate body
>
>   (sec. 28)

And then, not the pink of "cherry ripe" or "rose" but of a rooting pig.
"Love Songs" opens with one of its two most frequently cited sections, in
which "Pig Cupid" presides over the writing and instigates erotic encounters, or erotic memories. "Pig" makes a greedy and lurid muse, rooting
"erotic garbage" rather than shooting arrows, a drastically anticonven-
tional figure with neither the whimsy of echt Cupids nor the possible
transcendences of Amor.[50] Pig Cupid is the "Spawn of Fantasies"—the

ova from which fantasy arises, or the offspring of reproductive encounters.[51] He is as well a phallic disturber of the peace, sticking his snout into "erotic garbage"—those nice narratives of "'Once upon a time.'" Lusty Pig is, in short, a fusion of male-female-child, an erotic-satyric holy family. Loy calls attention to the fictive or scripted nature of the love plot in an arch, ironic, and bitter way:

> Spawn of Fantasies
> Silting the appraisable
> Pig Cupid
> His rosy snout
> Rooting erotic garbage
> "Once upon a time"
> (sec. 1)

From the beginning of the poem, Loy creates an excessive, or exaggerated, attention to the one act hidden in the carpe diem convention, although its constant point. By excess in a female voice, she swamps the convention's dependency on a certain delicacy, feminine resistance, or reluctance. She overrides the poetic convention of romance both by a sense of aggression (Carpe diem! you don't even have to ask!) where she represents herself continuously as a sexual woman, and by a sense of judgment, where she represents her skeptical, damaging analysis of what can happen after the "achievement" of bliss or completion promised in the convention of romance (Carpe diem / dies irae). A short list includes impotence, or awkward, ill-paced consummations, betrayals of trust, "ephemeral conjunction[s]" (sec. 27), jealousy, the apparently "superhuman" man reseen as a "weak eddy," "Little lusts and lucidities / and prayerful lies" (sec. 24).

Besides the lyric conventions of romance and love to which it is clear Loy responds, her modern sexual story differs from at least one other sex-radical narrative about sex, love, and intercourse. An important contemporaneous novel, *The Rainbow* (1915) by D. H. Lawrence, embeds sexual contact—kisses, courtships, and sexual acts—in a tumultuous context of *Bildung*.[52] Sexuality, an animating drive for the characters, is thoroughly contextualized as expressive of emotional and spiritual development, and both passion and revulsion (which are versions of each other) are impelled through the novel's three generations of erotic encounters like enormous weather fronts, clouding or illuminating, bursting upon or darkening

characters. Sexuality is also a force programmatically set against superficial meliorisms and moralities: education, regimentation, intellection,
and abstraction. Love-making is a dark and "subtle" exercise, in which an
insinuating ("stealthy," 420), "relentless" and "fecund" male figure, by
penetration, "shatters" certain resistances in a female figure, inducing her
to leave off light, and go into the dark: "The lighted vessel vibrated, and
broke in her soul, the light fell, struggled, and went dark. She was all
dark, will-less, having only the receptive will" (422). It is uncanny that
Loy's trope of lighting a lamp (sec. 1)—an orgasmic yet investigatory
lamp—creates the obverse of this blackout: female will, power, aggression, and judgment.

In our Loy poem, in contrast, there is no "typical" statement about
sexual intercourse. However, the images she does use do not concern pen-
ile penetration, but seem to be a variety of attempts to figure orgasm
itself ("inseparable delight") in which male and female are not especially
differentiated, and in which male does not lead female to some realization. Unlike Lawrence, Loy seems to question that core of the self that
sexuality can transform; hence sexual contact happens in a kaleidoscopic
variety of tones—comic, passionate, terse, distant, cold, judgmental—
that seem more like temporary, situational positions than a defining and
regrouping of one's innermost fibers.[53] Loy's representations of sexual intercourse are less narrated, less sequentially "filled in" with a moment-to-
moment, or play-by-play, set of movements than Lawrence's. They tend
to be a fragmented narration of thought, or of options; or a summary
report, as if there were some equation to solve. Representation, not conversion, is precisely at issue. Perhaps it is the syntactic fragmentation or
obscurity of the poem, but in Loy sexuality seems more a problem (that
is, as in math or logic); in Lawrence it has the status of solution. Her
representations are determinantly secular; allusions to sex are made with
the same passionate dispassion as any other topic of the poem. There is
no special, magical diction for sex, in contrast to the diction of spiritual
renewal in Lawrence.

In a work by Lawrence, sexual intercourse or kisses that are protosexual
are relatively rare in proportion to other narrated events. The scenes of
intercourse are thus indeed climactic: that is, they are proposed as narrative peaks. Narrative climax and orgasmic climax coincide. In contrast,
Loy's representations of intercourse occur in a loosely structured plot of
connection, loss, and analytic reprise, but they comprise a much greater

proportion of the work, and hence are not climactic but various. They put pressure upon and are pressured by the mixture of suspicion and desire, the playing out of equations for possibilities, that is constitutive of the sexuality depicted.[54] Because narrative climax does not coincide with sexual climax, Loy's mode is antiseptic. Because these acts provide no "crisis" in a narrative sense, they seem rather a series of repeated behaviors, conceptualized and reconceptualized, thought and rethought.

Finally, Lawrence confirms certain long-standing gender conventions, although acting within a libertarian sexual ideology about sexual intercourse: the polarized binaries of male versus female; and how the powerful magic wand of a penetrating penis transforms the female psyche.[55] Orgasm is a reconversion experience to sexual binaries away from modern womanhood and its terrible "frictions." Loy, in contrast, wants to find orgasm the only site in which sexual binaries of gender are rendered inoperable, where men and women lose their suspicion and become just grasping flesh: "the only point at which the interests of the sexes merge." But she cannot uphold this utopian finding. However, in the process, she helps to open lyric poetry as a genre by virtue of the feminist intelligence she brings to bear upon it.

NOTES

1. Jonathan Arac calls for this approach to the lyric in his subtle and far-reaching critique of an anthology called precisely *Lyric Poetry: Beyond New Criticism,* ed. Chaviva Hošek and Patricia Parker (Ithaca, 1985), p. 350. Arac criticizes the anthology for an inadequate reaching beyond the textual and rhetorical, inadequate use of historical scholarship, and an unwillingness to historicize literary genres and terms and to specify how these are related to "socio-cultural codes."

2. The evocation of an immediately "noncanonical" writer is a topos in feminist criticism; it is meant to signal the historical construction of narratives of mattering—who does matter? One may borrow a formulation about art history from Griselda Pollock and Rozsika Parker: there is a distinction between the material existence and activities of poems, poets, and their relationships (a history of literature) and "literary history"—the discipline according to which these facts are selected, sequenced, and institutionalized (*Old Mistresses: Women, Art and Ideology* (New York, 1981), p. xvii). Canons are properly described as a dialogized historical effect of ideologies of value, cultural choices, and mediated needs, and are always in motion, affirmed or criticized. (As canons are a kind of hegemony, it is no surprise that I echo Raymond Williams in *Marxism and Literature* [Ox-

ford, 1977].) Canons are therefore a kind of narrative. A story told. And by being told and retold, become a kind of comforting convention, a lulling law, in which what is not familiar deserves not to be familiar, what is not remembered deserves not to be remembered, what is excluded was always meant to be excluded. The work of Mina Loy (accompanied by the now dubiously familiar tags, "what?" or "who?") is an example of such a canon law in action. Once Loy mattered enough to have been reviewed by both Eliot and Pound. But her career as a writer was intermittent, intersecting with careers as visual artist and interior designer, and with other concerns. In a professionalized market, even nonmarket writers suffer dangerous effects from intermittent careers—compare some noncanonical "Objectivists" like George Oppen and Louis Zukofsky, who also had intermittent careers.

   3. Mina Loy, "Love Songs to Joannes," in *The Last Lunar Baedeker*, ed. Roger L. Conover (Highlands, N.C., 1982), pp. 91–107; hereafter cited in text as *LLB* (the text of the poem is cited parenthetically by section number). Also, as "Songs to Joannes," *Others* 3, no. 6 (Apr. 1917). Little attention is given to Loy, to date, except by positive but glancing mentions in literary-historical lists referring to those "also present": e.g., also present in the avant-garde array in Europe and the United States. Notable exceptions to this canon rule: Conover's introduction to this edition of the poems and the critical works of Virginia Kouidis, *Mina Loy: American Modernist Poet* (Baton Rouge, La., 1980); Carolyn Burke's striking biographical, contextual, and analytic studies on Loy (noted below) are to appear in her long-awaited biography (forthcoming). Both Kouidis and Burke treat "Love Songs"; and both do so both textually and contextually. Burke discusses elements of "Love Songs" at several junctures in her published articles to date, but gives no narrative overview of the poem, such as I propose. She offers a close reading of the first sections in a recent article that focuses on "the dominant mode of incompletion" in the work, contrasting "the ideal of romantic love and mutual divinity with the actual failure of sexual union and the difficulty of overcoming this primary [gender] division (Carolyn Burke, "Getting Spliced: Modernism and Sexual Difference," *American Quarterly* 39 (1987): 110. Other recent feminist work includes articles by Susan Stanford Friedman (on "Anglo-Mongrels and the Rose," another long poem) and Maeera Schreiber on "Love Songs" (in typescript) as well as analyses of Loy's life, in Gillian Hanscombe and Virginia Smyers, *Writing for Their Lives* (London, 1987), and Shari Benstock, *Women of the Left Bank* (Austin, Tex., 1986).

   4. The manifesto is conjecturally dated 1914, that is, virtually simultaneous with the poem, and just preceding it (?); possibly its critical force then is transferred to the poem "Love Songs," for although Conover notes Loy had written on the autograph manuscript "This is a rough draught beginning of an absolute

resubstantiation of the feminist question," the manifesto is apparently not continued beyond these few page (*LLB* 269–71 and 327). Carolyn Burke, to whose help I am indebted, kindly provided me with a copy of the autograph manuscript of the "Feminist Manifesto." A comparison of the Loy autograph and the version published in *LLB* reveals some notable changes, including: (1) the dropping of a whole statement; (2) decisive normalizations of Loy's punctuation, capitalization, and underlining; (3) significant copy editor's changes of Loy's syntax, such as alterations of the plural form "women" into the singular "woman," changes of word order, and the like; and (4) the rewriting of at least seven statements that significantly alters their tone, import, or meaning. To give an example of the latter, Loy wrote: "As conditions are at present constituted—you have the choice between *Parasitism, & Prostitution*—or *Negation*[.]" Conover reports for the last phrase "you have the choice between Parasitism, Prostitution, or Negation." This rendering significantly distorts Loy's allusion to feminist debate. When I cite from this document, I will use my own renderings of Loy's (easy-to-read) handwriting, with the *LLB* page number. Although such changes seem almost inconceivable, there is no indication of another text (e.g., a later typescript by Loy with her revision) from which Conover worked as he prepared this rendering.

5. See *LLB* 271: "In defiance of superstition I assert that *there is nothing impure in sex* except the mental attitude toward it. The eventual acceptance of this fact will constitute an incalculably wider social regeneration than it is possible for our generation to acquire." This version is decidedly different from what I read in the autograph manuscript, cited above in my text.

6. I am borrowing Bruce Clarke's incisive characterization of Marsden in "Dora Marsden's Egoism and Modern Letters: West, Weaver, Joyce, Pound, Lawrence, Williams, Eliot," *Works and Days* 2, no. 2 (1985): 29. Marsden, supported in part by Harriet Shaw Weaver, edited *The Freewoman* (one year, 1911–12), *The New Freewoman* (half a year in 1913), which then was renamed *The Egoist* (1914–19). Born in 1882, Loy studied art in London and Munich, lived in Paris in 1903–6, and in Florence from 1906 to 1916, but the circles she moved in make plausible, if not arguable, some direct encounter with Marsden's periodical. In 1913 she was alienated from her first husband; in 1914 she had affairs with Marinetti and Papini.

7. In both "Parasitism, & Prostitution" what radicals saw as the private ownership of women in marriage is implied. Loy was adamant that "economic legislation, vice-crusades and uniform education" are inadequate sops when nothing short of "Absolute Demolition" will change the sex-gender system (*LLB* 269).

8. Loy's feminism of individual agency and will still seems to consider women as a group, and indeed still uses the term *feminist*. In contrast, Marsden

was highly resistant to any consideration of Woman-as-type, by which she meant both stereotypes of women and any analysis considering woman in the mass— that is, analyses by gender. She announces her principles as follows: that "'Woman,' spelt with a capital, Woman-as-type, had no existence; that it is an empty concept and should be banished from language" ("Views and Comments," *The New Freewoman* 2, no. 1 [1913]: 24). Marsden also insisted that "'Feminism' was the natural reply to 'Hominism,'" suggesting that both were inadequate and unnecessary, because a higher and more specific individualist urge replaced these political positions—"[women] can be as 'free' now as they have the power to be" (Views and Comments," *The New Freewoman* 2, no. 12 [1913]: 244). This latter editorial announces the end of the "new freewoman" title, so that the review would no longer emphasize female specificity but be for "individualists of both sexes." The name change was precipitated by a letter from such male contributors as Ezra Pound, Allen Upward, and Richard Aldington.

9. Barbara Low had a review in *The New Freewoman* which stated there was no difference between men's and women's "sex-feelings" ("A New Altar," *The New Freewoman* 2, no. 1 [1913]: 36).

10. For the analysis of the sexual debates, I am indebted to Frank Mort, *Dangerous Sexualities: Medico-Moral Politics in England since 1830* (London, 1987), p. 148. And in general, to Jeffrey Weeks, *Sex, Politics and Society: The Regulation of Sexuality since 1800* (London, 1981).

11. Ellen Dubois and Linda Gordon, "Seeking Ecstasy on the Battlefield: Danger and Pleasure in Nineteenth Century Feminist Sexual Thought," *Feminist Studies* 9, no. 1 (1983): 15 and 7; but the whole article informs this analysis.

12. Loy's phrase, "the progression of realisations," citing a Loy letter to Carl Van Vechten (Kouidis, *Mina Loy*, p. 62). The terms of the desertion—indeed, whether it is a desertion in the classic sense—are actually more difficult to discern than I have suggested at this moment.

13. Laurence Lipking, *Abandoned Women and Poetic Tradition* (Chicago, 1988).

14. This is the statement cut by Conover.

15. "Sewn" is in the *Others* printing; it makes a pertinent pun about female and male work. I follow two revisions to the Conover edition in just this first section. Kouidis (*Mina Loy*, p. 64, n. 20) follows the manuscript not the 1915 publication in *Others*, which had errors apparently picked up by Conover. "Silting" (for "sitting") is one; "These" (for "there") is the other. In addition, Loy ideally wanted each section to be followed by a reciprocal page of blank space with a "large round" in it (Kouidis, p. 64). For the sake of clarity in this paper, I am reluctantly ignoring this issue and other differences in punctuation from *LLB*, such as a lavish use of the dash by Loy in the publication of the poem in *Others*.

16. Poets who used slide show and lantern show imagery include T. S. Eliot, "Preludes"; H. D., in "Projector," uses early cinema. A Bengal light is a firework with a brilliant blue light sometimes used for signaling. The combination of orgasmic connotations with images of scrutiny and signaling is irresistible.

17. Carolyn Burke, "The New Poetry and the New Woman: Mina Loy," in *Coming to Light: American Women Poets in the Twentieth Century,* ed. Diana Middlebrook and Marilyn Yalom (Ann Arbor, 1985). Burke reports in general Loy's "shocking . . . treatment of gender and sexuality in these so-called love songs. She alluded to the 'suspect places' of sexual intercourse with such frankness that no one could miss her meaning" (p. 51). The article—an important study of the link of free verse and free love—traces the considerable impact of Loy on the *Others* group and the New York avant-garde, and the impact on Loy of Margaret Sanger's birth control activism. My paper complements Burke and offers my sense of the specific meanings and textual implications of Loy's insistence on sexuality.

18. Carolyn Burke, "Supposed Persons: Modernist Poetry and the Female Subject (a Review Essay)," *Feminist Studies* 11, no. 1 (1985): 136.

19. I am alluding to Margaret Homans's argument that the masculine plot of desire constructs the romantic lyric, and female writers of adequate cultural mission or with certain historical leverage can offer critical rearrangements of this heterosexual love plot. Among the tactics are an erosion of exclusive specularity by textual and formal evocations of other senses, and a rearrangement of gender hierarchy by an evocation of intersubjectivity ("'Syllables of Velvet': Dickinson, Rossetti, and the Rhetorics of Sexuality," *Feminist Studies* 11, no. 3 [1985]: 569–93).

20. And not only this set of materials, but yet another at the end of the poem (secs. 24–30) returns to intercourse as its topos and ground.

21. "Welded," for instance, puns on and rejects the more familiar phrase "wedded together."

22. Elizabeth Arnold argues that the difference between this manifesto and this poem can be traced to Loy's adhesion to futurist principles in the manifesto (including "depersonalized and amoral sexual intercourse") but her reembrace of "romantic love and femininity" in the poem. That there was a distinct shift in Loy's attitude to the futurists between 1914 and 1917, and a critical regard of their masculinist ideology, Arnold's article makes plain. It did not intend to offer an adequate reading of the poem ("Mina Loy and the Futurists," *Sagetrieb* 8, no. 1 and 2 [1989]: 83–117).

23. Both sections 16 and 25 mention the Arno, which tends to frame this part of the poem. The narrative middle shows the "I" enmeshed in certain thralldoms in phrases like "at your mercy"; "Is it true / That I have set you apart";

"To love you most"; and after the fall: "I store up nights against you / Heavy with shut-flower's nightmares" secs. 11, 12, 15, 21).

24. In a letter (c. 1915) to Carl Van Vechten, cited from the Beinecke Library by Conover (*LLB* 326), Kouidis (p. 85), Burke ("Supposed Persons," 137), and Schreiber (typescript, p. 1). I have not yet seen the context for this remark within the whole letter and their correspondence.

25. *The Poems of Sappho,* tr. Susy Q. Groden (New York, 1966), p. 78.

26. Page numbers of Sappho in the Groden are 52, 4, 18, 44, 67, 136. I have spoken about H. D.'s need for Sappho in *H. D.: The Career of that Struggle* (Brighton, 1986), drawing upon Susan Gubar's "Sapphistries," *Signs* 10 no. 1 (1984): 43–62, with its exquisite drawing of the erotic longings (maternal, heterosexual, and lesbian) which Sappho encodes, and Hugh Kenner's *The Pound Era* (Berkeley, 1971) with its sense of the textual meaning of fragments to imagist poetic practice. I add to these, textual longings given the fragmentary survival of Sappho's work and a strong sense of cultural authority, acutely felt for women writers, achieved in claiming the ability to remake Sappho.

27. Ezra Pound, "Papyrus," in *Personae: The Collected Shorter Poems of Ezra Pound* (New York, 1926), p. 112. Sappho, in Groden, p. 45. This brief survey suggests Loy's strongly motivated intertextual match with Sappho: there may certainly be other instances of Loy's use.

28. Section 26 reads in toto: "Shedding our petty pruderies / From slit eyes / We sidle up / To Nature / that irate pornographist."

29. I.e., they have no identity, have false names, unlike herself. Or perhaps like herself, who changed her family name from the ethnic Jewish freight of Lowy to Loy in 1903.

30. I take this as the development of a new species within a genus, or the development of specialized organs, a word used of embryos or fetuses.

31. To recall, "Every woman [i.e., married or unmarried] has a right to maternity"; indeed "woman must become more responsible for the child than man"—the latter is either the most banal of her propositions, since it recapitulates what is, or the most radical in proposing dyadic (mother-child) families (*LLB* 270, 271).

32. Richard Brown, *James Joyce and Sexuality* (Cambridge, 1985), p. 63.

33. An unpublished paper by Maeera Schreiber, "'The Best Since Sappho': Mina Loy's *Love Songs,*" which I saw as I was completing this essay, suggests that within this poem Loy narrates an abortion; this point could be precisely argued, but it is Schreiber's, and she will do so.

34. I follow Susanne de Lotbinère-Harwood's ingenious suggestion (made in an unpublished essay), that Anglophones use a modified version of the French word *cyprin* for a word apparently missing in English.

35. The decision to have a child (to participate in "vital creation") Loy inter-

preted as the solemnization of "a definite period of psychic development in her life," that is, the life of "a superior woman" (*LLB* 271).

36. This is informed by a brief discussion by Teresa de Lauretis of an article by Lucy Bland ("The Domain of the Sexual," which appeared in *Screen Education* 39 [1981]), in *Technologies of Gender: Essays on Theory, Film, and Fiction* (Bloomington, Ind., 1987), p. 14.

37. In an otherwise thoroughly modern study called *Sex in Civilization,* ed. Victor F. Calverton (New York, 1929), A. Davison Ficke, the author of "A Note on the Poetry of Sex," pp. 659–76, cites himself depicting sexual intercourse: "My body was one tremulous sense / Of her slight body's eloquence. / I was a drowned man in the sea / Of her immaculate melody" (p. 675). The contrast of this poetic cupcake with Loy's work could not be more acute.

38. Michel Foucault, Introduction, *The History of Sexuality* (New York, 1980), 1:63. I have tried to do some of what he asks; some is exciting but not possible.

39. Homans, " 'Syllables of Velvet.' " Indeed, in another extension, "to write" for certain male lyric poets may be to court or seduce "Poetry" personified as female. Margaret Homans makes this point about Keats, in her brilliant "Keats Reading Women, Women Reading Keats" (typescript).

40. This situation is memorialized in Adrienne Rich's iconic image, out of Campion, and into a protofeminist critique. She speaks about "Corinna" (a name evocative of a Greek woman lyricist) bent over her lute singing, framed in the viewer's gaze as beauty itself, not as the creator of art. Adrienne Rich, "Snapshots of a Daughter-in-Law," in *Poems: Selected and New, 1950–1974* (New York, 1975), p. 49.

41. Homans uses Irigaray; and one might well adduce both feminist film criticism (Laura Mulvey, Mary Ann Doane) and Griselda Pollock's study of the sexual politics of looking in *Vision and Difference: Femininity, Feminism and the Histories of Art* (London, 1988) to suggest an increasingly sophisticated interest in the social and political construction of looking in its relation with questions of the lyric. I can only allude to this here.

42. I am basing my argument on my extension of Nancy Vickers, "Diana Described: Scattered Women and Scattered Rhyme," in *Writing and Sexual Difference,* ed. Elizabeth Abel (Chicago, 1982). And I have borrowed a little from my essay "Otherhow," in my *The Pink Guitar: Writing as Feminist Practice* (New York, 1990).

43. Virginia Woolf, *A Room of One's Own* (1929; rpt. New York, 1957), pp. 12–13; the two melodies in question are "There has fallen a splendid tear" and "My heart is like a singing bird."

44. David Lindley, *Lyric* (London, 1985), p. 12. Sandra Gilbert and Susan Gubar have begun this process in their multivolumed consideration of modern-

ism, *No Man's Land: The Place of the Woman Writer in the Twentieth Century* (New Haven, 1987), but the war metaphor—the battle of the sexes—at least in the first volume, disallows some of the historical complexity of gender debates.

45. About beauty, Loy was less critical, proposing a technique of "Auto-Facial-Construction" to preserve beauty through the exercise of individual techniques of control. This was written in 1919 (*LLB* 283–84 and 328) and aimed to be a sincere (if wacky) tactic to enter the beauty business. It is also notable, in Loy's attitude to beauty (and her own was considerable), to read in "Feminist Manifesto" that "woman must retain her deceptive fragility of appearance, combined with indomitable will, irreducible courage, abundant health, and sound nerves" (*LLB* 271). "Dress like a girl, think like a man, and work like a dog"?

46. Ezra Pound, "How to Read, or Why" (1929), rpt. in *Literary Essays* (Norfolk, Conn., 1954), p. 25; "dialogic" alluding to Bakhtin.

47. Ezra Pound, "Marianne Moore and Mina Loy," originally published in *Little Review* (March 1918), rpt. in *Marianne Moore: A Collection of Critical Essays,* ed. Charles Tomlinson (Englewood Cliffs, N.J., 1969), pp. 46–47.

48. A striking analysis of the hidden gender histories of key modernist stylistic features (parataxis, collage, dislike of connectives, logopoeia) is done by Carolyn Burke in "Getting Spliced"; the analysis of the relation of this to the gender issues in the lyric tradition are my own.

49. Kouidis discusses the red-white-green imagery of this poem to a certain extent (*Mina Loy,* pp. 81–82); it is important to see how traditional these colors are to love poetry and to pastoral. Yellow, or yellow-white ("cymophanous" means just that), then becomes a modernist, franker color of sex. Williams, very possibly inspired by the general frankness of Loy's poem, which was partially published in the July 1915 issue of *Others,* uses it in "Love Song [I lie here thinking of you]." He repeats "yellow" and "saffron" in an exclamation to, and about a "honey-thick stain" of love. Poem in two versions (1915 and 1917) in *The Collected Poems of William Carlos Williams,* ed. A. Walton Litz and Christopher MacGowan (New York, 1986), 1:53, 106.

50. More thick etymology: "root" could be a dialect form of the verb *rut,* meaning to be in a state of sexual excitement.

51. It cannot be irrelevant to Loy's imagination that the main character of her "Anglo-Mongrels and the Rose" (1923–25), the character closest to her self, is called Ova.

52. Lawrence is one precise kind of example. Clearly a more complete, and much longer, paper or monograph would attempt the analysis of more literary and social texts. And "modern sexual stories" are not exclusively ones that center on heterosexual intercourse. It is also clear that the very definition of the "sexual embrace" and its meanings might differ from discourse to discourse. Citations of *The Rainbow* from the London, 1928, edition; hereafter cited in text.

IDEOLOGY IN MINA LOY

53. Kaleidoscopic is an image suggested by an early section of the poem. Virginia Kouidis proposes that Loy was in the tradition of sexual reformers who urge spiritual change in a self (that is, in my terms, her ideology is like Lawrence's).

54. It does not escape me that I am comparing a novel and a relatively shorter poem sequence; one comment is—the proportion of sexual material in Loy is much more astonishing, given its genre and its seminarrative obliqueness.

55. Stephen Heath, on whom I draw here, has spoken about this dominant discursive convention of love-making in twentieth-century fiction (he calls it "the sexual fix"), which frames the penis-vagina connection, with its male-female binary, and makes a large "primordial and cosmic investment in 'sexuality'" as "culminations of a life and a novel." "Writing love-making is again a problem of complicity with and support for the sexual fix, going over and over the standard pattern. Here if anywhere, one might think, differences would be fundamental, a plurality of positions and inscriptions would be possible. Yet here [in a passage from *Lady Chatterley's Lover,* 1928] precisely the same is made and remade, the very fact of these scenes determined by the myth and its repetition; with the difficulty of writing otherwise, outside that repetition, immense" (*The Sexual Fix* [1982; rpt. New York, 1984], pp. 130, 131, 126).

12

TOCQUEVILLE AND THE IDEA
OF AN AMERICAN LITERATURE
1941–1971

ૹ

Cushing Strout

IT MIGHT SEEM PERVERSE to focus on the idea of an American literature by paying much attention to the opinions of a youthful French liberal aristocrat who had no opportunity of reading any of it. All he had to say about it after his visit in 1831 can be found in a few pages of *Democracy in America,* where he prophesies about the shape of modern democratic literature. Moreover, democracy for him is an ideal type or model of an egalitarian system, one mainly pertinent to a possible French future and only partially illustrated in American actuality, which in his view had some powerful antibodies against the bleak diseases of modernism that might isolate citizens under the soft despotism of a paternalistic administration.[1] For Tocqueville the sources of poetry in a democratic world centered around the nature of man himself, because the social space between the individual and the state would be empty of the aristocratic forms of life that had previously filled it. Reflecting on the examples of Chateaubriand, Lamartine, and Byron, he prophesied in the 1840 volume of his book that modern democratic writers would, by focusing on "passions and ideas" in "the hidden depths of man's spiritual nature," illuminate by exaggeration, as he put it, "certain dark corners of the human heart."[2]

Tocqueville's prophecy fell on deaf ears until 1941, but from then on, for the next two decades especially, an influential group of American literary critics praised his prescience about what they took to be the persistent American aspect of our classic nineteenth-century literature from Poe to James. Tocqueville often seemed pertinent because the critics were looking for ways to recognize a difference between American and English literature. In 1937 an introduction to a study of twentieth-century American literature described the modern writer as a cosmopolitan who "sees no distinction between American civilization and European civilization."[3] But it was this difference itself that fascinated critics in the following two decades. Summing up a conference of distinguished intellectuals on "The National Style," the historian Elting E. Morison confessed that it was "a little depressing that twenty-five learned Americans could find so little more to say about ourselves in 1957 than a single visiting Frenchman had said in 1835."[4] Tocqueville's hour had come because the hour of American power and of mass culture had also come.

It is not surprising, given Tocqueville's image of a privatized modern age, that northerners rather than southerners would seize upon his literary prophecy. It would be professors in New England and New York universities who would make the most of Tocqueville precisely because they responded so sympathetically to the abstract and metaphysical characteristics they saw in a canon of American classics from which southern writers were notably absent. It was not only because they had not yet quite developed that quarrel with themselves from which poetry is made but also because Tocqueville envisaged a poetic subject disengaged from society, and so his prophecy could not include the plantation novel, whether written by the southerner William Gilmore Simms or the northerner Harriet Beecher Stowe.

Tocqueville's reference to an exaggerated illumination of the heart's dark corners was congenial to the theorizing about the "romance" by his American contemporaries, whose "prevailing tendency was to see it as an escape or a flight from the actual, going above or beyond or inside—and this is the qualifying point—human experience."[5] As a compensation for lacking "social characteristics and historical connotations," this idea of the "romance" as "escape from the world and society" was rediscovered, in effect, by twentieth-century critics. F. O. Matthiessen's *The American Renaissance* applied Tocqueville's prophecy to Emerson and Whitman insofar as they had followed Tocqueville's idea that the chief subject of democratic poetry would be "Man himself, not tied to time or place, but face to face with nature and with God."[6] At the same time W. H. Auden, a recent émigré to America, defined classic American literature from Poe to James as "a literature of lonely people," symbolically exploring "a timeless and unlocated (because internal) psychomachia." Later, Auden would observe that if Tocqueville had truly characterized modern poetry, America had never known any other kind.[7]

In the following decade Lionel Trilling reinforced the asocial implications in Tocqueville's and Auden's denial of time and place. He thought Tocqueville saw "the greatness of isolation," in our major writers, and Trilling even found in them "a disenchantment or disgust with the very idea of society,"[8] something first fully seen by D. H. Lawrence in his *Studies in Classic American Literature.* Trilling influentially proposed a sharp contrast between the abstract, "desocialized" American romance and the concrete, socially dense English novel of manners. Other critics, such as Marius Bewley, R. W. B. Lewis, Charles Feidelson, Harry Levin, and especially Richard Chase, extended Trilling's idea so that metaphysical symbolism and mythicized characters became the hallmarks of American nationality in literature.

How do we account for this emergence of a paradigm about our literature over a hundred years after its formulation? The development is intelligible only in the light of the previous treatment of our literature, the intellectual prestige of symbolism, the political role of America in the war and postwar years, and the reception of American literature in Europe.

The striking thing about literary opinion in America before the 1940s was the long period of apology and condescension for American literature as a poor country cousin of its English ancestor. V. L. Parrington and Van Wyck Brooks finally escaped this colonial complex, but both of these critics were Jeffersonian in temper, lacking sympathy for writers who were either pessimistic or skeptical about democracy, human nature, and progress. Yet these traits marked the most powerful modernist poets and novelists, who were also alien to the vulgar Marxists of the 1930s, who confused their cult of the literature of a proletarian class with the propaganda of a party. Moreover, symbolism and myth were in the intellectual air as ways of coming to terms with the nonrational in human experience and also with the typical gestures of Modernism in the arts with its taste for a certain abstractness. Even in folk culture the modern critic found a nonnaturalistic tradition including "the abstraction of a Jonathan Edwards sermon, a Navajo blanket, a John Henry feat, and a Vermont hooked rug," and it was Marin rather than Norman Rockwell who was painting in it.[9]

Leslie Fiedler did not need to adopt his enfant terrible role to announce in 1958 that "the last thirty years have been a time of triumph for American literature. Throughout the world, our classic books have come to seem more and more not merely excellent or interesting but central to the development of contemporary literature everywhere—a challenge to other long-accepted traditions and an example to the writer in a mass culture." Fiedler also saw that Melville is "our age's darling, and this has meant not only a revision of the earlier estimates of him and his work, but a redefinition of the writers around him . . . indeed of our literature as a whole." The advantage of symbolism as a way of talking about American writers was to provide a "long overdue counterbalance to the never-satisfactory view of our literary history as a slow struggle upward from darkness toward realism." [10] Instead of apologizing for our classic writers for their lack of English robustness, as earlier critics had done, the New Critics could find in the idea of the romance a genre term to account for the qualities in American writing that distinguished it from English social realism. In this way the romance made something positive out of the lack of social density in the American novel in terms of English social class.

Near the end of the twenties Edmund Wilson had called for a criticism that would recognize how Hawthorne, Melville, and Poe "anticipated, in the middle of the last century, the temperament of our own day and invented methods for rendering it." [11] In 1953 Charles Feidelson answered the call in his *Symbolism in American Literature.* It substituted for Matthiessen's theme of our classic writers' "devotion to the possibilities of democracy" an aesthetic focus on "their devotion to the possibilities of symbolism." He was entirely candid about his modern interest in seeing our classic writers "as a proving ground for the issues to which the method of modern literature is an answer." [12]

In a symposium on myth in 1958 Claude Lévi-Strauss suggested that since the pattern of myth points both to past time and to all time, what has replaced its function in modern societies is political ideology. [13] The point can be reversed, for myth tended to replace politics for intellectuals who identified with the theme of Daniel Bell's *The End of Ideology*. It summed up a decade of political disenchantment with Marxist ideology by concluding that ideas were no longer "social levers" because the passing of chiliastic socialism had left a prosaic world in which to invest issues with "moral color and high emotional charge is to invite conflicts which can only damage a society."[14] This repudiation of intellectual and moral passion in politics inevitably made the political world much less interesting than the literary world of symbols and myths.

R. W. B. Lewis's *The American Adam,* published at the same time as the symposium on myth, invoked Tocqueville's prophecy to identify a recurring American story of an Adamic person, "at home only in the presence of nature and God," being "thrust by circumstances into an actual world and an actual age."[15] Lewis's reference to an actual world and an actual time was a valuable modification of Tocqueville's idea and of the self-referential modernism celebrated in Feidelson's insistence that symbolism's "characteristic subject is its own equivocal method" (73).

Other devotees of the Tocqueville theme, however, were more inclined, as in Daniel Hoffman's *Form and Fable in American Fiction,* to see the romance form as "an ahistorical depiction of the individual's discovery of his own identity in a world where his essential self is inviolate and independent of such involvements in history." But Hoffman too admitted at the back door the involvements in history that he had driven out the front by noting how in American folklore and fiction the America hero "must define himself in conflict with a more stable ritual-figure or society reflecting the American inheritance of European culture and its burdens of historical responsibility." Yet the Tocqueville theme inclined him to confuse literature with history by assuming that "the American had neither a class nor a history to fix his place in society, neither priest nor church to ameliorate his relation to the immensities."[16] These Americans without class or church to define them, however, are rather like mythical reflections of our national folklore with its hyperbole about the superiority of the New World to the Old. In this sense, as Hoffman himself recognized, our folklore and fiction reflect "the continuity of culture and the struggles of history" in the recurrence of New World opposition to the Old. Our writers have treated the latter critically whenever they have dealt with what Henry James called "the international theme," which entered as well into the work of Irving, Cooper, Hawthorne, Melville, and Howells.[17]

One of Trilling's most prominent students, Norman Podhoretz, saw that his teacher was influential because he was so much "in tune with the temper of a period which found Tocqueville a more reliable guide than Marx to the American reality." [18] For Trilling the intellectuals' idea of society was largely a construct of "the long war of the French intellectuals with the French bourgeoisie." In the 1950s Trilling spoke for many intellectuals who felt "the virtual uniqueness of American security and well being, and, at the same time, of the danger in which they stand." [19] Most of them had discovered in the crisis of the Second World War that they had, after all, a stake in American victory. Columbia intellectuals had a close relation to the *Partisan Review,* and one of its editors in 1952 heralded a "new sense of belonging to their native land" in the attitudes of our intellectuals and artists. A *New Yorker* writer once joked that *Partisan Review* typewriters must have had a special key labeled "alienation," but now the editor defined the artist as being suspended "between belonging and alienation." [20]

Politically, the *Partisan Review*'s courageous anti-Stalinism of the late 1930s had set it on a course opposed to the Popular Front, represented by the League of American Writers. The League tended to link American literary tradition with the left-liberal and fellow-traveling intellectuals, as Van Wyck Brooks did, while the anti-Stalinists saluted instead European writers like Kafka, Silone, Malraux, and Orwell. [21] By the end of the fifties, however, the new theorists of American literature had reoriented our classic writers in terms that made them partakers of abstractness, symbolism, and myth—the very qualities the critics admired in European modernists and contemporary writing. Van Wyck Brooks's admiration for Henry Wallace, whose Progressive party was manipulated by Communists in 1948, marked his distance from the anti-Stalinist orbit in political terms, but he was separated as well in literary terms every bit as far because for him what Melville saw in Hawthorne as "the power of blackness" could never be "the true voice of America," as it was for those who, like Harry Levin in his *The Power of Blackness,* hailed "the symbolic character of our greatest fiction and the dark wisdom of our deeper minds." [22]

Trilling saw in 1958 that a crucial change had come about through the war in the way we thought of American literature in relation to its English ancestry. The new sense of American destiny came with the decline of English power: "Only then, it seems, could we really begin to think of American literature as being a separate entity, with its own special qualities which existed of and by themselves, with its own history peculiar to itself, with its own kind of development." It seemed to him that now "all the world recognizes a particular quality in our literature which is American or nothing, and perhaps the English recognize it most of all; they see how different this quality is from the quality of their own literature."[23] Shortly, the *Times Literary Supplement* would publish a special number on American writing asserting in Trilling's own terms that for English readers "our own fiction, more than we ever realize until we set it against American, is rooted deeply in society; man for the English novelist is social man—and this is so even for Lawrence, who is as much obsessed with class as with sex—man as he exists in the context of a very old, exceedingly complex, hierarchical society; and though the society may be criticized or rebelled against, it remains inescapable."[24]

There was nothing parochial about this new critical interest in American literature, for it was shared by Europeans. Melville and Hawthorne had new translations in France after 1939, and their work now appeared as legitimate ancestors of the modern American novel, which was enjoying unprecedented and remarkable success in Europe. Henri Peyre observed in 1947 that three out of every four translations from the English language published in France, Italy, Russia, and South America in the last twenty years were from American works. For Europeans threatened by fascism, contemporary American books seemed "best attuned to a tragic era of incomprehensible violence and brutal inhumanity of man to man."[25] Sartre declared in 1946: "To writers of my generation, the publication of *The 42nd Parallel, Light in August, A Farewell to Arms,* effected a revolution similar to the one produced fifteen years earlier in Europe by the *Ulysses* of Joyce."[26] Appropriately, it was in the *French Review* of 1950 that a scholar showed how Tocqueville had "put his finger on certain qualities of this literature which only the future would unveil."[27]

In the sixties the asocial theme of Tocqueville's paradigm about democratic literature persisted, but critics began to take a more critical second look at the orthodoxy that had emerged. When the National Council of English in 1965 published a collection of essays aimed at the teacher of American literature, the editor recommended Chase, Fiedler, Levin, Feidelson, Hoffman, and Lewis, but one essay posted a dissent against Richard Chase's conflation of the romance form with all the values of modernist criticism.[28] Taking a second look at Hawthorne, Lionel Trilling now countered James's complaint about Hawthorne's "thinly composed" world by stressing the positive presence in it of an "iron hardness" for which the world was "ineluctably *there* in a stubborn way."[29] About this time a graduate student of Lewis's, A. N. Kaul, developed the argument that while our classic writers did not write the English social novel, they did, after all, deal with the search for a more satisfying community life, even if they did so on a personal or metaphysical level.[30]

Richard Poirier in *A World Elsewhere* continued and modified the desocialized theme that he, like Trilling, found in D. H. Lawrence's essays. Poirier usefully challenged the romance-novel distinction because he saw that "none of the interesting American novelists can be placed on either side of this dichotomy."[31] He expanded on Kaul's idea of "retreat from society into an ideal community" (119) as a recurrent American strain, but his book mainly celebrated the notion of an epic ego in the "hero-poet" who seeks some form of imaginative "relinquishment and possession" (90) and acts in Emersonian-Whitman style as "an imperialist of the inner lives of other people" (94). Poirier did not believe in connecting literary with historical events and proposed instead to see passages in American books as "examples of a modernist impulse" (4) to create through language "an essentially imaginative environment" (5). The American writer was just "the most persistent, the most poignantly heroic example of a recurrent literary compulsion, not at all confined to our literature, to believe in the possibilities of a new style" (39).

Quentin Anderson in *The Imperial Self,* as his title implies, applied Poirier's idea of the omnivorous hero-poet while exemplifying it by Emerson, Whitman, and James, but his perspective also challenged the tradition that he represented. He charged two generations of critics with having ignored "two tremendous nineteenth century inventions: the concept of society and the concept of history," so that literary works begot other literary works "under the aegis of symbol or myth," rather than "on a scene the historian could conceivably recognize."[32] Such a scene, he suggested, would relate character structure and familial relationships to culture, showing how Emerson spoke to a widespread loss of authoritative supporting structures, cracks opening up in "the grain of American communal existence." Tocqueville and Trilling were still benchmarks for Anderson, but his relation to both was revisionary.

Whatever abstractness Tocqueville observed in the American mind of the 1830s, Anderson knew that the eighteenth-century founding fathers had a socially concrete vocabulary, one that "posited rooted oppositions

between warring social interests" (39). While Anderson cited his colleague Trilling on the classic American writer's alleged neglect of the idea
of society as the scene of human action, he subverted the traditional notion by treating Hawthorne's *The Scarlet Letter* as being "much more
closely akin to the novels of Jane Austen, George Eliot, or Trollope than
it is to the late James" (77), because the New Englander viewed society
"as the unique ground of our triumphs and defeats" (86). James's reputa-
tion, however, had risen only with the waning of historically oriented
criticism. Where Trilling had vaunted James as the master of social observation, Anderson saw his "various and voluminous world" subdued
instead to an imaginative order in which (as with Emerson and Whitman)
"the compelling character of history, generational order, places and things
leaches out, tends to disappear" (223). Anderson himself sympathized
with another strain in American literature, present in Cooper, Hawthorne, Melville, Hemingway, and Faulkner, one that accepts "the constraints of associated life," but he focused instead on those who had some
affinity with the contemporary fashion of social disaffiliation, represented
by the counterculture protest of the 1960s, notably evident at the Morn-
ingside Heights campus, where Allen Ginsberg had been a student and
where Anderson taught (241).

Anderson's important revisions in this thirty-year tradition of interpreting American literature open the door to a more extensive reappraisal
of Tocqueville's idea of democratic literature. It may turn out his prophecy will have renewed life for its pertinence to our time rather than to the
nineteenth century. The major flaw in his crystal ball was the rigid polar-
ity of an aristocratic interest in the past contrasted to a democratic interest in passions and ideas.[33] Both of these interests, however, were always
conjoined in the best work of Cooper, Hawthorne, and Melville.

Tocqueville believed that America would some day have a literature
"peculiarly its own," no longer English in form and substance, but he
could only speculate about it (439). While describing America, he was
always thinking about Europe, and that concern had generated his journey to America. Indeed, America interested him not for itself, but typo-
logically as a society less revolutionary than France and more democratic
than England.[34] He was an inveterate generalizer, a French trait by his
own reckoning, and he knew that "an abstract word is like a box with a
false bottom; you may put in it what ideas you please and take them out
again unobserved" (450). Much of the critical theory of American litera-

ture suggests this gaffed box by its exaggeration of the asocial theme in American novels, as if it were the only American strain.

Matthiessen, who had introduced Tocqueville's idea into the discussion of American classic writers, had a reasonable regard for its limits. But one American critic, who earned three degrees in England, saw the American artist as dieting on "democratic abstractions" that have "no social context."[35] Richard Chase, one of Trilling's colleagues, did the most for linking the idea of the romance to respect for "the peculiar narrow profundity" of American classics, but he also unjustly accused them of lacking "a sense of history" as well as "a sense of society and culture."[36] This lingering trace of the apologetic tone of the genteel critics proves only that the New Critics saw clearly enough the abstractness of the American fictional world; what they often failed to see was that its symbolism was a method for exploring historical and cultural issues, rather than for transcending them. The major irony in this astigmatism is that Chase himself scorned myth criticism for ignoring "the whole reality of time and place," which the novel reflects more than other forms, and he had wanted in 1950 "to open up the category of political discussion again" among men of letters. But, characteristically, it was *the idea of politics,* rather than any concrete version of it, that he recommended.[37] His theory of the romance in *The American Novel and Its Tradition* tended to desocialize our classics, projecting on them his own abstract cast of mind.

Classic American protagonists, whether Deerslayer, Hester Prynne, Ishmael, Huckleberry Finn, Jay Gatsby, or the black Invisible Man, may not be fully a part of their society, but "to be outside society is not to be immune to its claims," as these characters always discover, "shuttling to and fro," as an English commentator has pointed out, "between a desire for order and a desire for freedom, a responsibility to the self and a responsibility to society."[38] Hawthorne's "psychological romance" (his term) did illustrate Tocqueville's prophecy by departing from literal realism to explore "the truths of the human heart," yet his symbols pointed not beyond history but to events in the moral history of New England. Emerson, Whitman, and Wolfe could have endorsed Tocqueville's point that "the nation itself calls for poetic treatment," but they would not have agreed that "the language, dress, and daily actions of democratic man are repugnant to conceptions of the ideal" (453–55).

Tocqueville's hope for a democratic poetry was balanced by a fear that poets, "abandoning truth and reality," would "create monsters," ending by describing "an entirely fictitious country" populated by "a fantastic breed of brainchildren who will make one long for the real world" (457). I suggest that it is the "irrealism" of some "postmodern" writers, obsessed with the fictive nature of contemporary life, who give substance to Tocqueville's fears. Lionel Trilling acutely heard this "irrealistic" note in the modern critic's vivacity when speaking of "imaginary gardens with real toads in them" as the essence of poetry. "Indeed," he went on to point out, "we have come to believe that the toad is the less real when the garden is also real." [39] An attentive student of postmodern fiction has pertinently observed that "history, escaped by Poirier's classic American writers to an elsewhere of language, can also be evaded in a here of 'fictualized' life." [40]

A nation's discovery of its own literature, as in Canada and Australia today, is a major historical development. One must appreciate, therefore, the role of these critics in the midwifery of bringing to birth the widespread recognition of our distinctive literary tradition. "As recently as thirty years ago," Malcolm Cowley remarked in 1954, "the United States had no national classic" in the sense of a work having clustered around it many values discovered in it or added to it by a generation of students, critics, and ordinary readers. [41] Even in 1941 H. G. Wells thought it was ridiculous for an American to call himself a professor of *American* literature. [42] In the next twenty-five years American professors would construct a canon in Cowley's sense and prove Wells wrong. If the canon now seems limited and skewed, as female critics are the first to charge, [43] the owl of Minerva, as Hegel remarked, flies only when the shades of dusk have fallen. American literature had first to be discovered. Now that the discovery is behind us, we can resettle the territory.

To "resettle" already means including the black and female writers left out of the canon because their commitment to the social definition of characters and plot badly squares with Tocqueville's prophecy; it also means the less obvious task of reconsidering the writers traditionally recognized as classic. The Tocqueville-quoting critics have tended to celebrate the writers of the American Renaissance as precursors of the modernists. In effect, they have applied a Puritan typological reading in which the modernists are seen as fulfilling the promise of the classic writers, much as in Puritan readings of the Bible the Old Testament prefigures the New. By this strategy we have found them pertinent to our own modern concerns at the price of justifying them by their contribution to our own consciousness. We need instead to see their deep engagement with matters of society and history, however abstract their methods. In this light Ralph Ellison's *Invisible Man,* with its echoing of classic first-person narratives like *Moby-Dick* and *Huckleberry Finn,* is a pertinent reminder because it condenses the history of black people in their Afro-American cultural setting, while using techniques of symbolism to dramatize democratic issues akin to Matthiessen's vision of our classic writers. Huck wanted to go to the Territory ahead of the rest, and our Tocquevillean critics have tended to see it as a world elsewhere, but of course it was really Oklahoma, where Ellison grew up.

NOTES

1. Cushing Strout, "Tocqueville's Duality: Describing America and Thinking of Europe," *American Quarterly* 21 (Spring 1969): 87–99.

2. Alexis de Tocqueville, *Democracy in America,* ed. J. P. Mayer and Max Lerner, tr. George Lawrence (New York, 1966), pp. 454–55; hereafter cited in text.

3. Vernon Loggins, *I Hear America: Literature in the United States since 1900* (New York, 1937), p. 8.

4. Elting E. Morison, in *The American Style: Essays in Value and Performance,* ed. Elting E. Morison (New York, 1958), p. 414.

5. Sergio Perosa, *American Theories of the Novel: 1793–1903* (New York, 1983), p. 51.

6. Tocqueville, p. 455; F. O. Matthiessen, *The American Renaissance: Art and Expression in the Age of Emerson and Whitman* (New York, 1941), p. 544. The first to cite Whitman as proof of Tocqueville's prescience was Katherine Harrison in "A French Forecast of American Literature," *South Atlantic Quarterly* 25 (1926): 350–60.

7. W. H. Auden, *New Year Letter* (London, 1942), p. 153. Later, Auden contrasted Huck and Oliver to illustrate the Anglo-American difference, defining the American mentality as the product "less of conscious political action than of nature." See "The Anglo-American Difference," *Anchor Review* 1 (1955): 219.

8. Lionel Trilling, "Family Album," in *Speaking of Literature and Society,* ed. Diana Trilling (New York, 1980), p. 238 and "An American View of English Literature," ibid., pp. 262, 265.

9. Stanley Edgar Hyman, *The Armed Vision: A Study in the Methods of Modern Literary Criticism,* rev. ed. (New York, 1955), p. 122.

10. Leslie Fiedler, "American Literature," in *Contemporary Scholarship: A Critical Review,* ed. Lewis Leary (New York, 1958), p. 157.

11. Edmund Wilson, "The Critic Who Does Not Exist," in *The Shores of*

Light: A Literary Chronicle of the Twenties and Thirties (New York, 1952), pp. 371–72.

12. Charles Feidelson, *Symbolism in American Literature* (Chicago, 1966), pp. 4, 75–76; hereafter cited in text.

13. Claude Lévi-Strauss, "The Structural Study of Myth," in *Myth: A Symposium*, ed. Thomas A. Sebeok (Bloomington, Ind., 1958), p. 52.

14. Daniel Bell, *The End of Ideology* (Glencoe, Ill., 1960), pp. 110, 288–89.

15. R. W. B. Lewis, *The American Adam: Innocence, Tragedy, and Tradition in the Nineteenth Century* (Chicago, 1955), p. 89. Lewis's sensitivity to socially oriented writing is shown by his citing of James Gould Cozzens as "the most neglected of our serious novelists in this century." See his "Contemporary American Literature," in *Contemporary Literary Scholarship*, ed. Lewis Leary, p. 215.

16. Daniel Hoffman, *Form and Fable in American Fiction* (New York, 1965), pp. x, xii, 7.

17. Hoffman, p. 9. See Cushing Strout, *The American Image of the Old World* (New York, 1963), for extensive treatment of "the international theme."

18. Norman Podhoretz, *Making It* (New York, 1967), p. 126.

19. Lionel Trilling, "The Situation of the American Intellectual at the Present Time," *A Gathering of Fugitives* (New York, 1956), pp. 73, 64.

20. William Phillips, "Our Country and Our Culture: A Symposium," *Partisan Review* 19 (1952): 586, 589.

21. See James Burkhart Gilbert, *Writers and Partisans: A History of Literary Radicalism in America* (New York, 1968), esp. pp. 161–282.

22. Harry Levin, *The Power of Blackness* (New York, 1958), pp. xxi, 18. Cf. Van Wyck Brooks, *Days of the Phoenix: The Nineteen Twenties I Remember* (New York, 1957), p. 154.

23. Lionel Trilling, "Reflections on a Lost Cause," in *Speaking of Literature and Society*, pp. 348–49.

24. "The Limits of the Possible," in *The American Imagination: A Critical Survey of the Arts from the* Times Literary Supplement (New York, 1960), p. 36.

25. Henri Peyre, "American Literature through French Eyes," *Virginia Quarterly Review* 23 (1947): 421.

26. Quoted by Peyre, p. 435.

27. Reino Virtanen, "Tocqueville on a Democratic Literature," *French Review* 23 (1950): 216.

28. Edwin H. Cady, "The Teacher and the American Novel: 1964," in *The Teacher and American Literature*, ed. Lewis Leary (Champaign, Ill., 1965), p. 25.

29. Lionel Trilling, "Hawthorne in Our Time," in *Beyond Culture: Essays on Literature and Learning* (New York, 1965), p. 199.

30. A. N. Kaul, *The American Vision: Actual and Ideal Society in Nineteenth-Century Fiction* (New Haven, 1963), p. 63.

31. Richard Poirier, *A World Elsewhere: The Place of Style in American Literature* (New York, 1966), p. 16; hereafter cited in text.

32. Quentin Anderson, *The Imperial Self: An Essay in American Literary and Cultural History* (New York, 1971), pp. 86, 229–30; hereafter cited in text.

33. See Cushing Strout, "From Trilling to Anderson: The Strange History of Tocqueville's Idea of a Democratic Poetry," *American Quarterly* 24 (1972): 601–6. Cf. Nicolaus Mills, *American and English Fiction in the Nineteenth Century: An Antigenre Critique and Comparison* (Bloomington, Ind., 1973), p. 23.

34. François Furet, "Naissance d'un paradigme: Tocqueville et le voyage en amérique (1825–1831)" *Annales: Economies, Sociétés, Civilisations* 39, no. 2 (1984): 225–37.

35. Marius Bewley, *The Eccentric Design: Form in the Classic American Novel* (New York, 1959), p. 15.

36. Richard Chase, "The Classic Literature: Art and Idea," in *Paths of American Thought,* ed. Arthur M. Schlesinger, Jr., and Morton White (Boston, 1963), p. 54. Chase by then was worried that an unhistorical entity called "the American imagination" would be taken as having been precipitated "once and for all" in its characteristics (p. 68).

37. Richard Chase, *The American Novel and Its Tradition* (New York, 1957), Appendix 2, pp. 245–46 and "Art, Nature, Politics," *Kenyon Review* 12 (1950): 593–94.

38. C. W. E. Bigsby, *The Second Black Renaissance: Essays in Black Literature* (Westport, Conn., 1980), pp. 66, 145.

39. Lionel Trilling, "William Dean Howells and the Roots of Modern Taste," in his *The Opposing Self* (New York, 1955), p. 83.

40. Charles Caramello, *Silverless Mirrors: Book, Self, and Postmodern American Fiction* (Tallahassee, Fla., 1983), p. 91. See also Cushing Strout, "The Fortunes of Telling," *The Veracious Imagination: Essays on American History, Literature, and Biography* (Middletown, Conn., 1981), pp. 13–14.

41. Malcolm Cowley, *The Literary Situation* (New York, 1955), p. 14.

42. Fred Lewis Pattee, *Penn State Yankee* (State College, Pa., 1953), p. 165.

43. Nina Baym, "Melodramas of Beset Manhood: How Theories of American Fiction Exclude Women Authors," *American Quarterly* 33 (1981): 130–31. Her critique includes Trilling, Bewley, Chase, and Poirier.

13

NOSTALGIA FOR THE FUTURE,

WAITING FOR THE PAST:

POSTMODERNISM IN PHILOSOPHY

ی۵

Berel Lang

> I *do* believe in beginnings, middles, and ends—but not neces-
> sarily in that order.
>
> —Godard

EVERYTHING IS NOW PERMITTED," we tell ourselves, knowing as
Dostoyevsky only imagined that God has in fact been found dead; confident, where Nietzsche could only speculate, that language itself no longer
constrains us ("I fear we are not yet rid of God," Nietzsche would write
apprehensively, "because we still believe in grammar"). We may inhabit
the first period in history that has suspected everything that *can* be suspected—we as heirs of the nineteenth-century pioneers, those classical
philosophers of suspicion, who were so convincing in their descriptions of
life underground that other stories about life on the surface now seem to
us as distant even in their charm as the flights of Greek myth or the
experiments of medieval alchemy.

It is not just skepticism that has come to hold us, certainly not the
tendentious skepticism of Descartes who, like Job, in the end found all
his worldly losses restored, not even of the Pyrrhonists or even of Gorgias,
who would commit no more of himself to life or logic than the wiggle of
a finger. The transformational grammars—of the psyche, of economics,
of language itself—were yet to be construed, and only with those revisions do we begin to understand how difficult the labor of suspicion is:

not a simple two-termed relation in which reality has to prove itself against appearance, but one in which the supposedly elementary distinction between appearance and reality is itself doubted. The institutions of the human world—art, political structures, science, social relations—are disclosed first as appearances moved by other forces: psychological, economic, literary—and then *these* examples of stratification: superstructure driven by base, sublimation by libido, historical representation by imagination—are in their turn suspected, no longer turned upside down as Marx had prescribed for Hegel but sideways, where there *could* be no privileged origins or conclusions. So the forces that Marx and Freud still, for all their revolutionary zeal, took as fundamental, foundational, and stable turn out also to be contingent features of experience; they, too, require explanation, with the concept of explanation itself also altered, no longer hoping for inclusive laws or models, but spinning new, individual narrative threads, flattening even causality into a virtual and noncausal present.

At the edge of postmodernism, then, no theory or word or even feeling is above suspicion, and whatever postmodernism does or says seems to take that fact, perhaps *only* that fact, as given.[1] This starting point turns out to be more demanding than that which challenges the oracle or the soothsayer: all *they* have to do is to predict a future woven from the same fabric as that used in the past—a continuity that offers both comfort and a means: with a modest reliance on Delphic ambiguity, most of us could do reasonably well as prophets. Postmodernism, however, not only has to predict but to constitute, since when nothing is given, when everything is possible (and more than that, *equally* possible), what is proposed cannot fall back on analogy or any other logical or literary figures, all of which presuppose versions of continuity; it is obliged to spin of whole cloth. How would Joyce (let alone anyone who was not Joyce) have *predicted* *Finnegans Wake?* Well, in a sense, Joyce *did* make the prediction—when he wrote it. At that point, all the speculation that had preceded his writing about an impending revolution in consciousness, the possibility or impossibility of a contemporary epic, and so on, appeared suddenly in a different light. *Finnegans Wake* itself—his prediction realized, the performance—was there, available to sight and touch, even in some loose way, since it must have been shaken up by the performance, to the mind.

We have then only an *apparent* choice in trying to anticipate the directions of postmodernism (whether in philosophical discourse or some other) in terms similar to those we would apply to *other* plans for the future. We might, on the one hand, speak *about* that future, extrapolating from the present (somehow overriding the postmodernist claim of a sharp gap between past and present, the *dis*analogy); or we might, on the other hand, try ourselves to *do* the work of postmodernism, accepting as a premise that traditional philosophy, with its search for foundations and its representational theory of truth, is passé, over, done. But in both these accounts the work of postmodernism is defined only negatively, by what it *rejects* in the past and so by what it is *not*. This common and negative starting point, it seems, discloses an important feature of postmodernism, although perhaps not a feature that it recognizes in itself; it also points to the general thesis I shall be arguing here, that one thread of discourse in the history of philosophy has been continually, repeatedly, postmodernist. How this is so turns out to be important for understanding both the history—and the present—of philosophy, on the one hand, and the phenomenon of postmodernism, on the other.

Let me rehearse a composite, and so bland but also standard, account of the history of philosophy, as postmodernism, in such figures as Heidegger, Derrida, and Rorty, impatiently looks back at it. We mark off here the approximate distance between Plato and Hegel in a circle with a perimeter 2,400 years long. At the center of this circle is a motivating distinction between, on the one hand, the apparent world—loose, disjointed, occasional; and, on the other hand, a second world that appearance both conceals and discloses, one that *includes* the apparent world and has enough left over to explain why the apparent world looks as it does without actually being it. The claim of displacement made by this second world, together with the related claim of truth as a form of representation, draws on a variety of ostensive powers: the role of a logos or god or causality that determines aspects of everything else; the idea of substance—an underlying stuff (or two or three) that is then somehow differentiated into a greater number of things; the doctrine of a soul or mind that is as invisible and active as the body it animates is palpable and inert. What appears in these numerous accounts at first as a genuine variety in the history of philosophical thought, however, discloses itself *formally* as no more than a series of variations on a single theme—that of hierarchical reverence: appearance subordinated to reality, plurality to the One. And just this suspicion—that it is a reverence for authority, the desire for a center (and then for its representation), that has motivated the history of philosophy—is the starting point of the postmodernist diagnosis of that philosophical history. It is in the diagnosis of that origin, moreover—the moment of *rupture,* in Derrida's term—that what had announced itself in the history of philosophy as the will for truth or wisdom is revealed as no more than a disguise for nostalgia, a form of wistfulness and finally of self-deception where the will, not the mind, has been accorded the last word. We ought, then, to interpret the traditional discourse of philosophy rather as expression than as idea, as manifestation, not assertion; there is no object or foundation driving the process, only *other* expressions and manifestations that philosophers in their weakness have reified after the fact, finding objects where there had been initially only tracks or traces.

Now it might well be argued that this revisionist history is based on fragmentary, and at points no evidence (suspicion, after all, is for some people a pleasure in itself). And it is, I think, a matter of fact that none of the several versions of philosophical deconstruction sponsoring the efforts of postmodernist philosophy has come close to explaining *why* the history of Western thought should have gone astray as deeply and consistently as it allegedly has, resulting in a measure of falsification not much slighter than that of Original Sin (and like it, too, apparently, in being passed on as transgression to every following generation). But no matter—for this is history as the postmodernist imagines and so, we may suppose, lives it; and so there, again, at the alleged core of that history, the aspiration for authority, for structure, for beginnings, species, essences, categories, centers, natures, explanations, causes—all of these reflecting a malady that we now, postmodernly, are in a position to identify and then to overcome. At least we are able to reduce the symptom—but, we are told, that is all there *is* to the malady since there is nothing that is *not* surface, even in illness—and we cure these, moreover, mainly by the recognition that they *are* symptoms (an invitingly docile malady, that). So speech, for Wittgenstein, is reconceived as a part, not a contrivance of the organism; the ghost in the machine, for Gilbert Ryle, turns out to be only the cogs and levers that anybody not put off by the fear of blood will find for himself if he has the courage to look inside; for Sartre, human nature is precisely the absence of any such nature; for Derrida discourse is about discourse and even then, more about its absence than its presence—in any event, not about subjects and certainly not about objects. The motivating image here is also of a circle, but undifferentiated now, designedly antihierarchical and thus verging on the possibility that everything is itself only by being everything else as well, that distinctions are intrinsically suspect, unnatural. Given this starting point, even to ask simply "What now?" is already to beg the question, since it revives from the past an ideological commitment to the *what* of things—and to a *now:* the present as implying a precedent, something it is not. And although these may be evoked by the headiest of nostalgias (our own), they too must be suspected.

There are, it seems to me, two possibilities open to postmodernist thinking beyond this point, the one consistent but self-defeating; the other, inconsistent, revisionary even of the starting point in its conception of history, but nourishing a hope of survival. We can think of the difference between these as a difference between two theories of time. On the first (consistent) one of these accounts, the linear conception of time dominant in Western history is alleged to be part of the problem. Lines imply beginnings and ends; they also imply continuity, inferring from the reality of a past the probability of a future. If, then, as this first version of postmodernism maintains, we are not entitled to such claims, then time must be *dis*continuous, unmotivated—and we are talking here of separation not only between periods of time (years or generations) but between moments or instants, where even personal identity becomes an arbitrary and mystifying fiction, where proper names or the meanings of common terms cannot count on reidentification either. Not only institutional or corporate continuity is denied here but also continuity as it has been alleged for individual persons or objects; the very conception of an identity is suspect.

It can, I think, be reasonably objected to this (consistent) version of inconsistency that little in the appearances of culture—in ethics or law, in science, in the arts—is in accord with it. In the phenomenon of "style" (of individuals or groups), one recognizes the dependence of expression on the assumption of continuity or, still more rudimentary, of repetition. If these are required for style—perhaps, in Freud's suggestion, for the mind itself—the sacrifice of cultural or human anatomy might seem too high a price to pay for a new theory no matter how enticing it otherwise is. To be sure, the phenomenon of style itself—its domestication of novelty, its reliance on categories that pass themselves off as nature—has been accused of an all too easy nostalgia, but this objection itself has a price: to live only with the supposed neutrality of "stylessness" would be to threaten nature and not only art (even without assuming a notion of "natural" style). We would find ourselves here in a domain of pure contingency where the purpose of all writing or thinking is mainly to defeat expectations, to deny reference, and thus to reiterate continually the absence of continuity. The prospect, it needs to be said, is not entirely unfamiliar. Dadaism, surrealism, the so-called experimental novel, have been partial attempts to move in this direction, and without judging them in other ways, we recognize one feature common to them all: much of their power comes precisely from the expectations they work to defeat. Like the jujitsu wrestler, they get strength for their throw from their opponent's rush; without that, they have no more power than he has by himself. They flourish, then, by contrast, by reaction—and although this may be a way *into* the future, it hardly promises survival there; it is also, of course, itself a form of continuity insofar as it presupposes the past. Moreover, the philosophical or theoretical past that postmodernism (on this first view) simply writes off has, even in postmodernism's own terms, had unmistakably compelling consequences—in poetry, in science, in social institutions.

By contrast, the new present announced by postmodernism has as yet been mainly declamatory (Yeats and Eliot were reactionaries politically and arguably poetically as well—but postmodernist theory applied in practice has not come close to producing rival poetic imaginations). Hegel suggested that philosophy's Owl of Minerva would fly only at dusk, and perhaps, as postmodernism now intimates, he was mistaken; perhaps criticism, theory, philosophy, can *anticipate* rather than follow objects of experience such as literary texts or paintings. But even then they would not need to be identical to the latter; thus the strain is evident when postmodernist critics and theorists of art, for example, represent their own work as displacing the art from which they ostensively had set out. (There is an analogy here to a more traditional failure in which the artist views his work as the equivalent of theory.)

Still, there is no assurance that the second, contrasting version of postmodernism, as it disputes the alleged rupture in the history of Western thinking, promises any improvement. Such an alternative, it might be argued, would forfeit not only a potent criticism of the past but also the new beginning in the present that might be extracted from that criticism. But it is precisely this sense of a beginning, it seems to me, that can best be sustained by the alternative outlined above. Here, in the interest of postmodernist survival, I appeal to a military analogy—but irenically, designed to beat the swords of deconstruction into the ploughshares of pragmatism. The analogy is in the distinction between a conception of *strategy,* on the one hand, in which it is ends or goals or principles that are asserted, and the idea of *tactics,* on the other hand, where it is the means, even beginnings, that are sought and those only in order to serve the context in which they appear. Characteristically, postmodernism has opposed itself not only to *particular* strategies in one or another critical system, but to the possibility of strategies altogether. What happens to strategists, on this account—here the analogy to military history is pointed—is ossification, reification. Generals, we know, are constantly preparing to fight the war just past (this is true even when they have been victorious, but especially if they have been defeated—as in criticism they always are). And the strategic ends are still more implacable: only the incidental names of the enemy change over time, and even then, in cultural warfare, not by much. Looking out on the debris of the battlefield, we might thus willingly say with the postmodernist, "Enough and no more; after this only tactics—the response to a moment, and always in a context, *always* in the spirit of contingency, that is, with the present always in part absent. A celebration, in effect, of mortality itself."

And here we note the beginning of a small deceit as it grows, like most deceits, from a small truth. That rupture in the history of Western philosophy, the diagnosis and then rejection of logocentrism: might we not suspect that this claim is itself open to suspicion? Do we not have, in the distinction between strategy and tactics, a weapon to be turned against the *reading* of history as well as against history itself? My thesis here comes in two parts: first, that the traditional discourse of metaphysics, supposedly ruptured once and for all at its first moment, was itself—notwithstanding its high talk of God, substance, soul, logos—a sequence of tactical variations that only *came to be seen* (by advocates and critics alike) as committed to strategic ends. Its own intention reflected a design that was contextual not transcendent, historical not atemporal, practical, not theoretical. And, secondly, that the postmodernist attack on philosophy's history is itself a tactic much in the tradition of other tactics in that history—not, as it professes, a strategy, not even a metatactic, to end all strategies.

These are large claims to make good on: the ascription of such a tactical impulse to the full history of philosophy is not easily substantiated, and I do not mean to suggest that the impulse is everywhere apparent (certainly not in the same measure) in that history. What I am recommending in fact is only the prudence of an even hand: that where logocentrism or reification is alleged, we look for the occasion of those charges in the dramatizing eyes of the beholder, among the reader-historians of logos, as well as in the supposedly guilty texts themselves. There is considerable evidence that *this* mote too may be in the eye of the reader, not of the author; ideology, after all, does not play favorites.

I can hardly defend this general claim for all the texts and philosophers that have been accused of deviant practices (the history of philosophy written by postmodernists has closer textual affiliations to the Marquis de Sade and Kraft-Ebbing than to more recognizably philosophical sources). But since the Greeks were on most versions of postmodernist history orig- inally responsible for the Fall into logocentrism, let me refer to them and in particular to Plato, who is in so many ways a "paradeigma" of the doctrine of presence. It is easy enough, in reconstructing Plato's dia- logues, to regard the questions he raises in them also as establishing their answers: "What is justice?" "What is piety?" "What is knowledge" "What is courage?"—we hear, finding in this catalogue of questions the merely assumed existence of the "things" in question which are thus given life immaculately, without having labored, virtually a priori. Around them the representational world of the philosopher then turns; nothing more, it is inferred, need be added by Plato except for a brief and always ad hoc specification in the definition itself. There, in the questions he asks (and then, unsurprisingly, in his answers to them), we have Plato's theory of Forms: immobile, abstract, otherworldly—patterns to be known and then imitated by the rational self, at once explanations and directives for action.

The one thing missing from this common portrait, however, is Plato himself, specifically the act—the motives, the reasons, the practice—of his writing and philosophizing. *Is* the genre of the philosophical dialogue a means of objectification and representation, or even of assertion? Do Plato's dialogues provide definitions or rules—for justice or temperance or courage or piety or whatever—that demand allegiance, or at least im- itation, from the reader? *Is* the Good quite other than the individual items that experience sails past in its tours? One need not agree to the flat No by which I should answer these questions myself to concede its plausibil- ity—and this in itself suffices as a wedge to loosen the rigid distinction that the ideologists of the historiography of philosophy have in general

taken for granted. It hardly makes a crypto-Marxist of Plato to acknowledge that his eye for the work of the shoemaker, the sailor, the horse
trainer was the same eye with which he looked for and then at the Forms.
What many readers of Plato have done on the assumption that psychology
duplicates ontology, is to read backwards from the Forms to experience—
rather than the other way round, which is the way that Plato himself
almost certainly proceeded and in any event assumed that his reader
would.

This historical revision does not deny that, once conceived, the Forms
might or did take on a life of their own—but it is at least a cautionary
warning that Plato (and then the Forms) may have found their hands
forced by the evidence, that they may have been the driven rather than
the driver. In any event, it underscores the importance of avoiding interpretive placebos (like nostalgia) to explain Plato's allegiance to the
Forms as long as other less reductive explanations (including Plato's own)
are available. Perhaps the theory of the Forms is not strictly *required* to
account for the possibility of Platonic experience—but Kant's transcendental formulation is surely relevant to understanding how Plato or his
readers could possibly take the Forms seriously. To be consistently or even
occasionally suspicious may well argue that we should not take philosophers at their own words, but this hardly entails that we should not take
their words at all.

One advantage of the account I have begun here is that it suggests an
explanation of what it is that the deconstructionists have objected to in the
history of philosophy itself—something to which Heidegger, Derrida,
and Rorty have, it seems to me, given little more than a few firm moments of intuition and a metaphysics of history then cobbled together out
of them. There is no conspiracy theory of history required here, no need
for the invidious contention lurking in the work of these figures that we—
or at least, *they*—are more astute, more circumspect, more enlightenedly
suspicious than past figures, singly or together, in the history of Western
thought. It turns out for one thing—what the readers of ancient philosophers, like the readers of the ancient poets, can hardly be surprised at—
that the occasions of philosophical experience from which those writers
set out resemble our own. Abuses that occur, moreover—fetishism, for
example—may be endemic to the process of thinking itself rather than
peculiar to the history of a single-minded ideology. So, for example, the
fallacy, in Whitehead's phrase, of "misplaced concreteness," where the

price exacted by abstraction for the power it provides to memory (itself, as Nietzsche argued, a human creation) is forgetfulness of its origins. This theoretical version of religious idolatry appears when symbols, signs, constructs, representations become things-in-themselves, when their history is repressed. And there is, of course, an irony in the association of this particular fallacy with the deconstructionist view of the history of Western thought: that the latter view, meant to destroy the idols of the past, is true only or largely as it is false, when it itself totalizes or fetishizes history.

One could go further here, incorporating even the rupture announced by postmodernism into the very history it claims to have ruptured. For if we ask now, not why the past was misread, but, more substantively, why the claim should now be made that the history of philosophy is over, finished, that it has, in Heidegger's words "come to term," we see *that* declaration too, in full hyperbole, as continuous with the past of philosophy. Not only is it not the first time that philosophers have seen themselves as starting anew, shrugging free of the past which they pronounce as over, finished—but this is what philosophers have repeatedly asserted. Aristotle, Descartes, Locke, Kant had little "philia" left for their predecessors; they were not more inclined than the more recent and explicit advocates of postmodernism have been to place themselves in a continuous line of indebtedness. The voice speaking in the preface of a literary work is as close as we ever come to the person of the author; and the history of prefaces to philosophical writing—Descartes in the *Discourse,* Locke in the *Essay,* Kant in the *First Critique*—is in fact a history of revolt, less nicely, of murder, where the sons pit themselves against the fathers, promising a future that is now to begin with the present authors themselves. That such writing condemns the past does not necessarily mean for its authors that there is no future for philosophy (as Heidegger and Rorty propose)—but for the former as for the latter, it is the rejection of the past that determines a radically different future.

The impulse behind this rejection is more than psychological; it is, we might say, philosophical, an appeal to reflection where the assertion of distance is a prerequisite for the act of discourse itself. The life of philosophy is in these terms paradoxical—since we know that the claims of distance, of detachment, have repeatedly been superseded, upended by history itself as it works to close the gap. (Nature may abhor vacuums in principle, but for history they are unintelligible in practice.) Thus philos-

ophy succeeds only when it fails, when it evokes the past by rejecting it
in favor of the present, when it wins access to the moment by imagining
the whole. The moral that emerges here may seem Calvinist in its anticipation of defeat, but it has the large advantage of addressing the history
of philosophy as a history. To win the partial glimpse that is in the end
what philosophy settles for is along the way to presuppose a rejection of
one whole and to seek after, to desire, another. An *original* impulse for
fragmentation or partiality promises at worst fetishism, at best a glimpse
of pleasure—but little, in either direction, of a habitable world, let alone
of the reflections of philosophy. Lionel Trilling suggests that the concept
of modernism soon came, in one of its main proponents, Matthew Arnold, to lose its standing as a chronological category: "By [his] definition,
Periclean Athens is a modern age, Elizabethan England is not." Can we not
then think of postmodernism in the same way—not simply as a present
possibility, now, at *this* moment, but a possibility attached to the present
whenever the present occurs?

The historical occurrence of this prospect is not difficult to find. Descartes's eventual claim of certainty for what he knew came neither as a
straightforward rejection of his philosophical past nor merely as a step
added to it: in the very skepticism that he disputed, as it turned on itself,
he found a ground for its denial and then for personal, eventually for
systematic, certainty. That alteration, we understand, was more than an
appeal to rhetorical irony; it was a redirection of speculation back to its
own means, conveying the force of a "postmodernist" break with its past,
something on the order of a "paradigm shift" in philosophical discourse
and method. Similarly, Kant, responding to Hume's critique of causality,
turns the mechanism of cognition inside out, assigning to the subject or
knower the power that Hume had conclusively found wanting in the object—a strong example of the way in which the means of discourse, as
the poststructuralists (themselves heavily indebted to the Kantian tradition) have insisted, can be turned back on itself, deconstructed. There is,
then—although the general claim requires further elaboration—a *history*
of "postmodernist" moments within the history of philosophy. It might
be argued that the notion of *the* history of philosophy itself is tied to
another one of those moments, in the Romantic assertion of philosophical
hegemony over time—specifically in the Hegelian account of philosophical time. Also in that account we note a ready source for the postmodernist fascination with the death of philosophy: as Hegel himself heralded

the deaths of art and religion, he might well appreciate the cunning of history that would then go on to write an obituary for the author of those death notices.

But what then, looking from *this* present, of the postmodernist future in philosophy? For even if the much-qualified version of postmodernism presented here were granted for the sake of argument, there is nothing predictive about it; and we also have the constant obligation of responding to those thinkers who, standing at the brink, have cordially pronounced the death of metaphysics—not the beginning of a new version, but simply the end. There is Wittgenstein for whom, mimicking his compatriot Karl Kraus's words about psychoanalysis, philosophy was the disease it had been supposed to cure; there is Heidegger who found that Nietzsche had once and for all unsettled the traditional philosophical accounts; there is Derrida for whom discourse is now disclosed as entirely its own object and in which, then, philosophy, no more than the other addictive sciences of representation, has a future. Could philosophy survive such confident obituaries?

One path here might be toward quietism—in the prescription of a character of Unamuno's, simply "to catalogue the world and return it to God all in order." There has indeed been something of this conservative affirmation of things-as-they-are in the mood of those thinkers themselves, and it is important to keep in mind how this comes about. Consciousness itself, Nietzsche had proposed, was to be suspected as a malady—and with *that* suspicion, it is understandable that tactics no less than strategy should be viewed with a wary eye, hinting that there was no particular goal either to reach or to avoid, no distinctions to stand on, no references to hold to. Pleasure and the will might at first seem likely replacements for truth and understanding, since the latter could inevitably harden into abstraction—categories, foundations, ends-in-themselves. But then we find that the former may also become objectified, also doctrinaire, also punitive. And if the will can ensue in foundations and principles, then what starts there as tactic also loses its sense of origins?

I have suggested here that this impulse for displacing its past may be native to philosophy—repeatedly to privilege the present over what has been judged in the past. But looking at the recent present also as a past, we also may see something omitted there, something that philosophers in the tradition were more candid about, even if they could not, any more than the philosophers of suspicion, respond to it conclusively: the possibility that philosophy begins not in suspicion but in the quite different phenomenon of wonder. The difference between those two is much like the distinction emphasized by Kierkegaard between fear and anxiety, between the problem and the mystery that Gabriel Marcel distinguished—with each of the former terms reacting to a specific object, in contrast to the latter terms whose reference was diffused, a general feature of experience. I do not propose here to define a concept of wonder except in its least technical sense which still suffices to mask it as at once a postmodernist and constant feature of philosophy. For wonder, unlike suspicion, is attached exclusively to the present, a function of the here-and-now. As a motive of philosophy, then, wonder compels philosophy to begin in the present, that is, always to start anew—thus, to reject the past even with the full knowledge that this rejection is a function of the present as present, not the rejection of some particular past. So we understand the mild irony of the ninth-century Arab writer Ibn Qutayba, when he reminds his readers that "God has so ordered it that every ancient was modern in his own time." To which might now be added ". . . and that some ancients were also postmodern in their own time."

This may seem to offer a peculiarly disembodied view of the history of philosophy (past and future), with its fate left entirely in the hands of individual philosophers (as individuals) who, whether they will it or not, will always be breaking free of their philosophical pasts and even of the world itself. In these terms, postmodernism would be not an option but a necessity—a supposed consequence that, for the postmodernist, would be as much an outrage as an irony. There is, indeed, a social history of philosophy yet to be written, one that reflects on that history as history and not just as word and which, in doing this, describes the contexts of meaning for philosophical discourse that the discourse has not said for itself. I suggest, as a link between this unwritten history and the more formal analysis I have been giving, that philosophy has itself been openly ambivalent about its social status. Nietzsche objected that the idea of a married philosopher was a joke, and we might predict from this the harsh words that he would also supply about "institutional" philosophy on a scale larger than that of the family. Philosophy seems itself to have realized well before this challenge that the phrase "institutional philosophy" was arguably an oxymoron—that even if philosophical discourse might evolve *in* institutions, it could never be honestly *of* them. One way of understanding the recent proclamations of the end of philosophy, in fact, is as a reaction to the institutionalization of philosophy that occurs mainly in the nineteenth century, associated there with the more general phenomena of bureaucracy and professionalization of which philosophers now, permitting themselves a guarded optimism, might hope to be the tail end.

I do not mean here to draw an image of the philosopher as an outsider or an alienated consciousness (insofar as this holds at all, it applies to only a small number of figures in the history of philosophy)—but rather to suggest that there is a difference worth building on further between institutional philosophy and a conception of philosophy as "polyphonic," in which the voice of any one philosopher is recognizable as an overlay of many other individual voices. The latter, it seems to me, has in fact been a recurrent feature of philosophical discourse that has come increasingly—and recently—to be discounted in the conception of a "heroic" history of philosophy. As the arts in the Renaissance discovered and then celebrated the artist as individual, so philosophy, tardily, would then in the eighteenth and nineteenth centuries learn to forget the metonymic function that proper names serve in the history of ideas—ostensively referring to an individual but standing in fact for a practice. We have recently heard much about the "death of the author" (proposed by authors who seem willing to observe that phenomenon for everyone but themselves); but it seems likely in fact that philosophy in its most compelling moments has long known about that death, indeed that it has even willed it. This is but one more way in which proclamations of the "end of philosophy" have continually shaped its history.

None of this is to claim that the noninstitutional philosopher, unlike his counterpart, will manage to escape the constraints of ideology—that because he is unfettered in this way, he can hope somehow to jump out of his skin. There are always certain matters that will not be spoken of: repression in its many guises will see to some of this, and when repression fails, finitude itself may suffice. Thus, philosophical wonder itself will also turn out to be partial, embodying particular interests and idioms, and so always with an object not fully of the philosopher's own choosing. But there is a difference between speaking *for* a context and speaking *out of context*—and it is the latter, as a violation of the taboos of the understanding, that philosophy seems to me to accomplish when it succeeds. That we can in retrospect find ways of neutralizing these violations is less unsettling than is the effort of those who would, even if only in principle, escape all retrospection. The denial of ideology occurs at the point where ideology is most active and most determinant. And like positivism and existentialism, which have thought to privilege themselves in this way, postmodernism in the fundamentalist version criticized here has victimized itself by the same denial.

Thus, irresolute and absent-minded an answer as it may seem, a plausible response to the question posed for philosophy, "What now?" is, "Go and do it." For as wonder is spontaneous and cannot be coerced, neither can its objects or shape be anticipated. There is at work here a theory of time that escapes both the lockstep of historical determinism that postmodernism finds in the prepostmodernist history of philosophy and the radical discontinuity or randomness that the latter would substitute for the former. Is it so improbable that the present can be new without being quite other than the past? Or that it can be indebted to the past without merely repeating it? This conception of philosophy's history would offer a means of thinking in the present without being quite of it; it would also, along the way, validate one side of postmodernism's view of the history of philosophy without the menace of its other consequences—founded again and again, in the present without the claim of a miraculous creation (again and again) ex nihilo.

This all may seem to promise a future for philosophy that is either hopelessly amorphous or, still worse, that bears an uncanny resemblance to the past—that is, a "new" present in which nothing has changed. But consistent with these alternatives is another one—and this is the "possibility of everything," the postmodernist theme with which the discussion here began and which turns out now to be an illusion (a creative illusion, its own "Noble Lie") by which philosophy has constantly lived in the past, watching what it envisages as tactics continually turn into strategies. What this means is that also in its own design, philosophy, waiting always on the new present, will be tactical, setting out from the immediacy of particular moments of experience. We may indeed look forward then to the philosophical "conversations" that Rorty anticipates, although these may not be as novel or unfamiliar as Rorty's readers have been led to expect. They will—if we are fortunate—be like (perhaps even *be*) Plato's dialogues, Montaigne's essays, Descartes's meditations, Hegel's phenomenologies, Kierkegaard's points of view for his work as an author. Like them, but of course also not like them—by as much, at any rate, as those works themselves were, are, like and not like each other. Does not this leave matters exactly as they had been? What would be *post*modernist about this? But the occasions will be different, the angles of vision will vary, the intersections of history will be occurring for the first time—and with these differences, also the constantly new question of address, of tactics. What this amounts to, then, is the appropriation into the present of a past that can be advanced, subverted—or, with the tactics of post-modernism, turned on its side: certainly not for the first time, probably not for the last, but nonetheless. Thus, everything *is* possible—including philosophy when it flatly asserts that not everything is possible. In this way, Aristotle argued for the law of noncontradiction as itself not requir-ing or even as capable of demonstration. The proof of *its* ground, even of its possibility, was for him the actuality of everything else around it— and there too we may find if not a foundation, at least the origins of a discourse that, in the testimony of the past, turns out to be philosophical. To demand more than this is to will oneself either a captive of the past or a fugitive in the future; on these terms, the next step is only to come back once more to the present work of philosophy, at once familiar and novel. Nostalgia, when it is spontaneous, is for the future; anticipation, when it is not merely wistful, is of the past. This is why philosophers would in their history say at first—and then again and again—"Let us begin." Let us, then, begin. Again.

NOTES

1. I do not attempt to assess here the numerous (sometimes conflicting) definitions that have been given of postmodernism; originally quite modest in its applications to architecture and to poetry, the term now stands as a general (if vague) term of cultural reference. See for the historical background to the term Jerome Mazzaro, "The Genesis of Post-modernism," in *Postmodern American Poetry* (Urbana, Ill., 1980), pp. 1–31; also, Marjorie Perloff, *The Poetics of Inde-terminacy* (Princeton, 1981), pp. 28–44, and Richard Palmer, "Towards a Post-modern Hermeneutics of Performance," in *Performance in Postmodern Culture* (Milwaukee, 1977). For a more speculative historical reconstruction, see J.-F. Lyotard, *The Postmodern Condition: A Report on Knowledge,* tr. G. Benington and B. Massumi (Minneapolis, 1984). Its latest transformation has been an ingenious turn into the "post-contemporary." See Stanley Fish, *Doing What Comes Naturally* (Durham, N.C., 1989), although this too, it may be predicted, is not the last word.

2. Although coming from a different starting point, this formulation con-

verges on Habermas's objection to postmodernism as a form of *anti*modernism, with its aestheticism a cloak for conservative or reactionary ideology: the post-modernists "remove into the sphere of the far-away and the archaic the sponta-neous powers of imagination, self-experience and emotion" (J. Habermas, "Modernity—an Incomplete Project," in *The Anti-Aesthetic: Essays on Postmodern Culture,* ed. H. Foster [Port Townsend, Wash., 1983], p. 14). See also in the same volume, Fredric Jameson, "Postmodernism and Consumer Society," pp. 114–18. Jameson, associating postmodernism with the genre of the "pastiche," argues still more sharply for the incapacitating social consequences of postmod-ernism.

CONTRIBUTORS

CONTRIBUTORS

DAVID BOUCHER has been a senior lecturer at La Trobe University, Melbourne, The Australian National University Canberra, and is currently a senior lecturer in politics at University College of Swansea, Swansea, Great Britain. He is the author of *Texts in Context* (1985), *The Social and Political Thought of R. G. Collingwood* (1989), and with Andrew Vincent, *Pure Citizenship: The Contribution of Henry Jones to Social and Political Argument in Great Britain 1880–1922* (forthcoming). He has edited *Essays in Political Philosophy* by R. G. Collingwood (1989) and *The New Leviathan,* revised edition, by R. G. Collingwood (forthcoming).

NORMAN BRYSON teaches art history at Harvard University. His most recent books are *Looking at the Overlooked: Four Essays on Still Life Painting* (1990) and *Visual Theory: Painting and Interpretation,* co-edited with Michael Ann Holly and Keith Moxey (1991).

RALPH COHEN is Kenan Professor of English, Director of the Commonwealth Center for Literary and Cultural Change at the University of Virginia, and editor of *New Literary History.* His most recent article,

"Genre Theory, Literary History, and Historical Change," appeared in *Theoretical Issues in Literary History,* edited by David Perkins (Harvard English Studies 16, 1991).

RACHEL BLAU DUPLESSIS is Professor of English, Temple University. Her recent publications include *The Pink Guitar: Writing as Feminist Practice* (1990), *Tabula Rosa* and *Drafts 3–14* (Potes and Poets, 1987 and 1991). She edited *The Selected Letters of George Oppen* (1990) and, with Susan Friedman, co-edited *Signets: Reading H. D.* (1990).

DELL HYMES is Commonwealth Professor of Anthropology and Commonwealth Professor of English at the University of Virginia. He has taught at Harvard, Berkeley and the University of Pennsylvania, and has been active in developing the field of sociolinguistics through his own writings and through the editing of the journal *Language in Society.* His first research was with the languages and traditions of Native Americans of the Pacific Northwest, a subject to which he has returned in recent years.

MURRAY KRIEGER is University Professor of English at the University of California, with Irvine as his home campus. He is the author of many books. The most recent are *Words about Words about Words: Theory, Criticism and the Literary Text, A Reopening of Closure: Organicism against Itself,* and currently *Ekphrasis: The Illusion of the Natural Sign.*

BEREL LANG is professor of philosophy and humanistic studies at the State University of New York at Albany. His most recent books are *Act and Idea in the Nazi Genocide* (1990), *The Anatomy of Philosophical Style* (1990), and *Writing and the Moral Self* (1991).

RICHARD LEHAN, Professor of English at the University of California, Los Angeles, has written books on F. Scott Fitzgerald, Theodore Dreiser, and literary existentialism. His most recent book is *The Great Gatsby: The Limits of Wonder* (1990).

DEBORAH E. MCDOWELL is Associate Professor of English at the University of Virginia. She is author of the forthcoming "'The Changing Same': Studies in Fiction by Black Women" and editor of the Beacon Black Women Writers Series.

R. K. MEINERS is Professor of English at Michigan State University and Editor of *The Centennial Review.* He has published books on Allen Tate and Robert Lowell, a book of poetry, and essays, poems, and reviews in many journals. The essay in this volume is part of a book-in-progress on the relation of poetic and critical discourses in recent literary history.

FRANCO MORETTI, born in 1950, has taught at various universities in Italy and the United States, and is at present Professor of English and Comparative Literature at Columbia University. His work in English includes *Signs Taken for Wonders* (1983, 2d enlarged ed. 1988) and *The Way of The World* (1987).

LINDA ORR is Professor of French at Duke University. She is the author of *Jules Michelet: Nature, History and Language* (1976), a critical edition of Michelet's *La Montagne* (1987), and *Headless History: Nineteenth-Century French Historiography of the Revolution* (1990).

ANN RIGNEY teaches literary theory, and is attached to the Research Institute for History and Culture, at the University of Utrecht. She is author of *The Rhetoric of Historical Representation: Three Narrative Histories of the French Revolution* (1990).

CUSHING STROUT is the Ernest I. White Professor of American Studies and Humane Letters, Emeritus, at Cornell University. His most recent work in American intellectual and literary history includes *The Veracious Imagination: Essays on American History, Literature, and Biography* (1981) and *Making American Tradition: Vision and Revision from Ben Franklin to Alice Walker* (1990).